Macmillan Vocabulary Practice Series

Science

Keith Kelly

MACMILLAN

Table of contents

Introduction

About this book

If you study science through the medium of English and you have trouble
remembering specific science words, this book is for you. Science is the first
volume in the *Macmillan Vocabulary Practice Series*. The series is designed
with students in mind whose first language is not English to help them practise
their vocabulary, but native speakers of English may find it useful too. The book
contains 28 key science topics with word lists and activities and can be used
alongside your regular science book.

Here is how you can use it:

- each topic starts off with a word list in which you can look up the words.
  Choose the topic you are focussing on in class and study the words that you
  need: each word has a definition in English, but there is also space for you to
  write down a translation in your own language. Some words also have an
  example sentence to make their meaning even clearer.
- once you feel comfortable with the words, you can practise them by doing
  the activities which follow on from the word list. There are word activities in
  the **Working with word**s sections to practise individual words. Try to write
  them down as well as pronounce them – the pronunciation of each word is
  in the word list as well. The following section is called **Working with
  sentences** and these activities are designed to help you use the words in the
  correct context. When you feel you are very familiar with the words you can
  attempt the activities under **Working with texts** which allow you to practise
  your knowledge of the words in larger contexts.
- at the back of the book is an index in which you can find all the words from
  the word lists in the book. If you come across an unfamiliar word which is not
  on your topic word list, look in the index to see where else in the book you
  can find it. If it is not in the book, the *Macmillan School Dictionary* or the
  Macmillan English Dictionary are very useful resources as well.
- if your book also contains an answer key, you can look up the answers to all
  activities at the back of the book in the Answer key section.
- the book can also be used as a quick reference tool to help look up the
  words you are struggling with in your regular text book. All the definitions
  are written in clear, simple English.

If you have the book as well as the CD-ROM, you have even more opportunities
to practise your vocabulary. The CD-ROM has searchable word lists which include
an audio file with the pronunciation of each word. There are interactive activities
per topic and many topics also contain animations and diagrams. Last but not
least, there is a word map tool in each topic which allows you to make and save
your own word maps to help you revise and remember your science words.

Studying your school subjects in English can be challenging as well as fun.
This book will help make the language learning easier so you can concentrate
on learning about science!

1 Living organisms

abdomen
/ˈæbdəmən/
1 the front part of the body below the chest and above the pelvis. It contains the stomach and several other organs, including the intestines and the liver. noun [count]
2 the back part of the three parts into which the body of insects or some other arthropods is divided. The other parts are the head and the thorax. noun [count]

In a test called amniocentesis, a fine needle is passed through the abdomen of a pregnant woman into the amnion. Grasshoppers and other insects have breathing holes along the sides of their abdomen.

absorb
/əbˈzɔːb/
1 to absorb liquid into a living cell through its cell membranes, for example by osmosis. noun [uncount]
2 to take in nutrients through the walls of the intestines into the blood.

Root hairs absorb water containing plant nutrients.
Special lymph cells in the small intestine absorb fats.

anus
/ˈeɪnəs/
the opening at the end of the alimentary canal through which solid waste passes out of the body. noun [count]

Undigested food is passed out through the anus as faeces.

bladder
/ˈblædə/
the part inside the body like a bag where urine collects before being passed out of the body through the urethra. noun [count]

The ureter takes urine from the kidneys to the bladder.

blood
/blʌd/
the red liquid that is pumped around the body from the heart. Blood carries oxygen, hormones, and nutrients to the various parts of the body, and also helps to get rid of waste products. It consists of plasma which contains red blood cells and white blood cells, and platelets. noun [uncount]

Oxygen is carried in the blood.

brain
/breɪn/
1 the organ inside the skull in vertebrates that controls physical and nervous activity and intelligence. noun [count]
2 the place in the bodies of some invertebrates that is the main centre of nerve tissue. noun [count]

The illness had affected his brain.

The 'brains' of some invertebrates are no more than a network of nerve fibres.

breathe
/briːð/
to take air into the lungs through the nose or mouth and let it out again. verb [intransitive/transitive]

We begin the exercise by breathing deeply (=breathing large amounts of air).

bronchial tube
/ˈbrɒŋkɪəl ˌtjuːb/
one of the tubes in the chest through which air goes into the lungs. noun [count]

In a mammal each lung is linked to the trachea by a bronchial tube.

bronchus
/ˈbrɒŋkəs/
one of the two main tubes coming from the trachea that carry air into the lungs. It has many smaller tubes called bronchioles connected to it (plural: bronchi /ˈbrɒŋkiː/). noun [count]

carbon dioxide
/ˌkɑːbən daɪˈɒksaɪd/
the gas that is produced when humans and other animals breathe out and when fossil fuels are burned. It is used by plants in the process of photosynthesis. Carbon dioxide is a greenhouse gas. Chemical formula: CO_2 noun [uncount]

Carbon dioxide dissolves in rainwater to form weak carbonic acid.

cell
/sel/
the smallest unit from which all living things are made. All cells have a cell membrane, and plant cells also have a cellulose cell wall. A cell also has a nucleus that contains the organism's genetic information, cytoplasm, and very small parts called organelles. noun [count]

The brains of mammals contain millions of brain cells.

cell membrane
/ˈsel ˌmembreɪn/
the outer layer surrounding the cytoplasm of all cells. The cell membrane controls which substances go in and out of the cell. noun [count]

New viruses burst out through the cell membrane, destroying the cell.

cellular
/ˈseljʊlə/
relating to the cells of living things. adjective

Oxygen is used up by cellular respiration.

cellulose
/ˈseljʊləʊz/
a substance that forms the walls of plant cells and plant fibres. It is insoluble in water, and is used to make plastics, explosives, paper, fabrics, and other products. noun [uncount]

Cows have microorganisms in their stomachs to help them digest cellulose.

cell wall
/ˌsel ˈwɔːl/
a strong layer that surrounds each cell in organisms other than animals, protecting them and giving them shape. In most plants, the cell wall is made of cellulose, and in fungi it is made of chitin. noun [count]

Chlorella is a plant-like protist with a cellulose cell wall and a chloroplast.

chloroplast
/ˈklɒrəplɑːst/
the part of the cells of plants where photosynthesis takes place. It is shaped like a very small bag and it contains chlorophyll. noun [count]

Each cell of Spirogyra has a spiral-shaped chloroplast.

chromosome
/ˈkrəʊməˌsəʊm/
a structure that looks like a very small piece of string and that exists, usually as one of a pair, in the nucleus of all living cells. Chromosomes contain the genetic information that says whether a person, animal etc is male or female and what characteristics they get from their parents. noun [count]

During cell division each chromosome makes an exact copy of itself.

circulatory /ˌsɜːkjʊˈleɪt(ə)ri, ˈsɜːkjələt(ə)ri/	relating to the movement of blood around the body. **adjective**	*Smoking can lead to circulatory problems.*
cytoplasm /ˈsaɪtəʊˌplæz(ə)m/	the substance inside the cells of living things, apart from the nucleus. It contains several different chemicals and structures. **noun [uncount]**	*Many chemical reactions take place in the cytoplasm.*
digest /daɪˈdʒest/	to break down food in the alimentary canal into soluble substances that the body can absorb. **verb [transitive]**	*Pepsin works in the stomach to digest protein.*
digestion /daɪˈdʒestʃ(ə)n/	the process by which food is broken down by the body into simple soluble substances that the body can absorb and then use for growth and as fuel for energy. **noun [uncount]**	*Enzymes speed up the process of digestion.*
digestive /daɪˈdʒestɪv/	relating to digestion. **adjective**	*The digestive system is a tube running from the mouth to the anus.*
duodenum /ˌdjuːəʊˈdiːnəm/	the first section of the small intestine, just below the stomach. **noun [count]**	*The bile duct carries bile from the gall bladder to the duodenum.*
enzyme /ˈenzaɪm/	a protein produced by all organisms that behaves as a catalyst (=a substance that speeds up chemical reactions but does not itself change.) **noun [count]**	*Each enzyme does a particular job, e.g. sucrase breaks down sucrose.*
epithelial /epɪˈθiːliəl/	relating to the epithelium. **adjective**	*The cheek is lined with a layer of delicate epithelial cells.*
epithelium /epɪˈθiːliəm/	a thin layer of cells that lines organs and cavities within the body, and forms a protective cover over openings such as cuts. **noun [count]**	*Blood capillaries have an epithelium which is only one cell thick.*
excrement /ˈekskrəmənt/	the solid waste that the body gets rid of = faeces. **noun [uncount]**	*The walls were smeared with human excrement.*
excrete /ɪkˈskriːt/	to get rid of waste from reactions within the body. **verb [intransitive/transitive]**	*Sweat glands excrete a small amount of salts from the blood.*
excretion /ɪkˈskriːʃ(ə)n/	the process by which the body gets rid of waste products. Excretion includes the process of getting rid of carbon dioxide from the lungs, sweat from the sweat glands, and urea from the body in urine. **noun [uncount]**	*The lungs and kidneys are organs of excretion.*
excretory /ɪkˈskriːtəri/	relating to excretion. **adjective**	*Urea and carbon dioxide are both excretory products.*
exhale /eksˈheɪl/	to breathe air out through the mouth or nose. **verb [intransitive/transitive]**	*Take a deep breath and then exhale into the tube.*
faeces /ˈfiːsiːz/	solid waste from the body = excrement. **noun [plural]**	*Blood in the faeces is a sign of disease.*
fat /fæt/	**1** a soft white or yellow substance that mammals and birds store under the skin. It is used as an energy store and to protect the body against heat loss. **noun [uncount]** **2** a food substance like oil that is used by the body for energy. **noun [count/uncount]**	*Surplus food is converted to fat and stored.* *You should reduce the amount of fat in your diet.*
fibre /ˈfaɪbə/	**1** the parts of fruit, vegetables, and grains containing cellulose that help food to pass through the body but that the body does not use. **noun [uncount]** **2** one of the thin pieces that form the nerves and muscles in the body. **noun [count/uncount]**	*Wholemeal bread is high in fibre.* *A single nerve fibre can be up to 40 cm long.*
food vacuole /ˈfuːd ˌvækjuəʊl/	a space inside the cell where food is digested in some protozoa (=organisms consisting of one cell only). **noun [count]**	*Amoeba engulfs its prey to form a food vacuole in the cytoplasm.*
genetic /dʒəˈnetɪk/	relating to genes or to the study of genes. **adjective**	*We inherit genetic characteristics from our parents.*
gland /glænd/	a part of the body that produces a chemical substance that the body needs, for example a hormone. **noun [count]**	*The pituitary gland in the brain is often called the master gland.*
grow /grəʊ/	**1** if plants grow somewhere, that is where they are found. **verb [intransitive]** **2** if you grow plants, you look after them and help them to develop. **verb [transitive]** **3** if bacteria or other living cells grow or are grown, they develop. **verb [intransitive/transitive]**	*Alpine plants grow in mountainous areas.* *You can grow your own vegetables.* *Given the right conditions a sapling will grow into a healthy tree.*
growth /grəʊθ/	**1** an increase in the size or development of a living thing, usually as the result of an increase in the number of cells. **noun [singular/uncount]** **2** a lump on someone's body that is caused by a disease. **noun [count]**	*Vitamins are essential for normal growth.* *The doctors found a cancerous growth in the liver.*
growth hormone /ˈgrəʊθ ˌhɔːməʊn/	a hormone that helps the process of growth in animal and plant cells. In animals, it is produced in the pituitary gland. **noun [count]**	*Excess growth hormone in humans causes giantism.*

haemoglobin /ˌhiːməˈɡləʊbɪn/	a protein in red blood cells that carries oxygen from the lungs to all parts of the body. noun [uncount]	*Carbon monoxide combines with haemoglobin and prevents red blood cells from transporting oxygen.*
heart /hɑːt/	in humans and most other animals, the organ in the chest that pumps blood around the body. noun [count]	*I could hear his heart beating.* *Did you know he had a weak heart?*
inhale /ɪnˈheɪl/	to breathe air, smoke, or other substances into the lungs (= breathe (sth) in; ≠ exhale). verb [intransitive/transitive]	*We were told not to inhale the vapour.*
inherited /ɪnˈherətɪd/	inherited characteristic, inherited chromosome passed from parent animals, plants, or other organisms to their offspring through their genes. adjective	*Eye colour is an inherited characteristic.*
insulate /ˈɪnsjʊˌleɪt/	to cover something in order to prevent heat, cold, sound, or electricity from passing through it. verb [transitive]	*NASA uses Teflon to insulate wires and cables.*
intestine /ɪnˈtestɪn/	the long tube in the body between the stomach and the anus that is a major part of the digestive system. There are two parts of the intestine, the small intestine and the large intestine, where different stages of digestion take place. noun [count]	*The lining of the small intestine has projections called villi.*
kidney /ˈkɪdni/	one of the two organs in the body that clean the blood by removing waste products such as urea and also control the level of water that the blood contains. The waste passes into the bladder in the liquid form of urine, which is then passed out of the body (plural: kidneys). noun [count]	*Blood enters each kidney through the renal artery.*
larynx /ˈlærɪŋks/	the organ in the throat that contains the vocal cords, which produce sounds. noun [count]	*Men have a deeper voice than women because they have a larger larynx.*
liver /ˈlɪvə/	an organ in the body that changes toxins such as alcohol into less harmful substances, and produces bile, urea, and cholesterol. The liver controls the level of glucose and amino acids in the blood, and stores some important vitamins and minerals. noun [count]	*Excessive drinking can lead to liver failure.*
lung /lʌŋ/	one of the two organs in the chest that fill with air during breathing. Blood flowing to the lungs takes oxygen from the air breathed into the alveoli and puts in carbon dioxide which is then breathed out as a waste product. Air enters and leaves the lungs through the bronchial tubes. noun [count]	*He was suffering from lung cancer.*
membrane /ˈmembˌreɪn/	a thin layer of tissue that covers, separates, protects, or connects cells or parts of an organism. noun [count]	*The eye is protected by a thin membrane.*
mitochondrion /ˌmaɪtəʊˈkɒndrɪən/	a very small round or rod-shaped part in the cytoplasm of a cell. It contains enzymes for the respiration of food to release energy (plural: mitochondria /ˌmaɪtəʊˈkɒndrɪə/). noun [count]	*Each mitochondrion has an inner folded membrane to increase the surface area.*
molecule /ˈmɒlɪˌkjuːl/	the smallest part of an element or compound that could exist independently, consisting of two or more atoms. noun [count]	*A molecule of carbon dioxide contains one carbon atom and two oxygen atoms.*
multicellular /ˌmʌltɪˈseljʊlə/	a multicellular organism consists of many cells. adjective	*All multicellular organisms rely on cell division for growth.*
muscle /ˈmʌs(ə)l/	a piece of flesh that connects bones and produces movement of the parts of the body by contracting and relaxing. noun [count/uncount]	*These exercises are good for your stomach muscles.*
muscular /ˈmʌskjələ/	1 relating to the muscles or made of muscle. adjective 2 having big muscles. adjective	*The stomach is a muscular bag.* *Men are usually more muscular than women.*
nerve /nɜːv/	one of the groups of fibres in the body that carry messages between the sense organs, the brain, and the rest of the body, communicating pain, pressure, feelings of heat and cold etc. noun [count]	*The optic nerve leads from the eye to the brain.*
nervous system /ˈnɜːvəs ˌsɪstəm/	the system of nerves that control the body and the mind. noun [singular]	*The nervous system works rather like a telephone system.*
nucleus /ˈnjuːklɪəs/	1 the central part of an atom, consisting of protons and neutrons, and containing most of its mass. noun [count] 2 the central part of a living cell that contains its DNA and controls its growth and reproduction (plural: nuclei /ˈnjuːklɪaɪ/). noun [count]	*The nucleus of an atom has a positive charge.* *The nucleus contains chromosomes.*
oesophagus /ɪˈsɒfəɡəs/	a tube that carries food from the pharynx to the stomach. noun [count]	*Mucus lubricates food as it passes down the oesophagus.*
organelle /ˌɔːɡəˈnel/	a structure in a cell that is designed to do a particular job, for example a nucleus. noun [count]	*A ribosome, one organelle in a cell, is about 20 nm wide.*
organism /ˈɔːɡəˌnɪz(ə)m/	a living thing that is capable of growing and reproducing and consists of one or more cells. noun [count]	*A pest is an organism that damages crops.*

organ system /ˈɔːgən ˌsɪstəm/	a group of organs in the body that work together to do a particular thing, for example the digestive system. **noun [count]**	*One organ system cannot function without another.*
ovary /ˈəʊv(ə)ri/	a tube in the body of a female mammal that takes eggs from an ovary to the uterus = Fallopian tube. **noun [count]**	
ovum /ˈəʊvəm/	the female gamete or egg cell that can grow into a new animal after it has been fertilized. In mammals, this happens inside the female (plural: ova /ˈəʊvə/). **noun [count]**	*The fertilized ovum is called a zygote.*
oxygen /ˈɒksɪdʒ(ə)n/	an important element in the air that is a gas with no smell or taste. It makes aerobic respiration possible in organisms. It combines with most other elements. Chemical symbol: O. **noun [uncount]**	*Brain damage occurs when the supply of oxygen to the brain is interrupted. Blood absorbs oxygen from the air in the lungs.*
plasma /ˈplæzmə/	the yellow liquid that is part of blood. **noun [uncount]**	*Blood plasma contains various dissolved substances.*
protein /ˈprəʊtiːn/	**1** an organic compound that is made of amino acids. Proteins contain carbon, hydrogen, oxygen, and nitrogen. **noun [count]** **2** food such as meat, eggs, and milk that contain proteins and that people need in order to grow and be healthy. Protein is very important for building tissues such as muscles and for keeping them healthy. **noun [uncount]**	*The villagers' main source of protein is fish from the river.*
protoplasm /ˈprəʊtəplæz(ə)m/	the substance that the cells of living things are made of. It consists of the cytoplasm and the nucleus. **noun [uncount]**	*Organelles are found within the protoplasm of a cell.*
repair /rɪˈpeə/	the process of fixing something that is broken or damaged. **noun [count/uncount]**	*We need proteins for the growth and repair of damaged cells.*
reproduce /ˌriːprəˈdjuːs/	to have babies, or to produce young animals, plants, or other organisms. **verb [intransitive/transitive]**	*Viruses can only reproduce inside a living host cell.*
reproduction /ˌriːprəˈdʌkʃ(ə)n/	the process of having babies or producing young animals, plants, and other organisms. The form of reproduction that involves the combination of male and female gametes, for example in most animals and plants, is called sexual reproduction. Reproduction in which there is only one parent, for example in bacteria, is called asexual reproduction. **noun [uncount]**	*Asexual reproduction in hydra is called budding.*
reproductive /ˌriːprəˈdʌktɪv/	relating to sex, or to the process of having babies or producing young animals, plants, or other organisms. **adjective**	*Many flowers have both male and female reproductive organs.*
reproductive cell /ˌriːprədʌktɪv ˈsel/	a male or female cell that unites with a cell from the opposite sex to form a new organism in the process of sexual reproduction = gamete. **noun [count]**	*The male reproductive cell is called a sperm.*
respiratory /rɪˈspɪrət(ə)ri, ˈresp(ə)rət(ə)ri/	relating to the process of breathing. **adjective**	*Smoking can lead to respiratory diseases.*
secrete /səˈkriːt/	to produce a liquid such as saliva. **verb [transitive]**	*Cells in the stomach lining secrete digestive enzymes.*
skeletal /ˈskelət(ə)l, skəˈliːt(ə)l/	relating to the skeleton. **adjective**	*The skeleton of birds is very light but strong.*
skeleton /ˈskelət(ə)n/	the hard frame that supports the body of a human or other animal. In vertebrates it is usually made of bone that the muscles are attached to, and it protects the most important organs, for example the brain and the heart. **noun [count]**	*Skeletal muscles are attached to bones.*
sperm /spɜːm/	**1** the male gamete (=reproductive cell) produced by the male sex organs that fertilizes a female egg. The sperm are contained in seminal fluid, and together they form semen. They have half the number of chromosomes as other cells in the body. A single sperm is sometimes called a spermatozoon. **noun [count]** **2** the liquid from a man's penis that contains sperm = semen (plural: sperm). **noun [uncount]**	*The production of sperm is controlled by hormones.*
sperm duct /ˈspɜːm ˌdʌkt/	a long thin tube that carries sperms away from the epidydimis in the scrotum to the seminal vesicles where they will be stored until ejaculation. **noun [count]**	
spine /spaɪn/	**1** the row of bones down or along the middle of the back of a vertebrate = backbone, spinal column, vertebral column. **noun [count]** **2** a sharp point on a plant or animal. **noun [count]**	*She felt a chill run down her spine.* *Many cacti have sharp spines to protect them against being eaten.*
stomach /ˈstʌmək/	the organ at the bottom of the oesophagus where food goes after it is eaten. **noun [count]**	*She'll feel better when she has some food in her stomach.*

Term	Definition	Example
sweat /swet/	liquid containing waste substances that forms on the skin when someone is hot. The evaporation of sweat helps to cool the body. **noun [uncount]**	*She wiped the sweat off her forehead with a towel.*
sweat /swet/	to produce sweat on the surface of the skin when you are hot, nervous, or ill. **verb [intransitive]**	*She could feel the palms of her hands sweating.*
sweating /'swetɪŋ/	the process by which liquid containing waste produced by sweat glands forms on the skin as a result of hot conditions, physical exercise, illness, or nervousness. **noun [uncount]**	*Sweating is the body's way of cooling itself down.*
system /'sɪstəm/	**1** the body considered as a set of connected organs, tubes etc. **noun [count]** **2** a set of organs, tubes etc in your body that work together. **noun [count]**	*The drug stays in your system for hours.* *The circulatory system consists of the heart and blood vessels.*
thorax /'θɔːræks/	**1** the part of the body between the neck and the waist. **noun [count]** **2** the middle part of the body of an insect or arachnid that its legs and wings are joined to. **noun [count]**	*The thorax is surrounded by the rib cage.* *Spiders have a fused head and thorax.*
tissue /'tɪʃuː, 'tɪsjuː/	large numbers of similar cells working together. The four main types of tissue are nerve tissue, muscle tissue, connective tissue, and epidermal tissue. **noun [uncount]**	*Connective tissue helps to hold other tissues together.*
trachea /trə'kiːə/	the tube at the back of the throat that goes from the larynx to the bronchi. Air travels down it into the lungs = windpipe. **noun [count]**	*The trachea has rings of cartilage which keep it open.*
unicellular /juːnɪ'seljʊlə/	a unicellular organism consists of one cell only. Amoebas are unicellular organisms. **adjective**	*Most unicellular organisms live in water.*
ureter /jʊ'riːtə/	one of the two tubes that carry urine from the kidneys to the bladder in most mammals, or to the place where waste collects in some other vertebrates. **noun [count]**	*Urine passes from the collecting ducts of the kidney into the ureter.*
urethra /jʊ'riːθrə/	in most mammals, the tube that carries urine out of the body. **noun [count]**	*In male mammals the urethra also carries sperm during intercourse.*
urine /'jʊərɪn/	a liquid that contains waste products such as urea and salts from the body that are filtered out through the kidneys. Urine collects in the bladder and passes from the body through the urethra. **noun [uncount]**	*Glucose in the urine is a symptom of diabetes.*
vacuole /'vækjuəʊl/	a space inside a cell, filled with air, food, or waste products. **noun [count]**	*Plant cells contain large, permanent vacuoles.*
vascular /'væskjʊlə/	**1** relating to the blood vessels in the body. **adjective** **2** vascular tissue in plants carries water, mineral salts, and food from one part of the plant to another. **adjective**	*Blood is transported around the body by the vascular system.* *The vascular bundles of stems contain phloem tissue.*
vein /veɪn/	**1** one of the blood vessels in the body that carry blood towards the heart. The blood in nearly all veins, except for the pulmonary vein, has a low level of oxygen, as the oxygen has been used in respiration. **noun [count]** **2** one of the tubes that carry substances through a plant. **noun [count]**	*The hepatic portal vein carries food from the intestines to the liver.* *Leaves contain a network of veins.*
vertebra /'vɜːtəbrə/	one of the small bones that form a row down the centre of the back (plural: vertebrae /'vɜːtəbreɪ/). **noun [count]**	*Each thoracic vertebra has a long neural spine for muscle attachment.*
vessel /'ves(ə)l/	a tube in people, animals, or plants through which liquid flows. **noun [count]**	*He laughed so much he nearly burst a blood vessel!*

A   Working with words

1   Living organism word map

Fill in the gaps on the word map.

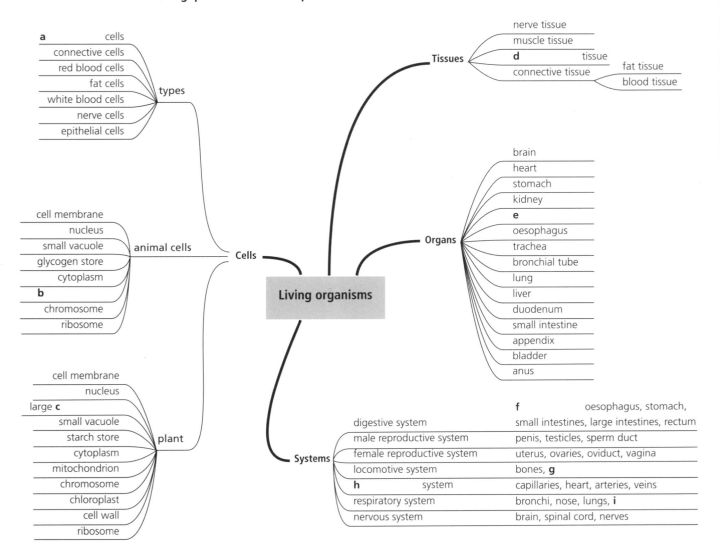

types

- **a** _____ cells
- connective cells
- red blood cells
- fat cells
- white blood cells
- nerve cells
- epithelial cells

animal cells

- cell membrane
- nucleus
- small vacuole
- glycogen store
- cytoplasm
- **b** _____
- chromosome
- ribosome

plant

- cell membrane
- nucleus
- large **c** _____
- small vacuole
- starch store
- cytoplasm
- mitochondrion
- chromosome
- chloroplast
- cell wall
- ribosome

Cells

Living organisms

Tissues

- nerve tissue
- muscle tissue
- **d** _____ tissue
- connective tissue
  - fat tissue
  - blood tissue

Organs

- brain
- heart
- stomach
- kidney
- **e** _____
- oesophagus
- trachea
- bronchial tube
- lung
- liver
- duodenum
- small intestine
- appendix
- bladder
- anus

Systems

digestive system	**f** _____ oesophagus, stomach, small intestines, large intestines, rectum
male reproductive system	penis, testicles, sperm duct
female reproductive system	uterus, ovaries, oviduct, vagina
locomotive system	bones, **g** _____
h _____ system	capillaries, heart, arteries, veins
respiratory system	bronchi, nose, lungs, **i** _____
nervous system	brain, spinal cord, nerves

2   Parts of animal cells

Label the parts of the animal cell.

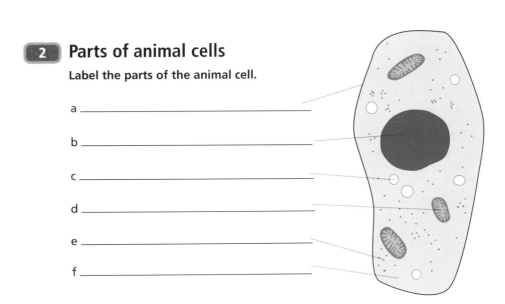

a _____

b _____

c _____

d _____

e _____

f _____

3 Animal cells and their functions

Write the correct cell name under each picture. Then add the functions of each cell as well.

Cell names	Cell functions
muscle cells	cause the body to move by contracting
red blood cells	have the job of carrying messages around the body
white blood cells	have the role of protecting the cells beneath them
nerve cells	kill bacteria and viruses
epithelial cells	transport oxygen around the body and help remove waste such as carbon dioxide

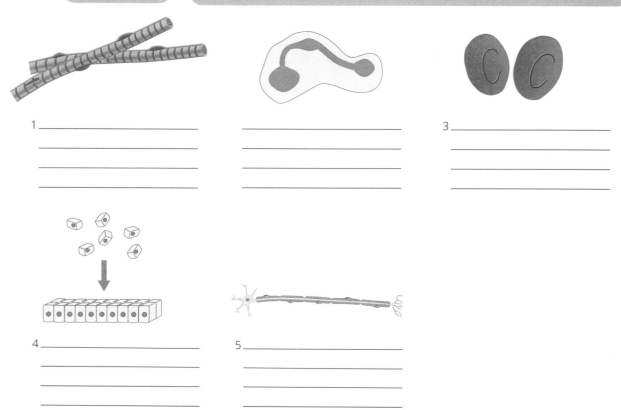

1 _____   _____   3 _____

_____   _____   _____

_____   _____   _____

_____   _____   _____

4 _____   5 _____

_____   _____

_____   _____

_____   _____

4 Systems and functions

Underline the correct word in each sentence.

1 The digestive system (breaks down / makes / removes) food for the body to absorb.

2 The circulatory system (drains / sucks / pumps) blood throughout the body.

3 The respiratory organs take oxygen into the body and (hold / remove / clean) the carbon dioxide.

4 The male reproductive organs (produce / change / transform) sperm.

5 The skeleton gives us our shape and (contains / carries / protects) the organs and helps the body to move.

6 The female reproductive system (absorbs / produces / controls) eggs and develops the foetus.

7 The excretory system (keeps / goes / removes) the waste from the body.

5 **System structures**

Complete the sentences with these words.

> blood vessels   bronchi   Fallopian tubes   large intestine
> muscles   penis   ovaries   oesophagus   sperm duct
> trachea   ureter   urethra

1   The digestive system includes the mouth, the _____, the stomach, the small

intestine _____ and the rectum.

2   The circulatory system is made up of the heart and the _____.

3   The respiratory system consists of the mouth, the _____, otherwise known as the

windpipe, the _____ and the lungs.

4   The male reproductive system is made up of the _____, the

_____ and the testicles.

5   The locomotive system includes the _____ and bones.

6   The female reproductive system consists of the _____, the

_____, the vagina and the uterus.

7   The excretory system consists of the _____, the bladder, the kidney and the

_____.

B   **Working with sentences**

6   **Organs and functions**

Match the beginnings and endings of the sentences.

Beginnings

1   The organ inside the skull in vertebrates that controls all activities including physical and nervous activity and intelligence is
2   The heart in humans and most other animals is
3   The kidney is
4   The organ in the throat that contains the vocal cords which produce sounds is
5   The oesophagus is a
6   The tube at the back of the throat that goes from the larynx to the bronchi where air travels down into the lungs is
7   The organ in the body that changes toxins such as alcohol into less harmful substances, and produces bile, urea, and cholesterol is
8   The duodenum is
9   The small intestine is
10   The small tube attached to the lower end of the small intestine in humans and some other mammals which has no known use in humans is
11   The bladder is
12   The anus is

Endings

a   tube that carries food from the mouth to the stomach.
b   called the brain.
c   called the trachea.
d   known as the appendix.
e   known as the liver.
f   one of the two organs in the body that clean the blood by removing waste products such as urea and also control the level of water and salts that the blood contains.
g   the first section of the small intestine, just after the stomach.
h   the larynx.
i   the opening at the end of the alimentary canal through which faeces pass out of the body.
j   the organ that pumps blood around the body.
k   the part inside the body like a bag where urine collects before being passed out of the body through the urethra.
l   the tube in the body that food goes into after it has passed through the stomach.

1 ☐   2 ☐   3 ☐   4 ☐   5 ☐   6 ☐   7 ☐   8 ☐   9 ☐   10 ☐   11 ☐   12 ☐

7 **Living organisms summary**

Put the phrases in the correct order to make sentences.

1 building blocks   Cells   of all living organisms.   are the

_____

2 multicellular organisms   while   only   one cell,   Unicellular organisms   of   many cells.   consist of   are   made up

_____

_____

3 are embedded.   the jelly-like material   The cytoplasm is   the cell in which   the organelles   inside

_____

_____

4 controls   The nucleus   of a cell.   of a cell   all the functions

_____

5 are the site of respiration   where energy   Mitochondria   from food.   in a cell,   is released

_____

_____

6 Plant cells   a cell wall and chloroplasts.   animal cells   have   a large central vacuole,   differ from   in that   most

_____

_____

C   Working with texts

8 **Plant and animal cells**

Read the text and sort the information into the diagram.

Plant cells and animal cells share a number of characteristics. Both plant and animal cells usually have a nucleus. Both types of cell also have cytoplasm where the chemical reactions occur. They also both have the cell powerhouses, the mitochondria. Plant cells have a rigid cell wall which means that there is little variation in the shape of plant cells. Animal cells have no cell wall and so there is more variety in cell shape according to function. While plant cells have chloroplasts animal cells do not. A characteristic of plant cells is the large central vacuole and plant cells may also have other small vacuoles. Animal cells have small vacuoles or none at all. Food stored in plant cells is stored as starch whereas in animal cells it is stored as glycogen.

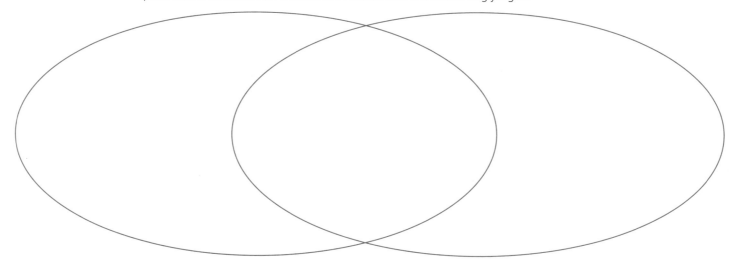

Plant cells contain …   Plant and animal cells both contain …   Animal cells contain …

2 Reproduction in plants

airborne /ˈeəˌbɔːn/	moving or carried in the air. **adjective**	
animal-pollinated /ˌænɪməl ˈpɒləˌneɪtɪd/	fertilized by having pollen moved from one plant to another by means of an animal. **adjective**	*Many tropical trees are animal-pollinated.*
anther /ˈænθə/	the male part of a flower that produces the pollen. It is the top part of the stamen. **noun [count]**	
auxin /ˈɔːksɪn/	a natural or artificial substance that controls the growth and development of plants. **noun [count]**	*Uneven distribution of auxin in a stem causes it to grow towards the light.*
binary fission /ˌbaɪnəri ˈfɪʃ(ə)n/	the process of reproducing by splitting into two new organisms which are exactly the same. **noun [uncount]**	*Amoebae reproduce asexually, by binary fission.*
bud /bʌd/	a part of a plant that opens to form a leaf or flower. **noun [count]**	*The rose bush was covered with yellow rose buds.*
bulb /bʌlb/	a structure growing underground that consists of a small stem, buds, and leaves that are swollen with food. The leaves provide food for the growth of a bud that makes a new plant. **noun [count]**	*An onion is a type of bulb.*
burr /bɜː/	the part of some plants that is covered all over with prickles and contains the seed. **noun [count]**	
burst open /ˌbɜːst ˈəʊpən/	to open quickly and suddenly. **verb**	*When the seed pod bursts open, the seed is scattered across a wide area.*
callus /ˈkæləs/	a mass of cells that develops from tissue taken from a parent plant, which can be used to form many new, identical plants. **noun [count]**	
capsule /ˈkæpsjuːl/	a small container in which seeds or eggs develop in some plants and animals. **noun [count]**	*The capsules of mosses contain the spores.*
clone /kləʊn/	an animal or plant that has been created artificially, using the DNA from one parent cell or organism to produce an animal or plant that is genetically the same as the parent, as opposed to one that inherits the genes of both parents through sexual reproduction. **noun [count]**	*Strawberry plants produce plants from runners which are clones.*
cloning /ˈkləʊnɪŋ/	the artificial production of new animals or plants that are genetically exactly the same as one parent, rather than having the genetic characteristics of two parents. **noun [uncount]**	*Identical oil palm plants are produced commercially by a cloning technique.*
corm /kɔːm/	a short swollen base of the stem in some plants that stores food underground that is used for the growth of new shoots in the next season. **noun [count]**	*Cocoyam corms are edible.*
cotyledon /ˌkɒtɪˈliːd(ə)n/	a leaf that is part of the embryo inside a seed before it germinates (=begins to develop into a plant). Scientists arrange plants into groups according to how many cotyledons their seeds have. **noun [count]**	*The cotyledons of some plants store food in the seed.*
cross-pollinate /ˌkrɒsˈpɒləˌneɪt/	to use the pollen from one plant to fertilize the flowers of another, or to be a plant that is usually fertilized in this way. **verb [intransitive/transitive]**	
dicotyledon /ˌdaɪkɒtɪˈliːd(ə)n/	a flowering plant that has two seed leaves (cotyledons) in each seed. Its other leaves have a pattern of veins. Many herbaceous plants, trees, and bushes are dicotyledons. **noun [count]**	
dispersal /dɪˈspɜːs(ə)l/	the process by which the seeds of plants are spread over a wide area. For example in wind dispersal, the seeds are carried by the wind. **noun [uncount]**	
disperse /dɪˈspɜːs/	to spread in different directions over a wide area, or to make things do this. **verb [intransitive/transitive]**	
endocarp /ˈendəʊkɑːp/	the inner layer of the pericarp of a fruit. **noun [count]**	
endosperm /ˈendəʊspɜːm/	the substance that surrounds the embryo inside a seed and provides food for it. **noun [uncount]**	*Maize grains store food in the endosperm.*

epicarp /ˈepɪkɑːp/	the outer layer of the pericarp of a fruit. **noun** [count]	
epigeal germination /ˈepɪˌdʒiəl ˌdʒɜːmɪˈneɪʃ(ə)n/	germination in which the cotyledons (= seed leaves) are lifted out of the ground to form the first leaves of the new plant. **noun** [uncount]	
filament /ˈfɪləmənt/	the long thin stem of a stamen of a flower. It supports the anther. **noun** [count]	
fungus /ˈfʌŋgəs/	a type of organism without chlorophyll that grows especially in wet conditions or on decaying matter. It reproduces by means of spores. There are many types of fungi, including mushrooms, yeasts, and moulds. Fungi are important to the environment as they naturally break down dead animal and plant material (plural: fungi /ˈfʌŋgiː/, funguses). **noun** [count/uncount]	
germinate /ˈdʒɜːmɪˌneɪt/	to develop from a seed and begin to grow into a plant, or to make a seed begin to grow. **verb** [intransitive/transitive]	*Seeds need water, warmth and oxygen to germinate and grow into a new plant.*
germination /ˌdʒɜːmɪˈneɪʃ(ə)n/	developing from a seed and beginning to grow into a plant, or making a seed beginning to grow. **noun** [uncount]	
graft /grɑːft/	to take a piece from a plant and join it to a cut that has been made in another plant, so that it can grow there. **verb** [transitive]	*Guavas are grown by grafting a bud from a plant that produces a good crop onto a healthy stock plant.*
guinep /ˈgenɪp/	a tropical evergreen tree that has edible fruit, also known as ackee. **noun** [count]	
hermaphrodite /hɜːˈmæfrədaɪt/	a person, other animal, or plant that has both male and female sex organs. **noun** [count]	*Most flowers are hermaphrodite because they have stamens (male) and pistils (female).*
hibiscus /haɪˈbɪskəs/	a bush with large brightly coloured flowers that grows mainly in tropical regions. **noun** [count]	
hilum /ˈhaɪləm/	a scar on a seed where it was attached to the plant. **noun** [count]	
husk /hʌsk/	the dry outer cover of some types of grain. **noun** [count]	*After harvesting, grains of wheat are threshed to remove the tough, outer husk.*
hypogeal germination /ˌhaɪpəʊdʒiəl ˌdʒɜːmɪˈneɪʃ(ə)n/	germination in which the cotyledons (= seed leaves) are left below the ground. **noun** [uncount]	
insect-pollinated /ˈɪnsekt pɒlɪˌneɪtɪd/	fertilized by having pollen moved from one plant to another by means of an insect. **adjective**	*Many common flowers are insect-pollinated.*
leafy branch /ˌliːfi brɑːntʃ/	a part of a plant or tree that grows out from the main stem or trunk, and has several leaves growing on it. **noun** [count]	
mesocarp /ˈmiːzəʊkɑːp/	the fleshy middle layer of the pericarp of a fruit, between the endocarp and the epicarp. **noun** [count]	
metabolic reactions /ˌmetəˈbɒlɪk riˈækʃn/	a chemical reaction within a living organism in which water, oxygen, food etc is converted into a form that the organism can use to live and grow. **noun** [count]	
micropyle /ˈmaɪkrəʊpaɪl/	a tiny hole in a seed, through which the pollen tube enters to fertilize it. **noun** [count]	
monocotyledon /ˌmɒnəʊˌkɒtɪˈliːd(ə)n/	a plant that has only one cotyledon in the seed, for example a grass. **noun** [count]	
moss /mɒs/	a soft green or brown plant that grows in a layer on wet ground, rocks, or trees. Mosses do not produce flowers or seeds and use spores to produce new plants. **noun** [count/uncount]	
nectar /ˈnektə/	a sweet liquid in flowers that insects and birds drink. Bees collect it and use it for making honey. **noun** [uncount]	
nectary /ˈnektəri/	the part of a flower that produces nectar (plural: nectaries). **noun** [count]	
ovule /ˈɒvjuːl/	a small structure containing the female gamete in a plant that becomes a seed after it has been fertilized. **noun** [count]	*Inside the ovary are ovules containing the female sex cell.*
perennating organ /ˈperəneɪtɪŋ ˌɔːg(ə)n/	part of a plant that stores food and can live for several years, usually with a period when it is dormant (= not growing or active). **noun** [count]	

perianth /ˈperiˌænθ/	the outer part of a flower, consisting of the sepals and the petals. noun [count]	
pericarp /ˈperiˌkɑːp/	the part of a fruit that develops from the wall of the ovary and that surrounds the seed or seeds. It forms the fruit's skin and flesh. noun [count]	
pin mould (Mucor) /ˈpɪn ˌməʊld/	a type of fungus that reproduces by spores that are released from a spore case at the end of a long fine thread, resembling a pin. noun [uncount]	
pistil /ˈpɪstɪl/	the female part of a flower used in reproduction. It consists of one or several carpels. noun [count]	*The pistil is made up of the stigma, style and ovary.*
Plasmodium /plæzˈməʊdiəm/	a protozoan organism that is the parasite that causes malaria. noun [count]	
plumule /ˈpluːmjuːl/	the first shoot of a plant embryo as it starts to grow. noun [count]	*The young shoot or plumule grows out of the seed and up through the soil.*
pollen grain /ˈpɒlən ˌɡreɪn/	a small individual particle of pollen (= the powder produced by flowers or cones in order to reproduce), containing the male sex cell. noun [count]	
pollen sac /ˈpɒlən ˌsæk/	the part of the anther (= male part) of a plant that contains the pollen. noun [count]	
pollen tube /ˈpɒlən ˌtjuːb/	a tube that develops from a grain of pollen. In a flowering plant, the tube grows down the style to the ovule which is fertilized and produces a seed. noun [count]	
pollinate /ˈpɒləˌneɪt/	to place pollen from one flower or cone onto another of the same type, and make fertilization possible. verb [transitive]	*The hibiscus flowers were pollinated by humming birds.*
pollination /ˌpɒləˈneɪʃ(ə)n/	the process by which plant pollen gets from the male stamen or cone to the female stigma or cone. In plants with flowers, this is often done by insects or the wind. noun [uncount]	
pollinator /ˈpɒləˌneɪtə/	something such as an insect or animal that moves pollen from one flower or cone to another of the same type, and makes fertilization possible. noun [count]	*Bees are the most well-known pollinators.*
pome /pəʊm/	a type of fruit such as an apple or pear, with a fleshy part consisting of a swollen receptacle (flower base), and a tough core containing the seeds. noun [count]	
poppy /ˈpɒpi/	a red flower with a black centre that produces small black seeds. noun [count]	
propagate /ˈprɒpəˌɡeɪt/	to make a plant produce more plants. verb [transitive]	*Fuchsias propagate easily from cuttings.*
propagation /ˌprɒpəˈɡeɪʃ(ə)n/	the process of making a plant produce more plants. noun [uncount]	*Propagation of cereal crops is mainly from seeds.*
radicle /ˈrædɪk(ə)l/	the part of a plant embryo that forms the root of the young plant. noun [count]	*The young root or radicle grows out of the seed and down into the soil.*
receptacle /rɪˈseptək(ə)l/	the wider, top part of the stem of a plant, where the flower joins the stem. noun [count]	
rhizome /ˈraɪˌzəʊm/	a thick plant stem that grows along the ground and produces roots and new plant growth. noun [count]	
runner /ˈrʌnə/	a stem that grows along the ground and has a new plant growing on it. noun [count]	
scatter /ˈskætə/	to throw or drop things so that they spread over an area. verb [transitive]	*New strawberry plants grow from runners.*
scion /ˈsaɪən/	a part that is cut from a plant and fixed to another plant in order to make it grow there. noun [count]	*The seed head breaks open and scatters the seeds.*
self-pollination /ˌselfpɒləˈneɪʃ(ə)n/	the process by which pollen passes from the anthers to the stigma of the same flower, or another flower on the same plant. noun [uncount]	*In grafting, a bud or other part of a plant – the scion – is attached to the stock where it grows.*
sepal /ˈsep(ə)l/	one of the parts of a flower that surround the petals and other inner parts before the flower has opened. The group of sepals is called the calyx. noun [count]	
shoot /ʃuːt/	a plant that has recently started growing, or a new part growing on a plant. noun [count]	
sporangium /spəˈrændʒiəm/	a spore case in which asexual spores are formed in plants such as ferns and fungi. noun [count]	

2 REPRODUCTION IN PLANTS

spore /spɔː/	a structure consisting of one cell that is produced, for example, by a fungus, moss, or fern, and that can develop into a new organism of the same type. **noun [count]**	
sprout /spraʊt/	if a plant sprouts, or if it sprouts something, new leaves or shoots begin to grow on it. **verb [intransitive/transitive]**	
stalk /stɔːk/	a long thin part of a plant with a flower, fruit, or leaf at the end. **noun [count]**	
stamen /ˈsteɪmən/	the male part of a flower that produces pollen. It consists of an anther and a filament. **noun [count]**	
stem /stem/	the long part of a plant that the leaves and flowers grow from. **noun [count]**	
stem tuber /stem ˈtjuːbə/	the swollen part of a plant such as a potato, that grows underground, stores food, and produces new plants. **noun [count]**	
sticky /ˈstɪkɪ/	made or covered with a substance that sticks to other things. **adjective**	*The tree produces sticky buds in spring.*
stigma /ˈstɪgmə/	the female part of a flower that receives pollen. **noun [count]**	
stock /stɒk/	a living plant onto which a bud or twig of another plant (a scion) is grafted. **noun [count]**	*The stock is prepared for the graft by making a cut in the bark.*
stolon /ˈstəʊlɒn/	a side stem that grows horizontally underground, and can start new roots and a new plant. **noun [count]**	
style /staɪl/	a long thin part of the carpel of a flower, at the top of which is the stigma. **noun [count]**	
sucker /ˈsʌkə/	a plant that grows from the bottom of another plant's stem or roots. **noun [count]**	*Banana and pineapple produce new plants from suckers.*
tap root /tæp ˌruːt/	the main straight root of a dicotyledon plant that has smaller roots growing out from its sides. Some vegetables, for example carrots, are tap roots. **noun [count]**	
testa /ˈtestə/	the hard layer that covers and protects the seed of a plant that produces flowers (plural: testae /ˈtestiː/). **noun [count]**	
tissue culture /ˈtɪʃuː ˌkʌltʃə/	**1** the process of growing tissue cells taken from an organism in a culture medium (=substance that helps something to grow) for medical or scientific purposes. **noun [uncount]** **2** an amount of tissue grown in a culture medium. **noun [count]**	*Oil palm plants are produced by a technique called tissue culture.*
tropism /ˈtrəʊpɪzm/	the movement of part of a plant in a particular direction as it grows. **noun [count/uncount]**	*Examples of tropism include growth towards light (phototropism) and growth towards water (hydrotropism).*
unisex /ˈjuːnɪseks/	containing only the male or female reproductive structure. **adjective**	*The coconut is a unisex flower.*
vegetative reproduction /ˈvedʒətətɪv ˌriːprəˈdʌkʃ(ə)n/	reproduction in which part of the parent plant gives rise to new plants, which can occur naturally or by artificial methods. **noun [uncount]**	
wind-pollinated /ˈwɪnd pɒlɪˌneɪtɪd/	the pollination of flowers or cones by pollen that is blown by the wind from other flowers or cones of the same type. **noun [uncount]**	*Wind-pollinated flowers do not produce nectar.*
yeast /jiːst/	a single-cell fungus that reproduces by budding, and that can convert sugar into alcohol and carbon dioxide. **noun [count/uncount]**	*Yeast is used in bread-making and brewing.*
zygote /ˈzaɪgəʊt/	a fertilized egg in living things that have sexual reproduction. **noun [count]**	*When the pollen cell nucleus and egg cell nucleus fuse together a zygote is formed which develops into a seed.*

A Working with words

1 Reproduction in plants word map

Write these words in the correct place on the word map.

bulb   cuttings   flower   petals   pollination   spores   stamen   style

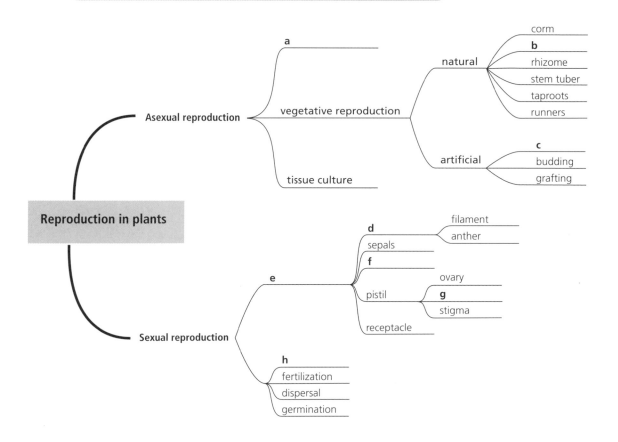

2 Some perennating organs

Label the illustrations with these phrases.

1 a carrot – example of a tap root as a storage organ
2 adventitious roots attached to stem
3 an Irish potato stem tuber
4 previous years' rhizomes
5 bud which will give rise to new rhizome
6 dormant bud
7 enlarged tap root containing food for growth of new plant
8 new shoot (x2)
9 new shoot formed at top of main root
10 lateral roots
11 swollen stem containing food for new shoot (x2)
12 the ginger rhizome

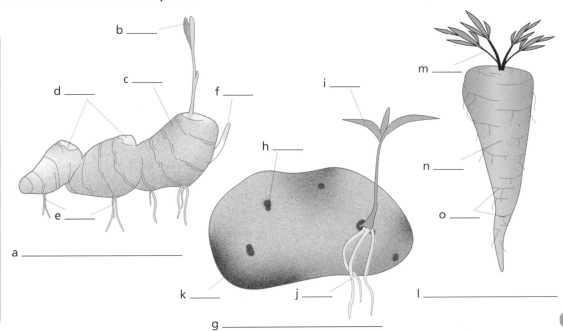

3 Reproductive structures in flowers

Look at the images and write labels.

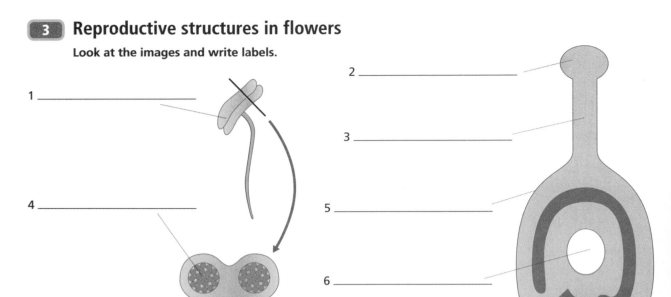

1 _____

2 _____

3 _____

4 _____

5 _____

6 _____

7 _____

4 Artificial methods of vegetative reproduction of plants

Fill the gaps with these words.

> cuttings   hormones   plants   potato   roots   soil   technique   types

1 Farmers and gardeners often use different _____ of artificial asexual reproductive techniques to increase the plants that they grow.

2 They choose high-quality _____ that grow well and reproduce them asexually so that they have more high-quality plants.

3 Some of these techniques are _____, budding and grafting.

4 Taking cuttings is a very simple _____ commonly used with hardwood plants such as sugar cane, cassava and hibiscus.

5 It involves cutting a leafy branch or stem through at an angle and placing it in _____ which contains lots of air.

6 The branch must be watered daily until _____ develop at the cut end of the stem.

7 Some people use plant _____ to encourage root growth.

8 Softwood plants such as sweet _____, cactus and Joseph's coat can also be grown from cuttings.

5 Fruit and seed dispersal

Complete the sentences by underlining the correct words.

1 The importance of fruit is in the (collection / dispersal / falling) of seeds.

2 If seeds (hang / fly / drop) beside the parent plant and germinate there, they will be competing with the parent for water, light and nutrients.

3 However, if they are carried some distance, there is a better chance of getting the (conditions / partitions / fractions) they need for germination and good growth.

4 Seeds are dispersed by different (times / places / methods), depending on the adaptations of the fruit.

5 This is often with the assistance of (superior / internal / external) agents, such as animals, water and wind.

B   Working with sentences

6   Differences between wind-pollinated and insect-pollinated flowers

Read the sentences and write them in the correct space in the grid.

… have feathery stigmas to catch airborne pollen grains.
… are generally directed upwards.
… hang down.
… produce a large amount of pollen.
… have large, brightly coloured petals.
… are odourless and produce no nectar.
… have relatively large pollen grains with a rough or sticky surface.
… have small, light and smooth pollen grains.
… produce a relatively small amount of pollen.
… have rigid and smooth stigmas, which are sticky at the tip.
… have stigmas and anthers which hang outside the flower for easy shaking in the wind.
… have stigmas and anthers which are usually inside or partly enclosed in the flower.
… have sweet scented flowers which usually produce nectar.
… are usually small with small petals that are not very conspicuous.

Characteristics	Insect-pollinated flowers …	Wind-pollinated flowers …
Petals		
Nectar production		
Direction of flowers		
Location of stigmas and anthers		
Stigmas		
Amount of pollen		
Pollen grains		

7   Natural vegetative propagation

Match these words with the correct paragraphs.

tap roots   stem tuber   runners   root tubers   rhizome   corm   bulb

1 _____ – a short, swollen, underground stem that grows vertically and is usually covered with papery leaves. The stem produces buds at the top, which give rise to the new shoots in the wet season, and roots that form on the lower surface.

2 _____ – a modified underground stem that is totally surrounded by large fleshy and scaly leaf bases. The fleshy leaf bases are the storage organ, and they are protected by outer dry scaly leaf bases. Onion and garlic are examples. The new plant develops from the terminal bud or from one or more lateral buds.

3 _____ – an underground swollen stem. It grows horizontally and has scaly leaves. The stem is firmly held in the soil by adventitious and contractile roots that form underneath the horizontal stem. Terminal buds give rise to new plants. As the plants produce food, they pass it down. Buds on the side may grow to form new lateral growths. Ginger, butterfly lily, Canna and arrowroot are examples.

4 _____ – the enlarged tip of an underground stem. Buds or 'eyes' appear at nodes or depressions where the leaves used to be. Under good conditions, one or more buds will sprout new plants. Irish or English potato is an example.

5 _____ – the sweet potato and cassava, are fibrous adventitious roots that become enlarged with food reserves. These fleshy enlarged roots serve as the storage organ, which provides the nutrients for the new shoot that arises from a bud.

6 _____ – carrots and turnips are examples of enlarged roots which contain stored food. The new shoot develops at the top.

7 _____ – natural methods of vegetative reproduction which are not storage organs. They are weak stems that grow horizontally above ground. They form roots and a shoot at their nodes. The root grows downwards to the soil which provides water and nutrients for the shoots to grow and become independent. The strawberry and water grass are the names of plants that reproduce asexually by sending these out.

C Working with texts

8 More on seed dispersal

Below is a text on ways of seed dispersal. The sentences are all jumbled up. Read the text. Then put the information about the two ways of seed dispersal in the correct columns.

Seed dispersal

Some seeds are dispersed by water. Other plants, such as the legumes, have a built-in mechanism that allows seeds to be scattered when the fruit suddenly bursts open when dry. Coconuts are the best known seeds that are dispersed by water. They have a buoyant husk which is the mesocarp of the fruit. As the fruit dries in self-dispersing plants, tension builds up in parts of the seed coat until it splits. Seeds with a buoyant husk can float long distances by sea before they are washed up onto the shore. Self-dispersing fruit split with a sudden 'explosion' which scatters the seeds quite widely. The waterproof epicarp of coconuts, the skin of the fruit, prevents them from becoming waterlogged during their journey.

Fruits dispersed by water	Self-dispersing seeds
1	5
2	6
3	7
4	

3 Reproduction in humans

Translation

acne /ˈækni/	a disease of the skin that causes spots to appear on the face, neck, and shoulders. noun [uncount]	*Many adolescents suffer with skin problems such as acne.*
acrosome /ˈækrəsəʊm/	an area inside the the tip of a sperm cell that contains enzymes (proteins) that break down the outer wall of the ovum (egg) during fertilization. noun [count]	
Adam's apple /ˌædəmz ˈæp(ə)l/	the lump at the front of a man's throat. noun [count]	*I could see his Adam's apple moving as he swallowed.*
adolescent /ˌædəˈles(ə)nt/	a young person who is going through puberty (= changing physically from being a child into being an adult). noun [count]	
AIDS /eɪdz/	acquired immune deficiency syndrome: a serious disease that destroys the body's ability to defend itself against infection. It is caused by the virus, HIV. noun [uncount]	*The best way to prevent the spread of AIDS is to keep the same sexual partner for life.*
amnion /ˈæmniən/	the inner of two membranes that forms around the embryo of a mammal, bird, or reptile. noun [count]	*The amnion breaks just before birth and releases the amniotic fluid.*
amniotic fluid /ˌæmniɒtik ˈfluːɪd/	the fluid inside the amnion that surrounds a foetus while it is developing inside its mother. noun [uncount]	
birth canal /ˈbɜːθ ˌkənæl/	a tube leading from the uterus to the outside of the body, along which a baby travels when it is born = vagina. noun [count]	
bladder /ˈblædə/	the part inside the body like a bag where urine collects before being passed out of the body through the urethra. noun [count]	*We learn to control our bladders when we are infants.*
caesarean /sɪˈzeəriən/ **or caesarean section** /sɪˈzeəriən ˌsekʃn/	a medical operation in which a baby is born by being removed through a cut in its mother's abdomen. noun [count/uncount]	
capillary /kəˈpɪləri/	the smallest type of blood vessel, with a wall that is only one cell thick. It carries blood to and from individual cells in the body (plural: capillaries). noun [count]	*All the body's organs have a network of capillaries.*
cervix /ˈsɜːvɪks/	the entrance to the uterus. noun [count]	
cilium	one of a great many extremely small hair-like parts on a cell and on some microorganisms. The cilia beat regularly to help the movement of fluids past the cell, or, in some microorganisms, to help them to move through liquid (plural: cilia). noun [count]	
clitoris /ˈklɪtərɪs/	the small sensitive part of the female sex organs, just above the entrance to the vagina. noun [count]	
colostrum /kəˈlɒstrəm/	the fluid that comes from a woman's breasts soon after she gives birth and before her breast milk, which contains a lot of nutrients and antibodies (= substances that help the baby's body to fight infections). noun [uncount]	
contraction /kənˈtrækʃ(ə)n/	a strong painful movement of a muscle in the uterus that helps to push a baby out during birth. noun [count]	*She knew she was in labour because her contractions were every 5 minutes.*
copulation /ˌkɒpjʊˈleɪʃ(ə)n/	sexual intercourse. noun [uncount]	*Copulation can result in pregnancy.*
corpus luteum /ˌkɔːpəs luːˈtiəm/	a structure that develops in a woman's ovary after an ovum (egg) has been released and produces the hormone progesterone, which prepares the woman's body for pregnancy. noun [count]	
deoxygenated blood /diˌɒksɪdʒəneɪtɪd ˈblʌd/	blood that has had oxygen removed from it, which becomes oxygenated when it passes through the lungs. noun [uncount]	
dilate /daɪˈleɪt/	if an opening in the body, especially a woman's cervix or a person's pupil, dilates, it becomes bigger and wider. verb [intransitive]	*Her cervix had dilated fully and she was ready to push the baby out.*
disintegrate /dɪsˈɪntəgreɪt/	to be completely destroyed by breaking into lots of very small pieces. verb [intransitive]	*If pregnancy does not occur, the womb lining disintegrates and is expelled during menstruation.*

ejaculate /ɪˈdʒækjʊˌleɪt/	if a man ejaculates, semen comes out of his penis. **verb [intransitive/transitive]**	
embedded /ɪmˈbedɪd/	firmly fixed in a surface or object. **adjective**	*A piece of metal was embedded in his leg.*
embryo /ˈembriəʊ/	an animal in its earliest stages of development, especially in the uterus of a female mammal or in the egg of a bird, reptile etc (plural: embryos). **noun [count]**	*The scan showed that the embryo was only about 8 weeks old.*
endocrine gland /ˈendəʊkraɪn ˌɡlænd/	a gland in the body that produces hormones that go directly into the blood or into the lymph vessels. **noun [count]**	
epididymis /epɪˈdɪdɪmɪs/	a coiled tube above a man's testes, which leads from the testes to the vas deferens (sperm duct). **noun [count]**	
erectile tissue /ɪˌrektaɪl ˈtɪʃuː/	tissue in the body that is capable of becoming erect (stiff and enlarged) by being filled with blood. **adjective**	
erection /ɪˈrekʃ(ə)n/	a penis that has become stiff and enlarged by being filled with blood. **noun [count]**	
expel /ɪkˈspel/	to force something out of a container or out of the body. **verb [transitive]**	*The unfertilized egg will be expelled from the body during menstruation.*
Fallopian tube /fəˌləʊpiən ˈtjuːb/	one of the two tubes in the body of a woman or other female mammal that carry eggs produced in the ovaries to the uterus = oviduct. **noun [count]**	*Eggs are fertilized by sperm in the Fallopian tube.*
fat deposit /ˈfæt dɪˌpɒzɪt/	a layer of fat that forms in a particular area of the body. **noun [count]**	*Most women have fat deposits on the buttocks and thighs.*
foetal /ˈfiːt(ə)l/	relating to a foetus. **adjective**	*The scan can detect some foetal abnormalities.*
foetus /ˈfiːtəs/	a mammal that is developing inside its mother's body, especially one that is not capable of existing independently. **noun [count]**	*Alcohol drunk by the mother can harm the developing foetus.*
finger-like projection /ˈfɪŋɡəlaɪk prəˈdʒekʃ(ə)n/	part of something that sticks out from a surface and has a long, thin shape like a finger. **noun [count]**	*The flowers have a central, finger-like projection.*
follicle /ˈfɒlɪk(ə)l/	a structure inside a woman's ovary where the ovum (egg) develops. **noun [count]**	*The eggs develop inside follicles in the ovary.*
foreskin /ˈfɔːskɪn/	the loose skin that covers the front part of a man's penis. **noun [count]**	*When males are circumcised their foreskin is removed.*
funnel-like /ˈfʌn(ə)llaɪk/	in the shape of a funnel, with a wider top part and a cylindrical lower part. **adjective**	*A funnel-like cloud had formed.*
gamete /ˈɡæmiːt/	a male or female cell that unites with a cell from the opposite sex to form a new organism in the process of sexual reproduction. Gametes have half the number of chromosomes of other cells. The egg and sperm cells in animals and the nuclei in grains of pollen are all gametes = reproductive cell. **noun [count]**	
genitalia /dʒenɪˈteɪliə/	a formal or technical word for the genitals (= the outer sex organs of a human or other animal). **noun [plural]**	
genitals /ˈdʒenɪt(ə)lz/	the outer sex organs of a human or other animal. **noun [plural]**	*During adolescence, hair begins to grow around the genitals and under the armpits.*
gestation period /dʒesˈteɪʃ(ə)n ˌpɪəriəd/	the period of time during which a human or animal baby develops inside its mother. **noun [count]**	*Human infants have a gestation period of nine months.*
glans /ɡlænz/	the rounded head of the penis. **noun [count]**	
hip /hɪp/	one of the two parts at either side of the body between the waist and the top of the legs. **noun [count]**	*She stood with her hands on her hips, waiting.*
hollow /ˈhɒləʊ/	empty inside. **adjective**	*The heart is divided into four hollow parts called chambers.*
hormone /ˈhɔːməʊn/	a chemical substance produced in animals and plants that controls things such as growth and sexual development. Hormones in animals are usually produced in the endocrine glands. **noun [count]**	*The hormone testosterone controls sexual development in boys.*
hymen /ˈhaɪmən/	a thin membrane that covers the entrance to the vagina in young girls. This is usually broken before puberty because of normal child activity in girls, but sometimes all or part of it remains until a woman first has sex. **noun [count]**	

immature /ˌɪməˈtʃʊə/	not fully grown or developed ≠ mature. **adjective**	*The immature birds are grey and the fully-grown adult birds are black.*
implant /ɪmˈplɑːnt/	to put something into someone's body (in a medical operation). **verb [transitive]**	*The fertilized egg develops into a ball of cells which implants in the spongy lining of the uterus.*
intact /ɪnˈtækt/	whole and not damaged or broken. **adjective**	*The seal on the jar was still intact.*
jaundice /ˈdʒɔːndɪs/	an illness that makes the skin and the white part of the eyes become yellow. **noun [uncount]**	*Premature babies often suffer from jaundice.*
labia /ˈleɪbiə/	the outer folds of skin of a woman's sex organs. **noun [plural]**	
labour /ˈleɪbə/	the time during which a mother has contractions in her uterus which push the baby out of her body so it can be born. **noun [uncount]**	*His wife was in labour for six hours.*
lining /ˈlaɪnɪŋ/	a layer that covers the inside surface of something such as a part of the body. **noun [count]**	*The lining of the uterus thickens in preparation for pregnancy.*
menopause /ˈmenəpɔːz/	the time in a woman's life when she no longer produces eggs, her periods stop, and she is no longer capable of getting pregnant. **noun [singular]**	
menstrual cycle /ˈmenstruəl ˌsaɪkl/	the repeated process in which a woman's uterus prepares for pregnancy, and which ends in a period if she does not get pregnant. The menstrual cycle usually lasts about a month, and ovulation usually takes place about halfway through it. **noun [count]**	
miscarriage /ˈmɪskærɪdʒ/	a process in which a foetus comes out of the uterus before it has developed enough to live independently. Very often there is no known reason for this, but it can be the result of illness in the mother, something wrong with the foetus itself, or an accident. **noun [count/uncount]**	
mood swing /ˈmuːd ˌswɪŋ/	a change from one emotion to another very different emotion. **noun [count]**	*He suffers from severe mood swings.*
mucus /ˈmjuːkəs/	a clear smooth liquid that is produced inside the nose and other parts of your body. **noun [uncount]**	
nocturnal emission /nɒkˌtɜːn(ə)l ɪˈmɪʃ(ə)n/	an ejaculation (release of semen from the penis) that takes place during sleep, as a result of a dream = wet dream. **noun [count]**	
nourishment /ˈnʌrɪʃmənt/	food or the substances in food that you need to live, grow and be healthy. **noun [uncount]**	*A foetus gets oxygen and nourishment through the mother's placenta.*
oestrogen /ˈiːstrədʒ(ə)n/	a hormone that makes women and other female mammals develop typical female sexual features. **noun [uncount]**	
ovary /ˈəʊv(ə)ri/	one of the two organs in the body of a woman or other female animal that produce eggs and the sex hormones progesterone and oestrogen. In mammals, the eggs travel from the ovaries down the Fallopian tubes to the uterus. If the eggs are fertilized, an embryo will develop (plural: ovaries). **noun [count]**	
oviduct /ˈɒvɪdʌkt/	a tube in the body of a female mammal that takes eggs from an ovary to the uterus = Fallopian tube. **noun [count]**	
ovulation /ˌɒvjʊˈleɪʃ(ə)n/	a time during which a woman or female mammal produces an egg in her body and can become pregnant. **noun [uncount]**	*In humans, ovulation takes place about every 28 days.*
ovum /ˈəʊvəm/	the female gamete or egg cell that can grow into a new animal after it has been fertilized. In mammals, this happens inside the female (plural: ova /ˈəʊvə/). **noun [count]**	*A baby develops after an ovum is fertilized by a sperm.*
oxytocin /ˌɒksɪˈtəʊsɪn/	a hormone which causes a woman or female mammal's uterus to contract when giving birth, and causes her to produce milk for her baby. **noun [uncount]**	
pelvis /ˈpelvɪs/	the large circular bones that support the lower part of the back. They are connected to the bones of the legs. **noun [count]**	
penetrate /ˈpenətreɪt/	if a man penetrates someone, he puts his penis into his partner's vagina or anus during sex. **verb [transitive]**	
period /ˈpɪəriəd/	the time about once a month when a woman who is not pregnant loses blood from the uterus. **noun [count]**	*She was not feeling well because she had her period.*
perspiration /ˌpɜːspəˈreɪʃ(ə)n/	the liquid that your skin produces when you are hot, ill, or nervous = sweat. **noun [uncount]**	

pituitary gland /pɪˈtjuːɪt(ə)ri ˌɡlænd/	the small gland at the base of the brain that produces the hormones that the body needs to control its growth and development. It is the main endocrine gland in the body, and controls many other endocrine glands. noun [count]	
placenta /pləˈsentə/	the organ through which a foetus is connected to its mother's blood supply in the uterus before birth. noun [count]	*The developing baby receives oxygen and food from its mother's blood through the placenta.*
postnatal /ˌpəʊs(t)(neɪt(ə)l/	relating to the period of time after the birth of a baby. adjective	*Postnatal care is important to ensure the health of a baby.*
pregnancy /ˈpreɡnənsi/	the condition of being pregnant, or the period of time when a woman is pregnant (plural: pregnancies). noun [count/uncount]	*Pregnancy in humans lasts for about 9 months.*
prenatal /ˌpriːˈneɪt(ə)l/	relating to the period of time when a woman is pregnant. adjective	*Pregnant women visit a special clinic for prenatal care.*
progesterone /prəˈdʒestərəʊn/	a hormone produced in the bodies of women and other female mammals that makes the uterus ready for pregnancy. noun [uncount]	
projection /prəˈdʒekʃ(ə)n/	part of something that sticks out from its surface. noun [count]	*The tongue has many small projections on it.*
prostate gland /ˈprɒˌsteɪt ˌɡlænd/	the organ in men and other male mammals that produces a liquid that combines with and carries sperm. noun [count]	*Semen is made up of sperm and fluids from the prostate gland.*
puberty /ˈpjuːbəti/	the stage of development in the lives of humans and other primates when they change from being a child to being an adult. This involves the development of physical characteristics such as the growth of breasts in females and the voice getting deeper in males. Females start to produce eggs and start to menstruate, and males begin to produce sperm. noun [uncount]	
rapid increase /ˌræpɪd ˈɪnkriːs/	an occasion when something rises very quickly in amount, number, size etc. noun [count/uncount]	*A rapid increase in weight is not good for your health.*
Rhesus factor /ˈriːsəs ˌfæktə/	an antigen that is present in the red blood cells of about 85% of humans and some other primates. noun [singular]	
rubella /ruːˈbelə/	an infectious viral disease that causes red spots on the skin. It is a minor illness in children and adults, but it can cause serious damage to the foetus if a pregnant woman catches it = German measles. noun [uncount]	
rupture /ˈrʌptʃə/	if something such as part of the body ruptures, it breaks or tears suddenly. verb [intransitive]	*His Achilles tendon ruptured.*
scar /skɑː/	a permanent mark on your skin where you have been injured or cut. noun [count]	*He has a scar under his left eye.*
scrotal sac /ˌskrəʊt(ə)l ˈsæk/	another word for scrotum (the bag of skin holding the testes). noun [count]	
scrotum /ˈskrəʊtəm/	the bag of skin holding the testes of a man or male animal. noun [count]	
sebaceous gland /səˈbeɪʃəs ˌɡlænd/	a gland in the skin that allows a type of oil called sebum to flow onto the skin and hair to keep them soft. noun [count]	
secretion /sɪˈkriːʃ(ə)n/	a liquid that is produced by a living thing, or the process of producing this liquid. noun [count/uncount]	*The prostate gland produces secretions that nourish the sperm.*
semen /ˈsiːmən/	the liquid that contains sperm produced by the male sex organs. noun [uncount]	
seminal vesicle /ˌsemɪn(ə)l ˈviːsɪkl/	a small gland that produces a thick, sticky fluid in which sperms are stored, that mixes with thin fluid from the prostate gland to form semen when the sperms are carried from the body during ejaculation. noun [count]	
sexual intercourse /ˌsekʃuəl ˈɪntəkɔːs/	sexual activity between a man and a woman in which the man puts his penis inside the woman's vagina. noun [uncount]	
sperm duct /ˈspɜːm ˌdʌkt/	a long thin tube that carries sperms away from the epididimis in the scrotum to the seminal vesicles where they will be stored until ejaculation. noun [count]	
spherical /ˈsferɪk(ə)l/	shaped like a ball. adjective	*The ovum is a spherical cell.*
spongy /ˈspʌndʒi/	light, soft and full of small holes. adjective	*Bone marrow is the spongy tissue inside bones.*

spontaneous abortion /spɒnˌteɪniəs əˈbɔːʃ(ə)n/	an occasion when a foetus is expelled from its mother's body before it has developed enough to live. noun [count]	*A study showed that the medication could cause spontaneous abortion.*
stiff /stɪf/	firm and difficult to bend. adjective	*Her fingers were swollen and stiff.*
stillbirth /ˈstɪlbɜːθ/	a birth in which the baby is born dead. noun [count/uncount]	
strenuous /ˈstrenjʊəs/	needing a lot of effort, energy or strength. adjective	*Pregnant women should avoid very strenuous exercise.*
sweating /ˈswetɪŋ/	the process by which liquid containing waste produced by sweat glands forms on the skin as a result of hot conditions, physical exercise, illness, or nervousness. noun [uncount]	*Drink plenty of water to replace the fluids lost through sweating.*
testis /ˈtestiːz/	one of two round male sex organs that hang in a sack of skin behind the penis (plural: testes /ˈtestiːz/). noun [count]	
testosterone /tesˈtɒstərəʊn/	a sex hormone that causes men to develop the physical features that are typical of males, for example hair on the face and a deep voice. Testosterone belongs to the group of hormones called steroids. noun [uncount]	
trigger /ˈtrɪɡə/	to cause something to happen. verb [transitive]	*The substance triggered an allergic reaction.*
ultrasound examination /ˈʌltrəˌsaʊnd ɪɡˌzæmɪˈneɪʃ(ə)n/	a medical examination in which sound waves are used to produce an image of an organ or of a baby developing inside its mother's uterus. noun [count]	*She had an ultrasound examination to find out how many weeks pregnant she was.*
umbilical cord /ʌmˌbɪlɪk(ə)l ˈkɔːd/	a long tube that connects a baby to its mother in the uterus and through which it receives food and oxygen It is cut immediately after birth. noun [count]	
undergo /ˌʌndəˈɡəʊ/	to experience something, especially a change or medical treatment. verb [transitive]	*He recently underwent knee surgery.*
urethra /jʊˈriːθrə/	in most mammals, the tube that carries urine out of the body. noun [count]	*The urethra passes through the penis and carries both urine and semen.*
urinary tract /ˈjʊərɪn(ə)ri (trækt/	the tube that carries urine from the bladder out of the body. noun [count]	
uterus /ˈjuːt(ə)rəs/	the organ in the body of a woman or female mammal where a fertilized egg grows and develops into a foetus = womb. noun [count]	
vagina /vəˈdʒaɪnə/	in female mammals, a sex organ consisting of a tube from the opening of the uterus to the outside. noun [count]	
vas deferens /ˌvæs ˈdefərənz/	a long thin tube that carries sperms away from the epidydimis in the scrotum to the seminal vesicles where they will be stored until ejaculation = sperm duct. noun [count]	
virgin /ˈvɜːdʒɪn/	someone who has never had sex. noun [count]	*She was still a virgin when she married.*
voice box /ˈvɔɪs ˌbɒks/	the part of the throat from which you produce sounds. noun [count]	*In adolescence the voice box of males enlarges and their voice deepens.*
vulva /ˈvʌlvə/	the outer parts of a woman's sexual organs. noun [count]	
wither /ˈwɪðə/	to stop living or growing, become smaller and then disappear. verb [intransitive]	*Without water the plants will wither and die.*
womb /wuːm/	the organ in the body of a woman or female mammal where a fertilized egg grows and develops into a foetus = uterus. noun [count]	
zygote /ˈzaɪɡəʊt/	a fertilized egg in living things that have sexual reproduction. noun [count]	*A zygote is formed when a sperm fertilizes an egg.*

1   Human reproduction word map

Fill in these words on the word map.

ejaculation   embryo   oviduct   puberty   sexual organs   sperm   testis

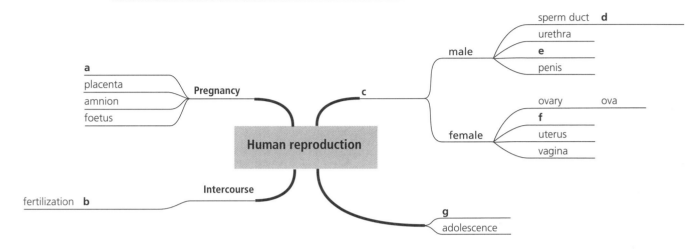

2   The female reproductive system

Look at the diagram and label the parts indicated.

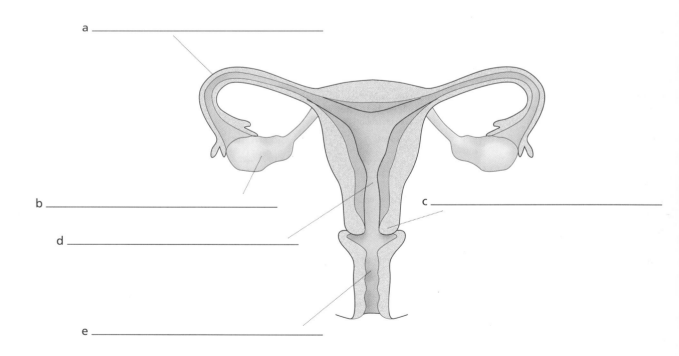

a _____

b _____

c _____

d _____

e _____

3 The role of the placenta

Fill in the gaps in the labels with these words.

> amnion capillaries deoxygenated embryo eye food oxygen (x2)
> placenta umbilical cord (x2) uterus waste

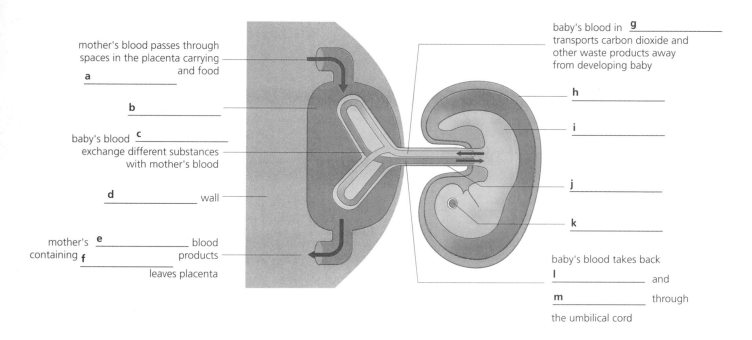

mother's blood passes through spaces in the placenta carrying _____ and food
a _____

b _____

baby's blood **c** _____ exchange different substances with mother's blood

d _____ wall

mother's **e** _____ blood containing **f** _____ products leaves placenta

baby's blood in **g** _____ transports carbon dioxide and other waste products away from developing baby

h _____

i _____

j _____

k _____

baby's blood takes back
l _____ and
m _____ through the umbilical cord

4 Sexual intercourse and fertilization

Read and fill in the gaps with these words.

> cervix ejaculation Fallopian tubes fertilization fertilize gamete (x2)
> nucleus ovum penetrate penis reproduction semen (x2) uterus

Sexual intercourse is the beginning of human 1_____. This process involves the insertion of the male's 2_____ into the vaginal passage of the female and with a rhythmic back and forth motion eventually 3_____ is expelled from the male's penis into the vagina. Sexual intercourse is the natural process by which the male 4_____ leaves the male's body and meets with the female 5_____ inside the female's body. The expelling of semen from the penis is called 6_____ . This deposits the sperm up towards the top of the vagina, near the 7_____. The human male ejaculates approximately 4 cm³ of 8_____, which may contain as much as 500 million sperm! These sperm then swim up along the lining of the 9_____ into the 10_____. Sperm that meet an egg in the Fallopian tube will compete to penetrate its protective membrane. However, only one sperm can 11_____ the egg. As soon as the head of the first sperm begins to 12_____ the surface of the egg, a membrane lifts from the egg's surface and water begins to fill the space between the surface of the egg and the fertilization membrane. This encloses the successful sperm and prevents any others from penetrating the surface. Only the head of the sperm enters the 13_____, the tail drops off and remains outside. The nucleus of the sperm will fuse with the 14_____ of the egg in the process of 15_____.

5   Male and female sex cells

Read these descriptions and put them in the correct places on the illustrations.

1 At the tip of the head is a sac of enzymes, called the acrosome.
2 The head contains a nucleus with the genetic information (chromosomes) that can be passed to the offspring from the father.
3 The internal structures of the cell are enclosed by a thin membrane and a jelly-like coat.
4 The long tail rapidly moves from side to side to allow the sperm to swim quickly.
5 The movement of the tail is powered by large numbers of mitochondria in the middle section of the sperm.
6 The nucleus of the ovum carries the genetic information from the mother that will be passed to the off-spring.
7 The ovum – the female gamete – is a single spherical cell with a diameter of about one millimetre.
8 The sperm, the male gamete, has three parts: a head, middle piece and a tail.
9 Enzymes break down the membrane of the female sex cell (ovum) during fertilization.

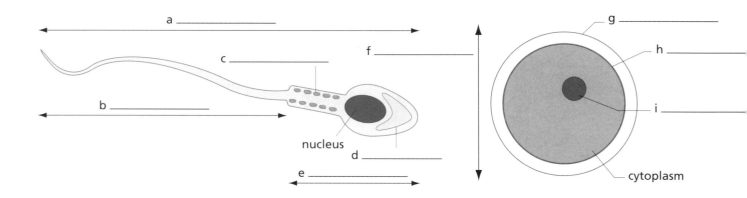

6   The menstrual cycle

Read the sentences and put them in the correct order.

a   About one week after ovulation, the corpus luteum produces a hormone called progesterone.

b   If the egg is not fertilized, the progesterone levels will gradually decrease causing the development of milk glands to stop and the lining of the womb to break down.

c   The hormone oestrogen, which is released by the ovary, starts the building of a soft lining in the uterus ready to receive a fertilized egg.

d   The menstrual cycle begins as an ovum matures inside a follicle in an ovary. When the ovum is mature it is released into the Fallopian tube.

e   The menstrual cycle starts in an adolescent girl indicating that she is capable of reproducing. It includes many changes in the ovaries and the uterus.

f   The progesterone has two effects: it stimulates the building of the lining on the walls of the uterus so that it becomes thicker and more spongy, to accommodate and protect the expected fertilized egg. It also stimulates the breasts to develop, making them ready to produce milk.

g   The released egg is slowly pulled along the Fallopian tube by cilia (fine hairs) towards the uterus.

h   The remains of the burst follicle in the ovary develops into a structure called the corpus luteum (yellow body).

i   This is called ovulation.

j   This will result in blood, mucus and the unfertilized egg leaving the body via the vagina during menstruation, commonly called the period.

1 ☐ 2 ☐ 3 ☐ 4 ☐ 5 ☐ 6 ☐ 7 ☐ 8 ☐ 9 ☐ 10 ☐

7 ## Summary of reproduction in humans

Match the beginnings and endings of the sentences.

Beginnings

1 The hormones that stimulate puberty
2 The female sex cell
3 The main male reproductive structures in humans
4 The main female reproductive structures in humans
5 The menstrual cycle takes about 28 days during which a mature ovum
6 Ovulation
7 Ejaculation
8 Fertilization in humans
9 The fertilized egg
10 Pregnancy
11 During pregnancy the placenta
12 Prenatal care
13 Both the mother and baby

Endings

a begins when the embryo becomes implanted in the wall of the uterus.
b are the testes, seminal vesicles, vas deferens and penis.
c are the ovaries, uterus and vagina.
d are oestrogen in girls and testosterone in boys.
e divides continuously to form the ball of cells known as the embryo.
f involves the release of semen through the urethra of the penis.
g is called ovum and the male sex cell is called the sperm.
h is released from an ovary, passes to the uterus and is shed along with the lining of the uterus during menstruation.
i is the care given to the mother before the birth of the baby.
j need postnatal care, after the birth.
k occurs approximately 14 days after the start of menstruation.
l occurs in the body of the woman when the nucleus of a sperm fuses with the nucleus of the egg in a Fallopian tube.
m provides all the food needed by the foetus, and removes all the waste products.

1 ☐ 2 ☐ 3 ☐ 4 ☐ 5 ☐ 6 ☐ 7 ☐ 8 ☐ 9 ☐ 10 ☐ 11 ☐ 12 ☐ 13 ☐

C Working with texts

8 ## Changes in young men and women

Read the text and sort the information into the right columns.

In females puberty starts between 8 and 16 years whereas in males it starts between 10 and 17 years. There is a marked increase in growth in females at the start of puberty. Males experience a rapid increase in height and weight. The female's breasts enlarge and develop and the male's shoulders widen and voice deepens as the voice box (Adam's apple) enlarges. There is also hair growth in both sexes, in the armpits and genital region of females and on the face, in the armpits, the genitals and sometimes on the chest of males. Hips get wider on females and fat deposits under skin increase here, giving a characteristic, curvier female shape whilst for males muscles get bigger and the penis and testicles enlarge. Females experience whitish, odourless vaginal secretions prior to the beginning of their menstrual cycle. It begins when ovaries start to release mature ova (ripe eggs). In males the testes are now able to produce sperm. Erections may be more frequent and may be accompanied by emissions of semen from the penis. If this happens during sleep, it is called nocturnal emission or 'wet dream'. In both sexes perspiration (sweating) begins and body odours are more noticeable. Acne may also result in both males and females although this is not common to all individuals and in males the endocrine (hormone) and sebaceous (oil secreting) glands increase their activity.

Females	Males

4 Heredity

amniotic fluid /ˌæmnɪɒtɪk ˈfluːɪd/	the fluid inside the amnion that surrounds a foetus while it is developing inside its mother. **noun [uncount]**	*Many plants are able to produce new plants by asexual reproduction.*
asexual /eɪˈsekʃʊəl/	without sex or sex organs. **adjective**	*Strawberry runners are an example of asexual reproduction.*
asexual reproduction /ˌeɪsekʃʊəl riːprəˈdʌkʃ(ə)n/	reproduction in which there is no joining of male and female gametes (=male or female reproductive cells), for example cloning or vegetative propagation. **noun [uncount]**	
cell division /ˈsel dɪˌvɪʒ(ə)n/	**1** process by which a cell divides into two smaller cells that each contain the same number of chromosomes as the original cell. It is the basis of asexual reproduction and ordinary cell division in living things = mitosis. **noun [uncount]** **2** a type of cell division in which a cell divides into four cells, each of which contains half the number of chromosomes of the original cell. It takes place when gametes (=reproductive cells) are formed = meiosis. **noun [uncount]**	
characteristic /ˌkærəktəˈrɪstɪk/	a typical quality or feature. **noun [count]**	*Personality characteristics are inherited from our parents.*
chromosome /ˈkrəʊməˌsəʊm/	a structure that looks like a very small piece of string and that exists, usually as one of a pair, in the nucleus of all living cells. Chromosomes contain the genetic information that says whether a person, animal etc is male or female and what characteristics they get from their parents. **noun [count]**	*Each body cell contains two sets of chromosomes.*
combination /ˌkɒmbɪˈneɪʃ(ə)n/	something that combines several things. **noun [count]**	*the combination of genes in a single cell*
corresponding /ˌkɒrɪˈspɒndɪŋ/	related to something, or similar to something. **adjective**	*Each of the 23 chromosomes from one parent pairs up with the corresponding chromosomes from the other parent.*
cystic fibrosis /ˌsɪstɪk faɪˈbrəʊsɪs/	a serious medical condition that mainly affects the lungs. It is caused by a gene that is passed from parents to their children. **noun [uncount]**	*John inherited cystic fibrosis from his parents.*
daughter cell /ˈdɔːtə ˌsel/	a cell that is formed when another cell divides. **noun [count]**	*During one type of cell division, a cell divides into two identical daughter cells.*
disease /dɪˈziːz/	a medical condition in humans or other animals and plants that can cause serious health problems or death. **noun [count/uncount]**	*Studies have revealed that fewer vegetarians suffer from heart disease. Smoking can cause fatal diseases.*
dominant /ˈdɒmɪnənt/	a dominant gene causes someone to be born with particular genetic features because it is stronger than other genes (≠recessive). **adjective**	*In eye colour the gene for brown is dominant to that for blue.*
duplicate /ˈdjuːplɪkeɪt/	**1** to make an exact copy of something. **verb [transitive]** **2** to repeat work that has been done already. **verb [transitive]**	*Sometimes a chromosome may duplicate itself.* *He is simply duplicating the work of other scientists.*
/ˈdjuːplɪkət/	**3** an exact copy of something. **noun [count]**	*The two 'daughter' cells are duplicates of the 'parent' cell.*
/ˈdjuːplɪkət/	**4** made as an exact copy of something else. **adjective**	*a duplicate cell*
exchange /ɪkˈstʃeɪndʒ/	**1** a situation in which something passes from one person or thing to another, in both directions. **noun [count/uncount]** **2** to pass something from one person or thing to another, in both directions. **verb [transitive]**	*an exchange of genetic information between chromosomes* *Genetic material is exchanged between chromosomes.*
faulty /ˈfɔːlti/	not working correctly, or not made correctly. **adjective**	*a faulty gene*
fertilization /ˌfɜːtəlaɪˈzeɪʃ(ə)n/	the joining together of a female and a male gamete (=reproductive cell) in order to make a zygote (=fertilized egg) that will develop into a completely new plant, human being or other animal etc. In mammals, birds, and reptiles, fertilization takes place inside the female's body. In plants, fertilization takes place inside the plant. In animals such as fish and amphibians, the eggs are fertilized in water. **noun [uncount]**	*a baby conceived by vitro fertilization*

fertilize /ˈfɜːtəlaɪz/	to provide the male gamete that will join with a female gamete to make a new organism. **verb [transitive]**	*A baby develops when a sperm fertilizes an egg.*
foetus /ˈfiːtəs/	a mammal that is developing inside its mother's body, especially one that is not capable of existing independently. **noun [count]**	*The developing foetus obtains food and oxygen from its mother in the womb.*
fuse /ˈfjuːz/	to join two substances together to form one thing, or to become joined together in this way. **verb [transitive]**	*The sperm cell fuses with the nucleus of the ovum.*
gamete /ˈgæmiːt/	a male or female cell that unites with a cell from the opposite sex to form a new organism in the process of sexual reproduction. Gametes have half the number of chromosomes of other cells. The egg and sperm cells in animals and the nuclei in grains of pollen are all gametes = reproductive cell. **noun [count]**	
gene /dʒiːn/	a section of DNA on a chromosome that is responsible for a particular characteristic. **noun [count]**	*We have genes for eye colour on our chromosomes.*
genetic /dʒəˈnetɪk/	relating to genes or to the study of genes. **adjective**	*We inherit genetic characteristics from our parents.*
genetic code /dʒəˌnetɪk ˈkəʊd/	the particular order of the sequence of nucleotides in the DNA in chromosomes that determines heredity. **noun [count]**	*A change in the genetic code is called a mutation.*
genetics /dʒəˈnetɪks/	the study of how features of living things are passed through their genes to their children. **noun [uncount]**	
heterozygous /ˌhet(ə)rəʊˈzaɪgəs/	a heterozygous cell or organism has two different forms of a particular gene for something such as eye colour. **adjective**	*Although the mouse was brown it was heterozygous for coat colour.*
homozygous /ˌhəʊməʊˈzaɪgəs/	having two of the same form of a particular gene for something such as eye colour. **adjective**	*She had blue eyes which meant she was homozygous for eye colour.*
identical /aɪˈdentɪk(ə)l/	exactly the same. **adjective**	*identical twins*
mate /meɪt/	if one animal mates with another, or if two animals mate, they have sex. **verb [intransitive]**	
meiosis /maɪˈəʊsɪs/	a type of cell division in which a cell divides into four cells, each of which contains half the number of chromosomes of the original cell. It takes place when gametes (=reproductive cells) are formed. **noun [uncount]**	*Eggs and sperm are produced by meiosis.*
mitosis /maɪˈtəʊsɪs/	the process by which a cell divides into two smaller cells that each contain the same number of chromosomes as the original cell. It is the basis of asexual reproduction and ordinary cell division in living things. **noun [uncount]**	*Growth in living things is a result of mitosis.*
offspring /ˈɒfˌsprɪŋ/	the young of any living thing, including humans (plural: offspring). **noun [count]**	
pair up /ˌpeə(r) (ˈʌp/	to form a pair. **phrasal verb**	*Each of the 23 chromosomes from one parent pairs up with the corresponding chromosomes from the other parent.*
parent cell /ˈpeərənt ˌsel/	the cell from which other cells are produced during cell division. During meiosis, the parent cell divides into four new daughter cells. **noun [count]**	
Punnett square /ˈpʌnɪt ˌskweə/	a diagram used for showing the possible combination of genes in a child with particular parents. **noun [count]**	
random /ˈrænd(ə)m/	chosen or happening without any particular method or pattern. **adjective**	*a random process of genetic change*
recessive /rɪˈsesɪv/	a recessive gene has to have been passed on by both parents in order to produce a particular feature in a child. **adjective**	*Sally had blue eyes because she inherited a recessive gene for blue eye colour from both parents.*
sickle cell anaemia /ˌsɪk(ə)l sel əˈniːmiə/	a blood disease in which the red blood cells are damaged, making the blood flow more slowly. This prevents oxygen from getting to the bones and organs. **noun [uncount]**	*Sickle cell anaemia is a hereditary disease.*
strand /strænd/	a single thin piece of something. **noun [count]**	*a strand of DNA*
suffer from /ˈsʌfə frəm/	to have a particular illness or physical problem. **verb [transitive]**	
survive /səˈvaɪv/	to stay alive after difficult conditions. **verb [intransitive/transitive]**	*Some of the offspring will survive to produce their own young.*
trait /treɪt/	a particular quality in someone's character. **noun [count]**	*the genes that determine our character traits*
variation /ˌveərɪˈeɪʃ(ə)n/	differences in living things. **noun [count/uncount]**	*Sexual reproduction results in variation between offspring.*

1 Heredity word map

Write these words in the correct place on the word map.

body cell   cystic fibrosis   division   recessive   homozygous   meiosis   parent

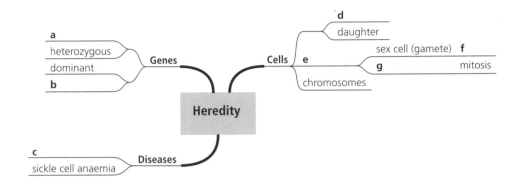

2 Genetic diseases

Fill in the gaps in the text with these words.

amniotic fluid   blood tests   faulty   foetus   gene
genetic disease   heterozygous   suffer from

In situations where there are individuals who have suffered from a 1 _____, it is possible that other close family members may be 2 _____ for that gene and carry one 3 _____ version without knowing it. If they marry someone from another family where there have been cases of the genetic disease, then they run the risk of having children with the genetic disease. A genetic counsellor can explain the chances that their children may 4 _____ the disease. In some cases 5 _____ may be taken from the parents to work out whether they carry the faulty version of the 6 _____. During pregnancy, samples of 7 _____ can be taken from around the 8 _____ inside the mother, to work out whether it will suffer from the disease.

3 Mitosis and meiosis

Put these phrases and sentences in the correct places on the diagrams.

Two pairs of similar chromosomes (total 4).
Before cell division starts, the chromosomes duplicate so each has two strands.
Cell divides in two – each new cell has two chromosomes.
Cell division occurs again – each chromosome strand is separated.
Each cell has copies of one chromosome from each original pair –
half the chromosome number of the parent cell.
Stages in meiosis
Pairs of chromosomes line up across centre of cell. Each chromosome duplicates to make two strands.
Stages in mitosis
The cell divides in two, each new cell has a full copy of the original chromosomes.
The chromosomes line up along the middle of the cell.
The strands of the chromosomes are pulled apart – one copy of each chromosome
goes to each side of the cell.
This body cell has 4 chromosomes – humans have 46.

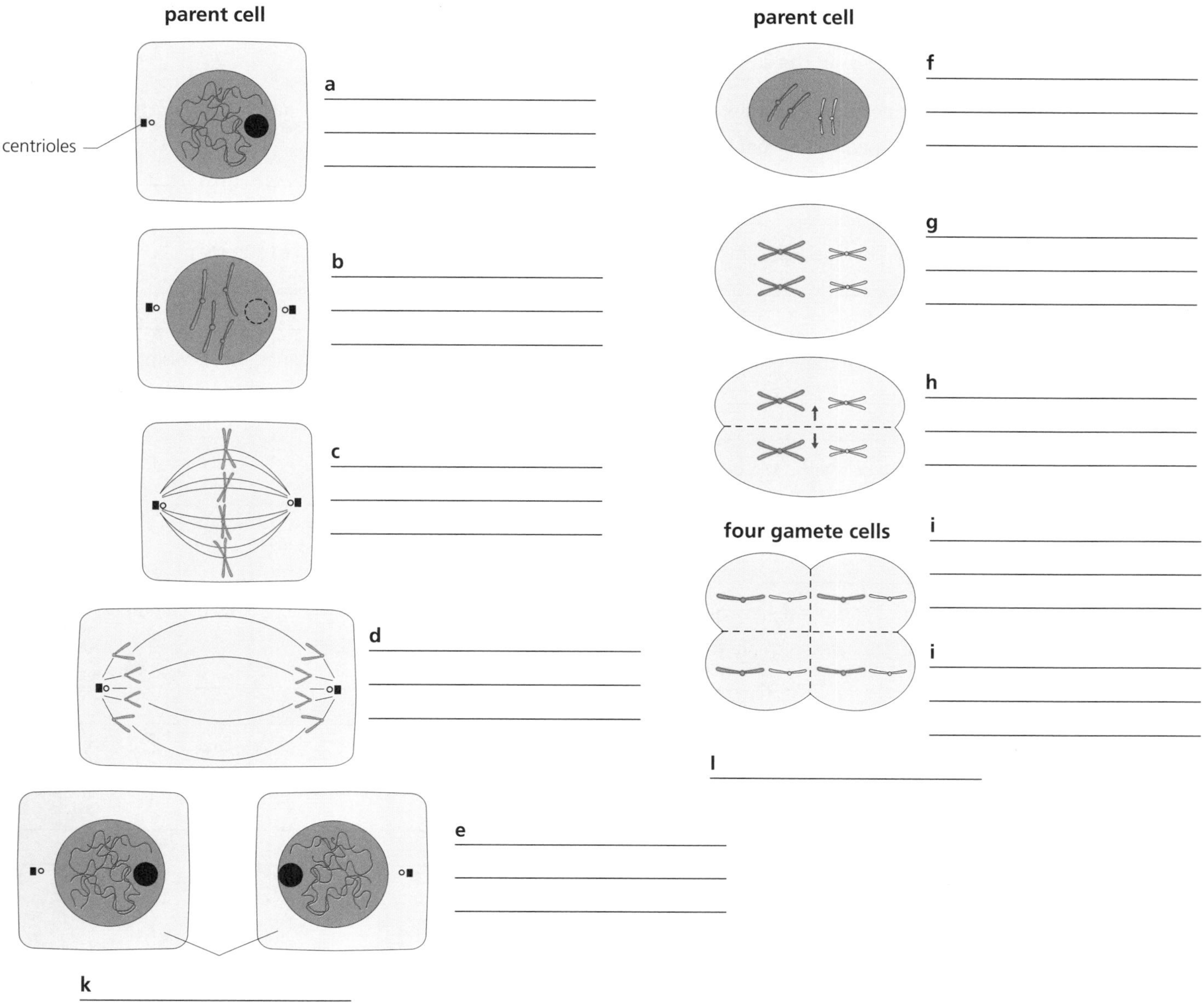

parent cell

centrioles

a _____

b _____

c _____

d _____

e _____

k _____

parent cell

f _____

g _____

h _____

four gamete cells

i _____

i _____

l _____

4 Homozygous and heterozygous

Match the beginnings and endings of the sentences.

Beginnings

1 When fertilization takes place
2 Each chromosome in a pair carries the same genes,
3 For example, there is a gene that
4 One version of the gene produces the physical characteristic of attached ear lobe,
5 You could inherit copies of the same version from both your parents,
6 If you have two copies of the same version of the gene,
7 If you have two different versions,

Endings

a but they may not carry the same version of the gene.
b and another version produces the characteristic of free ear lobe.
c you are said to be homozygous for that gene.
d each of the 23 chromosomes from one parent pairs up with the corresponding chromosome from the other parent.
e then you are heterozygous for the gene.
f or you might have inherited one copy of each version.
g controls the shape of your ear lobe.

1 ☐ 2 ☐ 3 ☐ 4 ☐ 5 ☐ 6 ☐ 7 ☐

5 How are gametes (reproductive cells) formed?

Put the phrases in the correct order to make sentences.

1 are formed not by mitosis   called meiosis.   but by a kind of cell division
   like the sperm and ovum in humans,   Reproductive cells,

   _____

   _____

2 divides   four new daughter cells.   In this kind of cell division   the parent cell   to form

   _____

   _____

3 has   Each of these cells   in the parent cell.   half the number of chromosomes   that was present

   _____

   _____

4 46 chromosomes in the parent cell,   In humans   so   the gametes
   there are   will have 23 chromosomes each.

   _____

   _____

5 becomes part of the new cell,   contain   It is random   different chromosomes from each other.
   so the gametes which are formed   which one of each chromosome pair

   _____

   _____

6 During fertilization,   so a new offspring   the full number of 46 chromosomes like the parents.
   fuses with   the nucleus of the sperm cell   will end up with   the nucleus of the ovum,

   _____

   _____

C Working with texts

6 Advantages and disadvantages of asexual and sexual reproduction

Read the text and make notes on the differences between asexual and sexual reproduction in the table. Make sure you also include the advantages and disadvantages of each.

Asexual reproduction is the result of mitosis, and sexual reproduction can only happen after there has been meiosis. Mitosis produces new cells that are exact copies of the original parent cell, but meiosis does not. Not only do they contain only half the number of chromosomes of the original cell, there is also exchange of genetic information between chromosomes during meiosis. This means that the new cells (gametes) do not have even an exact match of one half of the original chromosomes.

When one of the gametes fuses with a gamete from the other parent, the combination of genes that the child has will be different from either of its parents. And, because of the exchange of genetic material and the way the chromosomes behave during meiosis, each child will inherit a different combination of genes from their parents. This means that in sexual reproduction, every offspring is different and unique, in contrast to asexual reproduction where they are all the same. Each kind of reproduction has its own advantages and disadvantages.

- Asexual reproduction is best when conditions are good and unchanging because an individual that is well adapted to those conditions will produce more individuals that are well adapted. If conditions change so that the individual does not grow well, then all its offspring will also not grow well. They might all die out.
- Sexual reproduction is best when conditions are changing, because there will be variation between the offspring. Even if many of the offspring are not well suited to the changed conditions, there is a better chance that some of them will be and so will survive to produce their own young.
- Asexual reproduction means the individual does not need a mate. This can save time, but can also be important where it is difficult to find a mate as happens in some parasites.

The fact that most animals and plants have sexual reproduction in their life cycles suggests that variation in offspring, to cope with changing conditions, is the most important factor.

Characteristics	Asexual reproduction	Sexual reproduction
name		
production of new cells		
offspring		
chances of survival		
mating		

5 Photosynthesis

Term	Definition	Translation
apex /ˈeɪpeks/	the pointed end or tip of a leaf (plural: apexes /ˈeɪpeksɪːs/ or apices /ˈeɪpəsiːs/). noun [count]	
Benedict's solution /ˈbenədɪkts səˌluːʃ(ə)n/	a solution used for testing a sample for reducing sugars. If reducing sugars are present a red substance is formed when Benedict's solution is added to the sample. noun [uncount]	
Biuret test /ˈbaɪjuːret test/	a test for the presence of protein in which you add sodium hydroxide followed by copper sulphate solution. If protein is present the sample turns purple. noun [singular]	
blue-black /ˈbluːˌblæk/	a colour that is between blue and black. adjective	
brick-red /ˈbrɪkˌred/	a colour that is between red and brown. adjective	
chlorophyll /ˈklɒrəfɪl, ˈklɔːrəfɪl/	the green substance in chloroplasts in plant cells. It traps the energy from sunlight which is then used to make food through the process of photosynthesis. noun [uncount]	The presence of chlorophyll in leaves makes them green.
cloudy /ˈklaʊdi/	a cloudy liquid is not clear. adjective	If the mixture turns cloudy, fat is present.
complex sugar /ˈkɒmpleks ˈʃʊɡə/	a compound such as sucrose that consists of chains of glucose made during photosynthesis. noun [count]	Foods containing complex sugars are bread, rice and vegetables.
copper sulphate solution /ˌkɒpə ˈsʌlfeɪt səˌluːʃ(ə)n/	a solution of copper sulphate, used in the Biuret test for testing a sample for the presence of starch. noun [uncount]	
cuticle /ˈkjuːtɪk(ə)l/	the outer layer of a leaf that prevents it from drying out. noun [count]	Without a cuticle, the leaf would dry out, lowering the efficiency of photosynthesis.
dissolve /dɪˈzɒlv/	if a solid substance dissolves in a liquid, or if someone dissolves it, it mixes into the liquid and becomes included in it. verb [intransitive or transitive]	
dropper /ˈdrɒpə/	a small glass tube with a rubber piece at one end that you squeeze to let out single drops of liquid. noun [count]	Add a dropper full of Benedict's solution to the sample.
fizzing /ˈfɪzɪŋ/	the reaction of a liquid when it has small gas bubbles of the surface that burst and make a soft noise. noun [uncount]	Adding hydrochloric acid to the substance causes fizzing.
formation /fɔːˈmeɪʃ(ə)n/	the process of starting to develop something. noun [uncount]	Cellulose is used in the formation of cell walls.
glucose /ˈɡluːkəʊz/	a simple sugar that is produced in plants through photosynthesis and in animals from the breaking down of carbohydrates in the body. It is important for providing energy to all cells. Chemical formula: $C_6H_{12}O_6$. noun [uncount]	
grease spot /ˈɡriːs ˌspɒt/	a small circle of grease that forms on the surface of a liquid. noun [count]	If a grease spot forms, the sample contains fat.
iodine solution /ˈaɪədiːn səˌluːʃ(ə)n/	a solution of iodine in potassium iodide, used as a test for starch. It turns blue-black when starch is present. noun [count/uncount]	
lamina /ˈlamɪnə/	a thin layer of tissue that makes up the flat surface of a leaf. It is also called the blade (plural: laminae /ˈlamɪniː/). noun [count]	
leaf /liːf/	a flat, thin, usually green part of a plant that grows on a branch or stem. A leaf consists of an outer layer called the epidermis, inner layers of cells that contain chloroplasts, and veins that transport water, minerals, and food (plural: leaves /liːvz/). noun [count]	The autumn leaves were beginning to fall.
lower epidermis /ˌləʊə(r) epɪˈdɜːmɪs/	the lower part of the surface of a leaf that contains most of the stomata. noun [singular]	
margin /ˈmɑːdʒɪn/	the edge of a leaf. It can have many different shapes which can help identify the leaf. noun [count]	

midrib /mɪdrɪb/	a large thick vein running through the centre of a leaf. **noun [count]**	
non-reducing sugar /nɒn rɪdjuːsɪŋ 'ʃʊgə/	a type of sugar that does not produce a brick-red substance when you add Benedict's solution to it. **noun [count]**	
palisade mesophyll /'pælɪseɪd ˌmiːsəfɪl/	the part of a leaf close to its top surface made up of cells that contain chloroplasts. **noun [singular]**	
petiole /peti:əʊl/	the thin part of a leaf that attaches it to the stem. It is also called the leaf stalk. **noun [count]**	
photo- /ˌfəʊtəʊ/	relating to light; used with some nouns and adjectives. **prefix**	*Photosensitive plants react to light.*
photosynthesis /ˌfəʊtəʊ'sɪnθəsɪs/	the process in which green plants combine carbon dioxide and water, by using energy from light, to produce their own food. **noun [uncount]**	*Green plants produce oxygen through the process of photosynthesis.*
precipitate /prɪ'sɪpɪteɪt/	a solid substance that has been separated from the liquid that it was in. **noun [count]**	
reducing sugar /rɪ'djuːsɪŋ ʃʊgə/	a type of sugar that produces a brick-red substance when you add Benedict's solution to it. **noun [count]**	
root /ruːt/	the part of a plant that grows under the ground, through which the plant gets water and minerals, and where some plants store food. **noun [count]**	*Olive trees have deep roots.*
seedling /'siːdlɪŋ/	a young plant that has very recently grown from a seed. **noun [count]**	*The bean seeds germinated into small seedlings which eventually grew into mature bean plants.*
seed /siːd/	a usually small, hard part produced by a plant, that can grow into a new plant of the same type. A seed is an ovule that has been fertilized and contains the plant embryo and its food. **noun [count/uncount]**	*The traditional method of sowing seeds (=putting them on or in the ground) is by hand.*
spongy mesophyll /'spʌndʒi ˌmiːsəfɪl/	a part below the top surface of a leaf that has large air spaces between its cells. **noun [singular]**	
starch /stɑːtʃ/	a type of carbohydrate made from glucose molecules that is stored in rice, potatoes, and other vegetables. It is an important type of food that provides energy. It is also used to make some types of cloth, paper, and glue. **noun [count/uncount]**	*Plants convert glucose from photosynthesis into starch for storage.*
stem /stem/	the long part of a plant that the leaves and flowers grow from. **noun [count]**	*The stems of roses have sharp thorns on them.*
stomata /'stəʊmətə/	small air holes in the lower surface of a leaf. **noun [plural]**	*Leaves 'breathe' through holes in the leaves called stomata.*
sucrose /'suːkrəʊz/	a common type of sugar that comes from plants such as sugar cane and sugar beet. It is a disaccharide. **noun [uncount]**	*Sucrose is used to sweeten foods.*
synthesis /'sɪnθəsɪs/	the process of producing a substance by a chemical or biological reaction (plural: syntheses /'sɪnθəsiːz/). **noun [count/uncount]**	*Photosynthesis involves the synthesis of sugars from carbon dioxide and water.*
translucent /ˌtræns'luːs(ə)nt/	a translucent surface is clear enough for light to pass through, but not completely clear. If you look through a translucent surface, you can see the general shape and colour of objects on the other side, but not the details. **adjective**	*If a translucent spot forms, the sample contains fat.*
underside /'ʌndəsaɪd/	the bottom side or surface of something. **noun [count]**	*the underside of a leaf*
upper epidermis /ˌʌpə(r) epɪ'dɜːmɪs/	the top surface of a leaf. **noun [singular]**	
vein /veɪn/	one of the tubes that carry substances through a plant. **noun [count]**	*Leaves contain a network of veins.*

5 PHOTOSYNTHESIS

A   Working with words

1   Photosynthesis word map

Write these words in the correct place on the word map.

carbon dioxide   cells   cellulose   dissolved minerals   leaves   roots

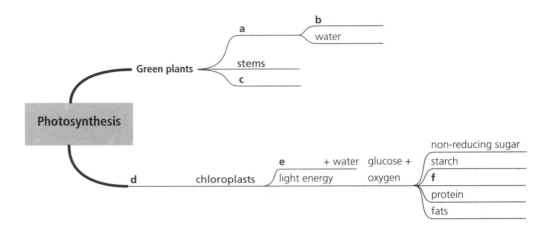

2   Parts of a leaf

Look at the diagram and label the parts with these words.

apex   lamina   margin   midrib   petiole   veins

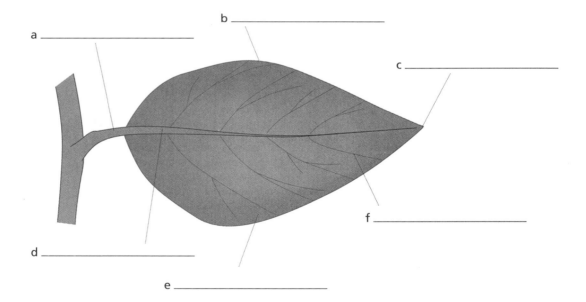

3   The process of photosynthesis

Label the diagram with these words, phrases and sentences.

carbon dioxide taken from the air
chlorophyll
Glucose made in the leaves is taken to all parts of the plant.
light energy
oxygen given out
sun
Water and minerals are taken from the soil by the plant's roots.

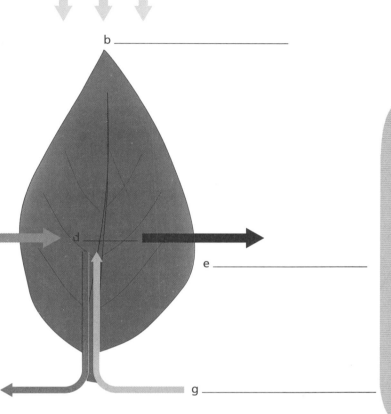

a _____

b _____

c _____

d

e _____

f _____

g _____

4   Respiration

Put the phrases in the correct order to make sentences.

1   are absorbed   from the soil   through the roots.   Water and minerals

_____

2   is transported   that is made during photosynthesis   The glucose   to other parts of the plant.

_____

3   for cell reactions.   Here   in respiration   it is used   to provide energy

_____

4   complex sugars   It also makes   like sucrose.   new materials   such as

_____

5   cell walls.   Cellulose   form   is   to   used

_____

6   are made from   absorbed from the soil with water.   Proteins and fats   the glucose   using minerals

_____

7   is also   for use at another time.   Glucose   converted to starch   stems, roots and seeds
    such as   which is stored in various parts of the plant

_____

5   Food test summary

Read the jumbled-up text and sort it into the correct columns and rows.

A blue-black colour indicates the presence of starch.

A brick-red precipitate indicates the presence of a reducing sugar.

A purple colour indicates the presence of protein.

Add 1 cm³ of 0.1 M sodium hydroxide followed by 2 drops of a 1% copper sulphate solution. This is called the Biuret test.

Add a few drops of dilute hydrochloric acid and warm gently. Neutralize the solution by gradually adding sodium carbonate until fizzing stops. Test with Benedict's solution.

Add a few drops of iodine solution.

Add one dropper full of Benedict's solution to a small sample of the food containing the reducing sugar.

If a translucent spot (grease spot) develops then the sample contains fat. A cloudy mixture indicates the presence of fat.

Rub the sample in paper and warm the area over a light bulb. Or add 2 cm³ ethanol to the food sample and shake vigorously.

The acid breaks the non-reducing sugar up into reducing sugars which produce a brick-red precipitate with Benedict's solution.

Type of food	Test	Results
Reducing sugars (e.g. glucose)		
Non-reducing sugar (e.g. sucrose)		
Starch		
Proteins		
Fats		

6 Nutrition

accumulation /əˌkjuːmjuˈleɪʃ(ə)n/	the process by which something increases in amount or is collected together over time. noun [uncount]	*slow accumulation of cholesterol in the arteries*
additive /ˈædətɪv/	a chemical substance that is added to food to make it last longer or look or taste better. noun [count]	*Some additives improve the colour and taste of food.*
anaemia /əˈniːmiə/	a medical condition in which there are too few red blood cells in the blood. noun [uncount]	*She was suffering from anaemia and felt tired all the time.*
antioxidant /ˌæntiˈɒksɪd(ə)nt/	**1** a substance that prevents oxygen from combining with other substances and damaging them. Antioxidants are used in industry for making substances such as rubber and plastic stronger, and they are often added to processed foods to make them stay fresh for longer. noun [count] **2** a substance in the body that prevents cells and tissue from being damaged by harmful substances. Some vitamins are antioxidants. noun [count]	*Antioxidants prevent some foods from going brown.*
arteriosclerosis /ɑːˌtɪəriəʊskləˈrəʊsɪs/	a serious medical condition in which the sides of the arteries become thick, hard, and stiff, so that the heart has to work harder to pump blood through the body. noun [uncount]	*Smoking can lead to arteriosclerosis.*
ascorbic acid /əˌskɔːbɪk ˈæsɪd/	vitamin C. noun [uncount]	*Orange juice is a good source of ascorbic acid, also known as vitamin C.*
balanced diet /ˌbælənst ˈdaɪət/	a diet that contains proteins, carbohydrates, fats, vitamins and minerals, in the correct amounts. noun [count]	*If you eat a balanced diet, you shouldn't need vitamin supplements.*
bleaching agent /ˈbliːtʃɪŋ ˌeɪdʒ(ə)nt/	an artificial substance in food that makes it whiter and more attractive. noun [count]	*White flour contains a bleaching agent.*
blindness /ˈblaɪndnəs/	the condition of being unable to see. noun [uncount]	*A lack of vitamin A can lead to night blindness.*
blood clotting /ˈblʌd ˌklɒtɪŋ/	the process by which blood becomes thick and stops flowing, forming a solid cover over any place where the skin has been cut or broken. noun [uncount]	*A scab is formed over a wound by blood clotting.*
boost /buːst/	**1** to help something to increase or improve. verb [transitive] **2** something that helps something to increase or improve. noun [singular]	*Does vitamin E boost the immune system?* *Eating a variety of healthy foods gives your body a boost.*
breastfeed /ˈbrestfiːd/	if a mother breastfeeds a baby, she feeds it with milk from her breasts. verb [intransitive/transitive]	*Women who are breastfeeding should eat a healthy balanced diet.*
brittle /ˈbrɪtl/	hard and easily broken. adjective	*brittle bones caused by calcium deficiency.*
broccoli /ˈbrɒkəli/	a vegetable consisting of green stems with many small green or purple parts on the ends. noun [uncount]	
bulky /ˈbʌlki/	big and thick. adjective	*Fibre in food creates bulkier faeces, which is easier to pass from the body.*
calciferol /kælˈsɪfərɒl/	vitamin D. noun [uncount]	
calcium /ˈkælsiəm/	a silver-white chemical element that is very important for the normal growth and health of most living things, especially for bones and teeth. It is also used to make things such as plaster and cement. Chemical symbol: Ca. noun [uncount]	*Milk is a good source of calcium.*
carbohydrate /ˌkɑːbəˈhaɪdreɪt/	an organic compound found in foods such as sugar, bread, and potatoes. Carbohydrates consist of oxygen, hydrogen and carbon, and they supply the body with heat and energy. noun [count]	*Rice and potatoes are important sources of carbohydrates.*
cobalamin /kəʊˈbæləmɪn/	vitamin B12. noun [uncount]	
colon cancer /ˈkəʊlɒn ˌkænsə/	cancer that begins in the lower part of the large intestine. noun [uncount]	*Eating lots of fruit, vegetables and whole grains helps prevent colon cancer.*
constipation /ˌkɒnstɪˈpeɪʃ(ə)n/	a condition in which someone cannot easily move solid waste out of their body. noun [uncount]	*Lack of fibre in the diet can lead to constipation.*

convert /kən'vɜːt/	to change something from one form to another, or to change in this way. verb [transitive/intransitive]	The body converts carbohydrates, sugars and starches into blood sugar.
cramp /kræmp/	a sudden painful contraction of a muscle, often caused by tiredness or strain. noun [count/uncount]	He had to stop swimming because he got cramp in his leg.
dairy product /'deəri ˌprɒdʌkt/	dairy products include milk and foods such as butter and cheese. noun [count]	Vitamin B12 is found in dairy products.
decay /dɪ'keɪ/	to be gradually broken down by bacteria or fungi. verb [intransitive]	Teeth may start to decay if they are not cleaned regularly.
deficiency /dɪ'fɪʃənsi/	a lack of something or a fault in something. noun [count/uncount]	diseases caused by mineral deficiencies in the body
deficient /dɪ'fɪʃ(ə)nt/	lacking something or not good enough. adjective	a diet deficient in vitamin C
deformity /dɪ'fɔːmɪti/	a part of someone's body that is not the normal shape. noun [count/uncount]	a disease in which the bones become soft, leading to fractures and deformity.
degeneration /dɪˌdʒenə'reɪʃ(ə)n/	the process of becoming worse. noun [uncount]	A lack of vitamin E can lead to tissue degeneration.
dehydrate /ˌdiːhaɪ'dreɪt/	if someone dehydrates, they lose so much water from their body that they feel weak or ill. verb [intransitive]	
dehydration /ˌdiːhaɪ'dreɪʃ(ə)n/	a dangerous lack of water in the body that results from not drinking enough or from extreme loss through sweating, vomiting, or diarrhoea. noun [uncount]	After 3 days in the desert he was suffering from dehydration.
diarrhoea /ˌdaɪə'riːə/	an illness in which the faeces are like liquid, usually as a result of food poisoning or another disease. Diarrhoea can be very dangerous, especially in young children and old people, as it prevents food and important minerals from getting into the body and can cause severe dehydration. noun [uncount]	
distinguish /dɪs'tɪŋgwɪʃ/	to recognise the difference between two things. verb [intransitive/transitive]	Our sense of smell allows us to distinguish different foods.
elimination /ɪˌlɪmɪ'neɪʃ(ə)n/	the process of getting rid of something that is not wanted. noun [uncount]	the elimination of food waste from the body
emulsifier /ɪ'mʌlsɪˌfaɪə/	a substance added to a food or drink to stop liquid and solid parts from separating. noun [count]	
enamel /ɪ'næm(ə)l/	the hard white outer layer of a tooth. noun [uncount]	Bacteria in the mouth attack the enamel of the teeth.
essential /ɪ'sentʃ(ə)l/	1 completely necessary. adjective 2 basic and important. adjective	Water is essential for the survival of an organism. the essential nutritional elements
essential amino acid /ɪ'sentʃ(ə)l əˌmiːnəʊ (æsɪd/	a substance in the body that combines to make proteins and must be provided by a person's diet. noun [uncount]	Eggs contain all eight essential amino acids.
extract /ɪk'strækt/ /'ekstrækt/	1 to remove something from something else. verb [transitive] 2 a substance that has been taken from a plant or from another substance. noun [count/uncount]	the process in which our body extracts energy from food yeast extract
faeces /'fiːsiːz/	solid waste from the body = excrement. noun [uncount]	Faeces can be a danger to health if not disposed of hygienically.
fat /fæt/	1 a soft white or yellow substance that mammals and birds store under the skin. It is used as an energy store and to protect the body against heat loss. noun [uncount] 2 a food substance like oil that is used by the body for energy. noun [count/uncount]	It is healthy to reduce the amount of fat in your diet.
fat-soluble /'fæt ˌsɒljəb(ə)l/	fat-soluble vitamins are absorbed from the fats and oils in our diet. adjective	fat-soluble vitamin A
fibre /'faɪbə/	the parts of fruit, vegetables, and grains containing cellulose that help food to pass through the body but that the body does not use. noun [uncount]	Wholegrain cereals are high in fibre.
fluorine /'flʊəriːn/	a poisonous yellow gas that is an element in the halogen group and is the most reactive element known. It is used in the treatment of water. Chemical symbol: F. noun [uncount]	Fluorine is sometimes added to drinking water to keep teeth healthy.
folic acid /ˌfəʊlɪk 'æsɪd/	an important B vitamin, found in green vegetables and liver. It is especially important for pregnant women. noun [uncount]	
goitre /'gɔɪtə/	a disease that affects your thyroid gland and makes your neck swollen. noun [count/uncount]	Goitre can develop because of a deficiency in iodine.

grain /greɪn/	the seeds from cereal plants such as wheat, rice, or barley that are used for food, or the plants that they grow on. noun [count/uncount]	*Wheat and other grains are a good source of vitamin B1.*
growth /grəʊθ/	**1** an increase in the size or development of a living thing, usually as the result of an increase in the number of cells. noun [count/uncount] **2** a lump on someone's body that is caused by a disease. noun [count]	*Vitamins are essential for normal growth.* *He had a cancerous growth on his liver.*
haemorrhoids /ˈhemərɔɪdz/	painful swollen areas around the anus. noun [plural]	*The common name for haemorrhoids is piles.*
hyperactivity /ˌhaɪpə(r)ækˈtɪvəti/	a higher than normal level of activity, in an organ or in a child's behaviour. noun [uncount]	*Some food colourings cause hyperactivity in children.*
hypertension /ˌhaɪpəˈtenʃ(ə)n/	a condition in which someone's blood pressure is extremely high. noun [uncount]	*drugs used to control hypertension*
infertility /ˌɪnfəˈtɪləti/	the problem of being physically unable to have children. noun [uncount]	*infertility treatments*
iodine /ˈaɪəˌdiːn/	a poisonous dark non-metal element. A solution in alcohol is put on cuts in the skin in order to prevent infection. Chemical symbol: I. noun [uncount]	*Iodine is sometimes used as an antiseptic.*
iron /ˈaɪən/	iron that exists in small quantities in some foods and in the body. Iron is found in foods such as red meat, eggs, nuts, and cereals and is important in order to make haemoglobin (=the substance that makes red blood cells able to carry oxygen around the body). Lack of iron in the body causes anaemia. noun [uncount]	
kilojoule /ˈkɪlədʒuːl/	a unit for measuring the energy content of food. noun [count]	*We put on about a pound of fat for every 15,000 kilojoules we eat in excess.*
kwashiorkor /ˌkwɒʃiˈɔːkɔː/	a serious disease that mainly affects children in Africa and is caused by a lack of protein in the food that they eat. noun [uncount]	*The starving children were suffering from kwashiorkor.*
lard /lɑːd/	white fat that is used in cooking. noun [uncount]	
legume /legjuːm/	**1** a seed such as a pea or bean that grows in a pod. noun [count] **2** the plant on which seeds with pods such as beans and peas grow. Legumes are important for the environment as the bacteria in their roots carry out nitrogen fixation. noun [count]	
lesion /ˈliːʒ(ə)n/	an area of damaged skin = wound. noun [count]	
lethargy /ˈleθədʒi/	the feeling of lacking energy and not wanting to do anything. noun [uncount]	*Not eating breakfast can cause lethargy later in the day.*
lipid /ˈlɪpɪd/	a chemical compound in organisms, mainly in the form of fats and oils. noun [count]	
make-up /ˈmeɪkʌp/	the individual qualities that combine to form the basic character of something. noun [count]	*features of our behaviour that are a result of our biological make-up*
malnutrition /ˌmælnjʊˈtrɪʃ(ə)n/	a medical condition in which you are very weak or ill because you do not have enough to eat, or you do not eat enough of the right foods. noun [uncount]	
marasmus /məˈræzməs/	a medical condition in which a young child gradually becomes extremely thin and weak as a result of not having enough food. noun [uncount]	*Children who are starving often suffer from marasmus.*
margarine /ˌmɑːdʒəˈriːn/	a yellow substance made from vegetable oil or animal fat that can be used instead of butter. noun [count/uncount]	
menadione /ˌmenəˈdaɪəʊn/	vitamin K3, a form of vitamin K. noun [uncount]	
mineral /ˈmɪn(ə)rəl/	an inorganic chemical in some foods that is important for good health, for example calcium. noun [count]	*Vitamins and minerals are an essential part of a healthy diet.*
monosodium glutamate /ˌmɒnəʊˌsəʊdiəm ˈ(glu:təˌmeɪt/	MSG. noun [uncount]	*Monosodium glutamate is added to foods to make them taste better.*
niacin /ˈnaɪəsɪn/	a type of vitamin that exists in milk and other foods. noun [uncount]	

nutrient /ˈnjuːtriənt/	a substance that all organisms need in order to live, grow, and be healthy. In animals, the nutrients are foods that contain energy, vitamins, and minerals. In plants, they are carbon dioxide, water, and mineral salts. noun [count]	
nutritional disorder /ˌnjuːtrɪʃn(ə)l dɪsˈɔːdə/	a condition or illness caused by a problem with someone's diet. noun [count]	*nutritional disorders such as anorexia nervosa*
obesity /əʊˈbiːsəti/	a condition in which someone is extremely fat in a way that is dangerous for their health. noun [uncount]	*People who overeat risk suffering from obesity.*
oil /ɔɪl/	a thick smooth liquid form of animal or vegetable fat, used in cooking and medicines. noun [count/uncount]	*Cook the chicken in oil.*
osteomalacia /ˌɒstiəʊməˈleɪʃə/	a disease in which the bones become soft and bend. It is caused by a lack of vitamin D in food or by a lack of sunlight on the skin. noun [uncount]	
pellagra /peˈlægrə/	a disease in which the skin becomes very rough. It is caused by a lack of niacin in food. noun [uncount]	
phosphorus /ˈfɒsfərəs/	a chemical element, especially a form called white phosphorus that starts to burn by itself when air touches it. Chemical symbol: P. noun [uncount]	*Phosphorus is important in our diet for healthy bones and teeth.*
poultry /ˈpəʊltri/	birds such as chickens that are used for meat or eggs, or the meat of these birds. noun [uncount]	*a bacteria which contaminates raw meat and poultry*
preserved food /prɪˌzɜːvd ˈfuːd/	food that has had salt or chemicals added to it in order to keep it fresh for a long time. noun [count/uncount]	*I prefer fresh food to preserved food.*
prevent /prɪˈvent/	1 to stop something from happening. verb [transitive] 2 to stop someone from doing something. verb [transitive]	*Fluorine in water prevents tooth decay.* *Poor health prevents her from joining in with the other children.*
protein /ˈprəʊtiːn/	1 an organic compound that is made of amino acids. Proteins contain carbon, hydrogen, oxygen, and nitrogen. noun [count] 2 food such as meat, eggs, and milk that contain proteins and that people need in order to grow and be healthy. Protein is very important for building tissues such as muscles and for keeping them healthy. noun [uncount]	*The villagers' main source of protein is fish from the river.*
protein energy malnutrition /ˌprəʊtiːn ˈenədʒi ˌmælnjuˈtrɪʃ(ə)n/	a condition in which a person is not getting enough food and their body begins to get energy from its tissues, rather than its fat, because there is no more body fat. noun [uncount]	
provisions /prəˈvɪʒ(ə)nz/	foods and other necessary supplies. noun [plural]	*ground provisions such as yams and potatoes*
pulses /ˈpʌlsɪz/	beans, peas, and other seeds that you can cook and eat. noun [plural]	
pyridoxine /pɪˌrɪdˈɒksiːn/	vitamin B6. noun [uncount]	
rare /reə/	not happening very often. adjective	*a rare blood disorder*
repair /rɪˈpeə/	1 to fix something that is broken or damaged. verb [transitive] 2 to improve a bad situation. verb [transitive] 3 the process of fixing something that is broken or damaged. noun [count/uncount]	*Skin has the ability to repair itself.* *The idea of the therapy is that by reliving a traumatic event, you can repair the emotional damage.* *Zinc is important for tissue repair.*
replenish /rɪˈplenɪʃ/	to bring something back to its previous level by replacing what has been used. verb [transitive]	*We eat to replenish the energy that we have used.*
reproduction /ˌriːprəˈdʌkʃ(ə)n/	The form of reproduction that involves the combination of male and female gametes, for example in most animals and plants, is called sexual reproduction. Reproduction in which there is only one parent, for example in bacteria, is called asexual reproduction. noun [uncount]	*The body needs energy for growth, repair and reproduction.*
requirement /rɪˈkwaɪəˌmənt/	something that is necessary. noun [count]	*a person's daily energy requirements*
retarded growth /rɪˌtɑːdɪd ˈgrəʊθ/	a condition in which someone is not as tall as he or she should be. noun [uncount]	*Zinc deficiency can cause retarded growth in children.*
riboflavin /ˌraɪbəʊˈfleɪvɪn/	a substance found in eggs, milk, liver, and green vegetables that the body needs for growth. Riboflavin is a vitamin. noun [uncount]	

rickets /ˈrɪkɪts/	a disease that mainly affects children in which the bones become soft and bend. It is caused by a lack of vitamin D in food or by a lack of sunlight on the skin. noun [uncount]	
roughage /ˈrʌfɪdʒ/	fibre in the food that you eat that cannot be digested and that helps the movement of food through the digestive system. It mainly consists of the cellulose that is found in grains, fruits, and vegetables. noun [uncount]	
scurvy /ˈskɜːvi/	an illness caused by not eating enough foods that contain vitamin C (=a natural substance found in fruit and vegetables). noun [uncount]	*Sailors in the olden days suffered from scurvy due to a lack of fresh fruit in their diet.*
seaweed /ˈsiːwiːd/	a simple green, red or brown plant that grows in the sea. noun [uncount]	
sedentary /ˈsedəntri/	involving a lot of sitting and not much exercise. adjective	*If you lead a sedentary life, you need less energy.*
shelf life /ˈʃelf laɪf/	the amount of time that something can be kept in a shop before it is too old to sell. noun [singular]	*Fresh fruit has a short shelf life.*
significant /sɪgˈnɪfɪk(ə)nt/	very important. adjective	*Significant amounts of pesticides remain on the foods we eat.*
sore /sɔː/	a small painful area of skin that is injured or infected. noun [count]	
spina bifida /ˌspaɪnə ˈbɪfɪdə/	a serious medical condition in which someone's spinal cord is damaged, making them paralysed (=unable to move parts of their body). noun [uncount]	*People suffering from spina bifida can get around in a wheelchair.*
spoilage /ˈspɔɪlɪdʒ/	the process of becoming decayed. noun [uncount]	*a bacteria which causes food spoilage*
stabiliser /ˈsteɪbɪlaɪzə/	a substance added to some prepared foods to stop the taste or appearance from changing. noun [count]	
staple /ˈsteɪp(ə)l/	a very basic and important food or product that people eat or use regularly. noun [count]	*Rice is a staple in the Chinese diet.*
starch /ˈstɑːtʃ/	a type of carbohydrate made from glucose molecules that is stored in rice, potatoes, and other vegetables. It is an important type of food that provides energy. It is also used to make some types of cloth, paper, and glue.	
strengthen /ˈstreŋθən/	to make someone or something stronger, or to become stronger. verb [transitive/intransitive]	*Vitamin D is used for strengthening the immune system.*
tartrazine /ˈtɑːtrəziːn/	a substance added to some prepared foods to colour them. noun [uncount]	
thiamine /ˈθaɪəmiːn/	a vitamin found in the outer layer of rice and other grains that is important for keeping the nerves healthy. It belongs to the B group of vitamins. noun [uncount]	
thyroid gland /ˈθaɪrɔɪd ˌglænd/	a gland in the neck that produces hormones that control the metabolism. noun [count]	*A lack of iodine in the diet causes the thyroid gland to swell.*
tiredness /ˈtaɪədnəs/	the feeling of being tired. noun [uncount]	*Anaemia causes weakness and tiredness.*
tocopherol /təˈkɒfərɒl/	vitamin E. noun [uncount]	
vitamin /ˈvɪtəmɪn/	a natural substance in food that is necessary for good health. noun [count]	*Vitamins are an important part of a healthy diet.*
water /ˈwɔːtə/	the clear liquid that falls as rain, covers two-thirds of the Earth's surface, and is used for drinking, washing, and cooking. Water is a compound of hydrogen and oxygen. It exists in frozen form as ice and in gas form as water vapour. It boils at 100°C and freezes at 0°C. Water is necessary to all living things on Earth and is necessary for most biological processes. Chemical formula: H_2O. noun [uncount]	*Wash your hands thoroughly with soap and water.*
weakness /ˈwiːknəs/	the state or condition of being weak. noun [uncount]	*Potassium deficiency can cause muscle weakness.*
yam /jæm/	a long vegetable that is the swollen root of a tropical vine. It has brown skin and white flesh. noun [count]	
yeast /jiːst/	a white substance that is used in making bread and beer. noun [uncount]	
yellowing /ˈjeləʊɪŋ/	the process of becoming yellow. noun [uncount]	*Too much fluorine can lead to the yellowing of teeth.*

1 Nutrition word map

Write these words in the correct place on the word map.

balanced diet disorder essential nutrients food colouring malnutrition minerals

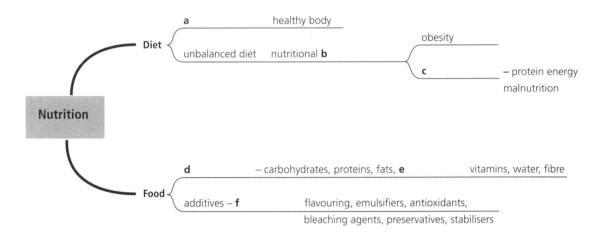

2 Carbohydrates

Fill in the gaps in the text with these words.

carbohydrates deficiency energy more quickly peas
plant cell walls provisions significant starch sugars

Carbohydrates include sugars, starch and cellulose. Cellulose is the material which forms

1 _____. It is very tough and difficult to digest, so most of our

2 _____ come from food containing 3 _____ and

4 _____.

    Carbohydrates are mainly found in plant foods, such as ground 5 _____ (yams,

potatoes), fruit, vegetables, 6 _____ and beans . Some animal products, such as milk,

yoghurt and cheese, also contain 7 _____ amounts of carbohydrates.

Carbohydrates provide us with 8 _____. We can get energy from protein and fats, but

carbohydrates are important when we are very active as they give us energy 9 _____.

A 10 _____ in carbohydrates can result in a lack of energy.

3 Food additives

Match the words with the explanations.

Words	Explanations
1 food colouring	a A lot of the taste of foods can be lost during food processing, so chemicals are used to restore it.
2 tartrazine	b Food changes during processing, so this is added so they look more attractive, or to make foods appear to contain something that they do not.
3 flavourings	c These are added to stop oil and water in the same mixture from separating out.
4 monosodium glutamate (MSG)	d These artificially whiten products which makes them more attractive to many people.
5 emulsifiers	e These maintain the physical state and preserve the texture and colour of the processed food.
6 antioxidants	f These prevent the growth of microorganisms that would cause the decay (spoilage) of food or food poisoning.
7 bleaching agents	g These prevent the spoilage of foods on exposure to air. They also prevent deterioration of flavour and colour that has been added to the processed food.
8 preservatives	h This is a bright yellow colouring often used in sweets and drinks and can cause hyperactivity in young children.
9 stabilisers	i This is added to savoury foods to improve the flavour, particularly south-east Asian foods.

1 ☐ 2 ☐ 3 ☐ 4 ☐ 5 ☐ 6 ☐ 7 ☐ 8 ☐ 9 ☐

B Working with sentences

4 Nutrition

Put the phrases in the correct order to make sentences.

1 for growth, repair and reproduction.   we eat   to provide energy needed   Nutrition is the study of   from the food   how the body uses the nutrients

_____

_____

2 carbohydrates, proteins fat, vitamins, and minerals.   these nutrients from   We get

_____

_____

3 our diet.   The foods   make up   every day   we eat and drink

_____

_____

4 we need to eat   To stay healthy,   nutrients.   the different kinds of   a good balance of

_____

_____

5 Changes in energy needs by sex

Read the sentences and look at the diagram and decide which sentences are true and which are false.

1   The daily energy needs of the body change at different times in our lives and are different for males and females.
2   When a baby is born the needs of females and males are approximately equal, slightly higher for males, at around 3000 kilojoules per day.
3   Between the ages of 1 to 3 daily energy needs are 5000 kilojoules per day for females and are a fraction higher for males.
4   The rise in daily energy needs continues to increase with a slightly higher daily rate for males until the age of 15 to 18 when they reach 8500 kilojoules for females and just over 11500 for men.
5   From the age of 19 to 59 the daily energy intake rises slightly from 10500 for males and around 8000 kilojoules for females, falling very slightly by the age of 59.
6   At the age of 60 the daily energy needs are the same again for both males and females.
7   At the age of 75 and above males need around 9000 kilojoules and females about 7500 per day.

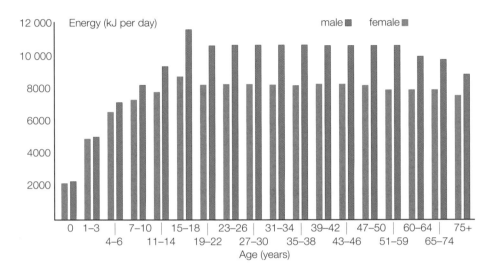

6 Energy required for carrying out different activities

Read the text and draw in the columns for the different activities. Sleeping has been given as an example

As we can see from the chart even the activity we take for granted uses up energy. Sleeping requires about 400 kilojoules per hour. Running is the activity which expends the most kilojoules per hour at around 2800. Reading is slightly better than sleeping. While reading we use up 500 kilojoules per hour. Swimming is a good activity for burning up kilojoules. According to the chart swimming burns up approximately 1700 kilojoules per hour. Even a good walk can burn off calories. Walking uses up 900 kilojoules per hour and according to the chart cycling burns up about 1400 kilojoules per hour.

7 Minerals

Read the text and make notes on the minerals mentioned, including their sources in food, their use in the body and the results of deficiency.

Calcium is found in dairy foods, for example, cheese and milk. It is also found in green vegetables, dried peas and beans. It is used in the body for the formation and hardening of bones and teeth. It also promotes the healthy functioning of the nerves and promotes the normal clotting of blood. In children, a deficiency can lead to rickets, where the bones of the legs bend as they cannot support the legs. In adults, the condition is called osteomalacia. It can also cause brittle bones and this can increase the risk of fracture.

The main source of sodium is in table salt, and sodium chloride in foods. In the body it helps the contraction of the muscles and the transmission of nerve impulses. A lack of salt in the diet can lead to painful muscle cramps and poor transmission of nerve impulses.

Iron comes from dark green leafy vegetables and pumpkin. Other sources are liver, kidney, fish and red meat. It is important in haemoglobin which carries oxygen in the blood. A diet deficient in iron can lead to anaemia which causes weakness and tiredness as less oxygen reaches cells for respiration and release of energy.

Magnesium is found mainly in green leafy vegetables, nuts, dried peas and beans. Magnesium is essential for effective nerve and muscle functioning and is important in energy production. A lack of magnesium can lead to tiredness and weakness.

Mineral	Sources in food	How it is used in the body	Result of deficiency

7 Health and safety

accident /ˈæksɪdənt/	an unexpected event that causes injury or damage. **noun [count]**	
accidental /ˌæksɪˈdentl/	not intended. **adjective**	
acid rain /ˈæsɪd reɪn/	rain that contains a high level of acid that can damage the environment. The acid forms when harmful gases from industry and vehicles mix with water in the atmosphere. **noun [uncount]**	
active ingredient /ˌæktɪv ɪnˈgriːdiənt/	a substance that produces a biological or chemical reaction. **noun [count]**	*Sodium hydroxide is the active ingredient in some household cleaners.*
aerosol /ˈeərəsɒl/	a container in which a liquid such as paint or perfume is kept under high pressure so that it can be sprayed. **noun [count]**	
air hole (burner) /ˈeə ˌhəʊl/	a hole at the base of the barrel of a Bunsen burner. When it is open it allows air to mix with the flammable gas so that it burns properly. **noun [count]**	*Make sure the air hole is closed before you light the burner.*
airtight /ˈeəˌtaɪt/	not allowing air to enter or leave. **adjective**	
ammonia /əˈməʊniə/	a poisonous gas, with a strong unpleasant smell, or the gas dissolved in water. It is used in cleaning products. **noun [uncount]**	*You mustn't inhale ammonia because it is poisonous.*
anti-histamine /ˌænti'hɪstəmiːn/	a drug that is used to treat allergies. **noun [count/uncount]**	*The doctor prescribed anti-histamines for his allergic reaction to strawberries.*
antiseptic /ˌænti'septɪk/	a substance that is used for cleaning injured skin and preventing infections. **noun [count/uncount]**	*Her mother put antiseptic on her grazed knee.*
apron /ˈeɪprən/	something that someone wears to protect the front of their clothes when they are cooking. **noun [count]**	*People working in food preparation should wear an apron.*
asthma /ˈæsmə/	a medical condition that makes it difficult to breathe. **noun [uncount]**	*His asthma made him breathless so he used his inhaler.*
Band-Aid /ˈbændeɪd/	a type of plaster used for covering a cut on your skin (American trademark). **noun [count]**	
barefoot /ˈbeəˌfʊt/	without any shoes or socks on. **adjective, adverb**	
bare hands /ˌbeə ˈhændz/	hands with no covering on them. **noun [plural]**	*You should not use strong cleaners such as oven cleaner with your bare hands.*
barrel (burner) /ˈbærəl/	the long tube that channels (=sends) the mixture of flammable gas and air to the mouth of a Bunsen burner. **noun [count]**	
base (burner) /beɪs/	the wide bottom part of a Bunsen burner. **noun [count]**	
bleach /bliːtʃ/	**1** a strong chemical that is used for killing bacteria or for making coloured things white. **noun [uncount]** **2** to remove the colour from something. **verb [transitive]**	*She poured bleach down the toilet to clean it.* *The cloth is bleached before being dyed.*
broken limb /ˌbrəʊk(ə)n ˈlɪm/	an arm or a leg that has a bone with a crack in it. **noun [count]**	*Sports such as rugby and football can sometimes result in broken limbs.*
Bunsen burner /ˌbʌns(ə)n ˈbɜːnə/	a piece of equipment that produces a gas flame, used in a laboratory for heating substances. **noun [count]**	*Pupils with long hair should tie it back when using a Bunsen burner.*
carbon monoxide /ˌkɑːb(ə)n mɒˈnɒksaɪd/	the poisonous gas that is produced by the engines of vehicles. Chemical formula: CO. **noun [uncount]**	*The fumes from the faulty gas heater contained carbon monoxide.*
caustic /ˈkɔːstɪk/	a caustic substance can cause burns to your skin and eyes because it is corrosive (=causes damage through chemical action). **adjective**	*Sodium hydroxide is caustic so protective clothing should be worn.*

caution /'kɔːʃ(ə)n/	**1** careful thought and lack of hurry in order to try to avoid risks or danger. noun [uncount]	*Bunsen burners produce a very hot flame and should therefore be treated with caution.*
	2 advice that you should be careful. noun [uncount]	*A word of caution: water and electricity don't mix!*
	3 to warn someone about a possible danger or problem. verb [transitive]	*The teacher cautioned them to be extremely careful when handling chemicals.*
chlorine /'klɔːriːn/	a non-metal element that is a strong-smelling poisonous gas. It is a halogen, and very reactive. It is added to water as a disinfectant. Chemical symbol: Cl. noun [uncount]	*The swimming pool water was treated with chlorine.*
choke /tʃəuk/	if you choke, or if something chokes you, you cannot breathe because there is not enough air, or because something is blocking your throat. verb [transitive/intransitive]	*Young children can easily choke on small objects.*
cleaning agent /'kliːnɪŋ ˌeɪdʒ(ə)nt/	a substance that is used to clean things, especially in the home. noun [count]	
collar (burner) /'kɒlə/	the metal ring near the bottom of a Bunsen burner that rotates to open and close the air hole. noun [count]	
contaminated /kən'tæmɪˌneɪtɪd/	made dirty, polluted, or poisonous by the addition of a harmful substance. adjective	
corrosive substance /kəˌrəʊsɪv sʌbstəns/	a substance that can cause damage through chemical action, for example to metal or stone or to someone's skin. noun [count]	
crush /krʌʃ/	to press something so hard that you damage it or break it into small pieces. verb [transitive]	
earmuffs /'ɪəˌmʌfs/	a pair of round pads connected by a band that you wear over your ears to protect them from the noise of machinery. noun [plural]	
earplug /'ɪəˌplʌg/	a small object that you put in your ear to keep noise or water out. noun [count]	
Elastoplast /ɪ'lɑːstəplɑːst/	a type of plaster used for covering a cut on your skin; British trademark. noun [count]	
electrical socket /ɪ'lektrɪk(ə)l ˌsɒkɪt/	a place on a wall or machine where you connect electrical equipment. It consists of holes into which you insert the plug of the machine you want to connect. noun [count]	
electrocution /ɪˌlektrə'kjuːʃ(ə)n/	death or serious injury caused by electric current flowing through your body. noun [uncount]	
exhaust fumes /ɪg'zɔːst ˌfjuːmz/	gases that are produced by the working of an engine, especially the engine of a vehicle. noun [plural]	
explosive /ɪk'spləʊsɪv/	a substance or object that can cause an explosion. noun [count/uncount]	*Fireworks contain explosives and must be handled with great care.*
fabric /'fæbrɪk/	cloth that is used for making things such as clothes or curtains. noun [count/uncount]	
face shield /'feɪs ˌʃiːld/	an object that is used to protect the face of a person who is working in an area where there is a risk of damage from hot or sharp flying objects, splashing chemicals etc. noun [count]	
faint /feɪnt/	to suddenly become unconscious for a short time. verb [intransitive]	
fire blanket /'faɪə ˌblæŋkɪt/	a thick piece of fabric that is placed over a fire in order to smother the flames. noun [count]	
fire extinguisher /'faɪə(r) ɪkˌstɪŋgwɪʃə/	a metal container that is filled with water or with a chemical that stops fires. noun [count]	
flammable /'flæməb(ə)l/	likely to burn very quickly and easily = inflammable (≠ non-flammable). adjective	*The chair caught fire easily because the material was flammable.*
foam /fəum/	**1** a lot of bubbles that stick together on the surface of a liquid. noun [uncount] **2** a soft, thick substance that contains a lot of bubbles. It is used for cleaning, washing or stopping fires. noun [uncount]	
fracture /'fræktʃə/	**1** a break or crack in a bone or piece of rock. noun [count] **2** if something hard such as a bone fractures, or if it is fractured, it breaks or cracks. verb [intransitive/transitive]	

frayed cord /ˌfreɪd ˈkɔːd/	an electrical wire connecting a piece of electrical equipment that has become damaged because the fibres covering it have become loose. **noun [count]**	
fuel /ˈfjuː(ə)l/	a substance such as oil, gas, coal, or wood that releases energy when it is burned. Coal and wood are sometimes called solid fuel. **noun [count/uncount]**	*Petrol is a highly flammable fuel.*
fumes /ˈfjuːmz/	smoke or gas that has an unpleasant smell, especially harmful smoke or gas. **noun [plural]**	*Traffic fumes raised pollution to record levels yesterday.*
gas hose (burner) /ˈgæs ˌhəʊz/	the tube that connects a Bunsen burner to the gas supply. **noun [count]**	
gasoline /ˈgæsəliːn/	petrol. **noun [count/uncount]**	
goggles /ˈgɒg(ə)lz/	special glasses that are worn to protect the eyes. **noun [plural]**	
grease /griːs/	a thick substance similar to oil, used on machine parts for making them work smoothly. **noun [uncount]**	
handle with care /ˌhænd(ə)l wɪð ˈkeə/	an instruction telling people to be careful when they touch or use something. **phrase**	*All chemicals must be handled with care.*
hatch (eggs) /hætʃ/	if a baby bird, fish, or insect hatches, or if it is hatched, it comes out of its egg. **verb [intransitive/transitive]**	
hazard /ˈhæzəd/	something that could be dangerous or could cause damage. **noun [count]**	
hazardous /ˈhæzədəs/	dangerous to people's health or safety. **adjective**	
heatproof mittens /ˌhiːtpruːf ˈmɪt(ə)nz/	gloves with one part for the thumb and another for the fingers that are made of a special fabric that does not allow heat to pass through. **noun [plural]**	
hydrocortisone /ˌhaɪdrəʊˈkɔːtɪzəʊn/	a hormone (=chemical substance) produced in the body that is used in medicine to treat parts of the body that have become swollen and painful. **noun [count]**	
inflammable /ɪnˈflæməb(ə)l/	something that is inflammable burns easily. **adjective**	
injury /ˈɪndʒəri/	physical harm. **noun [count/uncount]**	*an eye injury*
irritant /ˈɪrɪt(ə)nt/	something that makes part of the body become painful or swollen. **noun [count]**	*The scratchy cloth was an irritant and brought him out in a rash.*
larva /ˈlɑːvə/	a form that some insects and amphibians take after they have hatched from the egg and before they develop into their adult form. After a period of time, an insect larva changes into a pupa, inside which the adult insect develops (plural: larvae /ˈlɑːviː/). **noun [count]**	
lead-free /ˈledˌfriː/	lead-free petrol and paints do not contain lead. **adjective**	
lighting /ˈlaɪtɪŋ/	light of a particular type or quality, or the equipment that produces it. **noun [uncount]**	
mouth (burner) /maʊθ/	the part at the top of a Bunsen burner where the flame is applied to light it. **noun [count]**	
neutralization /ˌnjuːtrəlaɪˈzeɪʃ(ə)n/	the process by which one substance cancels out the effects of another, for example, the reaction between an acid and an alkali. **noun [uncount]**	
overalls /ˈəʊvərɔːlz/	a single piece of clothing with trousers and long sleeves that someone wears over their clothes to protect them while they are working. **noun [plural]**	
overheat /ˌəʊvəˈhiːt/	to become too hot, or to make something too hot. **verb [intransitive/transitive]**	
oxide /ˈɒksaɪd/	a chemical that consists of oxygen combined with another substance. **noun [uncount]**	
ozone /ˈəʊˌzəʊn/	a type of oxygen that exists high in the Earth's atmosphere. Each molecule consists of three atoms of oxygen. Chemical formula: O_3. **noun [uncount]**	*The ozone layer is gradually shrinking.*
pad /pæd/	a thick piece of a soft substance that you use for protecting something, making it more comfortable, or changing its shape. **noun [count]**	*knee pads*

pesticide /ˈpestɪˌsaɪd/	a chemical used for killing insects that damage crops. **noun [count/uncount]**	*Fruits that have been treated with pesticide should be washed before eating them.*
precaution /prɪˈkɔːʃ(ə)n/	something that you do in order to protect people or things against possible harm or trouble. **noun [count]**	*Doctors recommend taking precautions to protect your skin from the sun.*
prevent /prɪˈvent/	**1** to stop something from happening. **verb [transitive]**	*Rubber seals are fitted to prevent gas from escaping.*
	2 to stop someone from doing something. **verb [transitive]**	*Children should be prevented from playing near the stove while food is being cooked.*
protective eye gear /prəˌtektɪv ˈaɪ ˌgɪə/	equipment such as safety goggles that is worn to protect the eyes from damage. **noun [uncount]**	
protective wear /prəˌtektɪv ˌweə/	clothing and other equipment that is worn to reduce the risk of injury in places such as laboratories, workshops and factories. **noun [uncount]**	
protrude /prəˈtruːd/	to stick out from a surface. **verb [intransitive]**	
pupa /ˈpjuːpə/	an insect such as a moth while it is changing inside a cocoon or hard shell. A pupa is the stage between a larva and an adult insect (plural: pupae /ˈpjuːpiː/). **noun [count]**	
radioactive /ˌreɪdiəʊˈæktɪv/	**1** a radioactive substance such as uranium gives off energy in the form of streams of particles, caused by the way its unstable atoms decay. **adjective** **2** relating to or making use of radioactivity or the radiation that some substances give off. **adjective**	*There was a radioactive leak from the nuclear power station.*
recovery position /rɪˈkʌvəri pəˌzɪʃ(ə)n/	the position in which an unconscious person should be placed provided they are breathing and their heart is beating. In the recovery position the person is lying on their side with the upper leg bent and the lower arm stretched out. **noun [singular]**	
resuscitation /rɪˌsʌsɪˈteɪʃ(ə)n/	the process of making an unconscious person start breathing again, for example by breathing into their mouth. **noun [uncount]**	
scald /skɔːld/	to burn your skin with very hot liquid or steam. **verb [transitive]**	
scratch /skrætʃ/	to damage the skin or a surface by cutting it slightly or marking it with something sharp or rough. **verb [transitive]**	*She scratched her hand on a piece of broken glass.*
secure /sɪˈkjʊə/	**1** safe from attack, harm or danger. **adjective** **2** fastened firmly, in a safe way. **adjective**	*Make your home more secure with our burglar alarm system.* *Keep all chemicals in a secure place out of the reach of children.*
short-circuit /ˌʃɔːt ˈsɜːkɪt/	to have a short circuit, or to make a piece of electrical equipment have a short circuit. **verb [intransitive/transitive]**	
slip /slɪp/	**1** if you slip, your feet slide accidentally and you fall or lose your balance. **verb [intransitive]** **2** if something slips, it slides out of the position it should be in. **verb [intransitive]**	*Margaret slipped and broke her arm.* *The knife slipped and cut my finger.*
smother /ˈsmʌðə/	to stop a fire burning by covering it. **verb [transitive]**	
sodium hydroxide /ˌsəʊdiəm haɪˈdrɒksaɪd/	a chemical compound that is very alkaline and is used in making paper, soap, chemicals, and medicines = caustic soda. **noun [uncount]**	*Sodium hydroxide is corrosive.*
splinter /ˈsplɪntə/	**1** a small, sharp piece of wood or glass that has broken from a bigger piece. **noun [count]** **2** to break into small sharp pieces or to make something do this. **verb [transitive/intransitive]**	
sprain /spreɪn/	to injure a joint such as the wrist by suddenly turning it too much. **verb [transitive]**	
starve (fire) /stɑːv/	to deprive a fire of the fuel that it needs to burn, for example by switching off the gas or electricity supply. **verb [transitive]**	
steel toecap /ˌstiːl ˈtəʊkæp/	a piece of steel at the front of a boot or shoe that protects your toes from being damaged by heavy objects falling on them. **noun [count]**	
sting /stɪŋ/	a sudden pain caused by an insect making a hole in your skin. **noun [count]**	*Bee and wasp stings can cause a severe allergic reaction in some people.*

7 HEALTH & SAFETY

Word	Definition	Example
sulphur dioxide /ˌsʌlfə daɪˈɒksaɪd/	a poisonous gas with a strong smell. It is used for preserving things. noun [uncount]	
supervised /ˈsuːpəˌvaɪzd/	when people are supervised, they are watched by a person or group of people who make sure they work or behave correctly. adjective	*Students must be supervised at all times while in the laboratory.*
tackle a fire /ˌtæk(ə)l ə ˈfaɪə/	to try to deal with a fire by putting it out. phrase	*Only tackle a fire if you are sure you can do so safely.*
tapeworm /ˈteɪpˌwɜːm/	a long flat worm that can live inside the intestines of humans and other vertebrate animals and cause illness. The larva of the tapeworm usually gets into the human body from meat or fish that has not been completely cooked. noun [count]	
tetanus /ˈtet(ə)nəs/	a serious infection of the nervous system caused by an organism that is found in soil and animal waste. It gets into the body through a cut in the skin, and causes severe convulsions and often death. noun [uncount]	*Children are vaccinated against tetanus.*
trauma /ˈtrɔːmə/	a serious injury. noun [count/uncount]	
trip /trɪp/	to hit your foot on something and fall down, or to make someone hit their foot on something and fall down. verb [intransitive/transitive]	*I tripped over a rock.*
tumble /ˈtʌmb(ə)l/	to suddenly fall to the ground. verb [intransitive]	
twisted /ˈtwɪstɪd/	bent into a shape that is not normal. adjective	*A good treatment for a twisted ankle is to apply an ice pack wrapped in a towel.*
unconsciousness /ʌnˈkɒnʃəsˌnəs/	a state similar to sleep in which you do not see, feel, or think, usually because you are injured. noun [uncount]	
uneven /ʌnˈiːv(ə)n/	1 not smooth or level. adjective 2 not the same in size or length. adjective 3 not fairly balanced or equally shared. adjective 4 not of the same quality in all its parts. adjective	
unleaded /ʌnˈledɪd/	unleaded petrol does not contain lead. adjective	
unsupervised /ʌnˈsuːpəˌvaɪzd/	someone who is unsupervised does not have a responsible person in charge of them or looking after them. adjective	*Three young children were left unsupervised in the house.*
ventilate /ˈventɪleɪt/	to allow fresh air to enter a room or building. verb [transitive]	
well-labelled /ˌwelˈleɪb(ə)ld/	with writing on it that says clearly what it contains. adjective	*All chemicals should be well-labelled and securely closed.*

A   Working with words

1   Health and safety word map

Write these words in the correct place on the word map.

accidents   fire extinguisher   oxide of nitrogen   permission   protective wear   radioactive

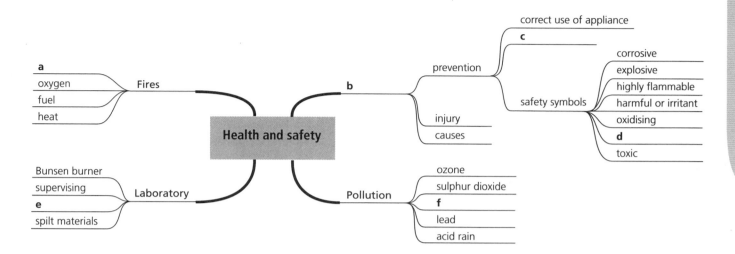

2   Universal safety symbols

Match these words with the correct safety symbols.

harmful or irritant   highly flammable   corrosive   explosive   oxidising   toxic   radioactive

 a _____

 b _____

 c _____

 d _____

 e _____

 f _____

 g _____

3 Health and safety

Fill in the gaps in the sentences with these words.

> air pollutants   carbon monoxide   fire   foam   fuel   hazard   injuries   precautions

1 _____ should be taken to avoid accidents.

2 Heat, _____ and oxygen are the conditions required for fire.

3 A _____ is extinguished if any one of these conditions is removed.

4 Water, carbon dioxide, dry chemical powder and _____ are used in different kinds of fire extinguisher.

5 _____ is poisonous because it bonds with haemoglobin and prevents it from carrying oxygen to the cells.

6 _____ have adverse effects on the environment and health of individuals.

7 Safety symbols are universal and colour-coded to indicate danger (red), _____ (yellow), no risk (green) and mandatory (blue).

8 First aid can be used for minor _____ but medical help should be sought for more major ones.

B Working with sentences

4 The effects of air pollution

Look at the illustration and label it with these words and sentences.

> 1 Acid rain damages plants, soil, water, stone and metal.
> 2 Acidified soils damage roots of plants and trees and essential minerals are washed out and poisonous minerals are released.
> 3 Lakes and rivers become acidified and poisoned from acid rain and water run-off.
> 4 Oxides of nitrogen, hydrocarbons and lead are emitted from chimneys and car exhausts.
> 5 Ozone also damages leaves so they lose minerals, turn yellow and are susceptible to disease.
> 6 Ozone: causes asthma, eats into rubber, textiles etc.
> 7 smoke and fumes
> 8 Sulphur dioxide corrodes metals, eats into the stonework of buildings and damages leaves.
> 9 sunlight

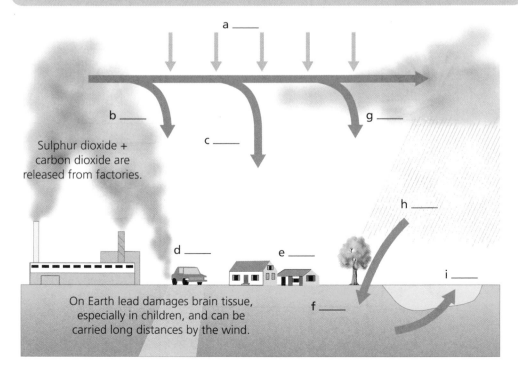

a _____

b _____

g _____

c _____

Sulphur dioxide +
carbon dioxide are
released from factories.

h _____

d _____   e _____

i _____

On Earth lead damages brain tissue,
especially in children, and can be
carried long distances by the wind.

f _____

5 **Houseflies and mosquitoes**

Label the diagrams with these phrases and sentences.

1 After 3 to 6 more days the pupae hatch into adults.
2 After 4 to 10 days the larvae turn into pupae.
3 An adult house fly – it feeds on your food, waste or faeces and lives for between 30 to 60 days.
4 The eggs are laid on water.
5 The adult female feeds on blood.
6 The eggs hatch after 6 to 24 hours into larvae.
7 The female fly lays eggs on meat.
8 The larva lives in water.
9 The larvae live in refuse.
10 The life cycle of a fly
11 The life cycle of a mosquito
12 The pupa lives in water.

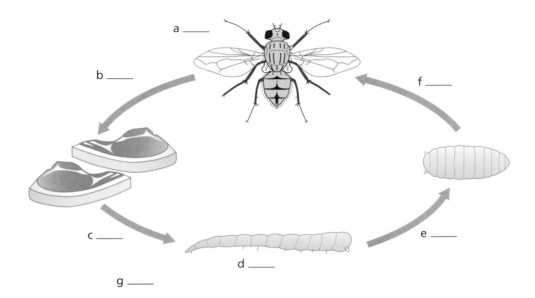

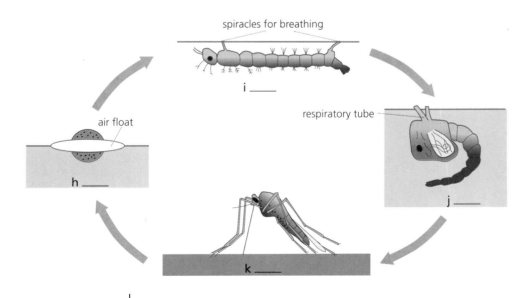

C   Working with texts

6   The life cycle of the beef tapeworm

A   Read the text and put the sentences in the correct order to form a complete paragraph.

a   After that, the eggs are eaten by a cow.
b   The next step is where the embryo is carried to cow's muscles where it forms a sac.
c   At this point the worm reproduces and the segments towards the end become full of eggs.
d   First of all, infected meat is eaten by a human.
e   In the small intestine inside the human, the head of the worm pops out of its sac.
f   Next, the embryo bores through the intestine wall into a blood vessel.
g   Once in the cow's intestine, the embryo is released from the egg.
h   Subsequently, the segments with eggs pass out with the host's faeces.
i   The head then attaches to the wall of the small intestine where it forms a chain of segments and grows to full size.

1 ☐   2 ☐   3 ☐   4 ☐   5 ☐   6 ☐   7 ☐   8 ☐   9 ☐

B   Now look at the picture and label it with the sentences.

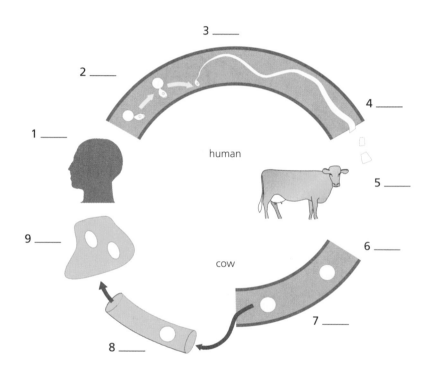

8 Health and disease

		Translation
abstinence /ˈæbstɪnəns/	the practice of avoiding something such as alcohol or sex. **noun [uncount]**	
Aedes mosquito /ˈiːdiːz mɒsˌkiːtəʊ/	a type of mosquito (=a small flying insect that bites people and takes their blood.) Aedes mosquitoes are dangerous because they carry the parasites (=organisms that live on another living creature) that cause dengue fever and yellow fever in humans. **noun [count]**	
AIDS /eɪdz/	acquired immune deficiency syndrome: a serious disease that destroys the body's ability to defend itself against infection. It is caused by the virus, HIV. **noun [uncount]**	*The AIDS virus is a serious problem in Africa.*
Anopheles mosquito /əˈnɒfəliːz mɒsˌkiːtəʊ/	a type of mosquito (=a small flying insect that bites people and takes their blood.) Anopheles mosquitoes are dangerous because they carry the parasites (=organisms that live on another living creature) that cause malaria in humans. **noun [count]**	
antibiotic /ˌæntibaɪˈɒtɪk/	a drug, for example penicillin, that cures illnesses and infections caused by bacteria. **noun [count]**	*She was prescribed antibiotics for her kidney infection.*
antibody /ˈæntiˌbɒdi/	a substance that the body produces to fight illnesses and infections. Antibodies are an important part of the immune system that protects the body against disease (plural: antibodies). **noun [count]**	*Breast milk contains antibodies which help babies fight infections.*
antigen /ˈæntɪdʒ(ə)n/	a harmful substance in the body that causes the body to produce antibodies to fight it. Bacteria, viruses, and some other chemicals are antigens. **noun [count]**	*Harmful antigens are destroyed by antibodies.*
antiseptic /ˌæntiˈseptɪk/	a substance that is used for cleaning injured skin and preventing infections. **noun [count /uncount]**	*The nurse bathed the wound with antiseptic.*
arsenic /ˈɑːsnɪk/	a poisonous grey solid element that is a metalloid. It is used to make alloys. Chemical symbol: As. **noun [uncount]**	*She poisoned him by putting arsenic in his tea.*
athlete's foot /ˈæθliːts ˈfʊt/	an infection in which the skin between the toes becomes sore, cracked, and itchy. **noun [uncount]**	
bilharzia /bɪlˈhɑːtsɪə/	a serious tropical disease caused by worms that live in rivers, lakes etc, which enter the body through the skin and live in the bloodstream. Bilharzia causes anaemia and fever. It is also called schistosomiasis. **noun [uncount]**	
birth rate /ˈbɜːθ ˌreɪt/	the official number of births in a particular year or place. **noun [count]**	*The birth rate was gradually falling.*
cervical cancer /səˌvaɪk(ə)l ˈkænsə/	cancer (=a serious disease in which the body's cells grow in an uncontrolled way) that affects the cervix (=the entrance to the uterus). **noun [uncount]**	
cervix /ˈsɜːvɪks/	the entrance to the uterus. **noun [count]**	*The cervix is a ring of muscle which relaxes when a baby is born.*
chickenpox /ˈtʃɪkɪnˌpɒks/	an infectious disease that most children get once, in which the skin is covered with red spots. **noun [uncount]**	*He stayed at home because he had chickenpox.*
chloroquine /ˈklɒrəkwaɪn/	a drug that you can take in order to prevent malaria (=a serious disease caused by mosquitoes). **noun [uncount]**	
clot /klɒt/	if blood or another liquid clots or something clots it, it becomes thick and stops flowing. **verb [transitive/intransitive]**	
cockroach /ˈkɒkˌrəʊtʃ/	an insect with hard flat wings and long antennae. It lives in warm places and where food is kept. **noun [count]**	
condom /ˈkɒndɒm/	a thin rubber tube that a man covers his penis with during sex in order to reduce the chance of a woman becoming pregnant. It also helps to protect against the spread of diseases. **noun [count]**	*Using a condom can help to reduce the spread of AIDS.*
contagious /kənˈteɪdʒəs/	a contagious disease spreads easily from one person or animal to another. A person or animal that is contagious has a disease that spreads easily to others. **adjective**	*He couldn't go to the party because his infection was contagious.*

8 HEALTH & DISEASE

contaminate /kən'tæmɪneɪt/	to make something dirty, polluted, or poisonous by adding a harmful substance. verb [transitive]	*Industrial sewage continues to contaminate our beaches.*
contraception /ˌkɒntrə'sepʃ(ə)n/	the methods that are used for preventing a woman from becoming pregnant, or the use of these methods. noun [uncount]	*No method of contraception is completely safe.*
contraceptive /ˌkɒntrə'septɪv/	a drug, method, or object that is used for preventing a woman from becoming pregnant. noun [count]	
Culex mosquito /'ku:leks mɒsˌki:təʊ/	a type of mosquito (=a small flying insect that bites people and takes their blood.) Culex mosquitoes are dangerous because they carry the parasites (=organisms that live on another living creature) that cause elephantiasis in humans. noun [count]	
DDT /ˌdi: di: 'ti:/	dichloro-diphenyl-trichloroethylane: a poisonous chemical used for killing insects. It destroys crops and also kills other animals and is dangerous to humans, and so it is no longer allowed in many countries. This kind of chemical is called a pesticide or an insecticide. noun [uncount]	
death rate /'deθ ˌreɪt/	the number of deaths in a particular area in one year. noun [count]	*The death rate was gradually rising.*
decrease /dɪ'kri:s/	**1** to become less. verb [intransitive] **2** to reduce something. verb [transitive] **3** the process of becoming less, or the amount by which something is less. noun [count/uncount]	*The rate of infection has decreased significantly.* *The new system decreases the risk to public health.* *Improved antenatal care has led to a substantial decrease in death rates among newborn babies.*
dengue fever /'deŋg 'fi:və/	a very serious illness that you get if a mosquito infected with a particular virus bites you. Dengue fever causes fever, headaches, and pain in the joints. noun [uncount]	
discharge /'dɪsˌtʃɑ:dʒ/	a liquid that comes out of someone's body when they are ill. noun [count/uncount]	*If there is a discharge from the wound, go and see your doctor.*
disinfectant /dɪsɪn'fektənt/	a chemical substance that kills bacteria, used for cleaning things. noun [count/uncount]	
droppings /'drɒpɪŋz/	the faeces of animals or birds. noun [count]	
dung /dʌŋ/	waste, especially from the body of a farm animal. It can be used to fertilize crops, or to produce biogas (fuel). noun [uncount]	
elephantiasis /ˌeləfən'taɪəsɪs/	a serious disease in which a leg or another part of the body becomes very swollen. It is caused by a parasite carried by the Culex mosquito. noun [uncount]	
flatworm /'flætˌwɜ:m/	an invertebrate worm with a long, soft, flat body. Many flatworms, for example tapeworms, are parasites. noun [count]	*Liver flukes are parasitic flatworms.*
flea /fli:/	a small jumping insect that feeds on the blood of mammals and birds. noun [count]	
foreign material /ˌfɒrən mə'tɪəriəl/	any material that does not form a normal part of the body and could enter it through a wound. noun [uncount]	
fungal parasite /ˌfʌŋg(ə)l 'pærəsaɪt/	a fungus (=an organism like a plant but with no leaves, flowers or green colour) that lives and feeds on another living organism such as a plant or an animal. Mould on decaying food and athlete's foot are both caused by fungal parasites. noun [count]	
fungicidal cream /ˌfʌŋgɪsaɪd(ə)l 'kri:m/	a cream that you put on your body to treat a skin fungus such as athlete's foot or ringworm. noun [count/uncount]	
genital herpes /ˌdʒenɪt(ə)l 'hɜ:pi:z/	a disease caused by a virus that can make painful spots (blisters) appear on the sex organs. It can be passed from a mother to her child during birth and increases the risk of cervical cancer. There is no cure for it. noun [uncount]	
German measles /ˌdʒɜ:mən 'mi:z(ə)lz/	an infectious disease that causes red spots on the skin. German measles is a minor illness but can cause serious physical damage to unborn children. The technical name for this disease is rubella. noun [uncount]	
gonorrhoea /ˌgɒnə'ri:ə/	a disease affecting the sex organs that is passed on during sex. If it is not treated, it can cause the infected person to become sterile (=unable to have children). noun [uncount]	

hatch (eggs) /hætʃ/	if a baby bird, fish, or insect hatches, or if it is hatched, it comes out of its egg. **verb [intransitive/transitive]**	
head lice /'hed ˌlaɪs/	tiny insects with six legs and no wings that live in the hair of humans. They bite the skin to suck blood, which causes itching. Their eggs are called nits (singular: head louse). **noun [plural]**	
HIV /ˌeɪtʃ aɪ 'viː/	human immunodeficiency virus: a virus that attacks the immune system and causes AIDS. The main ways HIV is spread are by having sex without condoms and sharing hypodermic needles. Babies of infected mothers can be born with HIV. It is also called HIV/AIDS. **noun [uncount]**	*Over half the children here were born with HIV.*
host /həʊst/	a plant or animal that has another organism, called a parasite, living on it. **noun [count]**	*Tapeworms live inside the intestines of their host.*
housefly /'haʊsˌflaɪ/	a very common flying insect that often lives in houses and is attracted by food. Houseflies can spread disease by landing on food, and also lay eggs in food that turn into maggots (plural: houseflies). **noun [count]**	
immune system /ɪˈmjuːn ˌsɪstəm/	the system in the body that protects against diseases by recognizing any cells, tissues, or organisms that do not belong to it such as bacteria or viruses and taking action against them. **noun [count]**	*People with AIDS easily catch diseases because HIV destroys the immune system.*
immunity /ɪˈmjuːnəti/	the protection that the body gives against a particular disease (plural: immunities). **noun [count/uncount]**	*Vaccinations give you immunity from specific diseases.*
incinerator /ɪnˈsɪnəˌreɪtə/	a machine that destroys rubbish or other material by burning it completely. **noun [count]**	*Some rubbish is disposed of by being burned in incinerators.*
incision /ɪnˈsɪʒ(ə)n/	a cut made into someone's body during a medical operation. **noun [count/uncount]**	
infection /ɪnˈfekʃ(ə)n/	**1** the process of becoming infected with a disease that is caused by bacteria or by a virus or a parasite. **noun [uncount]** **2** a disease that is caused by bacteria or by a virus or a parasite. **noun [count]**	*He was suffering from a throat infection.*
infectious /ɪnˈfekʃ(ə)s/	**1** an infectious disease is caused by bacteria or by a virus or a parasite and can spread from one person to another. **adjective** **2** a person or animal that is infectious has a disease that is caused by bacteria or by a virus or a parasite and that can spread from one person or animal to another. **adjective**	*The condition is highly infectious.* *Joe was still infectious with chicken pox so he couldn't go to the party.*
infestation /ˌɪnfesˈteɪʃ(ə)n/	a situation in which a lot of insects or animals are in a place and are causing damage or disease. **noun [count/uncount]**	*There was an infestation of rats in the barn so the farmer put down poison.*
inflamed /ɪnˈfleɪmd/	swollen and painful because of an infection or injury. **adjective**	*Her hand became inflamed because of the infection.*
inflammation /ˌɪnfleˈmeɪʃ(ə)n/	an area on your body that is swollen and painful because of an infection or injury. **noun [count/uncount]**	*A steroid cream can help reduce inflammation.*
insect repellent /'ɪnsekt rɪˌpelənt/	a substance that you put on your body or in a room to keep harmful insects such as mosquitoes away. **noun [count/uncount]**	*To avoid being bitten, cover up before dusk and use insect repellent on exposed parts of your body.*
insecticide /ɪnˈsektɪˌsaɪd/	a chemical used for killing insects. **noun [count]**	*The flies were killed by spraying them with insecticide.*
intrauterine device (IUD) /ˌɪntrəˈjuːtəraɪn dɪˌvaɪs/	a small object made of plastic or metal that is put inside a woman's uterus to prevent her becoming pregnant. It works by stopping a fertilized egg from becoming implanted in the wall of the uterus. **noun [count]**	
larva /'lɑːvə/	a form that some insects and amphibians take after they have hatched from the egg and before they develop into their adult form. After a period of time, an insect larva changes into a pupa, inside which the adult insect develops (plural: larvae /'lɑːviː/). **noun [count]**	*The caterpillar is the larva of a butterfly.*
latex rubber /'leɪteks ˌrʌbə/	a substance that is used for making condoms. **noun [uncount]**	
leptospirosis /ˌleptəʊspaɪˈrəʊsɪs/	a disease caused by bacteria that affects the kidneys and liver of humans and other mammals. **noun [uncount]**	
lymphocyte /'lɪmfəʊˌsaɪt/	a white blood cell that attacks antigens (=harmful substances that the body reacts to). **noun [count]**	*Lymphocytes produce antibodies.*
malaria /məˈleəriə/	a very serious illness that you can get if a mosquito infected with a particular parasite bites you. Malaria causes fever, shivering, and sweating, and it can be fatal. **noun [uncount]**	

8 HEALTH & DISEASE

measles /ˈmiːz(ə)lz/	a very infectious disease caused by a virus that causes red spots to appear on the body and a high temperature. Measles can cause death in young children. **noun [uncount]**	
meningitis /ˌmenɪnˈdʒaɪtɪs/	a serious illness affecting the brain and spinal cord. It is caused by a bacterium or a virus and can cause death. **noun [uncount]**	
microorganism /ˌmaɪkrəʊˈɔːɡənɪz(ə)m/	a very small living thing that you can see only with a microscope. **noun [count]**	*Bacteria are microorganisms.*
mucus /ˈmjuːkəs/	a liquid that is produced inside the nose and other parts of your body. **noun [uncount]**	
nausea /ˈnɔːzɪə/	the feeling that you are going to vomit. **noun [uncount]**	*Side effects of the drug can include headaches and nausea.*
navel /ˈneɪv(ə)l/	the small round place in the middle of the skin on the abdomen. **noun [count]**	*Your navel is the scar left by cutting the umbilical cord when you are born.*
nits /nɪts/	the eggs of insects called head lice that people sometimes have in their hair. **noun [plural]**	
opportunistic /ˌɒpətjuːˈnɪstɪk/	an opportunistic disease or infection is one that attacks someone who is already ill and has a weak immune system. **adjective**	*People with HIV are subject to opportunistic infections.*
overpopulation /ˌəʊvəˌpɒpjuˈleɪʃ(ə)n/	the problem of there being too many people in a particular place, so that they cannot all have a decent standard of living. **noun [uncount]**	*Overpopulation is one of the main causes of poverty.*
parasite /ˈpærəˌsaɪt/	an organism that lives in or on another living thing and feeds on it. Lice, fleas, and tapeworms are all types of parasite. The organism that a parasite lives on is called the host. **noun [count]**	
pathogen /ˈpæθəˌdʒən/	a microorganism such as a bacterium or virus that causes disease. **noun [count]**	*Many pathogens live and breed in dirty surroundings.*
pathogenic /ˌpæθəˈdʒenɪk/	causing disease. Pathogenic agents include viruses and bacteria. **adjective**	
penicillin /ˌpenəˈsɪlɪn/	a drug used for treating illnesses that are caused by bacteria. Penicillin is an antibiotic. **noun [uncount]**	*The doctor prescribed penicillin for her throat infection.*
phagocyte /ˈfæɡəʊˌsaɪt/	a cell in an organism that gets rid of bacteria and other harmful cells by taking them into itself and digesting them. **noun [count]**	
pheromone /ˈferəməʊn/	a chemical that an insect produces that spreads in the air and influences the behaviour of other insects of the same type. Pheromones can be used as a method of pest control. The pheromones are put into traps which attract and catch the male insects, so that the females cannot breed. **noun [count]**	
pinworm /ˈpɪnˌwɜːm/	a small thin worm that is a parasite of humans. They live in the intestines and are spread by contact as a result of poor hygiene. **noun [count]**	
pit latrine /ˈpɪt ləˌtriːn/	a type of outside toilet that consists of a hole in the floor built over a large hole in the ground (a pit). **noun [count]**	
Plasmodium /ˌplæzˈməʊdiəm/	a parasite (=an organism that lives on another living creature) that lives in female Anopholes mosquitoes and causes malaria. **noun [count]**	
population explosion /ˌpɒpjəˈleɪʃ(ə)n ɪkˌspləʊʒ(ə)n/	a very large increase in the number of people in a place over a very short period of time. **noun [count]**	*The human population explosion started in about 1800.*
premature /ˈpremətʃə/	a premature baby is born before it should be. **adjective**	*Although three weeks premature, the baby was healthy.*
prevent /prɪˈvent/	to stop something from happening. **verb [transitive]**	*Valves prevent blood from flowing the wrong way out of the heart.*
progestin /prəˈdʒesˌtɪn/	a hormone (=a chemical substance produced by the body) such as progesterone that prepares a woman's body for pregnancy (also called: progestogen). **noun [count]**	
rash /ræʃ/	an area of small red spots on the skin that is caused by a disease or by a reaction to something. **noun [count]**	*The doctor took a look at the rash and said it was measles.*
rat /ræt/	a small, furry mammal like a large mouse with a long tail. Rats are regarded as pests because they eat our food, destroy things and can spread disease. **noun [count]**	
resistant /rɪˈzɪst(ə)nt/	not harmed or affected by something. **adjective**	*a disease that is resistant to antibiotics*

rodent /ˈrəʊdənt/	a type of mammal that has long sharp front teeth, for example a rat or a porcupine. **noun [count]**	
rot /rɒt/	to decay by a gradual natural process, or to make something decay in this way. **verb [intransitive/transitive]**	*All those sweets will rot your teeth.*
roundworm /ˈraʊndˌwɜːm/	an invertebrate animal like a worm that is a parasite of humans, especially children. It lives in the intestines and can reproduce very quickly. **noun [count]**	
Schistosoma /ˌʃɪstəˈsəʊmə/	a type of flatworm (=invertebrate animal) that causes a serious disease called bilharzia or schistosomiasis. It is found in infected water and passes into humans through their skin. **noun [count]**	
schistosomiasis /ˌʃɪstəsəˈmaɪəsɪs/	a serious tropical disease caused by worms that live in rivers, lakes etc, which enter the body through the skin and live in the bloodstream. Schistosomiasis causes anaemia and fever. It is also called bilharzia. **noun [uncount]**	
sebum /ˈsiːbəm/	a substance like oil produced by the sebaceous glands that stops the hair and skin from drying out and also protects against some bacteria. **noun [uncount]**	*Sebum keeps the skin supple.*
septic tank /ˌseptɪk ˈtæŋk/	a large container buried under the ground and used for collecting waste from toilets. **noun [count]**	
sewer /ˈsuːə/	an underground pipe or passage that carries sewage (=human waste). **noun [count]**	
sludge /slʌdʒ/	an unpleasant thick wet substance. Sludge is produced when dung is made into biogas (=fuel) and can be used to fertilize crops. **noun [uncount]**	*Sludge is an excellent fertilizer because it is rich in substances that promote plant growth.*
sore /sɔː/	a small painful area of skin that is injured or infected. **noun [count]**	
spermicide /ˈspɜːmɪˌsaɪd/	a cream that kills sperm, used during sex to prevent a woman from becoming pregnant. **noun [count]**	
stagnant /ˈstæɡnənt/	stagnant water does not flow and often smells bad. **adjective**	*Mosquito larvae live in stagnant water.*
starvation /stɑːˈveɪʃ(ə)n/	a situation in which people or animals suffer or die because they do not have enough food. **noun [uncount]**	*Many children died of starvation during the famine.*
STD /ˌes tiː ˈdiː/	sexually transmitted disease: a disease that someone gets from having sex with an infected person.	*Wearing a condom can reduce the risk of spreading STDs.*
sterile /ˈsteraɪl/	**1** completely clean, with no bacteria. **adjective** **2** not able to produce children. **adjective**	*Make sure that the needles are sterile.* *Some common illnesses can make you sterile.*
syphilis /ˈsɪfəlɪs/	a serious disease caused by a bacterium that is passed on through sexual contact. **noun [uncount]**	*The STD syphilis can be treated with antibiotics.*
tapeworm /ˈteɪpˌwɜːm/	a long flat worm that can live inside the intestines of humans and other vertebrate animals and cause illness. The larva of the tapeworm usually gets into the human body from meat or fish that has not been completely cooked. **noun [count]**	
thallium /ˈθæliəm/	a chemical element in the form of a silver-white metal. Its symbol is TI. **noun [uncount]**	
the pill /ˌðə ˈpɪl/	a contraceptive pill that can be taken regularly by women to reduce the chance of becoming pregnant. **noun [count]**	*She was taking the pill because she didn't want any more children.*
tick /tɪk/	a small arachnid (=creature similar to a spider) that fastens itself onto the skin of a mammal and feeds on its blood. Ticks live on animals such as dogs and cats and can spread some diseases to humans. **noun [count]**	
transfusion /ˌtrænsˈfjuːʒ(ə)n/	a medical treatment in which blood from one person is put into another person's body, especially because the patient has lost a lot of blood from an injury or during a medical operation. **noun [count/uncount]**	*She needed a blood transfusion.*
tubal ligation /ˌtʃuːb(ə)l laɪˈɡeɪʃ(ə)n/	a surgical procedure that is done so that a woman cannot have any more children. It involves burning the Fallopian tubes or oviducts so that the eggs cannot pass down them to be fertilized. **noun [count]**	
unprotected sex /ˌʌnprəˌtektɪd ˈseks/	if people have unprotected sex, they do not use any form of contraception. This can result in pregnancy or the transmission of STDs. **noun [uncount]**	

unreliable /ˌʌnrɪˈlaɪəbəl/	someone or something that is unreliable cannot be depended on. **adjective**	*Withdrawal is an unreliable method of contraception.*
vaccination /ˌvæksɪˈneɪʃ(ə)n/	treating a person or animal with a vaccine in order to protect them against a disease. **noun [count]**	*A worldwide vaccination programme helped to wipe out small pox.*
vaccine /ˈvæksiːn/	a dead or weak microorganism that is put into the body in order to provide protection against a disease by causing it to make antibodies. **noun [count/uncount]**	*The nurse administered a vaccine against German measles to all the schoolgirls.*
vasectomy /vəˈsektəmi/	a medical operation in which the tube that a man's sperm passes through is cut. This makes him unable to have children (plural: vasectomies). **noun [count]**	*He had a vasectomy because he didn't want to father any more children.*
vector for disease /ˌvektə fə dɪˈzɪːz/	an insect or other small organism that carries diseases between larger animals, including humans, but is not itself harmed by the disease. Mosquitoes and ticks are vectors. **noun [count]**	
venereal disease /vəˈnɪəriəl dɪˌziːz/	a disease that is spread when people have sex. **noun [count/uncount]**	*STDs used to be referred to as venereal disease (VD).*
vomit /ˈvɒmɪt/	if you vomit, or if you vomit something, food comes up from your stomach and out through your mouth because you are ill. **verb [intransitive/transitive]**	*Symptoms of the disease include vomiting and diarrhoea.*
yellow fever /ˌjeləʊ ˈfiːvə/	a serious tropical illness caused by a virus and spread by a mosquito. It causes fever, bleeding, and the skin to turn yellow. **noun [uncount]**	

A   Working with words

1   Health and disease word map

Write these words in the correct places on the word map.

house flies   immunity against disease   mosquitoes   parasites   AIDS   pinworms

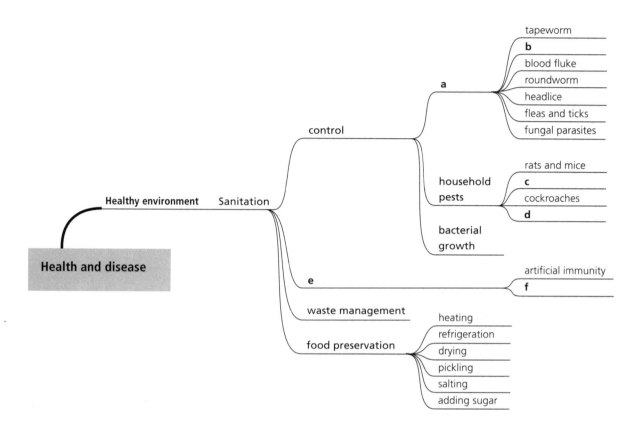

2   Artificial immunity

Read the text and fill in the gaps with these words.

antibodies   chickenpox   immunity   infection   lymphocytes   microorganism   vaccinations   vaccine

We can trick the body into responding to an 1_____ without actually becoming ill. Do you remember going to the doctor to get 2 _____ against 3 _____, hepatitis B and measles when you were younger? Vaccines are 'pretend' infections. The vaccine is either made from a very small amount of the dead 4 _____ or the toxins that it makes. When you receive the vaccine the white blood cells (5 _____) identify them and begin to make antibodies against the infection, but because the microorganism is dead (or not even there), you do not get ill. Just as with natural 6 _____ , these antibodies stay in the bloodstream for a very long time. So when you come into contact with the live microorganism, 7 _____ are produced rapidly and you will not become ill. This is known as artificial immunity. Many infections can now be avoided by being given the 8 _____ for them before we come into contact with the live versions.

3 Acquired Immune Deficiency Syndrome (AIDS)

Complete the text by filling in the missing information. Certain letters are given to help you.

Acquired Immune Deficiency Syndrome (AIDS) is the worst sexually 1 t_____d disease. It is caused by the Human Immunodeficiency 2 _____ (HIV) which attacks the immune system. The 3 i_____e system usually plays an important part in fighting off infections. HIV is transmitted through contact with the 4 i_____d person's body fluids, such as semen, blood and vaginal secretions. HIV is not only transmitted by sexual intercourse, but also in infected blood 5 t_____s, from an infected expectant mother to her unborn child, or between drug addicts sharing an infected needle. HIV reduces the protective function of the immune system by destroying the cells that produce 6 a_____s to fight against viruses and bacteria that enter the body. When the immune system breaks down, the person will then suffer many infections and diseases. These are called 7 o_____c infections because they take advantage of the body's weakened defences. This is what we call Acquired Immune 8 D_____y Syndrome (AIDS). A person can be infected with HIV for up to 10 years before showing any signs of AIDS. The person usually dies from one of these opportunistic infections, not from the HIV virus itself. To date there is no cure for HIV/AIDS. However, patients are usually treated for the various opportunistic infections. The drug AZT (azidothymidine) can cause the HIV virus to take much longer to develop into AIDS, and so prolong the life of an HIV-infected individual. It is also widely accepted that the use of a latex 9 c_____m while having intercourse will 10 p_____t the transfer of the virus from an infected individual to another.

4 Microorganisms and decay

Read the text. Some of the sentences contain incorrect words. These are underlined. Replace them with one of these words.

> bacteria   cycle   decay   ill   organisms   plants   rot   unpleasant

Have you ever had food stored at room temperature for a long time? What happens to it after a while? It begins to develop or decay. Microorganisms, including reptiles and fungi, feed on organic materials. During this process they cause the erosion or breakdown of the materials. They are an important part of the circle of minerals and nutrients between living organs because they break down complex substances into simpler ones that animals can use at the start of a food chain. Decay can cause problems for us because it makes our food nice to eat. It can also make us better because the microorganisms can release chemicals that are toxic or poisonous to us as they feed on it.

develop > _____   organs > _____

reptiles > _____   animals > _____

erosion > _____   nice > _____

circle > _____   better > _____

B Working with sentences

5 Health and disease

Match the beginnings and endings of the sentences.

Beginnings

1 Microorganisms, such as bacteria and fungi,
2 The growth and development of microorganisms
3 Food preservation methods
4 Parasites are microorganisms that
5 Pests may
6 Pesticides are chemicals that
7 Herbicides kill plant pests (weeds) while
8 The use of pesticides can
9 Biological pest control involves
10 The improper disposal of waste
11 Refuse can be classified as
12 Alternative methods of waste disposal
13 Your immune system protects you from infection

Endings

a act as hosts to human parasites.
b be hazardous to the environment and to the health of humans and other useful organisms.
c are affected by temperature, moisture, oxygen and acidity.
d biodegradable (decays) or non biodegradable (does not decay).
e by making antibodies.
f cause decay.
g feed on living material.
h include reuse, recycling and converting to energy (e.g. biogas).
i include salting, heating, refrigeration, drying, pickling and adding of sugar.
j insecticides kill insects.
k introducing the natural predator or parasite of the pest.
l kill pests.
m will result in many health problems and the spread of diseases.

1 ☐ 2 ☐ 3 ☐ 4 ☐ 5 ☐ 6 ☐ 7 ☐ 8 ☐ 9 ☐ 10 ☐ 11 ☐ 12 ☐ 13 ☐

C Working with texts

6 Leptospirosis

Read the text and sort the information into the table.

Leptospirosis is caused by a bacterium, *Leptospira*, which is found in the urine and faeces of infected rats, mice, and in the fleas that bite them. Humans become infected through contact with water, food or soil containing urine from the infected rodents, or through bites from infected fleas. Other animals, such as cattle, pigs, horses and dogs are also able to spread the disease if they are infected with the bacteria. The symptoms of leptospirosis include high fever, severe headache, chills, muscle aches and vomiting, and may include jaundice (yellow skin and eyes), red eyes, abdominal pain, diarrhoea or a rash. If the disease is not treated, the patient could develop kidney damage, meningitis, inflammation of the membrane around the brain and spinal cord, liver failure and respiratory distress, which may lead to death. Leptospirosis is treated with chemicals, such as doxycycline or penicillin (antibiotics), which should be given early in the course of the disease. However, control of the pests which carry the disease and can prevent infection is better. Avoid swimming or wading in water that might be contaminated with animal urine. Wear protective clothing or footwear when exposed to contaminated water or soil. Do not allow rubbish to accumulate in or around the house which will attract rodents.

Cause	
Ways of infection	
Symptoms	
Consequences	
Treatment	
Prevention	

7 Food preservation

Read the text and complete the table.

Heating – This kills many microorganisms that grow on our food. We use it when we boil, sterilise, pasteurize and roast our food. However, it does not destroy many toxins from microorganisms, so this will not make 'bad' food safe to eat. This method is also used in the food canning industry, where foods are first processed in this way before being sealed in airtight cans.

Refrigeration – The temperature inside a refrigerator is low enough to slow the growth of microorganisms but not to stop it. This can help us keep food for longer before we eat it. The lower temperatures in a freezer stop the growth of most microorganisms and the decay they cause, and so preserve foods for even longer. However, they start growing again as food thaws, which is why you should not defrost frozen food and then refreeze it.

Drying – This involves removing moisture from the food, which the microorganisms need for all the chemical processes both inside and outside them. This process is mainly used for preserving fruits, vegetables and some kinds of meats and fish.

Pickling – This is adding an acid to, or storing food in, an acidic solution which is usually vinegar. Many of the microorganisms that spoil food are unable to grow or survive in acid conditions.

Salting – This is probably one of the oldest methods of preserving food. Placing food in a large amount of salt removes water from it by osmosis. This is effectively another way of making the food dry or dehydrated, which prevents the growth of microorganisms. This process is mainly used on meats and fish.

Adding sugar – The addition of sugar works on the same principle as another process. A high concentration of it removes water from the food. This method is used in preserving fruit such as jellies and jams.

Technique used	Name of method(s)	How	Type of foods
temperature			
extraction of moisture			
use of acid			

9 The circulatory system

agglutination
/ə,gluːtɪ'neɪʃ(ə)n/
the process by which particles such as blood cells clump together. noun [uncount]

If a patient is given the wrong blood this can lead to agglutination, which can be fatal.

angina
/æn'dʒaɪnə/
a medical condition in which not enough blood gets to your heart, so that you get pains in your chest. noun [uncount]

antibody
/'æntɪ,bɒdi/
a substance that the body produces to fight illnesses and infections. Antibodies are an important part of the immune system that protects the body against disease (plural: antibodies). noun [count]

anti-D
/,ænti'diː/
an injection of a blood product that is given to Rh- mothers in order to prevent rhesus disease in their Rh+ baby. noun [uncount]

RhD-negative women are offered anti-D injections during pregnancy.

antigen
/'æntɪ,dʒ(ə)n/
a harmful substance in the body that causes the body to produce antibodies to fight it. Bacteria, viruses, and some other chemicals are antigens. noun [count]

aorta
/eɪ'ɔːtə/
the main artery that carries blood with a high oxygen level from the heart to other parts of the body. noun [count]

artery
/'ɑːtəri/
one of the blood vessels in the body that carries blood from the heart to the rest of the body. The blood in most arteries has a high level of oxygen, except for the pulmonary artery that takes blood from the heart to the lungs (plural: arteries). noun [count]

The coronary artery supplies the heart tissue with blood.

arteriosclerosis
/ɑ;tɪəriəusklə'rəusɪs/
a serious medical condition in which the sides of the arteries become thick, hard, and stiff, so that the heart has to work harder to pump blood through the body. noun [uncount]

Arteriosclerosis is a common condition in old age.

atherosclerosis
/,æθə'rəusklə'rəusɪs/
a medical condition in which the diameter of the artery becomes narrower due to the build up of fatty deposits of cholesterol on the wall. noun [uncount]

atrio-ventricular
/,eɪtriəu ven'trɪkjulə/
relating to the atrial and ventricular chambers of the heart, or the connection between them. adjective

The atrio-ventricular valves control the flow of blood between the heart's chambers.

atrium
/'eɪtriəm/
one of the two upper spaces in the heart which force blood into the ventricles (plural: atria or atriums). noun [count]

backflow
/'bækˌfləu/
the process by which a liquid such as blood flows back through a valve because the valve does not close properly. noun [uncount]

Backflow can cause heart failure.

biconcave
/,baɪkɒn'keɪv/
a biconcave object is concave (=curved inwards) on both sides. adjective

Red blood cells have the shape of a biconcave disc.

bicuspid valve
/baɪ'kʌspɪd ,vælv/
the mitral valve on the left side of the heart that stops blood from flowing back into the ventricle from the atrium. noun [count]

bleed
/'bliːd/
to have blood flowing from your body, for example from a cut. verb [intransitive]

He was bleeding from a wound in his shoulder.

bleeding
/'bliːdɪŋ/
the process of losing blood from your body, for example from a cut. noun [uncount]

They had to act quickly to stop the bleeding.

blood film
/'blʌd ,fɪlm/
a slide made from a drop of blood. Blood films are usually made in order to look for illnesses of the blood. Blood smear means the same. noun [count]

blood group
/'blʌd ,gruːp/
one of the groups that human blood can be divided into. The four main groups are A, B, AB, and O. noun [count]

Her blood group was AB, which is quite rare.

blood smear
/'blʌd ,smɪə/
a slide made from a drop of blood. Blood smears are usually made in order to look for illnesses of the blood. Blood film means the same. noun [count]

blood vessel
/'blʌd ,ves(ə)l/
a tube that carries blood around the body. Veins, arteries, and capillaries are all blood vessels. noun [count]

A blood vessel in her eye burst.

blue baby
/,bluː 'beɪbi/
a baby whose skin looks blue when it is born because its Rh+ blood cells have been attacked by Rh- antibodies from its mother, causing the baby's blood to agglutinate. noun [count]

Term	Definition	Translation
bone marrow /ˈbəʊn ˌmærəʊ/	the soft red substance inside the spaces in the bones. Red blood cells, platelets, and some white blood cells are formed in the bone marrow. **noun [uncount]**	
burst /bɜːst/	if an object bursts, or if you burst it, it breaks suddenly. **verb [intransitive/transitive]**	
capillary /kəˈpɪləri/	the smallest type of blood vessel, with a wall that is only one cell thick. It carries blood to and from individual cells in the body (plural: capillaries). **noun [count]**	*All the body's organs have a network of capillaries.*
cardiac muscle /ˈkɑːdiæk ˌmʌs(ə)l/	a type of muscle that the heart is made of. It only exists in the heart and never gets tired. **noun [uncount]**	*When cardiac muscle contracts, it squeezes blood out of your heart.*
cholesterol /kəˈlestərɒl/	a substance that is found in the blood and the cells of the body. It can cause diseases of the heart and the arteries if there is too much of it. **noun [uncount]**	*It is important to have your cholesterol level checked regularly.*
circulation /ˌsɜːkjʊˈleɪʃ(ə)n/	the movement of blood around the body. **noun [uncount]**	*His hands were often cold because he had bad circulation.*
circulatory system /sɜːkjʊˈleɪtri ˌsɪstəm/	the system that moves blood around the body. It consists of the blood, the blood vessels and the heart. **noun [count]**	
clenched fist /ˌklentʃt ˈfɪst/	a clenched fist is a hand that is tightly closed. **noun [count]**	
clotting /ˈklɒtɪŋ/	clotting is the process by which blood or another liquid becomes thick and stops flowing. **noun [uncount]**	*Platelets assist in the clotting of blood.*
clump /klʌmp/	when particles clump, they come together to form a solid mass. **verb [transitive/intransitive]**	*Anti-A antibodies react with A-antigens and cause clumping.*
contract /kənˈtrækt/	if a muscle contracts, it gets tighter and shorter. **verb [transitive/intransitive]**	*The muscular walls of the ventricles contract to push blood into the arteries.*
coronary artery /ˈkɒrən(ə)ri ˌɑːtəri/	either of the two arteries that carry blood to the heart. **noun [count]**	
coronary bypass /ˌkɒrən(ə)ri ˈbaɪpɑːs/	an operation to bypass (=go round) an area of a coronary artery that has become clogged. A blood vessel from the patient's leg is used to create a new tube so that the blood can flow freely to the heart muscles. **noun [count]**	*Since having a coronary bypass, he has been fit and well.*
diastolic pressure /daɪəˌstɒlɪk ˈpreʃə/	a person's blood pressure when the heart is relaxing. It is the second of the two numbers given when saying what someone's blood pressure is. **noun [uncount]**	
digest /daɪˈdʒest/	to break something down into soluble substances that can be absorbed. **verb [transitive]**	*Phagocytes destroy bacteria by digesting the organisms inside them.*
donor /ˈdəʊnə/	someone who gives something such as blood, sperm, or an organ to help someone else. **noun [count]**	*Being a blood donor can help save lives.*
elastic /ɪˈlæstɪk/	able to stretch or bend and then return to the original shape. **adjective**	*The walls of blood vessels are elastic.*
endothelium /ˌendəʊˈθiːliəm/	the tissue which forms the lining of the whole of the circulatory system. It is only one cell thick. **noun [uncount]**	
engulf /ɪnˈgʌlf/	to cover something in a way that destroys it. **verb [transitive]**	*Phagocytes first engulf invading organisms and then digest them.*
erythrocyte /eˈriːθrəsaɪt/	the technical name for a red blood cell. Unlike most cells they do not contain a nucleus. **noun [count]**	
fatty deposit /ˈfæti dɪˈpɒzɪt/	an amount of a fatty substance that gradually forms on a surface. **noun [count]**	*The build-up of fatty deposits on the artery walls can lead to health problems.*
fibrin /ˈfaɪbrɪn/	a type of protein that is produced by the blood near a wound. It forms a network of threads that trap red blood cells and platelets to form a clot. **noun [count/uncount]**	
fibrous /ˈfaɪbrəs/	containing fibres, or similar to fibres. **adjective**	*Arteries and veins are surrounded by a fibrous layer.*
foreign material /ˌfɒrən məˈtɪəriəl/	any material that does not form a normal part of the body and could enter it through a wound. **noun [uncount]**	
form a clot /ˌfɔːm ə ˈklɒt/	to cause blood to become thick and make a lump which seals a wound and prevents further bleeding. **phrase**	
haemoglobin /ˌhiːməˈgləʊbɪn/	a protein in red blood cells that carries oxygen from the lungs to all parts of the body. **noun [uncount]**	
haemolytic disease /ˌhiːməˈlɪtɪk dɪˌziːz/	a condition which can affect a Rh+ baby of a Rh- mother. If the condition is not treated, the mother's antibodies pass through the placenta and attack the baby's Rh+ blood cells, causing serious health problems and even the death of the baby. Rhesus disease means the same. **noun [uncount]**	

heart attack /'hɑːt əˌtæk/	an occasion when someone suddenly has a lot of pain in the chest because the heart stops working normally. **noun [count]**	*The heart attack was caused by a blockage in the coronary artery.*
hepatitis B /ˌhepəˌtaɪtɪs 'biː/	an infectious disease of the liver. **noun [uncount]**	
hypertension /ˌhaɪpə'tenʃ(ə)n/	a condition in which someone's blood pressure is extremely high. **noun [uncount]**	*He suffered from hypertension as a result of his stressful job.*
lumen /'luːmən/	the central space in an artery or vein through which the blood flows. **noun [count]**	
lymphocyte /'lɪmfəʊˌsaɪt/	a white blood cell that attacks antigens (=harmful substances that the body reacts to). **noun [count]**	
malaria /mə'leəriə/	a very serious illness that you can get if a mosquito infected with a particular parasite bites you. Malaria causes fever, shivering, and sweating, and it can be fatal. **noun [uncount]**	
mesh /meʃ/	a network of something such as threads or fibres that traps small particles, for example to form a blood clot. **noun [count/uncount]**	
muscular /'mʌskjʊlə/	**1** having big muscles. **adjective** **2** affecting your muscles. **adjective**	*muscular legs*
narrow /'nærəʊ/	if something is narrow, there is only a short distance from one side of it to the other. **adjective**	
one-way valve /ˌwʌnweɪ 'vælv/	a valve (=a part of an organ or tube that opens and closes to allow liquid to flow) that only allows blood to flow in one direction, for example, towards the heart. **noun [count]**	
oxygenate /'ɒksɪdʒəˌneɪt/	to add oxygen to something. **verb [transitive]**	*Blood is oxygenated in the lungs.*
phagocyte /'fægəʊˌsaɪt/	a cell in an organism that gets rid of bacteria and other harmful cells by taking them into itself and digesting them. **noun [count]**	
pigment /'pɪgmənt/	a natural chemical compound that gives colour to animal or plant tissues. **noun [count/uncount]**	*Red blood cells contain a red pigment.*
plasma /'plæzmə/	the yellow liquid that is part of blood. **noun [uncount]**	
platelet /'pleɪtˌlət/	a small piece of a cell in the blood of humans and other mammals that helps the blood to clot. **noun [count]**	
poison /'pɔɪz(ə)n/	a substance that can kill someone or make them very ill if they eat, drink, or breathe it. **noun [count/uncount]**	
prevent /prɪ'vent/	to stop something from happening. **verb [transitive]**	*Valves prevent blood from flowing the wrong way out of the heart.*
protective coat /prəˌtektɪv 'kəʊt/	a layer that forms or is put on a surface in order to protect it. **noun [count]**	*A scab is a hard protective coat that forms over a wound.*
pulmonary artery /ˌpʌlmən(ə)ri 'ɑːtəri/	one of two arteries that carry blood from the right ventricle of the heart to the lungs (plural: pulmonary arteries). **noun [count]**	
pulmonary circulation /ˌpʌlmən(ə)ri sɜːkju'leɪʃ(ə)n/	the pumping of blood from the right side of the heart to the lungs. **noun [uncount]**	
pump /pʌmp/	to send liquid or gas somewhere, especially by using a pump. **verb [transitive]**	*The heart pumps blood around the body.*
recipient /rɪ'sɪpiənt/	someone who receives something. **noun [count]**	*The donor heart must be transplanted into the recipient within five hours.*
red blood cell /ˌred 'blʌd ˌsel/	a blood cell that contains haemoglobin and gives the blood its red colour. Red blood cells have no nucleus and are formed in the bone marrow. **noun [count]**	
regular intervals /ˌregjulə 'ɪntəvəlz/	if something happens at regular intervals, it happens repeatedly and with the same amount of time between each occurrence. **phrase**	*The human heart beats at regular intervals of about 70 times a minute.*
repetitive /rɪ'petətɪv/	involving repeating the same action over long periods of time. **adjective**	
Rhesus disease /'riːsəs dɪˌziːz/	a condition which can affect a Rh+ baby of a Rh- mother. If the condition is not treated, the mother's antibodies pass through the placenta and attack the baby's Rh+ blood cells, causing serious health problems and even the death of the baby. Haemolytic disease means the same. **noun [uncount]**	
Rhesus factor /'riːsəs ˌfæktə/	an antigen that is present in the red blood cells of about 85% of humans and some other primates. **noun [singular]**	

Term	Definition	Translation
rupture /ˈrʌptʃə/	if something ruptures, or if you rupture it, it bursts or tears suddenly. **verb [transitive/intransitive]**	*She suffered a ruptured vein in her leg.*
rush /rʌʃ/	if a liquid rushes somewhere, it moves there quickly and with force. **verb [intransitive]**	*The muscles in the artery walls stretch when blood rushes into the artery.*
scab /skæb/	a hard layer of dried blood that forms on a cut on your skin. **noun [count]**	*The child's knees were covered in scabs.*
semilunar valve /ˌsemiluːnə ˈvælv/	a valve in the aorta and pulmonary artery. It prevents blood from flowing back into the ventricles.	
septum /ˈseptəm/	a layer of muscle that separates the two sides of the heart. **noun [count]**	
single file /ˌsɪŋg(ə)l ˈfaɪl/	a line of people or things in which one is directly behind the other. **noun [count/uncount]**	
spherical /ˈsferɪk(ə)l/	shaped like a ball. **adjective**	
sphygmomano-meter /ˌsfɪgməˌmæˈnɒmɪtə/	an instrument that is used to measure blood pressure. It consists of an inflatable cuff that is put round the arm and connected to a column of mercury which measures the blood pressure as the air is released from the cuff. **noun [count]**	
squeeze /skwiːz/	**1** to press something firmly. **verb [transitive/intransitive]** **2** to press something such as a liquid out of something. **verb [transitive]** **3** to fit something into a small space with difficulty, or to fit into a small space with difficulty. **verb [transitive/intransitive]**	
stethoscope /ˈsteθəˌskəʊp/	a piece of equipment that doctors use to listen to your heart or to your breathing. **noun [count]**	
suffocation /ˌsʌfəˈkeɪʃ(ə)n/	death caused by lack of oxygen. **noun [uncount]**	
systematic circulation /sɪstəˌmætɪk səːkjuˈleɪʃ(ə)n/	the pumping of blood from the left side of the heart to the rest of the body. **noun [uncount]**	
systolic pressure /sɪsˌtɒlɪk ˈpreʃə/	a person's blood pressure when the heart is contracting. It is the first of the two numbers given when saying what someone's blood pressure is. **noun [uncount]**	
thrombosis /ˌθrɒmˈbəʊsɪs/	a serious medical condition in which the blood gets thicker and forms a clot that stops it from flowing normally (plural: thromboses /θrɒmˈbəʊsiːz/). **noun [count/uncount]**	*A coronary thrombosis can cause a heart attack.*
toxin /ˈtɒksɪn/	a poisonous substance. **noun [count]**	*The liver removes toxins from the blood.*
transfusion /ˌtrænsˈfjuːʒ(ə)n/	a medical treatment in which blood from one person is put into another person's body, especially because the patient has lost a lot of blood from an injury or during a medical operation. **noun [count/uncount]**	*She needed a blood transfusion.*
tricuspid valve /traɪˈkʌspɪd ˌvælv/	a valve on the right side of the heart. It prevents blood from flowing back from the right ventricle into the atrium. **noun [count]**	
vein /veɪn/	one of the blood vessels in the body that carry blood towards the heart. The blood in nearly all veins, except for the pulmonary vein, has a low level of oxygen, as the oxygen has been used in respiration. **noun [count]**	
vena cava /ˌviːnə ˈkeɪvə/	one of the two large veins that carry blood into the right side of the heart. The anterior vena cava brings blood from the upper body and the head, and the posterior vena cava brings blood from below the chest (plural: venae cavae /ˌviːniː ˈkeɪviː/). **noun [count]**	
ventricle /ˈventrɪk(ə)l/	one of the two lower parts of the heart that pumps blood to the rest of the body. **noun [count]**	
white blood cell /ˌwaɪt ˈblʌd ˌsel/	a type of blood cell. Many types of white blood cells protect the body against infection and produce antibodies. Unlike red blood cells, white blood cells have a nucleus. They are formed in the bone marrow and lymph nodes. **noun [count]**	
wound /wuːnd/	an injury in which your skin or flesh is seriously damaged. **noun [count]**	*a head wound*

1 The circulatory system word map

Write these words in the correct places on the word map.

> artery   blood vessels   left side   plasma   platelets   pumps blood to lungs   right atrium

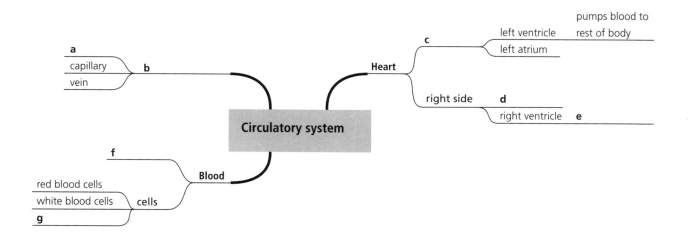

2 The heart

Read the text and put the words in the right places.

> aorta   atria   cardiac   lower   pulmonary   pumping   septum   upper   valves   vena cava

Although the heart has the major role of 1 _____ blood around the entire body it is a small organ. The wall of the heart is very muscular. This is a special type of muscle called 2 _____ muscle which does not get tired. The heart is divided into two parts, left and right sides, which are separated by a layer of muscle called the 3 _____. Each side of the heart has two chambers: each 4 _____ chamber is an atrium, the plural is atria, and the 5 _____ chambers are called the ventricles. Between the atria and ventricles on each side of the heart are 6 _____ that prevent blood flowing the wrong way through the heart. Blood enters the heart through veins and leaves the heart through arteries. On the right side of the heart, blood arrives from the body via the 7 _____. On the left side blood from the lungs enters the heart through the 8 _____ vein. Blood passes from the veins into the 9_____, then to the ventricles, and then out through the arteries. On the right side it leaves through the pulmonary artery to go to the lungs, and on the left side it leaves through the 10 _____ to go to the rest of the body. Blood flowing on the right side of the heart is low in oxygen (deoxygenated blood) and high in carbon dioxide because it has come from the body. When it returns from the lungs to the left side of the heart it is high in oxygen, oxygenated blood, and low in carbon dioxide.

3 Blood circulation in humans

Look at the diagram and place these labels in the correct places.

capillaries in the body   deoxygenated blood from body   deoxygenated blood from the head
deoxygenated blood to the lungs   from body   from head   head, neck and arms   lungs
oxygenated blood to the body   oxygenated blood to the head   oxygenated blood to the head and body   to heart

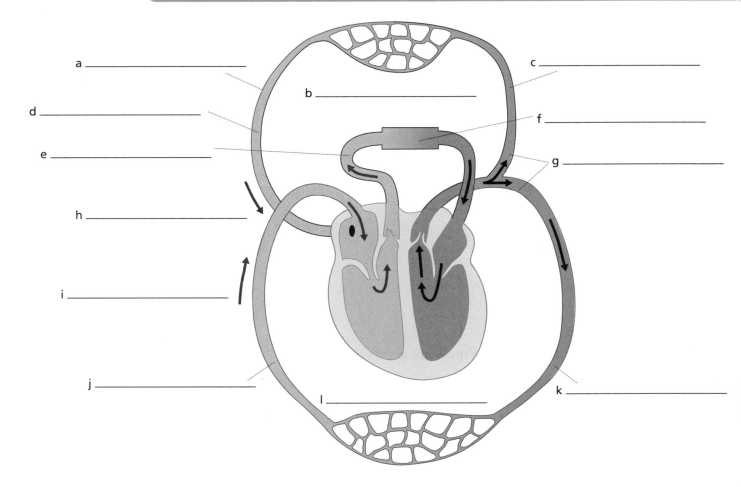

a _____

d _____

e _____

h _____

i _____

j _____

b _____

c _____

f _____

g _____

l _____

k _____

4 The internal structure of the heart

Look at the diagram and put these labels in the correct places.

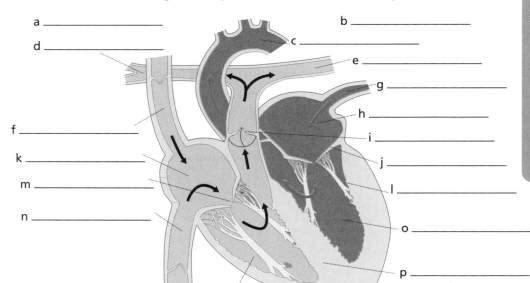

a _____

d _____

f _____

k _____

m _____

n _____

b _____

c _____

e _____

g _____

h _____

i _____

j _____

l _____

o _____

p _____

q _____

aorta   bicuspid valve
left atrium
left pulmonary artery
left pulmonary vein
Left Side   left ventricle
right atrium
right pulmonary artery
Right Side
right ventricle
semilunar valves   septum
tendon   tricuspid valve
vena cava from the head
vena cava from the lower
part of the body

5 ## Three types of blood vessel

Look at the diagrams and put these labels in the correct places.

artery   capillary   endothelium   endothelium – one cell thick   fibrous layer (x2)
large lumen   lumen – red blood cells pass in single file   muscle and elastic layer
small lumen   thin muscle and elastic layer   vein   wall composed of a single layer of cells

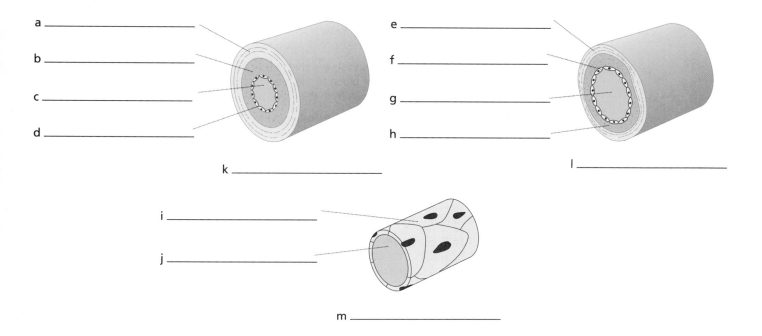

a _____

b _____

c _____

d _____

k _____

e _____

f _____

g _____

h _____

l _____

i _____

j _____

m _____

6 ## The blood and protection

Underline the correct word from the three choices given in the sentence.

1   Antibodies will destroy invading cells by causing them to either stick together or burst, making it easier for the (phagocytes / erythrocytes / platelets) to clear them up.

2   Lymphocytes are also able to convert (thrombosis / toxins / cholesterol) or poisons released into the bloodstream into less toxic substances.

3   Platelets are fragments of cells formed in the bone marrow which help in the (clumping / meshing / clotting) of blood in open wounds.

4   Platelets near the wound cause the blood to produce thread-like proteins called (fibrous / fibrin / mesh).

5   The fibrin forms a mesh of fibres that trap the blood cells and eventually (forms / makes / organises) a clot which seals the wound and prevents further bleeding.

6   The clot dries up to form a hard protective coat called a (scab / knot / skin), which keeps the wound clean and protects it until a new layer of skin is formed.

7   In areas where there is a wound you will also find many white blood cells which are attracted to the wound area to remove any (mesh / foreigners / foreign material) that may have entered the body through the cut.

7 Diseases of the heart and circulation

Match these diseases and problems with the paragraphs below.

> angina   arteriosclerosis   atherosclerosis   heart attack   hypertension   thrombosis

1 _____ – If this occurs in the coronary artery, it can stop the heart beating. To start the heart beating again, it needs to be massaged or given electrical shocks. In the longer term it can be treated by giving the patient a coronary bypass. This is an operation in which a piece of blood vessel is taken from the person's leg and used to create a new passage for the flow of blood to the heart muscles, bypassing the blocked area.

2 _____ – This is a condition with severe chest pains. The pains result from the hardening of the coronary arteries which restrict the flow of blood to the heart muscles. The heart keeps pumping because it gets a continuous supply of food and oxygen from the blood passing through the coronary arteries.

3 _____ – This is also known as high blood pressure. This is when the pressure of the blood passing through the blood vessels is higher than the norm. When someone suffers from this it means that great force is exerted on the arteries, especially when the heart contracts. So their systolic reading will be much higher than 120.

4 _____ – This is the hardening of arteries which makes them lose their elasticity. This makes it impossible for the artery to stretch to accommodate the blood which is being forced through it.

5 _____ – This is when the diameter of the artery becomes narrower due to the build-up of fatty deposits of cholesterol on the artery wall.

6 _____ – This occurs when the cholesterol build-up in an artery creates a very rough surface through which the blood passes. This can result in the formation of a blood clot which is released into the blood flow. If the blood clot is large enough, it can block the narrower passages in an artery and stop the blood flow through it.

8 The circulatory system

Read the sentences and choose the best ending.

> **Endings**
> along the veins   and capillary   around the body   away from the heart   become veins
> blood vessels   blood in the veins   cell in your body   cells of the body   easily damaged
> elastic fibres   from the heart   heart beats   one cell thick   the capillaries
> them bursting   walls of the veins   when you walk

1 The human circulatory system consists of three main structures: the heart, blood and

_____.

2 The blood vessels are tubes through which the blood travels _____.

3 There are three types of blood vessels, the artery, vein _____.

4 Arteries transport blood _____.

5 Blood leaving the heart is at high pressure, so arteries have thick muscular and elastic walls to stop

_____.

6 The muscles in the walls stretch when blood rushes into the artery _____.

7 As the muscles relax they continue to put pressure on the blood that is passing through them, helping to

smooth out the differences in pressure between _____.

8 This is important because blood flows into narrower and narrower vessels until it reaches

_____.

9 The capillaries have walls that are _____.

10 Blood flow through the capillaries needs to be constant and even as they are

_____.

11 The very thin walls allow for the rapid exchange of materials between the blood and the

_____.

12 There are so many capillaries that they run close to every _____.

13 The capillaries join up to form larger and larger blood vessels which eventually

_____.

14 Veins are wider tubes than arteries with thinner walls that contain less muscle and

_____.

15 Body muscles that surround the veins squeeze them when they contract, such as the muscles in your leg

_____.

16 This helps to push the blood _____.

17 However, to make sure the blood only moves towards the heart, there are 'one-way' valves along the

_____.

18 The valves prevent the backflow of _____.

9 How does the heart pump blood?

Put the phrases in the correct order to make sentences.

1 is due to   of the cardiac muscle.   the regular and repetitive   The pumping action of your heart
contractions and relaxations

_____

_____

2 around   keeps   This   your body.   constantly   the blood flowing

_____

3 the atria   the heart muscles   relax,   blood   on both sides.   When   enters

_____

4 open,   with blood.   The valves   to be filled   allowing the heart

_____

5 immediately.   contract   The heart muscles   then

_____

6 the atria   squeeze   begin   at the top of   The contractions   downwards.   and

_____

_____

7 the valves.   into the ventricles   the blood   This forces   through

_____

8 and   then contracts,   of the ventricle walls   squeezes upwards.   but this starts   The muscle
from the bottom

_____

_____

9 and the blood   between the atria   the arteries.   The valves   are forced shut   is pushed into
and ventricles

_____

_____

10 is   more muscular   of the left ventricle   than   the right ventricle.   The wall

_____

11 all around   Blood from   needs to be   the body.   pushed   the left side of the heart

_____

_____

12 a heartbeat   about 70 times per minute   and   is called   it occurs   of contraction and relaxation This cycle   while resting.

_____

_____

C   Working with texts

10   Blood groups

The table below shows the correct matching of blood groups. Correct matching of blood groups is important to prevent antibodies reacting with antigens. Read the text and put a cross (X) in the boxes when the two blood groups cannot match. Put a tick (✓) in the boxes when the blood groups match.

Recipient's blood type	Donor's blood type			
	A (antigen A)	B (antigen B)	AB (antigens A and B)	O (no antigens)
A (antibodies, anti-B)	1	2	3	4
B (antibodies, anti-A)	5	6	7	8
AB (no antibodies)	9	10	11	12
O (antibodies, anti-A and anti-B)	13	14	15	16

Humans have four types of blood groups A, B, AB and O. The blood group of an individual is determined by the presence of antigen on the surface of the red blood cells and antibodies in the plasma. People who have:

● A-antigens on their cells have anti-B antibodies in their plasma, and are type A blood group;
● B-antigens on their cells have anti-A antibodies in their plasma, and are type B blood group;
● both A- and B-antigens on their cells and no antibodies are type AB blood group;
● no antigens on their cells and anti-A and anti-B antibodies in their plasma are type O blood group.

The antibodies in the plasma must be different from the antigen on the cells because they react and make the cells stick together. For example, anti-A antibodies react with A-antigens and cause clumping, or agglutination. This could lead to death!

If a person needs blood, for example during an operation or after an accident, they can be given a blood transfusion. People called blood donors usually donate this extra blood and it is stored in a blood bank, at the hospital. Because getting the wrong type of blood can be deadly, it is very important that the blood group of the patient is matched with the blood they are being given. A person with type O blood can donate blood to anyone. Therefore they are called 'universal donors'. This is because antibodies in the recipient's blood have no antigens in the donor blood to react with. However, a person with AB type blood can receive blood from people with any blood group. So they are called 'universal recipients'. This is possible because they do not have any antibodies in the plasma to react with antigens of the other blood types.

Translation

acidic /əˈsɪdɪk/	containing acid. **adjective**	*The inside of the stomach is an acidic environment.*
acidity /əˈsɪdəti/	the amount of acid in a substance, often measured in pH. **noun [uncount]**	*The acidity of the stomach kills germs in food.*
alimentary canal /ˌælɪˌment(ə)ri kəˈnæl/	the system of organs in humans and other animals that breaks down food into a form that the cells can absorb and use. The oesophagus, the stomach, and the intestines are all part of the alimentary canal. **noun [singular]**	
alkaline /ˈælkəˌlaɪn/	containing an alkali or consisting of an alkali. **adjective**	*Bile salts from the liver are alkaline and neutralize the stomach acid.*
amino acid /əˌmiːnəʊ ˈæsɪd/	one of the substances in the body that combine to make proteins. **noun [count]**	
amylase /ˈæmɪˌleɪz/	an enzyme that helps the body to make a type of sugar from starch. Amylase is found in saliva, in the pancreas, and in plants. **noun [uncount]**	
appendix /əˈpendɪks/	a small tube attached to the lower end of the small intestine in humans and some other mammals. There is no known use for the appendix in humans (plural: appendixes). **noun [count]**	
bile /baɪl/	a bitter greenish-brown liquid that is produced by the liver and stored in the gall bladder. It helps the body to digest food. **noun [uncount]**	*He could taste the bile at the back of his throat.*
bolus /ˈbəʊləs/	a ball of chewed food which is swallowed and moves down the oesophagus to the stomach by peristalsis. **noun [count]**	
caecum /ˈsiːkəm/	the first section of the large intestine. It is shaped like a bag and is open at one end (plural: caeca /ˈsiːkə/). **noun [count]**	
canine /ˈkeɪˌnaɪn /	one of the four pointed teeth towards the front of the mouth. The front teeth between the canines in humans are called incisors, and the large square teeth behind them are called premolars and molars (also called: canine tooth). **noun [count]**	
catalyst /ˈkætəˌlɪst/	a substance that causes a chemical reaction to happen more quickly but is not affected itself. An enzyme is a type of catalyst. **noun [count]**	
chemical digestion /ˌkemɪk(ə)l daɪˈdʒestʃ(ə)n/	the breaking down of the large molecules of foods containing proteins, carbohydrates, and fats by enzymes in the alimentary canal, so that they become small enough to pass through the cell membranes of the intestine wall. **noun [uncount]**	*Chemical digestion occurs in the mouth when food is digested by enzymes in saliva.*
chewing /ˈtʃuːɪŋ/	the action of using your teeth to break food in your mouth into small pieces. **noun [uncount]**	*Chewing starts the process of digestion.*
chyme /tʃaɪm/	a mushy liquid produced in the stomach when food is broken down by mixing with gastric juices. **noun [uncount]**	
contraction /kənˈtrækʃ(ə)n/	a movement in which a muscle tightens or shortens. **noun [count/uncount]**	*Contraction of the muscles in the gut wall push the food along.*
crown /kraʊn/	the part of a tooth that shows above the gum, which is covered in hard white enamel. **noun [count]**	
crush /krʌʃ/	to press something hard that it is broken into small pieces. **verb [transitive]**	
cusp /kʌsp/	one of the points on the surface of a molar or premolar tooth. **noun [count]**	
decay /dɪˈkeɪ/	the gradual destruction of something as a result of a natural process of change. **noun [uncount]**	*Sweets cause tooth decay.*
defecation /ˌdefəˈkeɪʃ(ə)n/	the action of getting rid of solid waste from the body through the anus. **noun [uncount]**	
dentine /ˈdenˌtiːn/	the hard substance, under the layer of enamel, that teeth are made of. **noun [uncount]**	*His teeth were badly decayed, exposing the dentine.*

Term	Definition	Translation
diaphragm /ˈdaɪəˌfræm/	the large sheet of muscle that separates the cavity (=area) in the chest from the cavity in the abdomen. It moves up and down, affecting the pressure in the chest and causing air to move in and out of the lungs. noun [count]	*When we breathe in the diaphragm contracts and flattens.*
digest /daɪˈdʒest/	to break something down into soluble substances that can be absorbed. verb [transitive]	*Phagocytes destroy bacteria by digesting the organisms inside them.*
duodenum /ˌdjuəʊˈdiːnəm/	the first section of the small intestine, just below the stomach. noun [count]	
eliminate /ɪˈlɪmɪˌneɪt/	to get rid of something from the body that is not wanted or needed. verb [transitive]	*Undigested food is eliminated by defecation.*
enamel /ɪˈnæm(ə)l/	the hard white outer layer of a tooth. noun [count/uncount]	*Teeth are protected by a layer of tough enamel.*
endothermic /ˌendəʊˈθɜːmɪk/	an endothermic reaction is a chemical reaction in which heat is absorbed, not produced. adjective	
enzyme /ˈenzaɪm/	a protein produced by all organisms that behaves as a catalyst (=a substance that speeds up chemical reactions but does not itself change.) noun [count]	*Each enzyme does a particular job, e.g. sucrase breaks down sucrose.*
epiglottis /ˌepɪˈɡlɒtɪs/	the small piece of flesh at the back of the tongue that closes the windpipe when food is swallowed. noun [count]	
exothermic /ˌeksəʊˈθɜːmɪk/	an exothermic reaction is a chemical reaction in which heat is produced, not absorbed. adjective	
fatty acid /ˌfæti ˈæsɪd/	one of a large group of acids that, together with glycerol, are found in animal and vegetable fats and oils. noun [count]	*In digestion, fats are broken down into fatty acids and glycerol.*
fructose /ˈfrʌktəʊz/	a type of sugar found in some fruits and honey. noun [uncount]	*Fructose is not as sweet as sucrose.*
gall bladder /ˈɡɔːl ˌblædə/	the organ in the body that stores bile. noun [count]	*He had an operation to remove his gall bladder.*
gastric gland /ˌɡæstrɪk ˈɡlænd/	a gland in the lining of the stomach wall that secretes gastric juices. noun [count]	
gastric juice /ˌɡæstrɪk ˈdʒuːs/	substance containing the enzyme pepsin and hydrochloric acid, that is secreted in the stomach to help to digest food. noun [plural]	
glucose /ˈɡluːˌkəʊz/	a simple sugar that is produced in plants through photosynthesis and in animals from the breaking down of carbohydrates in the body. It is important for providing energy to all cells. Chemical formula: $C_6H_{12}O_6$. noun [uncount]	*In digestion, starch is broken down into glucose.*
glycerol /ˈɡlɪsərɒl/	a substance that is produced when fats and oils are digested in the body. noun [uncount]	
glycogen /ˈɡlaɪkəˌdʒən/	a polysaccharide that is found especially in the liver. Muscles use it to release the energy they need. noun [uncount]	*Glucose is converted to glycogen and stored in the liver.*
grind /ɡraɪnd/	to break something into very small pieces by crushing it between two hard surfaces. verb [transitive]	*The molars are used for grinding food.*
gut /ɡʌt/	the tube in the body that carries food away from the stomach. noun [count]	*Fibre in the diet helps to move food through the gut.*
harmful /ˈhɑːmfʊl/	causing harm. adjective	*the harmful effects of cigarette smoke*
hydrochloric acid /ˌhaɪdrəˌklɒrɪk ˈæsɪd/	a strong liquid chemical that is used in industry and in laboratory work. Hydrochloric acid is present in the stomach in a weak form, and helps make conditions suitable for digestion. noun [uncount]	
ileum /ˈɪliəm/	the last section of the small intestine. It produces enzymes that help to digest food (plural ilea /ˈɪliə/). noun [count]	*The end-products of digestion are absorbed into the blood in the ileum.*
incisor /ɪnˈsaɪzə/	one of the sharp teeth at the front of the mouth. noun [count]	
ingestion /ɪnˈdʒestʃ(ə)n/	the process of taking food or drink into the body. noun [uncount]	
inhibitor /ɪnˈhɪbɪtə/	an enzyme that slows down a biological process. noun [count]	
jaw /dʒɔː/	one of the two hard parts around the mouth in vertebrates that are used for biting and for eating food. The upper jaw is joined to the skull while the lower part, the mandible, moves up and down. noun [count]	
lacteal /ˈlæktɪəl/	the central lymph vessel inside one of the villi (tiny projections covering the wall of the ileum), that absorbs fatty acids. noun [count]	

Term	Definition	Example
lipase /ˈlaɪˌpeɪz/	an enzyme in the pancreas. It helps the body to turn lipids into fatty acids and glycerol. noun [uncount]	
lymph /lɪmf/	a clear liquid in the body that cleans the tissues and helps to remove harmful bacteria from the blood. noun [uncount]	*The lymph glands swell when the body is fighting an infection.*
maltose /ˈmɒlˌtəʊz/	a sugar produced by the breaking down of starch. noun [uncount]	
molar /ˈməʊlə/	one of the large teeth at the back of the mouth that you use for chewing food. noun [count]	
muscular /ˈmʌskjələ/	relating to the muscles or made of muscle. adjective	
neutralize /ˈnjuːtrəˌlaɪz/	if a chemical neutralizes a substance, it makes it neither an acid nor a base. verb [transitive]	*Bile salts neutralize stomach acid.*
oesophagus /ɪˈsɒfəgəs/	a tube that carries food from the pharynx to the stomach. noun [count]	
pancreas /ˈpæŋkriəs/	the small organ behind the stomach that produces insulin and enzymes to help with the process of digestion. noun [count]	
particle /ˈpɑːtɪk(ə)l/	an extremely small piece of matter. noun [count]	*Digestion breaks food down into small particles.*
pepsin /ˈpepsɪn/	an enzyme produced in the stomach that changes proteins into simpler compounds. noun [uncount]	
peristalsis /ˌperɪˈstælsɪs/	the regular movement of the muscles in the alimentary canal which contract and relax, pushing food along. noun [uncount]	
peristaltic /ˌperɪˈstæltɪk/	peristaltic movement is the regular contracting and relaxing of the muscles in the alimentary canal, which pushes food along. adjective	
pH /ˌpiː ˈeɪtʃ/	a number that describes how acid or alkaline a substance is. Pure water has a pH of 7, with a lower number showing a level of acidity and a higher number showing a level of alkalinity. noun [singular]	*The stomach juices have a low pH because they are acidic.*
physical digestion /ˌfɪzɪk(ə)l daɪˈdʒestʃ(ə)n/	physical processes in the body that break down food. These include chewing and the backward and forward motion of the stomach walls, which mixes food with gastric juices. noun [uncount]	
plaque /plæk, plɑːk/	a substance that forms on the teeth and in which bacteria can grow. noun [uncount]	*Brushing the teeth helps to remove plaque and prevent tooth decay.*
polypeptide /ˌpɒliˈpeptaɪd/	a smaller unit formed when protein is broken down by an enzyme such as pepsin or trypsin. noun [count]	
premolar /ˌpriːˈməʊlə/	one of the two teeth on each side of both jaws that are immediately in front of the molars and behind the canines. They are used for chewing and grinding. noun [count]	
pulp cavity /ˈpʌlp ˌkævəti/	the area inside a tooth where the pulp is. noun [count]	
pyloric sphincter /paɪˌlɒrɪk ˈsfɪŋktə/	a ring of muscles at the base of the stomach which control the movement of chyme (partly-digested food) from the stomach into the small intestine. noun [count]	
rectum /ˈrektəm/	the lowest part of the tube through which faeces leave the body. noun [count]	
relaxation /ˌriːlækˈseɪʃ(ə)n/	a movement in which a muscle becomes less tight. noun [count/uncount]	*The food moves down the oesophagus by regular contraction and relaxation of the muscles.*
saliva /səˈlaɪvə/	the liquid that is produced in the mouth. It makes food easier to chew and swallow, and contains enzymes that help with the digestion of carbohydrates. noun [uncount]	
salivary gland /səˈlaɪvəri ˌglænd/	a gland that produces saliva in the mouth. noun [count]	
secrete /səˈkriːt/	to produce a liquid such as saliva. verb [transitive]	*The incisors slice and cut food.*
slice /slaɪs/	to cut something into flat pieces using something sharp. verb [transitive]	
stool /stuːl/	a piece of faeces (solid waste from the body). noun [count]	
swallow /ˈswɒləʊ/	to make food or drink go down into your oesophagus. verb [transitive/intransitive]	*She quickly swallowed the rest of her coffee.*

trachea /trəˈkiːə/	the tube at the back of the throat that goes from the larynx to the bronchi. Air travels down it into the lungs = windpipe. **noun [count]**	*The epiglottis closes over the trachea when you swallow to prevent food from going down it.*
trypsin /ˈtrɪpsɪn/	an enzyme produced in the pancreas that breaks down protein into polypeptides and amino acids. **noun [uncount]**	
undigested /ˌʌndaɪˈdʒestɪd/	not broken down into smaller units that the body can use. **adjective**	*Undigested food is passed out of the body as waste.*
urea /jʊˈriːə/	a substance found in urine that is used for making fertilizers and for some types of medicine. **noun [uncount]**	
villus /ˈvɪləs/	one of a large number of small parts that stick out from the inner wall of the small intestine. They increase the amount of surface that is available for the absorption of food substances (plural: villi /ˈvɪlaɪ/). **noun [count]**	*Each villus contains a network of blood capillaries.*
wave-like /ˈweɪvˌlaɪk/	moving with a regular motion that is similar to that of a wave. **adjective**	*The wave-like motion was making him feel sick.*
wisdom teeth /ˈwɪzdəm ˌtiːθ/	the four large teeth that grow at each of the back corners of the mouth of an adult. **noun [count]**	

A Working with words

1 Digestion word map

Write these words in the correct places on the word map.

anus   digested food   enzymes   gastric juices   inhibitors   premolar   teeth

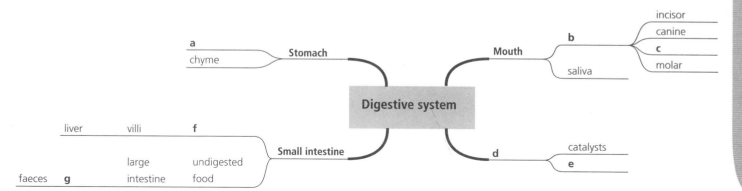

2 The human digestive system

Look at the diagram of the digestive system and write the labels in the correct places.

anus   appendix   caecum   diaphragm   duodenum
epiglottis closes entrance to trachea when food is being swallowed
gall bladder stores bile   ileum   large intestine removes water from undigested food
liver produces bile   oesophagus   pancreas   rectum   salivary gland produces saliva
small intestine digests and absorbs food   stomach mixes food with gastric juice
teeth cut and grind food   tongue mixes food with saliva   trachea (breathing tube into lungs)

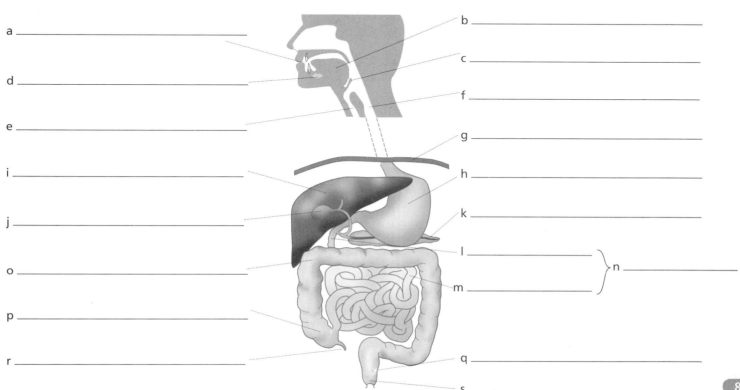

3 **The role of the teeth in digestion**

Fill in the gaps with these words.

> canine crush digestion grind human incisors jaw molars premolars wisdom

There are four different types of teeth found in the 1 _____ mouth, set in an upper jaw and a lower jaw. Each type plays a particular role in the physical 2 _____ of large chunks of food. In a single jaw the teeth are arranged symmetrically and the arrangement of the teeth in each jaw is identical. In one half of an adult jaw there are a number of different types of teeth. There are two 3 _____ in a half-jaw, at the front of the mouth. They are chisel-shaped and are used for cutting and biting bits of food. The single 4 _____ lies just behind the incisors. It is pointed or dagger-shaped and is used for tearing foods. The two 5 _____ lie just behind the canine tooth. They have broad bumpy surfaces, which allow them to 6 _____ and 7 _____ food. The three 8 _____ lie behind the premolars, and they are adapted for crushing and grinding foods. They differ from the premolars in that they are larger and wider at the surface. The 9 _____ of an adult human has a total of 16 teeth, which means there is a total of 32 teeth in the mouth of an adult. However, up to the age of 16 years you might not have your last set of molars in each jaw. These molars are usually called 10 _____ teeth and usually appear some time after your 17th birthday.

4 **Teeth**

Look at the diagrams and label them with these words.

> canine   dentine   enamel
> incisors   jaw bone   molars
> premolars   pulp cavity

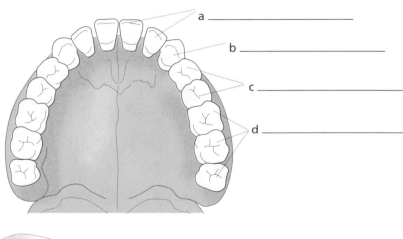

a _____

b _____

c _____

d _____

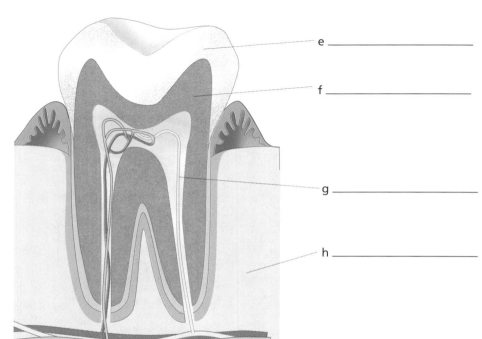

e _____

f _____

g _____

h _____

5 The human digestive system

Read the text and fill in the missing words.

The digestive system is mainly a long tube that runs from the 1 _____ to the 2 _____. This tube is called the 3 _____, or alimentary canal. The alimentary canal is associated with the organs of the liver, gall bladder and pancreas. These organs assist digestion by secreting 4 _____ that help break down the food so that it can be easily absorbed by the body. The digestion of food begins in the mouth with chewing and ends in the 5 _____. Any undigested food is eliminated from the body via the anus. There are two forms of digestion. 6 _____ involves the mechanical processes of chewing in the mouth and churning due to the backward and forward motion of the stomach walls. 7 _____ is the use of enzymes to break down the food into smaller particles that can be absorbed into the body.

6 Digestion – parts and terms

Match the terms with their definitions.

Terms	Definitions
1 digestion	a Enzymes are also described with this term.
2 the epiglottis	b These are finger-like projections which increase the surface area of the ileum to increase the rate of absorption of digested foods.
3 the ileum and the duodenum	
4 the ileum	c These are the four types of teeth humans have.
5 the villi	d These are the organs which make up the small intestine.
6 defecation	e This is the instrument which prevents swallowed food, bolus, from entering the windpipe.
7 incisors, canines, premolars and molars	
8 enamel	f This is the job of inhibitors.
9 the pulp cavity	g This is the name of the hard white coating on the teeth.
10 biological catalysts	h This is the only living portion of the tooth which contains blood vessels and nerve endings.
11 to slow down biological processes	i This is where the absorption of digested food takes place.
	j This is the process by which faeces are eliminated from the body.
	k This is the process by which food is broken down to smaller molecules, which the body can easily absorb.

1 ☐ 2 ☐ 3 ☐ 4 ☐ 5 ☐ 6 ☐ 7 ☐ 8 ☐ 9 ☐ 10 ☐ 11 ☐

B   Working with sentences

7 Absorption

Read the text and complete it with these sentences.

> Anything in the ileum that is water-soluble, such as water-soluble vitamins, minerals, water, glucose, fructose and amino acids, is absorbed into the blood capillaries.   Inside the villus is a network of many blood vessels. The process of absorption begins in the ileum.   The villi increase the surface area for absorption.

1 _____

The walls of the ileum are covered in tiny finger-like projections called villi.

2 _____

The surface layer of each villus is only one cell thick which allows the digested food to be absorbed easily.

3 _____

It also contains a central lymph vessel called the lacteal which will transport the food molecules that have been absorbed.

4 _____
_____

The blood transports them to the liver. Fat-soluble products, such as fatty acids, glycerol and fat-soluble vitamins, are absorbed into the lacteal and then transported to the liver.

8 Digestion

Match the beginnings and endings of the sentences.

Beginnings

1 Water-soluble digested products are
2 Fat-soluble products are
3 Water is absorbed from the undigested
4 Digestion in humans involves
5 The digestion of carbohydrates begins
6 The stomach contains gastric juices
7 Bile from the liver neutralizes
8 Pancreatic juice contains three enzymes:

Endings

a physical and chemical digestion.
b absorbed directly into the bloodstream and transported to the liver.
c in the mouth by the action of the enzyme salivary amylase.
d and hydrochloric acid which digest the food.
e absorbed into the lacteal and transported to the liver.
f the acid chyme.
g amylase, lipase and trypsin which break down sugars, fats and proteins in the food.
h food in the colon leaving behind the soft solid waste called faeces.

1 ☐ 2 ☐ 3 ☐ 4 ☐ 5 ☐ 6 ☐ 7 ☐ 8 ☐

B Working with texts

9 Digestion in the small intestine

Read the text and fill in the grid. Leave the cells blank if the information is not in the text.

Unlike the stomach, the small intestine is alkaline since the digestive juices released here cannot function under acidic conditions. The small intestine is divided into two parts: the duodenum, the upper section, and the lower section which is called the ileum.

As the chyme enters the duodenum, pancreatic juice is secreted from the pancreas and bile is released from the liver. The pancreatic juice contains three enzymes. Trypsin is the enzyme which continues the digestion of protein into polypeptides and also into even smaller units called amino acids. Amylase continues the digestion of starch which began in the mouth. Any starch that is still present is digested to maltose and glucose units. Lipase begins the digestion of fats and oils into smaller units called fatty acids and glycerol.

The bile from the liver is very alkaline and so it neutralizes the chyme. By the time the food reaches the ileum, most of the complex food substances have been broken down into very small particles. Enzymes released in the ileum complete the digestion process by breaking down polypeptides, from protein foods, into their smallest unit – amino acids. The enzymes also break down fats, from fats and oils, to fatty acids and glycerol. Sugars such as maltose, from carbohydrate foods, are broken down to their smallest units – fructose and glucose. Vitamins, minerals and water in the food do not need to be broken down into smaller units because they are small enough to be absorbed as they are.

Parts of small intestine		
Receives juices from …		
Type of juice (name)		
Juice consists of …		
Digestion of … by …		
Digested into …		

11 Respiration

Translation

aerobic respiration /eəˌrəʊbɪk respəˈreɪʃ(ə)n/	the process by which the body uses oxygen in order to break down food and produce energy. **noun [uncount]**	
aggravate /ˈægrəveɪt/	to make something bad become worse. **verb [transitive]**	*His asthma was aggravated by the traffic fumes.*
ailment /ˈeɪlmənt/	a minor illness. **noun [count]**	*Many people visit their doctor with ailments such as coughs and colds.*
air sac /ˈeə ˌsæk/	**1** an alveolus. **noun [count]** **2** in birds, a space formed by the growth of the lungs into the bones. It reduces the bones' total weight. **noun [count]** **3** in insects, a wider area formed in the tubes that carry air through the body. It helps respiration. **noun [count]**	*Each air sac is surrounded by blood capillaries.*
alcoholic fermentation /ælkəˌhɒlɪk ˌfɜːmenˈteɪʃ(ə)n/	a process in which glucose in an organism such as yeast is broken down without oxygen, producing alcohol and carbon dioxide as waste products. **noun [uncount]**	
allergy /ˈælədʒi/	a medical condition in which someone becomes ill as a reaction to something that they eat, breathe, or touch (plural: allergies). **noun [count/uncount]**	*Asthma attacks are sometimes brought on by an allergy to pollen in the air.*
alveolus /ælˈvɪələs/	an extremely small air sac (=space like a bag) with very thin walls, of which there are a great many in the lungs. In the alveoli, oxygen is taken into the blood from air that is breathed into the lungs, and carbon dioxide is passed into the air that is breathed out (plural: alveoli /ælˈvɪəlaɪ/). **noun [count]**	
anaerobic respiration /ˌænərəʊbɪk respəˈreɪʃ(ə)n/	respiration that takes place where there is little or no oxygen. This produces less energy than aerobic respiration, and a lot of it is lost as heat. Examples of organisms that use anaerobic respiration are some bacteria and yeast. In animal muscles, it is responsible for making lactic acid as a waste product. **noun [uncount]**	
asbestos /æsˈbestɒs/	a substance that was used in buildings in the past, which can cause respiratory problems or lung cancer in people who inhale it. **noun [uncount]**	*The building was demolished because it was found to contain asbestos.*
asthma /ˈæsmə/	a medical condition that makes it difficult to breathe. **noun [uncount]**	*Inhaling the smoke brought on an asthma attack.*
atmospheric air /ˌætməsferɪk ˈeə/	the air in the atmosphere that we breathe. **noun [uncount]**	
bronchiole /ˈbrɒŋkiəʊl/	a very small tube inside the lungs that is connected to one of the bronchi (=the two main tubes inside each lung). **noun [count]**	
bronchitis /brɒŋˈkaɪtɪs/	an illness that affects people's breathing and makes them cough. **noun [uncount]**	
bronchus /ˈbrɒŋkəs/	one of the two main tubes coming from the trachea that carry air into the lungs. It has many smaller tubes called bronchioles connected to it (plural: bronchi /ˈbrɒŋkiː/). **noun [count]**	
bubble /ˈbʌbl/	a ball of air or gas in a liquid or other substance. **noun [count]**	*Bubbles of carbon dioxide in the drink make it fizzy.*
bunch together /ˌbʌntʃ təˈgeðə/	to form a group or a tight round shape, or to make something do this. **verb [transitive/intransitive]**	*The chemical causes soil particles to bunch together.*
carcinogen /kɑːˈsɪnədʒ(ə)n/	a substance that can cause cancer. **noun [count]**	*Some food additives have been found to contain carcinogens.*
cartilage /ˈkɑːtəlɪdʒ/	a type of very strong tissue that is found, for example, at the end of bones and between the vertebrae. It also forms parts of the ear, nose, and throat. It is a type of connective tissue. **noun [uncount]**	*The trachea and bronchi have rings of cartilage to keep the airways open.*
chest cavity /ˈtʃest ˌkævəti/	the space inside the chest that contains the heart and lungs. **noun [count]**	*Doctors had to open his chest cavity.*

chronic cough /ˌkrɒnɪk ˈkɒf/	a cough that lasts for a long time and is difficult to treat. noun [count]	*Smokers often suffer with chronic coughs.*
clog /klɒg/	to block something such as a pipe, or to become blocked. verb [intransitive/transitive]	*Cholesterol can clog the arteries, leading to high blood pressure and heart disease.*
composition /ˌkɒmpəˈzɪʃ(ə)n/	the way in which something is formed from separate parts. noun [uncount]	*The composition of rain water varies according to many factors.*
detect /dɪˈtekt/	to prove that something is present by using scientific methods. verb [transitive]	*The machine detected high levels of radiation in the area.*
diaphragm /ˈdaɪəˌfræm/	the large sheet of muscle that separates the cavity (=area) in the chest from the cavity in the abdomen. It moves up and down, affecting the pressure in the chest and causing air to move in and out of the lungs. noun [count]	*When we breathe in the diaphragm contracts and flattens.*
dissolve /dɪˈzɒlv/	if a solid substance dissolves in a liquid, or if someone dissolves it, it mixes into the liquid and becomes included in it. verb [transitive/intransitive]	*Gases dissolve in the moist surface of the air sacs.*
dough /dəʊ/	a mixture of flour, water, fat etc that is baked to make bread or pastry. noun [count/uncount]	*Leave the bread dough in a warm place to rise.*
dust particle /ˈdʌst ˌpɑːtɪk(ə)l/	a very small individual piece of the dirt or other substance that forms a layer on surfaces. noun [count]	*A cloud of dust particles was visible in the room.*
emphysema /ˌemfɪˈsiːmə/	a very serious illness that affects your lungs. noun [uncount]	*He suffered from emphysema as a result of inhaling coal dust in the mines.*
exhalation /ˌeksəˈleɪʃ(ə)n/	the process of exhaling. noun [count/uncount]	
exhale /eksˈheɪl/	to breathe air, smoke, or other substances out from the lungs through the mouth or nose (≠ inhale). verb [transitive/intransitive]	*Take a deep breath in, then exhale slowly.*
froth /frɒθ/	a mass of small air bubbles that form on the surface of a liquid. noun [singular]	*There was a froth on the top of his coffee.*
gaseous /ˈgæsɪəs/	in the form of a gas or similar to a gas, rather than a solid or liquid. adjective	*Ozone is a gaseous air pollutant.*
gill /gɪl/	one of the organs behind the head of a fish that it uses to breathe. noun [count]	*Gills allow fish to extract oxygen from water.*
gill filament /ˈgɪl ˌfɪləmənt/	the finely divided structure in the gill of a fish where the exchange of gases occurs. noun [count]	
gill raker /ˈgɪl ˌreɪkə/	one of many fine structures in the gill of a fish that filter the water, removing any rough particles from it before it passes over the gill filament. noun [count]	
inflammation /ˌɪnfləˈmeɪʃ(ə)n/	a condition in which part of your body is swollen and painful because of an infection or injury. noun [count/uncount]	*She was suffering from an inflammation of the bladder.*
inhalation /ˌɪnəˈleɪʃ(ə)n/	the process of inhaling (≠ exhalation). noun [count/uncount]	
inhale /ɪnˈheɪl/	to breathe air, smoke, or other substances into the (lungs = breathe (sth) in; ≠ exhale). verb [transitive/intransitive]	
intercostal muscle /ˌɪntəkɒst(ə)l ˈmʌs(ə)l/	one of the muscles that are between the ribs. noun [count]	*The intercostal muscles contract to raise the ribcage when we breathe in.*
lactic acid /ˌlæktɪk ˈæsɪd/	a substance that forms in muscles after physical exercise as a result of anaerobic respiration. It can cause cramp. noun [uncount]	
lamella /ləˈmelə/	a thin layer or part, such as one of the filaments in the gills of a fish (plural: lamellae /ləˈmeliː/). noun [count]	
larynx /ˈlærɪŋks/	the organ in the throat that contains the vocal cords, which produce sounds. noun [count]	*He had had his larynx removed so could not speak.*
moisten /ˈmɔɪs(ə)n/	to make something slightly wet. verb [transitive]	*He swallowed to moisten his throat.*
nasal congestion /ˌneɪz(ə)l kənˈdʒestʃ(ə)n/	a condition in which your nose is blocked, for example with mucus. noun [uncount]	*A cold is a common cause of nasal congestion.*
nasal passage /ˌneɪz(ə)l ˈpæsɪdʒ/	one of the two tubes in your nose that end in your nostrils, through which you breathe and smell. noun [count]	*The aroma filled her nasal passages.*
nitrogen /ˈnaɪtrədʒ(ə)n/	an element that is a gas with no colour or smell. It makes up about 78% of the Earth's atmosphere. Chemical symbol: N. noun [uncount]	*We breathe out the same amount of nitrogen as we breathe in.*
noble gas /ˈnəʊb(ə)l ˌgæs/	a gas that does not react with other substances, from the group of gases that includes helium and neon. noun [count]	

operculum /əˈpɔːkjʊləm/	the structure that covers and protects a fish's gills. noun [count]	
oxygen /ˈɒksɪdʒ(ə)n/	an important element in the air that is a gas with no smell or taste. It makes aerobic respiration possible in organisms. It combines with most other elements. Chemical symbol: O. noun [uncount]	*Blood absorbs oxygen from the air in the lungs.*
persistent /pəˈsɪstənt/	continuing to exist for a long time. adjective	*He went to the doctor complaining of a persistent cough.*
phlegm /flem/	a thick substance that develops in the nose and throat, especially when someone has a cold. noun [uncount]	*She coughed up lots of phlegm.*
pleural fluid /ˈplʊərəl ˌfluːɪd/	the liquid found inside the membrane layer that surrounds the lungs. noun [uncount]	
pleural membrane /ˈplʊərəl ˈmembreɪn/	the layer of tissue that lines the inside of the chest cavity and surrounds the lungs. noun [count]	
pneumonia /njuːˈməʊniə/	a serious infection of the lungs. noun [uncount]	*He caught pneumonia as a result of falling into the freezing water.*
pollutant /pəˈluːt(ə)nt/	a substance that is harmful to the environment, especially a chemical. Large amounts of noise, heat etc can also be pollutants. noun [count]	*Inhaling airborne pollutants can damage the lungs.*
reaction site /riˈækʃ(ə)n ˌsaɪt/	the place where a reaction, for example the reaction that breaks down glucose in aerobic or anaerobic respiration, takes place. noun [count]	
respiration /ˌrespəˈreɪʃ(ə)n/	the process of making the energy present in organic compounds able to be used by the cells of living things. Oxygen is usually needed for this to take place, and this is called aerobic respiration. When oxygen is not used, it is called anaerobic respiration. The exchange of gases that is necessary for respiration to take place is called gaseous exchange, which takes place in the lungs of animals, leaves of trees, gills of fish etc. In humans and many other animals oxygen is taken into the lungs by breathing. noun [uncount]	
respiratory /rɪˈspɪrət(ə)ri, ˈresp(ə)rət(ə)ri/	relating to the process of breathing. adjective	*The lungs form part of the respiratory system.*
respire /rɪˈspaɪə/	to release energy from food so that it can be used by the body. verb [intransitive]	*All living things respire.*
rib /rɪb/	one of the long curved bones in the chest. noun [count]	*She fell off her bike and broke a rib.*
rise /raɪz/	to move upwards or increase in size. verb [intransitive]	*The bread dough has to be left to rise.*
sinus /ˈsaɪnəs/	one of several empty spaces that are in the bones of the face in the area behind the nose. noun [count]	*His sinuses were inflamed and painful.*
smoking /ˈsməʊkɪŋ/	the activity of breathing smoke from cigarettes, pipes etc into the mouth and lungs. Smoking is very addictive, and causes many serious diseases, including cancer and heart disease. noun [uncount]	
spasm /ˈspæz(ə)m/	a sudden uncontrollable movement of a muscle. noun [count/uncount]	*He felt a painful spasm in his back.*
trachea /trəˈkiːə/	the tube at the back of the throat that goes from the larynx to the bronchi. Air travels down it into the lungs (= windpipe). noun [count]	
vigorous /ˈvɪɡərəs/	strong and energetic. adjective	*Doctors recommend vigorous exercise at least twice a week.*
viral infection /ˈvaɪrəl ɪnˌfekʃ(ə)n/	an infection caused by a virus rather than by bacteria. noun [count]	
water vapour /ˈwɔːtə ˌveɪpə/	water in the form of a gas produced by evaporation below its boiling point. noun [uncount]	*The air we breathe out contains water vapour.*
wheezing /ˈwiːzɪŋ/	noisy, uncomfortable breathing, caused by an illness or condition such as asthma. noun [uncount]	*He uses an inhaler when his wheezing gets bad.*
windpipe /ˈwɪn(d)ˌpaɪp/	the tube that carries air into the lungs from the nose or mouth (= trachea). noun [count]	*The child had an obstruction in his windpipe.*
yeast /jiːst/	a microorganism that is used in making bread and beer. noun [uncount]	

A   Working with words

1   Respiration word map

Fill in these words on the word map.

aerobic   animals   bronchi   gills   humans   pneumonia   stomata

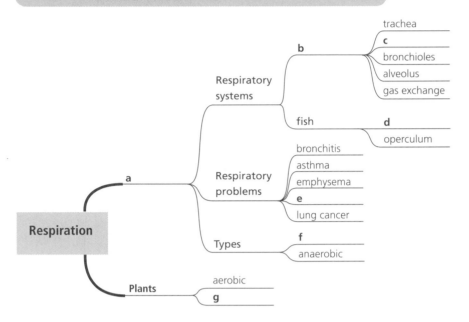

Respiratory systems
- **b** ____
  - trachea
  - **c** ____
  - bronchioles
  - alveolus
  - gas exchange
- fish
  - **d** ____
  - operculum

Respiratory problems
- bronchitis
- asthma
- emphysema
- **e** ____
- lung cancer

Types
- **f** ____
- anaerobic

Plants
- aerobic
- **g** ____

a ____

Respiration

2   The human respiratory system

Look at the diagram and label it with these words or phrases.

air sacs/alveoli   bronchiole
diaphragm   heart
external intercostal muscle
internal intercostal muscle
larynx (voice box)   left bronchus
left lung   mouth
movement of air   nose
pleural fluid   pleural membrane
rib   ring of cartilage   trachea
trachea opens to mouth and nose

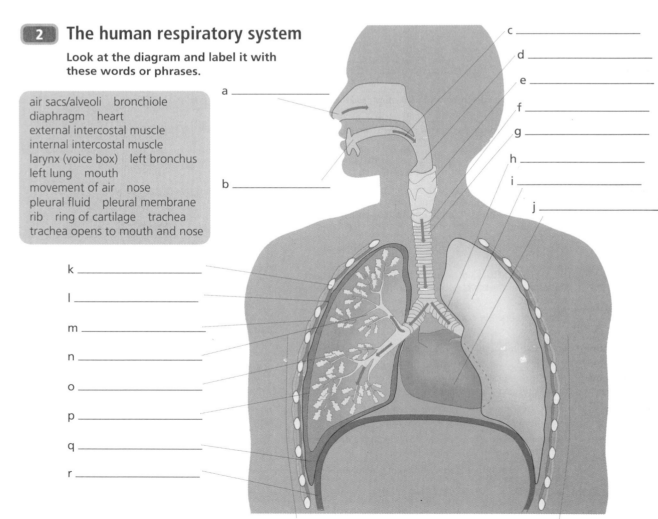

a ____

b ____

c ____

d ____

e ____

f ____

g ____

h ____

i ____

j ____

k ____

l ____

m ____

n ____

o ____

p ____

q ____

r ____

3 Respiration

Underline the correct word from the three choices given in the sentence.

1 Respiration is the chemical breakdown of (food / carbohydrates / fuels) in cells to produce energy.

2 There are two types of respiration, (upper and lower / aerobic and anaerobic / active and passive) respiration.

3 Aerobic respiration occurs in the (isolation / absence / presence) of oxygen and the products are carbon dioxide, water and energy.

4 Anaerobic respiration (creates / occurs / develops) in the absence of oxygen.

5 In yeast, anaerobic respiration is also known as alcoholic fermentation as it produces alcohol. (Carbon dioxide / Alcohol / Oxygen) is a waste product.

6 In muscle cells and bacteria, anaerobic fermentation produces (alcohol / oxygen / lactic acid).

7 Aerobic respiration releases much more (gas / energy / acid) than either form of anaerobic respiration.

8 The main gases in pure air are oxygen (21%), carbon dioxide (0.03%), (royal / lord / noble) gases (about 1%), nitrogen (78%), and water vapour in very small amounts.

9 Breathing is a (biometric / mechanical / chemical) process in which air is drawn across the respiratory surface.

10 The human respiratory system consists of the (oesophagus / epiglottis / trachea), bronchi and lungs.

11 In humans, gas exchange occurs in the air (sacs / balloons / bags), or alveoli, in the lung.

12 Fish breathe with (tubes / chambers / gills).

13 Plants respire day and night but they also (photosynthesize / synthesize / transpire) during the day.

B Working with sentences

4 Anaerobic respiration

Read each sentence. Some are correct, but some have a word which should not be there. Tick (✓) each correct sentence. If a sentence has a word which should not be there, write it next to the sentence.

1 There are two main types of human anaerobic respiration. _____

2 In yeast and other microorganisms glucose is broken down without oxygen to release energy. _____

3 This forms alcohol and carbon dioxide as the waste products in a process that is called carbonated alcoholic fermentation. _____

4 However, anaerobic exercise respiration only breaks down glucose to alcohol. _____

5 The alcohol molecule still contains a lot of energy. _____

6 So much less energy is released in this nuclear reaction than in aerobic respiration. _____

7 Anaerobic respiration of a different kind occurs in some cells of humans and other animals, and in bacteria. _____

8 When we are do vigorous exercise continuously, we use up all the oxygen that was in the muscle cells. _____

9 Although we breathe faster and our heart pumps harder, we can still be unable to get enough oxygen to the muscle cells so that they can continue with aerobic respiration. _____

10 In these cases, anaerobic respiration takes place in the leg muscle cells instead. _____

11 Glucose is broken down to a substance called lactic acid with no other waste products. _____

12 The lactic acid molecule still contains a lot of alternative energy, so this form of anaerobic respiration also releases only a small amount of energy. _____

5 Respiratory problems caused by environmental pollution

Match these words with the correct paragraphs.

asthma   bronchitis   emphysema   pollutants and respiratory problems   lung cancer   pneumonia

1 _____ An inflammation of the lung caused by infection with bacteria or viruses, which sometimes develops from a simple viral cold or influenza.

2 _____ This is a long-term condition that occurs when the main air passages of the lungs, the bronchial tubes, become inflamed and go into spasm. Extra mucus is also produced along the lining of the bronchi. The spasms and the build-up of mucus clog or partially block the respiratory passage.

3 _____ This is the uncontrolled growth of abnormal cells in one or both of the lungs. These abnormal cells reproduce rapidly and form tumours, which destroy that part of the lung so that it does not work properly.

4 _____ We obtain our continuous supply of oxygen from the air around us. However, the air we breathe may contain pollutants that harm us. Many of the pollutants found in air are dust particles, toxic or harmful gases released in smoke, microorganisms and other substances that irritate the linings of the respiratory organs.

5 _____ This is the abnormal enlargement of alveoli (air spaces) in the lung, which also causes them to lose elasticity. As a result the alveoli are unable to efficiently exchange gases between the lung and the blood.

6 _____ This involves an inflammation of the bronchial tubes (the air passage between the trachea and the lungs), which causes a persistent cough and produces a significant amount of phlegm or mucus.

C   Working with texts

6 The structure of the alveoli and gas exchange

Replace the wrong words in the text with these words. The wrong words are underlined.

a blood   b body   c capillaries   d greater   e lower   f increased
g moist   h quick   i rapidly   j reverse   k sacs   l small   m thin

The alveoli are little 1 bags that are bunched together like grapes. They are covered with a network of blood capillaries that bring 2 water close to them. The blood entering the capillary network comes from the 3 air where there has been respiration. So the blood has a 4 higher concentration of oxygen and an 5 decreased concentration of carbon dioxide (a waste product of respiration) compared with the air in the alveoli. As this blood passes through the 6 arteries over the alveoli two diffusion gradients are created. There is a 7 smaller concentration of oxygen in the alveoli (in the lung) than in the blood therefore the oxygen diffuses from inside the lung into the blood. The 8 same happens with carbon dioxide. The diffusion of gases across the respiratory surface is very 9 slow because there are large numbers of alveoli. Also, the alveoli and the blood capillaries both have very 10 thick walls so the distance over which diffusion takes place is very 11 large. Lastly, the respiratory surfaces are 12 dry so that the gases dissolve, allowing them to diffuse more 13 slowly across the respiratory surface.

1 ☐ 2 ☐ 3 ☐ 4 ☐ 5 ☐ 6 ☐ 7 ☐ 8 ☐ 9 ☐ 10 ☐ 11 ☐ 12 ☐ 13 ☐

Exchange of gases in the lungs

Read the text and write in the information in illustrations given.

The alveoli are covered with blood capillaries. Blood being transported by a capillary to the alveoli has little oxygen in it. This is called deoxygenated blood. This blood has a high concentration of carbon dioxide. Blood being transported by a capillary from the lungs is oxygenated. This means that it has a high concentration of oxygen. This blood also has a low concentration of carbon dioxide. There is a network of capillaries surrounding the alveoli. This is where the exchange of gases takes place. Firstly, deoxygenated blood flows in a capillary surrounding an alveolus. The wall of the capillary is only one cell thick. This allows gases to move in and out of the blood cells. Here, carbon dioxide leaves the deoxygenated blood and this is exhaled as we breathe. At the same time oxygen we breathe in passes through the alveolus wall, which is also only one cell thick, into the blood. Finally, the newly oxygenated blood is transported away from the lungs.

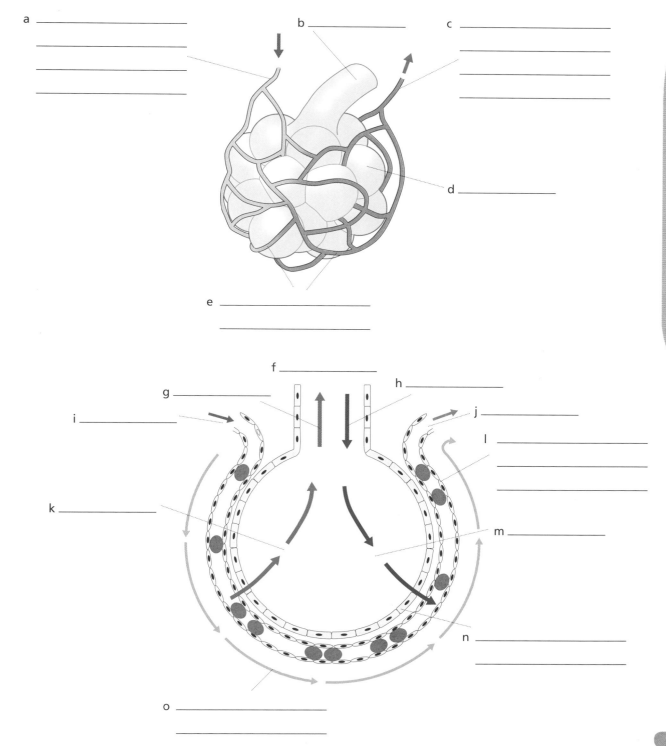

a _____
_____
_____
_____

b _____

c _____
_____
_____
_____

d _____

e _____
_____

f _____

g _____

h _____

i _____

j _____

l _____
_____
_____

k _____

m _____

n _____
_____

o _____
_____

12 Transport in plants

adhesion /əd'iːʒ(ə)n/	the tendency of one thing to stick to another, for example for one type of molecule to stick to another type of molecule. **noun [uncount]**	*the adhesion of water molecules to glass molecules*
artificial /ɑːtɪ'fɪʃ(ə)l/	not natural or real, but made by people. **adjective**	*The growers use both natural and artificial light.*
barrier /'bæriə/	something that separates one thing from another. **noun [count]**	*The grease forms a barrier on the surface that stops water from penetrating.*
bromine vapour /'brəʊmaɪn ˌveɪpə/	the dark red element bromine (chemical symbol: Br) in the form of a gas. **noun [uncount]**	
bump /bʌmp/	to hit against something solid. **verb [intransitive]**	*The ball rolled around, bumping into furniture.*
cactus /'kæktəs/	a plant with thick stems and sharp points that grows in deserts (plural: cacti /'kæktaɪ/). **noun [count]**	
capillarity /'kəpɪleərəti/	the tendency of water to move up the inside of a tube because the water molecules are attracted to the walls of the tube and climb up it, bringing other molecules with them = capillary action. **noun [uncount]**	
clumped together /ˌklʌmpt tə'geðə/	very close to each other, forming a tight group or solid mass. **adjective**	*His hair was dirty and all clumped together.*
cohesion /ˌkəʊ'hiːʒ(ə)n/	the tendency of things such as molecules to stick together. **noun [uncount]**	*Clay particles are attracted to each other, but sand particles do not exhibit cohesion in the same way.*
concentration /ˌkɒns(ə)n'treɪʃ(ə)n/	the amount of a substance that is present in something. **noun [count/uncount]**	*The concentration of cell sap is greater than that of the solution around soil particles.*
conduct /kən'dʌkt/	to carry out something such as an experiment or test. **verb [transitive]**	*We are conducting experiments to test this theory.*
constant /'kɒnstənt/	continuous or regular, or continuing at the same rate or level, over a period of time. **adjective**	*The temperature in the lab has to be kept constant.*
cortex cell /'kɔːteks ˌsel/	one of the cells that makes up the cortex (main outer layer of tissue) of a plant stem or root. **noun [count]**	
dehydrated /ˌdiːhaɪ'dreɪtɪd/	someone who is dehydrated feels weak or ill because they have lost a lot of water from their body. **adjective**	*If plants become dehydrated they wilt.*
dicotyledonous /daɪˌkɒtɪ'liːd(ə)nəs/	having two seed leaves (cotyledons) in each seed. Many herbaceous plants, trees, and bushes are dicotyledonous. **adjective**	*Geraniums are dicotyledonous plants.*
diffusion /dɪ'fjuːʒ(ə)n/	movement of molecules or ions from an area of high concentration to one of lower concentration. **noun [uncount]**	*Water vapour passes out of plant leaves into the air by diffusion.*
dilute solution /daɪˌluːt sə'luːʃ(ə)n/	a solution that has a high concentration of water molecules and a low concentration of other particles. **noun [count/uncount]**	*a dilute solution of hydrochloric acid*
double /'dʌb(ə)l/	to become twice as big, twice as much, or twice as many or to make something do this. **verb [transitive/intransitive]**	*The school has doubled its number of students in five years.*
dropper /'drɒpə/	a small glass tube with a rubber piece at one end that you squeeze to let out single drops of liquid. **noun [count]**	
dye /daɪ/	a substance used for changing the colour of something such as cloth or hair. **noun [count/uncount]**	*For the test, a dye is injected into the vein.*
effective /ɪ'fektɪv/	working well and producing the result that was intended. **adjective**	*The new vaccine is highly effective against all strains of the disease.*
elongated /'iːlɒŋɡeɪtɪd/	longer and narrower than is usual, or than most things of the same kind. **adjective**	*a plant with elongated leaves*
epidermis /ˌepɪ'dɜːmɪs/	the outer layer of tissue in a plant, or the outer layer of skin in an animal. **noun [count/uncount]**	*The epidermis of a leaf is covered with a waxy layer called the cuticle.*
evaporation /ɪˌvæpə'reɪʃ(ə)n/	a process in which a liquid becomes a vapour without being boiled. **noun [uncount]**	*Water is lost from the surface of the leaf through evaporation.*
exchange /ɪk'stʃeɪndʒ/	to give or release something and take or absorb another thing at the same time. **verb [transitive]**	*Diffusion is one way of exchanging materials between an organism and its environment.*

exposed /ɪkˈspəʊzd/	not covered, hidden, or protected from something. **adjective**	*You should wear sunscreen on any exposed areas of skin.*
extension /ɪkˈstenʃ(ə)n/	something that develops or sticks out from something else. **noun [count]**	*We observed tubular extensions on the membrane.*
get rid of /ˌget ˈrɪd ˈəv/	**1** to throw away, give away or sell something that you no longer want or need. **phrase** **2** to do something so that you stop being affected by someone or something that is annoying or unpleasant. **phrase**	
gradient /ˈgreɪdiənt/	the rate of change of something such as temperature or pressure. **noun [count]**	*Oxygen gas passes out of leaves down a diffusion gradient.*
halve /hɑːv/	to reduce something to half its original size or amount, or to become half the original size or amount. **verb [transitive/intransitive]**	*The concentration of the original solution has halved after ten minutes.*
haphazard /ˌhæpˈhæzəd/	done in a way that is not carefully planned or organized. **adjective**	*The molecules move in a haphazard way.*
humidity /hjuːˈmɪdəti/	the amount of water vapour that is in the air. **noun [uncount]**	*Banana trees are well adapted to growing in areas of high humidity.*
intense /ɪnˈtens/	very great, extreme, or concentrated. **adjective**	*The pain was intense.*
lignin /ˈlɪgnɪn/	a chemical compound that makes the walls of plant cells hard and stiff. It is the main substance that wood is made of. **noun [uncount]**	
membrane /ˈmemˌbreɪn/	a thin layer of tissue that covers, separates, protects, or connects cells or parts of an organism. **noun [count]**	*Gases diffuse across the plant cell membrane.*
meniscus /məˈnɪskəs/	the curved surface of a liquid in a tube as a result of surface tension. It is usually concave as the liquid is pulled towards the sides of the container, and convex if it is not. **noun [singular]**	
moist /mɔɪst/	slightly wet. **adjective**	*Plants grow best in moist soil.*
moisture /ˈmɔɪstʃə/	very small droplets of water or another liquid in the air, on the surface of something, or in a substance. **noun [uncount]**	*High humidity means there is a lot of moisture in the air.*
molecule /ˈmɒlɪˌkjuːl/	the smallest part of an element or compound that could exist independently, consisting of two or more atoms. **noun [count]**	*Water molecules contain one atom of oxygen and two atoms of hydrogen.*
net movement /ˌnet ˈmuːvmənt/	the overall total effect of all the movements that have taken place, for example of molecules during osmosis. **noun [singular]**	*Water molecules move in both directions, but the net movement is towards the more dilute solution.*
osmosis /ɒzˈməʊsɪs/	the process by which a solvent, usually water, slowly passes through a semipermeable membrane from a weaker solution to a stronger one, until they both have the same concentration. **noun [uncount]**	*Water enters the roots of a plant by osmosis.*
permeable /ˈpɜːmiəb(ə)l/	a permeable substance or material is one that a liquid or gas can pass through. **adjective**	*The cell membranes of plant cells are permeable to water.*
phloem vessel /ˈfləʊem ˌves(ə)l/	one of the tubes in the phloem (vascular tissue) of a plant, which takes food from the leaves to other parts of the plant. **noun [count]**	
pith /pɪθ/	the white substance inside the stems of some plants. **noun [uncount]**	
potassium permanganate /pəˌtæsiəm pɜːˈmæŋgəˌneɪt/	a dark purple compound used in dyes. **noun [uncount]**	
root hair /ˈruːt ˌheə/	a small thin growth from the root of a plant that takes water and minerals from the soil. **noun [count]**	
root pressure /ˈruːt ˌpreʃə/	the pressure inside the root of a plant, which increases when water enters the root. **noun [count/uncount]**	
scent /sent/	a smell. **noun [count/uncount]**	*The scent of bread baking filled the air.*
selective /sɪˈlektɪv/	affecting only some things. **adjective**	*Modern pesticides are more selective, and do not kill all insects.*
single-celled /ˌsɪŋg(ə)l ˈseld/	consisting of only one cell. **adjective**	*single-celled organisms such as amoebae*
solute /ˈsɒljuːt/	a substance that has dissolved in a solvent and become part of the liquid so that they form a solution. **noun [count/uncount]**	*Plant root hairs absorb water with various dissolved solutes.*
solution /səˈluːʃ(ə)n/	a liquid mixture that is formed when a solute dissolves in a solvent and becomes part of the liquid. **noun [count]**	*Soil water is a solution of several mineral salts.*

speed up /ˌspiːd ˈʌp/	to move or happen faster, or to make something move or happen faster. **phrasal verb**	*The sun's heat speeds up the process of evaporation.*
spray /spreɪ/	to force very small drops of a liquid out of a container through a small hole. **verb [transitive/intransitive]**	*The chemical is sprayed onto the crops once a week.*
spread /spred/	to gradually affect a larger area, or to make something do this. **verb [transitive/intransitive]**	*The gas gradually spread throughout the building.*
stele /ˈsteleɪ/	a structure containing the xylem and phloem which runs through the centre of a root. **noun [count]**	
stir /stɜː/	to cause a liquid to mix or move by moving an object in it. **verb [transitive]**	*Stirring the solution will make it dissolve more quickly.*
stomata /ˈstəʊmətə/	the plural of stoma.	*Gases pass into and out of the leaf through the stomata.*
summing together /ˌsʌmɪŋ təˈgeðə/	the action of adding or combining two or more amounts to find a total. **noun [singular]**	*The overall total is calculated by a summing together of all these figures.*
supply /səˈplaɪ/	to provide someone or something with something that they need or want. **verb [transitive]**	*Circulating blood keeps the brain supplied with oxygen.*
surface area /ˈsɜːfɪs ˌeəriə/	the total area of a surface or surfaces, especially the outside surfaces of an object. **noun [count]**	*Leaves have a large surface area because they are flat and thin.*
transpiration /ˌtrænspɪˈreɪʃ(ə)n/	the process in which water that has travelled from the roots of a plant up to its leaves passes out into the air. The holes that the water evaporates from are called stomata. **noun [uncount]**	*The transpiration rate increases in hot, windy conditions.*
transpiration stream /ˌtrænspɪˈreɪʃ(ə)n ˌstriːm/	another term for transpirational pull. **noun [singular]**	
transpirational pull /ˌtrænspɪˈreɪʃ(ə)nl ˌpʊl/	the effect by which water is pulled in through the roots and up through the xylem tube of a plant when water evaporates from the leaves. **noun [singular]**	
transport system /ˈtrænspɔːt ˌsɪstəm/	the way in which something is moved from one place to another, for example the way that food and water are moved around within a plant. **noun [count]**	
transverse section /ˌtrænzˌvɜːs ˈsekʃ(ə)n/	an image that shows what you would see if you cut through something. **noun [count]**	*The diagram shows a transverse section of a human brain.*
unicellular /ˌjuːnɪˈseljʊlə/	a unicellular organism consists of one cell only. Amoebas are unicellular organisms. **adjective**	*Chlorella is a unicellular, plant-like organism.*
uptake /ˈʌpteɪk/	a process in which living creatures use substances such as food or water to breathe, produce energy etc. **noun [uncount]**	*a plant's uptake of water and nutrients from the soil*
vascular bundle /ˈvæskjʊlə (bʌnd(ə)l/	the structure inside the stem or root of a plant that consists of the phloem and xylem. **noun [count]**	
visking tubing /ˈvɪskɪŋ ˌtjuːbɪŋ/	an artificial substance that can be used as a selectively permeable membrane in laboratory experiments. **noun [uncount]**	
wind current /ˈwɪnd ˌkʌrənt/	a movement of the wind in a particular direction. **noun [count]**	*Spores are blown in on wind currents.*
wind speed /ˈwɪnd ˌspiːd/	the speed at which the air is moving when the wind is blowing. **noun [count/uncount]**	*Today we had wind speeds of over 50 miles per hour.*
xylem vessel /ˈzaɪləm ˌves(ə)l/	one of the strong, hard tubes in the xylem (vascular tissue) of a plant, which transports water to all parts of the plant. **noun [count]**	

1 Transport in plants word map

Fill in these words and phrases on the word map.

cohesion   phloem vessels   root pressure   roots   transpiration   vascular bundle

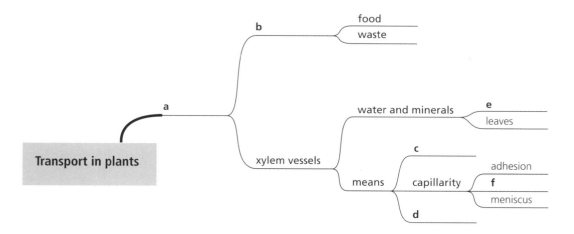

2 Sections of stems and roots

Label the diagrams with these words and phrases.

a number of phloem tubes lie close together   a number of xylem vessels lie close together
a transverse section through the stem of a dicotyledonous plant   cortex (x2)   epidermis (x2)
made up of a number of phloem vessels   made up of a number of xylem vessels   phloem (x2)
pith   stele   the transverse section of a root of a dicotyledonous plant   vascular bundle   xylem (x2)

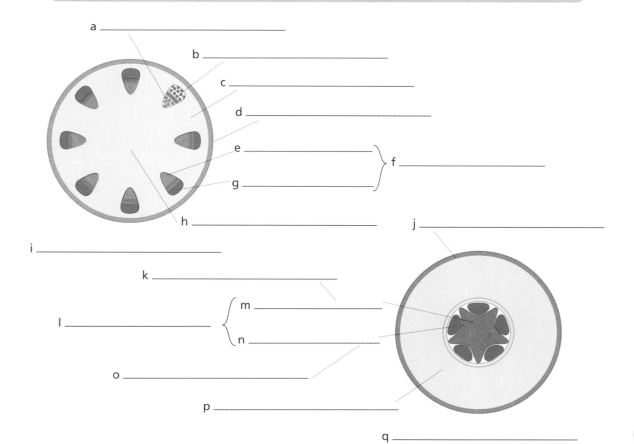

B   Working with sentences

3   Transport system in plants

Match the beginnings and the endings of the sentences.

Beginnings

1   The transport vessels in plants
2   The phloem and the xylem
3   The phloem vessels
4   The xylem vessels
5   Water enters plants
6   Water moves up plants in the xylem vessels,
7   The rate of transpiration is affected

Endings

a   are found in the vascular bundles.
b   are the phloem and xylem.
c   by osmosis through the roots.
d   by root pressure, capillary action and transpiration pull.
e   by temperature, wind, humidity and the surface area of leaves
f   transport food.
g   transport water and dissolved minerals.

1 ☐   2 ☐   3 ☐   4 ☐   5 ☐   6 ☐   7 ☐

C   Working with texts

4   How water moves in a plant

Read the text. It describes three ways in which water moves in a plant. The information has been jumbled up. Sort out the information into the correct sections. One sentence has been given to help you.

a   As a result the water molecules next to the walls begin to climb up the insides of the tubes bringing along those next to them.
b   This will leave fewer water molecules in the surrounding cells, so pulling water from the nearby cells. This effect continues through all the cells back to the xylem vessels. As water molecules are strongly attracted to each other, those at the top of the xylem tube will pull those below them up the tube.
c   Capillary action can only cause the water level to rise by about 3 metres in the xylem vessels, so how can water get to the leaves of plants that are taller than this?
d   In the very narrow xylem vessels, water can rise to a height of about 3 metres by capillarity.
e   The answer is that it is pulled up by transpiration. Transpiration is the evaporation of water from the plant parts above ground, mainly the leaves. Water molecules escape through the stomata in the leaves when there are fewer molecules in the air than in the spaces between leaf cells. If there are fewer water molecules in the air spaces than in the leaf cells, water will evaporate into the spaces.
f   This pull happens all the way down to the bottom of the xylem tube, drawing water in from the root cells and causing more water to enter the roots (by osmosis). This pull is called the transpirational pull or transpiration stream
g   As water enters the roots, the pressure in the roots increases. This pushes water up the xylem.   .
h   You can see the effect by the curved shape of the water surface in a tube, called the meniscus. The narrower the tube, the higher the water molecules can climb.

The water moves up the xylem vessels because of three factors:

Root pressure
1
Capillarity
2 Water molecules are strongly attracted to each other. They are also strongly attracted to the walls of tubes.
3
4
5
Transpiration
6
7
8
9

13 Excretory system

Translation

aorta /eɪˈɔːtə/	the main artery that carries blood with a high oxygen level from the heart to other parts of the body. noun [count]	*The coronary artery supplies the heart tissue with blood.*
accumulate /əˈkjuːmjʊˌleɪt/	to increase in quantity over a period of time. verb [intransitive]	*Waste products accumulate in the blood.*
ADH /ˌeɪ diː ˈeɪtʃ/	anti-diuretic hormone: a hormone (chemical substance produced in the body) that controls the amount of water taken back in through the kidneys, in order to keep the concentration of water in the body's cells at a normal level. noun [uncount]	
amino acid /əˌmiːnəʊ ˈæsɪd/	one of the substances in the body that combine to make proteins. noun [count]	
ammonia /əˈməʊniə/	a poisonous gas, with a strong unpleasant smell, or the gas dissolved in water. It is used in cleaning products. noun [uncount]	*The liver converts ammonia compounds to urea.*
arise /əˈraɪz/	(of a problem or complication) to begin to exist or develop. verb [intransitive]	*Complications can arise when the body loses too much water through sweating.*
Bowman's capsule /ˈbəʊmənz ˌkæpsjuːl/	one of many structures shaped like a cup inside the kidney, that contains the glomerulus. noun [count]	
capillary /kəˈpɪləri/	the smallest type of blood vessel, with a wall that is only one cell thick. It carries blood to and from individual cells in the body (plural: capillaries). noun [count]	*All the body's organs have a network of capillaries.*
carbohydrate /ˌkɑːbəˈhaɪdreɪt/	an organic compound found in foods such as sugar, bread, and potatoes. Carbohydrates consist of oxygen, hydrogen and carbon, and they supply the body with heat and energy. noun [count]	*Rice and potatoes are important sources of carbohydrates.*
coil /kɔɪl/	to twist to form several circles, one on top of the other. verb [transitive/intransitive]	*The intestines are coiled so they fit into the abdominal cavity.*
compound /ˈkɒmˌpaʊnd/	a chemical substance that consists of two or more elements that together form a molecule. Each different compound has a fixed ratio of elements, for example the water compound (H_2O) always consists of two hydrogen atoms and one oxygen atom. noun [count]	
convoluted tubule /ˌkɒnvəˌluːtɪd ˈtjuːbjuːl/	a small tube-shaped part in the nephrons of the kidney that has many twists and turns. noun [count]	
cortex /ˈkɔːteks/	the outer layer of the kidney that contains the nephrons. noun [count]	*The kidney has an outer cortex and an inner medulla.*
crystallise /ˈkrɪstəˌlaɪz/	to change into crystals, or to make something change into crystals. verb [transitive/intransitive]	*Urea is crystallised in the excretory products of birds.*
cup-like /ˈkʌpˌlaɪk/	in the shape of a cup. adjective	*The flower is surrounded by a cup-like calyx.*
deamination /ˌdiːæmɪˈneɪʃ(ə)n/	the process in which ammonia is removed from blood in the liver, so it can be converted to urea and excreted. noun [uncount]	
dermis /ˈdɜːmɪs/	the thick sensitive layer of skin that is just below the epidermis. It contains blood, the ends of the nerves, blood vessels, and sweat glands. noun [singular]	
dialysis /daɪˈæləsɪs/	a medical treatment that artificially removes waste substances from the blood of someone whose kidneys are not working properly. noun [uncount]	*He was having dialysis whilst waiting for a kidney transplant.*
digest /daɪˈdʒest/	to break something down into soluble substances that can be absorbed. verb [transitive]	*Phagocytes destroy bacteria by digesting the organisms inside them.*
distal /ˈdɪstəl/	further away from the centre of the body or to the point where something is attached to the body (≠ proximal). adjective	*the distal end of the tibia*
duct /dʌkt/	a narrow tube inside the body that carries liquid. noun [count]	*tear ducts*

13 EXCRETORY SYSTEM

Term	Definition	Translation
egestion /ɪˈdʒestʃ(ə)n/	the process by which the body gets rid of solid waste through the anus. noun [uncount]	
eliminate /ɪˈlɪmɪˌneɪt/	to get rid of something that is not wanted or needed. verb [transitive]	
erector (muscle) /ɪˈrektə/	a muscle that can move a part of the body, such as a hair, into an upright position. noun [count]	
evaporate /ɪˈvæpəˌreɪt/	if a liquid evaporates, it slowly changes into a vapour at a temperature below its boiling point. verb [intransitive]	*Sweat evaporates from the surface of the skin.*
excess /ekˈses/	more than is usual, needed, or healthy. adjective	*Avoid foods containing excess salt.*
excretion /ɪkˈskriːʃ(ə)n/	the process by which the body gets rid of waste products. Excretion includes the process of getting rid of carbon dioxide from the lungs, sweat from the sweat glands, and urea from the body in urine. noun [uncount]	*Excretion is the process of eliminating waste products from the body.*
excretory organ /ɪkˈskriːtəri ˌɔːgn/	one of the organs in the body that remove waste products not needed by the body. The lungs, the skin, and the kidneys are the three main excretory organs. noun [count]	
extend /ɪkˈstend/	to continue for a particular distance or in a particular direction. verb [intransitive]	*The pain had extended over a large area of his body.*
faeces /ˈfiːsiːz/	solid waste from the body = excrement. noun [plural]	
fluid /ˈfluːɪd/	a liquid or gas. A fluid flows easily, takes the shape of its container, and is affected by pressure on it. noun [count/uncount]	*Urine is a pale yellow fluid.*
follicle /ˈfɒlɪk(ə)l/	a small hole in the skin that contains the root of a hair. noun [count]	
glomerulus /ɡlɒˈmerʊləs/	one of many small structures in the kidney consisting of a fine network of tiny blood capillaries that filter the blood. noun [count]	
get rid of /ˌget ˈrɪd əv/	to deal with something that is not wanted or needed, so you do not have it any more. phrase	*The kidneys get rid of excess water from the body.*
interfere /ˌɪntəˈfɪə/	to prevent something from happening or developing in the correct way. verb [intransitive]	*Some drugs can interfere with the body's ability to absorb nutrients.*
intestine /ɪnˈtestɪn/	the long tube in the body between the stomach and the anus that is a major part of the digestive system. There are two parts of the intestine, the small intestine and the large intestine, where different stages of digestion take place. noun [count]	*The lining of the small intestine has projections called villi.*
kidney /ˈkɪdni/	one of the two organs in the body that clean the blood by removing waste products such as urea and also control the level of water that the blood contains. The waste passes into the bladder in the liquid form of urine, which is then passed out of the body.	
located /ləʊˈkeɪtɪd/	existing in a particular place. adjective	*The gland is located near the centre of the brain.*
loop of Henlé /ˌluːp əv ˈhenleɪ/	part of a kidney tubule which forms a long loop in the medulla. noun [count]	
medulla /meˈdʌlə/	the inner part of the kidney, which contains the loops of Henlé. noun [singular]	
nephron /ˈnefrɒn/	one of many small structures in the kidney that consists of the glomerulus, the Bowman's capsule, and its tubules (small tubes). noun [count]	
nitrogenous waste /naɪˌtrɒdʒənəs ˈweɪst/	waste products from the body that contain nitrogen. noun [uncount]	
osmoregulation /ˌɒzməʊˌregjʊˈleɪʃn/	the process of keeping the right balance of salts and water in the blood and cells of the body. noun [uncount]	
pelvis /ˈpelvɪs/	the wide part at the top of the ureter where it joins the kidney, where urine from the kidney is collected. noun [count]	
proximal /ˈprɒksɪm(ə)l/	nearer to the centre of the body or to the point where something is attached to the body (≠ distal). adjective	*the proximal small intestine*
receptor /rɪˈseptə/	a nerve in a sense organ such as the skin or the nose that sends messages to the central nervous system. noun [count]	*a touch receptor (=one that tells the brain you are touching something)*
removal /rɪˈmuːv(ə)l/	the process of removing someone or something. noun [count/uncount]	*the removal of excess water from the body*

renal artery the blood vessel which takes blood containing waste products
/ˈriːn(ə)l/ to the kidney. noun [count]

The kidneys receive a blood supply via the renal arteries.

respire to release energy from food so that it can be used by the body.
/rɪˈspaɪə/ verb [intransitive]

All living things respire.

sebaceous gland a gland in the skin that allows a type of oil called sebum to
/səˌbeɪʃəs ˈɡlænd/ flow onto the skin and hair to keep them soft. noun [count]

secrete to produce a liquid such as saliva. verb [transitive]
/sɪˈkriːt/

soluble able to dissolve in a liquid and become part of the solution
/ˈsɒljʊb(ə)l/ (≠ insoluble). adjective

Urine contains urea, salts and other soluble substances.

sphincter muscle a muscle that surrounds and controls an opening in the body,
/ˈsfɪŋktə ˌmʌs(ə)l/ especially in the anus. noun [count]

The sphincter muscle at the neck of the bladder is under voluntary control.

spine the row of bones down or along the middle of the back of a
/spaɪn/ vertebrate. noun [count]

She had suffered an injury to her spine.

substance a particular type of liquid, solid, or gas. noun [count]
/ˈsʌbstəns/

Some substances are toxic if they build up in the blood.

sweat gland a gland in the skin that produces sweat. noun [count]
/ˈswet ˌɡlænd/

Sweat contains small amounts of urea and salts, so sweat glands can be thought of as excretory organs.

sweat pore a small hole in the skin through which sweat can leave the
/ˈswet ˌpɔː/ body. noun [count]

swell to become larger than normal, or to make something larger
/swel/ than normal. verb [transitive/intransitive]

The condition causes the liver to swell.

transplant a medical operation in which a new organ is put into
/ˈtrænsˌplɑːnt/ someone's body. noun [count/uncount]

She was waiting for a kidney transplant.

tubular shaped like a tube, or made from tubes. adjective
/ˈtjuːbjʊlə/

a long tubular gland

twist to bend or turn in a curved shape. verb [transitive/intransitive]
/twɪst/

If the umbilical cord twists, there may be problems for the baby.

ultrafiltration the process that takes place in the nephrons of the kidney,
/ˌʌltrəfɪlˈtreɪʃ(ə)n/ where small molecules such as glucose, water, salt and urea
are removed from the blood. noun [uncount]

urea a substance found in urine that is used for making fertilizers
/jʊˈriːə/ and for some types of medicine. noun [uncount]

ureter one of the two tubes that carry urine from the kidneys to
/jʊˈriːtə/ the bladder in most mammals, or to the place where waste
collects in some other vertebrates. noun [count]

urethra in most mammals, the tube that carries urine out of the body.
/jʊˈriːθrə/ noun [count]

urine a liquid that contains waste products such as urea and salts
/ˈjʊərɪn/ from the body that are filtered out through the kidneys. Urine
collects in the bladder and passes from the body through the
urethra. noun [uncount]

vena cava one of the two large veins that carry blood into the right side
/ˌviːnə ˈkeɪvə/ of the heart. The anterior vena cava brings blood from the
upper body and the head, and the posterior vena cava brings
blood from below the chest (plural: venae cavae /ˌviːniː ˈkeɪviː/).
noun [count]

waste the unwanted materials, substances, or parts that are left after
/ˈweɪst/ you have used something. noun [count/uncount]

The kidneys remove waste from the blood.

waste product an unwanted material or substance that is left after you have
/ˈweɪst ˌprɒdʌkt/ used something. noun [count]

Waste products of the body include carbon dioxide and urea.

1 Excretory system

Fill in these words and phrases on the word map.

> digested food   egestion   excreted via lung   part not required   sweat pore   urethra

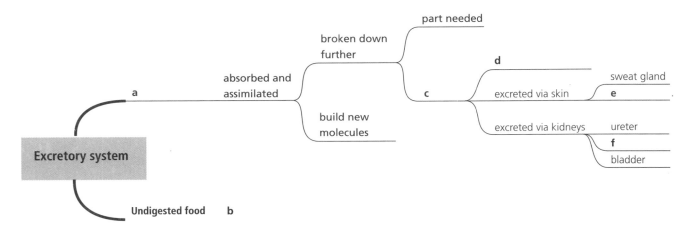

2 The nephrons

Label the diagram with these words and phrases.

> blood coming to kidney   blood leaving kidney   Bowman's capsule   capillaries   collecting duct
> cortex   distal convoluted tubule   glomerulus (knot of capillaries)   loop of Henlé   medulla
> proximal convoluted tubule   urine

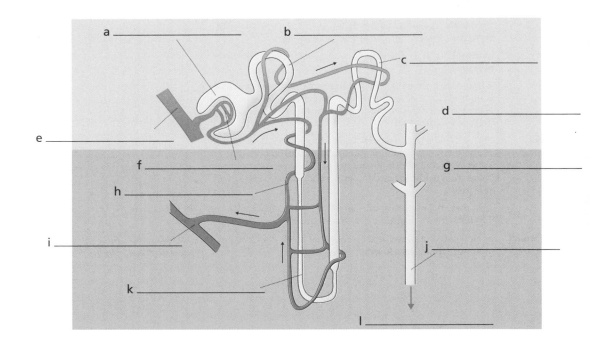

3 The waste products of digestion

Read the text and complete with these words.

> amino acids   carbohydrates   deamination   digested   excess   kidneys   respiration   small intestine   urea

When proteins are 1 _____ they are broken down into amino acids which are absorbed in the
2 _____. The body uses the 3 _____ it needs to make its own protein for growth and
repair of body cells. If we absorb more amino acids than the body needs, we cannot store the
4 _____. These are transferred to the liver where the amino group (–NH₂) is removed as ammonia.
This is known as 5 _____. Ammonia is highly toxic to cells so it is converted to a less toxic
compound called 6 _____. The rest of the amino acid is converted to 7 _____, which
can be stored as glycogen and later used in respiration to provide energy. Urea is a waste product because it is
not needed by the body. The carbohydrate is not a waste product because it is stored and then used by the body
during 8 _____. The urea must be removed from the body because it can affect reactions in the
cytoplasm, so it is transported by the blood to the 9 _____ where it is filtered and excreted from the
body as urine.

4 Vertical section through the human skin

Label the diagram with these words and phrases.

> capillary network   dermis   epidermis   fatty layer below skin   hair erector muscle
> hair follicle   nerve fibre   pain receptor   pressure receptor   sebaceous gland
> sweat gland   sweat pore   temperature receptor

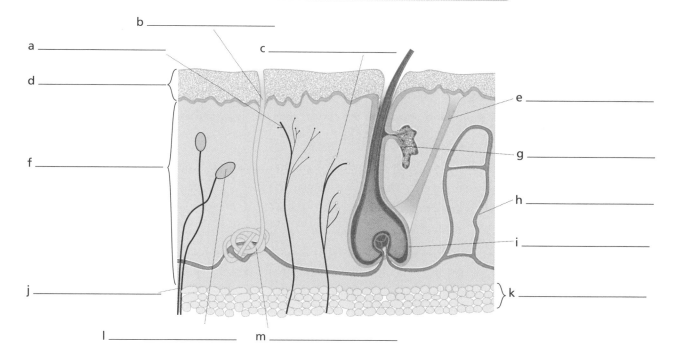

5   How sweat is excreted through the skin

The text describes how sweat is excreted through the skin. The steps have been mixed up. Look at the diagram and place these sentences in the correct order on the picture.

> The sweat is transported to the surface of the skin via the sweat duct.
> Blood carrying a lot of water flows along the capillaries and the waste diffuses from the blood into the sweat gland.
> The base of the glands are near to blood capillaries which allows easy diffusion of waste products from the blood into the gland. The mixture of water, urea and salt, which is excreted from the sweat glands, forms a solution called sweat.
> The blood continues along the capillary but contains less water.
> The skin contains many sweat glands which are tubular structures that extend into the skin's surface.
> The soluble substances, urea and salts, remain on the surface of the skin.
> The water evaporates from the skin's surface.

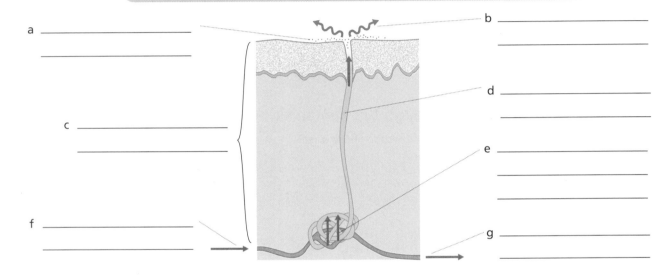

a _____

_____

b _____

_____

c _____

_____

d _____

_____

e _____

_____

_____

f _____

_____

g _____

_____

6   Excretion of waste products in flowering plants

Put the words and phrases in the correct order to make sentences.

1   also   form   Plants   products.   waste

_____

2   a complex excretory system   like humans   because   can be re-used   do not require   in other processes. most of their products   Plants

_____

_____

3   a waste product of photosynthesis,   can be considered   is a waste product of respiration.   Oxygen while carbon dioxide

_____

_____

4   on the underside of the leaves.   oxygen and carbon dioxide,   Both gases,   via the stomata will diffuse out of the leaves

_____

_____

5   and at night   During daylight   made in respiration   may be used in photosynthesis,
    may be used in respiration.   much of the carbon dioxide   oxygen that was made during photosynthesis

_____

_____

6   by the plant   made during respiration   that is not needed   through transpiration through the stomata.
    Water   will be lost

_____

_____

7   are   excretory organs   in plants.   The leaves   the main

_____

8   after some time.   from other chemical reactions   in the plant   like the leaves and seeds,
    may be stored in different parts,   Waste products   which are destined to drop off the plant

_____

_____

9   a large amount of waste   in the vacuoles   may store   of their leaves.   Some plants

_____

10   and drops off.   and is lost   eventually crystallises,   The accumulated waste   the leaf dies   when

_____

7 The lung as an organ

Match the beginnings and the endings of the sentences.

Beginnings

1   The lungs excrete the gaseous
2   The carbon dioxide that is formed in the cells during
3   On reaching the lungs the blood flows through a network of
4   The carbon dioxide diffuses into the lungs along with
5   Both the carbon dioxide and water (vapour) are excreted

Endings

a   capillaries over the alveoli, which is the point of gaseous exchange in the lungs.
b   from the lungs into the atmosphere when you exhale.
c   some water from the cells of the alveoli.
d   respiration diffuses into the blood stream, which transports it to the lungs.
e   waste product of respiration, carbon dioxide.

1 ☐   2 ☐   3 ☐   4 ☐   5 ☐

8 Excretory organs of the human body

A Read the texts about the lungs and the kidneys. The information has been mixed up. Sort the texts into the two columns.

1 Both the carbon dioxide and water vapour are excreted from the lungs into the atmosphere when you exhale.
2 Each kidney is about 12.5 cm long and 7.5 cm wide.
3 On reaching the lungs the blood flows through a network of capillaries over the alveoli, which is the point of gaseous exchange in the lung.
4 The carbon dioxide diffuses into the lung along with some water from the cells of the alveoli.
5 This carbon dioxide which is formed in the cells during respiration diffuses into the bloodstream, which transports it to the lungs.
6 The kidneys are the main excretory organs in the human body.
7 The lungs excrete the gaseous waste product of respiration, carbon dioxide.
8 The main function of the kidneys is to remove excess water and nitrogenous waste from the blood.
9 This waste is urea, which was formed from the breakdown of amino acids in the liver.
10 We have two of them, which are located to the back of the body just above the waist on either side of the spine.

The lung as an excretory organ	The kidney as an excretory organ

B Now put the sentences in the correct order to form two paragraphs.

The lung as an excretory organ	The kidney as an excretory organ

antagonistic pair a pair of muscles that always work together, so that when one
/æn,tægənɪstɪk 'peə/ is contracting the other is relaxing. noun [count]

appendicular the appendicular skeleton in humans consists of all bones
skeleton except for the skull, the vertebral column with the rib cage.
/ə,pendɪkʊəl(ə)r noun [count]
'skelɪt(ə)n/

armour hard layers that cover the bodies of some animals, such as a
/'ɑːmə/ rhinoceros or an armadillo. noun [uncount]

arthropod a type of invertebrate that has jointed legs, a body divided
/'ɑːθrəpɒd/ into several parts, and an external skeleton. Insects, arachnids, centipedes, and crustaceans are arthropods. noun [count]

articulation the ways in which the different parts of a structure or system
/ɑː,tɪkjʊ'leɪʃn/ are connected. noun [uncount]

atlas the first cervical vertebra in humans. noun [uncount]
/'ætləs/

axial skeleton the axial skeleton in humans consists of the skull, the
/'æksiːəl 'skelɪt(ə)n/ vertebral column with the rib cage. noun [count]

axis the second vertebral column in humans. noun [uncount]
/'æksɪs/

backbone the row of small bones that goes down the middle of the back *Shivers ran down her backbone.*
/'bæk,bəʊn/ = spine, vertebral column. noun [count]

ball-and-socket a joint in the body of a person or animal where a bone with
joint a round end fits into another bone that has a concave part,
/'bɔːl ənd 'sɒkɪt allowing the bones to move easily in many directions. The
,dʒɔɪnt/ hip is an example of a ball-and-socket joint. noun [count]

biceps the muscle between the shoulder and elbow on the front of *The bodybuilder's biceps were huge.*
/'baɪseps/ the arm. noun [count]

breastbone the flat bone in the middle of the chest = sternum. *Birds have a large breastbone to*
/'brest,bəʊn/ noun [count] *support the powerful flight muscles.*

calcify to become hard or to make something hard, by the addition
/'kælsɪfaɪ/ of a substance that contains calcium. verb [intransitive]

canal a passage in the body shaped like a tube. noun [count] *the alimentary canal*
/kə'næl/

cardiac muscle the type of muscle found in the heart. noun [uncount]
/'kɑːdɪæk ,mʌs(ə)l/

carpal one of the small bones in the wrist. noun [count]
/'kɑːp(ə)l/

cartilage a type of very strong tissue that is found, for example, at the *He had an operation to remove some*
/'kɑːtəlɪdʒ/ end of bones and between the vertebrae. It also forms parts *cartilage from his knee joint.*
of the ear, nose, and throat. It is a type of connective tissue.
noun [uncount]

caterpillar the larva of a butterfly or moth. It has a worm-like body,
/'kætəpɪlə/ with three pairs of true legs and several pairs of false legs.
noun [count]

centrum the solid central part of a vertebra (plural: centrums or centra).
/'sentrəm/ noun [count]

cervical vertebra one of the vertebrae (spinal bones) found in the neck (plural:
/sɜːvaɪk(ə)l vertebrae /'vɜːtəbreɪ/). noun [count]
'vɜːtəbrə/

chitin a strong substance that forms part of the outer layer protecting
/'kaɪtɪn/ some insects and other arthropods, and the cell walls of some
fungi. noun [count]

clavicle one of the pair of bones that go across the top of the chest
/'klævɪk(ə)l/ from the shoulder to the bottom of the neck = collarbone. *She fell and fractured her clavicle.*
noun [count]

coccyx the small bone at the bottom of your spine. noun [count]
/'kɒksɪks/

collarbone /ˈkɒləˌbəʊn/	the bone along the front of the shoulder = clavicle. **noun [count]**	
connective tissue /kəˌnektɪv ˈtɪʃuː/	the parts of the body that connect or support organs and other parts of the body. Connective tissue can consist of fat, bone, cartilage etc. **noun [uncount]**	
contract /kənˈtrækt/	when a muscle contracts, it gets tighter and shorter. **verb [transitive/intransitive]**	*As he lifted the heavy weight you could see his arm muscles contract.*
crab /ˈkræb/	a sea crustacean with two large claws that walks sideways. **noun [count]**	
cranium /ˈkreɪniəm/	the skull. **noun [count]**	
endoskeleton /ˈendəʊˌskelɪt(ə)n/	the hard structure, usually made of bone, inside the body of a vertebrate. **noun [count]**	*Our endoskeleton supports our body and gives it shape.*
exoskeleton /ˈeksəʊˌskelɪt(ə)n/	a hard covering on the outside of organisms such as crustaceans, insects, and turtles, that provides support and protection.	*The exoskeleton of some insects is brightly coloured.*
extend /ɪkˈstend/	to stretch out a part of your body, for example your arm or leg, so that it is straight. **verb [transitive]**	*He stood with his arms extended towards her.*
extensor muscle /ɪkˈstensə ˌmʌs(ə)l/	a muscle that is used when extending part of the body. **noun [count]**	
facet /ˈfæsɪt/	one of two parts on each vertebra that link to the vertebrae above and below. They allow a small amount of movement but stop the spine from twisting too much. **noun [count]**	
fascicle /ˈfæsɪk(ə)l/	a bundle of structures, such as nerve or muscle fibres. **noun [count]**	
femur /ˈfiːmə/	the bone in the top part of the leg, above the knee. **noun [count]**	*The femur is also called the thigh bone.*
fibril /ˈfaɪbrɪl/	a small thin muscle fibre. **noun [count]**	
fibula /ˈfɪbjʊlə/	the outer narrow bone in the bottom part of the leg. The wider bone next to it is called the tibia. **noun [count]**	*The fibula and tibia together make up the lower leg bones.*
flex /ˈfleks/	to bend a part of your body such as your arm or leg. **verb [transitive]**	*This muscle is used when you flex your arm.*
flexor muscle /ˈfleksə ˌmʌs(ə)l/	a muscle that is used when bending part of the body. **noun [count]**	
fore /ˈfɔː/	the fore parts of an animal are the part at the front. **adjective**	
gristle /ˈgrɪs(ə)l/	a strong substance that surrounds the joints of animals and is difficult to eat when you find it in meat. **noun [uncount]**	
hind /ˈhaɪnd/	the hind legs or feet of an animal are its back legs or feet. **adjective**	
hinge joint /ˈhɪndʒ ˌdʒɔɪnt/	a joint in the body that allows movement up and down in one direction only. The joints at the knees and elbows are hinge joints. **noun [count]**	
hip /hɪp/	one of the two flat bones at either side of the body between the waist and the top of the legs. **noun [count]**	*He fell downstairs and broke his hip.*
humerus /ˈhjuːmərəs/	the bone that connects the shoulder to the elbow. **noun [count]**	*The humerus is sometimes called the 'funny bone'.*
insect /ˈɪnsekt/	an arthropod (=type of invertebrate) that has six legs and usually two pairs of wings, such as a bee, a fly, or a beetle. An insect's body is divided into three parts: the head, the thorax, and the abdomen. **noun [count]**	*Some insects, especially sucking insects, are responsible for the spread of diseases.*
intervertebral disc /ˌɪntəˈvɜːtəbrəl ˌdɪsk/	one of the layers of cartilage separating the vertebrae (bones) in the spine. **noun [count]**	
involuntary muscle /ɪnˈvɒləntri ˌmʌs(ə)l/	muscle such as heart muscle, that is involved in processes in the body that a person cannot consciously control. **noun [uncount]**	
jawbone /ˈdʒɔːˌbəʊn/	the mandible. **noun [count]**	*The teeth are embedded in the jawbone.*
jellyfish /ˈdʒeliˌfɪʃ/	a soft transparent invertebrate sea animal that can sting you. A sting from a jellyfish can be very dangerous, and can even kill (plural: jellyfish). **noun [count]**	
joint /dʒɔɪnt/	a part of the body that can bend where two bones meet. It usually consists of connective tissue and cartilage. **noun [count]**	*a knee joint*

kneecap /'niːkæp/	the bone at the front of the knee = patella. noun [count]	
ligament /'lɪgəmənt/	a strong band or sheet of tissue inside the body that holds bones together and keeps organs in place. noun [count]	*She tore a ligament in her knee.*
limb /lɪm/	an arm or a leg. noun [count]	
lumbar vertebra /'lʌmbə ,vɜːtəbrə/	one of the vertebrae (spinal bones) found in the lower back (plural: vertebrae /'vɜːtəbreɪ/). noun [count]	
mandible /'mændɪb(ə)l/	**1** the lower jaw of humans and vertebrates. noun [count] **2** one of the two parts of an insect's mouth that it uses for biting. noun [count]	*Bees use their mandibles for moulding wax.*
marrow /'mærəʊ/	the soft substance inside bones, where blood cells develop = bone marrow. noun [uncount]	*The young child was waiting for a life-saving bone marrow transplant.*
metacarpal /ˌmetəˈkɑːp(ə)l/	one of the five bones in the hand. noun [count]	-
metatarsal /ˌmetəˈtɑːs(ə)l/	one of the bones in the foot. noun [count]	
mollusc /'mɒləsk/	an invertebrate animal that has a soft body with no bones and is usually covered by a hard shell. Snails, octopuses, and mussels are all molluscs. noun [count]	
muscle fibre /'mʌs(ə)l ,faɪbə/	one of the thin pieces that form the muscles in the body. noun [count/uncount]	
muscle /'mʌs(ə)l/	a piece of flesh that connects bones and produces movement of the parts of the body by contracting and relaxing. noun [count/uncount]	*These exercises are good for your stomach muscles.*
nerve cord /'nɜːv ,kɔd/	a long set of nerve fibres running along an animal's body, especially in an invertebrate. noun [count]	
neural /'njʊərəl/	relating to your nerves or your nervous system. adjective	
patella /pəˈtelə/	the bone at the front of the knee (= kneecap). noun [count]	*Tapping the knee just below the patella causes the lower leg to jerk upwards.*
pectoral /'pekt(ə)rəl/	in or relating to the chest. adjective	
pelvic /'pelvɪk/	relating to the pelvis. adjective	
pelvis /'pelvɪs/	the large circular bones that support the lower part of the back. They are connected to the bones of the legs. noun [count]	*Elderly people often fracture their pelvis in a fall.*
phalanx /'fælæŋks/	one of the bones of a finger or toe (plural: phalanges /fəˈlændʒiːz/). noun [count]	
process /'prəʊses/	a part that sticks out from a bone. noun [count]	
radius /'reɪdiəs/	the larger outer bone in the lower arm, next to the ulna (plural radiuses or radii /'reɪdiaɪ/). noun [count]	*Rotating the palm of the hand downwards causes the radius to cross over the ulna.*
rib /rɪb/	one of the long curved bones in the chest. noun [count]	*The ribs protect the heart and lungs.*
rib cage /'rɪb ,keɪdʒ/	the bones that curve around and protect the organs in the chest. noun [count]	*You can see someone's rib cage rise when they breathe in.*
sacral vertebra /'sækrəl ,vɜːtəbrə/	one of the vertebrae (spinal bones) found in the bottom part of the back between the hip bones (plural: vertebrae /'vɜːtəbreɪ/). noun [count]	
scapula (shoulderblade) /'skæpjʊlə/	one of the two bones on the sides of the upper back = shoulder blade (plural: scapulae or scapulas). noun [count]	*There is a ball-and-socket joint between the scapula and the humerus.*
shed /ʃed/	to have something fall off as part of a natural process. verb [transitive]	*Snakes regularly shed their skin.*
shinbone /'ʃɪn,bəʊn/	the bone in the lower front part of the leg, between the knee and the ankle = tibia. noun [count]	*During the football game he received a painful kick on the shinbone.*
shoulderblade /'ʃəʊldə,bleɪd/	one of the two flat bones at the top of the back, near the shoulders = scapula. noun [count]	
sinew /'sɪnjuː/	the strong substance that connects muscles to bone, or a piece of this = tendon. noun [count/uncount]	

skeleton /ˈskelɪt(ə)n/	the hard frame that supports the body of a human or other animal. In vertebrates it is usually made of bone that the muscles are attached to, and it protects the most important organs, for example the brain and the heart. noun [count]	
skull /skʌl/	the bones of the head. noun [count]	*The bones of the skull are fused together.*
slug /slʌg/	a small mollusc that lives on land, similar to a snail without a shell. noun [count]	
smooth muscle /ˌsmuːð ˈmʌs(ə)l/	the type of muscle found inside the gut, that is not made of long fibres and is not under voluntary control. noun [uncount]	
spider /ˈspaɪdə/	an arachnid with eight legs that spins webs in order to catch insects. noun [count]	
spinal cord /ˈspaɪn(ə)l ˌkɔːd/	the thick length of nerve tissue that goes down the hole in the spine, from the bottom of the brain to the bottom of the back. It is part of the central nervous system. noun [count]	*The brain and spinal cord together make up the central nervous system.*
spine /spaɪn/	the row of bones down or along the middle of the back of a vertebrate = backbone, spinal column, vertebral column. noun [count]	*She was paralysed after breaking her spine in a car accident.*
spongy /ˈspʌndʒi/	light, soft, and full of small holes. adjective	*spongy tissue*
stag beetle /ˈstæg ˌbiːt(ə)l/	a large dark beetle with large jaws that resemble the antlers (the horns on the head of a male deer). noun [count]	
sternum (breastbone) /ˈstɜːnəm/	the flat bone in the middle of the chest = breastbone. noun [count]	*The ribs are attached to the sternum at the front of the chest.*
striated muscle /straɪˈeɪtɪd ˌmʌs(ə)l/	the type of muscle that you have in your arms or legs, made of long fibres. noun [uncount]	
support /səˈpɔːt/	to hold something such as a structure in place so that it does not move in the wrong way. verb [transitive]	*Four major ligaments support the knee.*
suture /ˈsuːtʃə/	the stitch or stitches used for closing the edges of a cut. noun [count/uncount]	*The wound needed a suture.*
synovial fluid /saɪˌnəʊviəl ˈfluːɪd/	liquid within the joints of the body that allows the bones to move smoothly. noun [uncount]	*The oil in a car engine performs the same job as the synovial fluid in joints.*
synovial membrane /saɪˌnəʊviəl ˈmembreɪn/	the membrane surrounding a synovial joint (= a type of joint that contains fluid helping it to move smoothly). noun [count]	
tarsal /ˈtɑːs(ə)l/	one of the bones of the tarsus (bones of the ankle and upper part of the foot). noun [count]	
tendon /ˈtendən/	a band of strong tissue that connects a muscle to a bone. noun [count]	
thigh bone /ˈθaɪˌbəʊn/	the bone in the top part of the leg, above the knee = femur. noun [count]	
thoracic vertebra /θəˈræsɪk ˌvɜːtəbrə/	one of the twelve vertebrae (spinal bones) found in the upper part of the back, to which the ribs are attached (plural: vertebrae /ˈvɜːtəbreɪ/). noun [count]	
tibia /ˈtɪbiə/	the wide bone at the front of the lower leg, between the knee and the ankle and next to the fibula = shinbone. noun [count]	
tough /tʌf/	difficult to break or damage. adjective	*Cartilage is very tough.*
transverse /ˌtrænzˈvɜːs/	placed sideways or at an angle across something.	
triceps /ˈtraɪˌseps/	the muscle at the back of the upper arm. noun [count]	*The biceps and triceps muscles work together to bend and straighten the arm.*
ulna /ˈʌlnə/	the longer of the two bones that connect the wrist to the elbow, next to the radius (plural: ulnas or ulnae /ˈʌlniː/). noun [count]	*The bony part of your elbow is the end of your ulna.*
vertebra /ˈvɜːtəbrə/	one of the small bones that form a row down the centre of the back, forming the spine (plural: vertebrae). noun [count]	*She damaged a vertebra in her neck.*
vertebral column /ˌvɜːtəbrəl ˈkɒləm/	the backbone or spinal column. noun [count]	
visceral muscle /ˈvɪsərəl ˌmʌs(ə)l/	muscle found in the internal organs such as the intestines. noun [count/uncount]	*The small bones of the vertebral column protect the spinal cord.*
voluntary muscle /ˈvɒləntrɪ ˌmʌs(ə)l/	muscle that you can control, for example any of the muscles that you use for moving your arms and legs. noun [count/uncount]	

A   Working with words

1   Locomotion word map

Fill in these words and phrases on the word map.

ball-and-socket   biceps   extensor muscle   joints   lumbar   skeleton   vertebral column

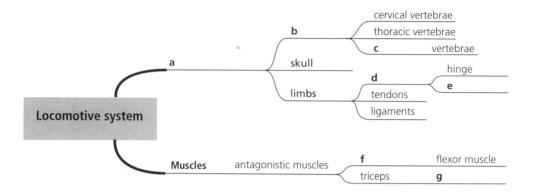

2   Movement in a human limb

Label the diagrams with these words and phrases.

articular cartilage – functions as a shock absorber   bone moved to the left   bone moved to the right
compact bone   contracted muscle (x2)   ligament (x2)   muscle at rest   relaxed muscle (x2)   spongy bone
synovial fluid – lubricates joint reducing friction during movement   synovial membrane   bone

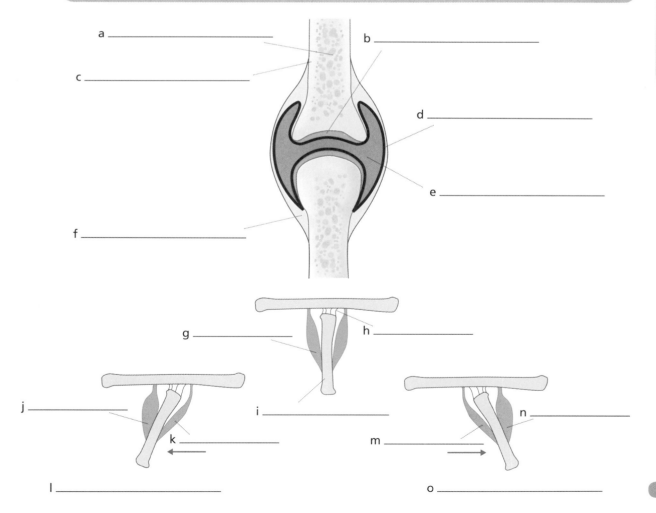

3 Structure of the skeleton

Label the diagram with these words and phrases.

carpals clavicle cranium
face femur fibula humerus
metacarpals metatarsals patella
pelvis phalanges (x2) radius
ribs scapula sternum tarsals
tibia ulna vertebral column

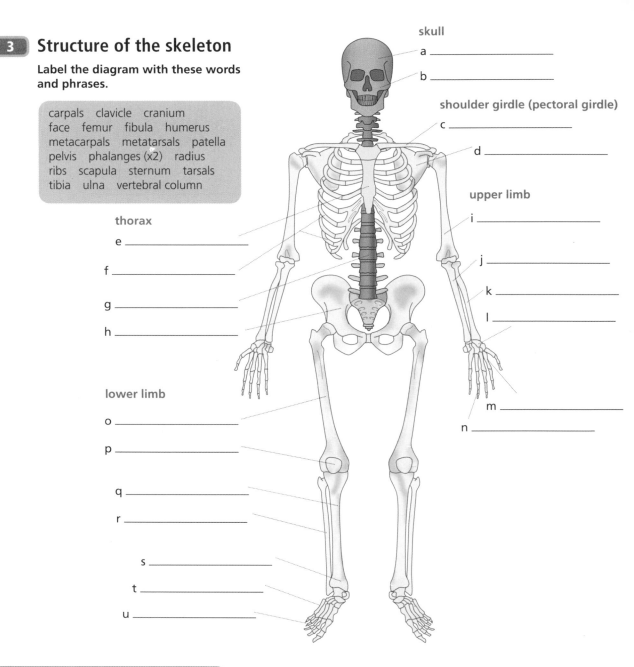

skull

a _____

b _____

shoulder girdle (pectoral girdle)

c _____

d _____

upper limb

i _____

j _____

k _____

l _____

m _____

n _____

thorax

e _____

f _____

g _____

h _____

lower limb

o _____

p _____

q _____

r _____

s _____

t _____

u _____

B Working with sentences

4 Locomotive system summary

Read the sentences and match the beginnings with the endings.

Beginnings

1 Movement is
2 There are a number of reasons
3 The human skeleton has
4 The skeleton forms
5 The axial skeleton consists of
6 The vertebral column is made up of
7 The appendicular skeleton consists of
8 The skeleton is made up of many
9 Movement is brought about by
10 There are many kinds of

Endings

a joints, immovable, partially movable and movable joints.
b a framework inside the human body and is made up of the axial and appendicular skeletons.
c bones joined together; movement is seen at these joints.
d a characteristic of life.
e many bones called vertebrae and includes the cervical, thoracic and lumbar vertebrae.
f many functions, one of which is movement.
g muscles, tendons and ligaments at these joints.
h the cranium and the vertebral column.
i the limbs and ribcage.
j why animals move.

1 ☐ 2 ☐ 3 ☐ 4 ☐ 5 ☐ 6 ☐ 7 ☐ 8 ☐ 9 ☐ 10 ☐

5 ## Sections of the vertebra

Look at the diagrams. Then read the sentences and sort them out into the correct section.

The centrum is big and well developed to support the weight of the body.
They have a large neural canal since these are closest to the brain.   The neural canal is small.
They have a heavy, wide neural spine.   They have a short neural spine.
They have a very long neural spine for attachment of the back muscles.
They have long transverse processes for muscle attachment.   They have short transverse processes.
They have short transverse processes to accommodate rib bones on either side.
The neural canal is smaller than in the cervical vertebrae as these are further from the brain.
Vertebrarterial canals are present.

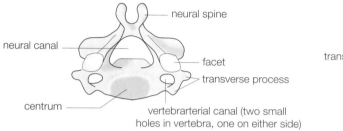

cervical vertebra – has two small holes apart from the large neural canal

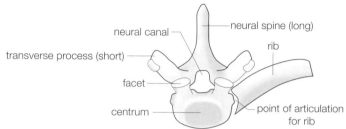

thoracic vertebra – articulate with ribs as well as other vertebrae

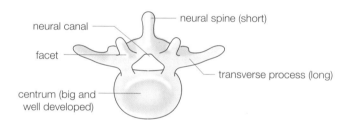

lumbar vertebra – has large centrum and long transverse processes

cervical vertebrae
1
2
3
4
thoracic vertebrae
5
6
7
lumbar vertebrae
8
9
10
11

6   Movement in the arms

Read the text and label the diagram using these words or phrases.

arm bends or flexes   arm extends   biceps muscle (contracts) (flexor muscle)
biceps muscle (relaxes)   extending the arm   flexing the arm   radius   radius (pulled)
tendons, attach muscle to bone   triceps muscle (contracts) (extensor muscle)
triceps muscle (relaxes)   ulna   ulna (pulled)

The muscles of the arm move the bones of the arm to flex or extend the arm in the same way. The bones are attached to each other by ligaments and attached to muscles by tendons. They have special names (triceps and biceps) and contract or relax to move the bones. All the bones of the body need muscles to help them move. Imagine the coordination of contraction and relaxation of muscles needed to cup the fingers around a bottle, then move the bottle to the lips to take a drink of water.

Movement is brought about the contraction and relaxation of antagonistic muscles. Antagonistic muscles are pairs of muscles that always work together: when one is contracting the other is relaxing. They move many bones of the human skeleton. In the joint of the upper arm, the triceps and biceps are antagonistic muscles. They are attached to the bones by tendons which are non-elastic. A muscle shortens when it contracts and lengthens when it relaxes. Movement of the bone is brought about when the muscles pull on the bones.

When the biceps contracts (and triceps relax), it pulls the bones of the lower arm upwards so the arm bends or flexes. The biceps is called a flexor muscle. When the triceps contracts (and biceps relax), it pulls the bones of the lower arm so that the arm straightens or extends. The triceps is called an extensor muscle.

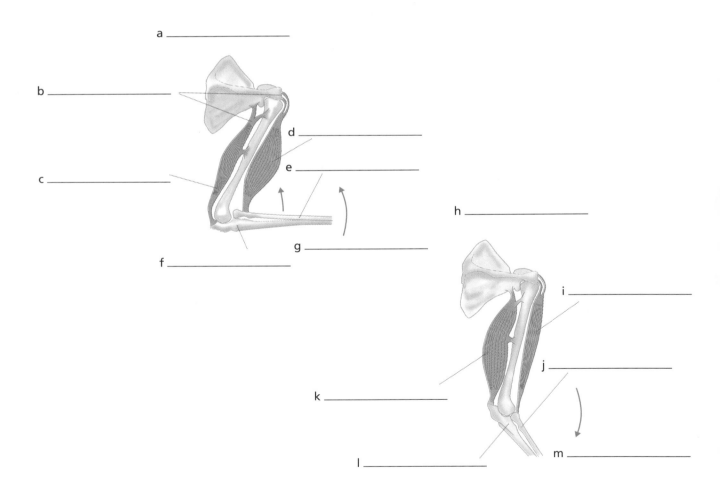

a _____

b _____

c _____

d _____

e _____

f _____

g _____

h _____

i _____

j _____

k _____

l _____

m _____

15 Temperature, thermometers and heat transfer

absolute zero
/ˌæbsəluːt ˈzɪərəʊ/
-273 °C, the lowest temperature that scientists believe is possible. **noun [uncount]**

agitation
/ˌædʒɪˈteɪʃ(ə)n/
the action of shaking or being shaken. **noun [uncount]**
Temperature measures the agitation of molecules in a liquid or gas.

air conditioner
/ˈeə kənˌdɪʃ(ə)nə/
a piece of electrical equipment that makes the air inside a building, room, or vehicle colder. **noun [count]**

atom
/ˈætəm/
the smallest unit of all matter that has all the chemical properties of a particular element. An atom consists of a nucleus that is made of protons, which are positive, and neutrons, which are neutral. The nucleus has electrons, which are negative, travelling around it. The numbers of protons and electrons are equal so that atoms are neutral. **noun [count]**

bend
/bend/
to become curved or folded and not straight, or to cause something to do this. **verb [transitive/intransitive]**
The metal bends when heated.

bimetallic thermometer
/baɪməˌtælɪk θəˈmɒmɪtə/
a device for measuring temperature made of two strips of different metals, that expand at different rates when heated. **noun [count]**

boiler
/ˈbɔɪlə/
a machine that heats water and provides hot water for a heating system. **noun [count]**
You should insulate your hot water tank or boiler.

bore
/bɔː/
the hollow tube inside something such as a thermometer or gun. **noun [count]**
The liquid-in-glass thermometer has a very fine bore.

brass
/brɑːs/
a shiny yellow metal that is a mixture of copper and zinc. **noun [uncount]**
a brass door handle

breeze
/briːz/
a light wind. **noun [count]**
a gentle breeze

brick
/brɪk/
a small block used as a building material to make walls, houses etc. **noun [count/uncount]**
The church was built entirely of brick.

bulb thermometer
/ˈbʌlb θəˌmɒmɪtə/
a device for measuring temperature that has a glass bulb at one end containing a liquid that expands into a narrow tube when heated = liquid-in-glass thermometer. **noun [count]**

capillary tube
/kəˈpɪləri ˌtjuːb/
a narrow tube inside a thermometer into which liquid expands when heated, measuring the temperature. **noun [count]**

Celsius
/ˈselsiəs/
a system for measuring temperature in the metric system. Symbol: C. **noun [uncount]**
The freezing point of water is zero degrees Celsius.

chilled
/tʃɪld/
chilled food or drink has been made cold in order to make it more pleasant or to keep it fresh. **adjective**
a bottle of chilled water

circulate
/ˈsɜːkjʊˌleɪt/
to move around continuously inside a system or area, or to make something do this. **verb [intransitive/transitive]**
The diagram shows how warm air circulates around the system.

clinical thermometer
/ˌklɪnɪkl θəˈmɒmɪtə/
a device for measuring the temperature of the human body. **noun [count]**

collide
/kəˈlaɪd/
if things collide, they crash into each other. **verb [intransitive]**
The particles inside the liquid move around and collide with each other.

conduction
/kənˈdʌkʃ(ə)n/
the process by which heat or electricity passes through a substance. **noun [uncount]**
As she touched the hot iron the heat travelled into her hand by conduction.

conductor
/kənˈdʌktə/
a substance that conducts heat or electricity (=allows heat or electricity to move through it). **noun [count]**
Copper is a good heat conductor.

constriction
/kənˈstrɪkʃ(ə)n/
a narrow part, for example inside a thermometer, that makes it difficult for something such as a liquid to pass. **noun [count]**
He felt a constriction in his throat and could not speak.

convection
/kənˈvekʃ(ə)n/
the process by which the very small parts in a liquid or gas move and give out heat. **noun [uncount]**
Land and sea breezes are caused by convection currents in the air.

convection current /kənˈvekʃ(ə)n ˌkʌrənt/	a constant movement of warm particles upwards and cooler particles downwards. **noun [count]**	The air in an oven circulates by convection currents.
convenient /kənˈviːniənt/	easy for you to do, or suitable for your needs. **adjective**	If it's convenient, call me tomorrow.
cooling effect /ˈkuːlɪŋ ɪˌfekt/	the effect of making someone or something feel cooler. **noun [singular]**	The concrete floor produces a pleasant cooling effect inside the building.
copper /ˈkɒpə/	a red-brown metal element that is a good conductor of electricity and heat. It is used to make electric wires, water and gas pipes, and alloys. Chemical symbol: Cu. **noun [uncount]**	The saucepan had a copper bottom.
cork /kɔːk/	a soft light substance from the bark of some cork trees. **noun [uncount]**	Cork tiles feel warm to touch because they don't conduct heat.
dense /dens/	a dense substance is heavy in relation to its size. **adjective**	Cold water is denser than warm water, so it sinks.
disposable /dɪsˈpəʊzəb(ə)l/	designed to be thrown away after being used once or a few times. **adjective**	disposable floor wipes
dyed /daɪd/	coloured using a dye. **adjective**	His hair looked dyed.
ectothermic /ˌektɒˈθɜːmɪk/	ectothermic animals are animals whose body temperature is affected by the temperature of their surroundings (=cold-blooded). **adjective**	
electromagnetic waves /ɪˌlektrəʊmægˌnetɪk ˈweɪvz/	a wave of energy within the electromagnetic spectrum. **noun [count]**	Heat reaches us from the Sun by electromagnetic waves of radiation.
endothermic /ˌendəʊˈθɜːmɪk/	endothermic animals are animals whose body temperature stays constant whatever the temperature of their surroundings (=warm-blooded). **adjective**	
erector muscle /ɪˈrektə ˌmʌs(ə)l/	a muscle that can move a part of the body, such as a hair, into an upright position. **noun [count]**	
evaporate /ɪˈvæpəˌreɪt/	if a liquid evaporates, it slowly changes into a vapour at a temperature below its boiling point. **verb [intransitive]**	
extend /ɪkˈstend/	to continue for a particular distance or in a particular direction. **verb [intransitive]**	Your heart is in the centre of your chest and extends into the left side of your chest.
Fahrenheit /ˈfærənhaɪt/	a system for measuring temperature in which water freezes at 32°F and boils at 212°F. **noun [uncount]**	It was a really hot day, over 100 degrees Fahrenheit.
fibreglass /ˈfaɪbəɡlɑːs/	a light hard substance made from very thin pieces of glass. **noun [uncount]**	a hollow fibreglass tube
flick /flɪk/	to move or tap something quickly and suddenly. **verb [transitive]**	He flicked the gauge to try and make it work.
freeze /friːz/	if a liquid freezes or something freezes it, it becomes solid because it has cooled and reached its freezing point. When water freezes, at 0°C, it becomes ice. **verb [transitive/intransitive]**	Liquid nitrogen freezes at –209 °C. The lake freezes in winter.
furnace /ˈfɜːnɪs/	a large enclosed container in which fuel is burned. It is used for heating a building or for industrial processes such as heating metal. **noun [count]**	
graduation /ˌɡrædʒuˈeɪʃ(ə)n/	one of a series of marks on a piece of equipment, such as a thermometer, used for measuring something. **noun [count]**	a thermometer that measures in Celsius with 0.1°C graduations
handle /ˈhænd(ə)l/	the part of something that you use for holding it. **noun [count]**	copper pans with plastic handles
heat transfer /ˈhiːt ˌtrænsfɜː/	the process of moving heat from one place or material to another. **noun [uncount]**	
inaccurate /ɪnˈækjʊrət/	not accurate or correct. **adjective**	The device gave an inaccurate measurement.
indicate /ˈɪndɪkeɪt/	to show something. **verb [transitive]**	The position of the mercury in the tube indicates the temperature.
infrared radiation /ˌɪnfrəred reɪdiˈeɪʃ(ə)n/	electromagnetic radiation that cannot be seen and has wavelengths that are longer than those of light that can be seen, but shorter than those of radio waves. **noun [uncount]**	Heat travels through space by infrared radiation.
infrared thermometer /ˌɪnfrəred θəˈmɒmɪtə/	a device that measures the temperature of an object without touching it, using an infrared beam that is directed at the object. **noun [count]**	

insulate /ˈɪnsjʊˌleɪt/	to cover something in order to prevent heat, cold, sound, or electricity from passing through it. **verb [transitive]**	*His thick, fur-lined coat insulated him from the cold.*
insulator /ˈɪnsjʊˌleɪtə/	a substance that reduces the amount of heat, cold, sound, or electricity that can pass through something. **noun [count]**	*Wood and plastic are examples of insulators.*
interval /ˈɪntəvəl/	a period of time between two events, or a space or distance between two things. **noun [count]**	*We measured the temperature at five-minute intervals.*
Kelvin scale /ˈkelvɪn ˌskeɪl/	the SI unit for measuring temperature. Symbol: K. **noun [singular]**	*Absolute zero is zero degrees on the Kelvin scale.*
kinetic energy /kaɪˌnetɪk ˈenədʒi/	the energy that an object has as a result of moving. This energy depends on the mass and velocity of the object. **noun [uncount]**	*Heating something gives the particles inside it more kinetic energy.*
knock /nɒk/	to hit something, or hit against something. **verb [transitive]**	*As the particles are heated they move and knock into one another more.*
lagging /ˈlæɡɪŋ/	a thick material used for covering things such as water pipes or boilers, so heat is not lost. **noun [uncount]**	*Lagging can save you money on your heating bills.*
lead /led/	a soft heavy grey metal element whose compounds can be poisonous. It is used to make containers that protect against harmful radiation. It is also a bad conductor of electricity that does not corrode easily. Chemical symbol: Pb. **noun [uncount]**	
liquid crystal thermometer /ˌlɪkwɪd ˌkrɪstəl θəˈmɒmɪtə/	a device for measuring temperature that consists of a plastic strip containing liquid crystals that are different colours at different temperatures. **noun [count]**	
loose-fitting /ˈluːsˌfɪtɪŋ/	loose-fitting clothes are large, comfortable, and not tight. **adjective**	*Wear comfortable, loose-fitting clothes.*
markings /ˈmɑːkɪŋz/	a pattern of marks that have been made on a surface to show a particular thing. **noun [plural]**	*The regular markings on the thermometer show the temperature scale.*
matter /ˈmætə/	the physical substances that everything in the universe is made of. Matter exists in the form of a solid, a liquid, or a gas. **noun [uncount]**	
maximum-minimum thermometer /ˌmæksɪməm ˌmɪnɪməm θəˈmɒmɪtə/	a device for measuring temperature that shows the highest and lowest temperature over a period of time. **noun [count]**	
measure /ˈmeʒə/	to find the exact size, amount, speed, or rate of something. **verb [transitive/intransitive]**	*We measured the temperature of the water.*
measurement /ˈmeʒəˌmənt/	the exact size, amount, speed, or rate of something, expressed in standard units. **noun [count]**	*They took measurements of noise levels inside the building.*
mercury /ˈmɜːkjʊri/	a very heavy silver metal element that is liquid at room temperature. It is used in thermometers and for making pesticides. Chemical symbol: Hg. **noun [uncount]**	*The mercury in the thermometer rose as the temperature increased.*
microwave /ˈmaɪkrəˌweɪv/	a type of electromagnetic wave used in radio communication, radar, and cooking. **noun [count]**	*Microwaves cook food by giving the particles inside more kinetic energy.*
motion /ˈməʊʃ(ə)n/	the process of action of moving. **noun [uncount]**	*The motion of the particles increases at higher temperatures.*
narrow /ˈnærəʊ/	if something is narrow, there is only a short distance from one side of it to the other. **adjective**	*The thermometer contains a narrow glass tube.*
non-conductor /ˌnɒnkənˈdʌktə/	a substance that does not conduct heat or electricity (does not allow it to pass through it). **noun [count]**	*Non-conductors are used as insulators.*
nylon /ˈnaɪlɒn/	a strong artificial substance that is used in making plastic and clothes. **noun [uncount]**	*Clothes made from nylon do not absorb moisture as well as natural fibres.*
packed /pækt/	having a lot of something in a small space. **adjective**	*The molecules are tightly packed.*
particle /ˈpɑːtɪk(ə)l/	**1** an extremely small piece of matter, for example an atom or a molecule. **noun [count]** **2** a subatomic particle that is part of an atom, for example an electron, proton, or neutron. **noun [count]**	
pointer /ˈpɔɪntə/	a long thin part of a measuring device that points to a particular number. **noun [count]**	*The pointer in the petrol gauge was on zero.*
polyester /ˌpɒliˈestə/	a light cloth made from artificial fibres. **noun [uncount]**	*I prefer cotton shirts to polyester.*
property /ˈprɒpəti/	a quality or feature of something. **noun [count]**	*We are learning about the properties of metals.*
quantitatively /ˈkwɒntɪtətəvli/	in a way that can be described or measured using numbers. **adverb**	*The improvement can be quantitatively measured.*

radiate /ˈreɪdiˌeɪt/	to produce energy in the form of electromagnetic waves such as heat, light, or radio waves. **verb [transitive/intransitive]**	*The heat radiated from the glowing coals.*
radiation /ˌreɪdiˈeɪʃ(ə)n/	**1** a type of energy that is sent out in the form of radioactive waves, for example, heat, light, or radio waves. **noun [uncount]** **2** a method by which heat can travel through empty space. **noun [uncount]**	*Heat reaches us from the Sun by radiation.*
rayon /ˈreɪɒn/	a light smooth artificial cloth made from cellulose. **noun [uncount]**	
reading /ˈriːdɪŋ/	a number or amount shown on a piece of measuring equipment. **noun [count]**	*The readings told us that we had gone off-course.*
refrigerator /rɪˈfrɪdʒəˌreɪtə/	a machine that keeps food and drinks cold, usually with a part for freezing food too. **noun [count]**	*Keep the milk in the refrigerator.*
relative /ˈrelətɪv/	used for comparing one situation with a more extreme one. **adjective**	*There was relative calm after the violence of the previous night.*
sense of touch /ˌsens əv ˈtʌtʃ/	the ability to tell what something feels like through your skin, or when you put your fingers on it. **noun [singular]**	*Sculpture can be appreciated through your sense of touch as well as through your eyes.*
shake /ʃeɪk/	to make lots of quick small movements up and down, or from side to side, or to make someone or something do this. **verb [transitive/intransitive]**	*She shook the flask to mix up the liquids.*
streak /striːk/	a line or long mark that is a different colour from the colour surrounding it. **noun [count]**	*The bird has a dark streak on its breast.*
styrofoam /ˈstaɪrəˌfəʊm/	a light plastic material, used especially for making containers and as an insulator (Trademark). **noun [uncount]**	
supply /səˈplaɪ/	an amount or quantity of something that is available to use. **noun [count]**	*The hospital's power supply was interrupted.*
synthetic fibre /sɪnˌθetɪk ˈfaɪbə/	fibre made from artificial materials or substances, not natural ones. **noun [count/uncount]**	*Many of the latest sports clothes are made from high-tech synthetic fibres.*
temperature /ˈtemprɪtʃə/	a measurement of how hot or cold a place or object is. **noun [count/uncount]**	*The usual temperature range here in winter is from 0 to 10°C.*
temperature range /ˈtemprɪtʃə ˌreɪndʒ/	all the temperature measurements that are included within particular limits, from the lowest to the highest. **noun [count]**	
temperature-sensitive /ˌtemprɪtʃə ˈsensətɪv/	reacting to changes in temperature. **adjective**	*The ring is made of a temperature-sensitive material that will change colour according to the warmth of your skin.*
thermal expansion /ˌθɜːm(ə)l ɪkˈspænʃ(ə)n/	the principle that substances expand when heated. **noun [uncount]**	*Bulb thermometers work because of thermal expansion.*
thermos flask /ˈθɜːməs ˌflɑːsk/	a vacuum flask that keeps liquids hot or cold (Trademark).	*She took some tea in a thermos flask.*
thermostat /ˈθɜːməʊˌstæt/	a piece of equipment that controls the temperature in a building, machine, or engine. It consists of a switch containing metals that expand to a different degree when heated. The thermostat switches the heat off as the temperature rises, and switches it on as the temperature falls. **noun [count]**	
transpiration /ˌtrænspɪˈreɪʃ(ə)n/	the process in which water that has travelled from the roots of a plant up to its leaves passes out into the air. The holes that the water evaporates from are called stomata. **noun [uncount]**	
uniformly /ˈjuːnɪˌfɔːmli/	in a way that is the same for all things in a group. **adverb**	*The two different metals in the device do not expand uniformly when heated.*
upright /ˈʌpraɪt/	vertical and straight. **adjective**	*The thermometer can be read in an upright position.*
utensil /juːˈtensɪl/	something that you use for cooking or eating with. **noun [count]**	*They manufacture cooking utensils.*
vacuum /ˈvækjʊəm/	an enclosed space with all the air and other gases removed from it. **noun [count]**	*Radiation is the only type of heat energy that can travel through a vacuum.*
vibrate /vaɪˈbreɪt/	to shake very quickly with small movements. **verb [intransitive]**	*The particles vibrate more vigorously as they are heated.*
vigorously /ˈvɪgərəsli/	in a way that involves a lot of energy. **adverb**	*You should exercise vigorously two or three times a week.*
wilt /wɪlt/	if a plant wilts, it gradually bends towards the ground because it needs water or is dying. **verb [intransitive]**	

1   Temperature, thermometers and heat transfer word map

Write the words in the correct places on the word map.

fish   bimetallic   conduction   cooling   warm blooded   plants   thermometers

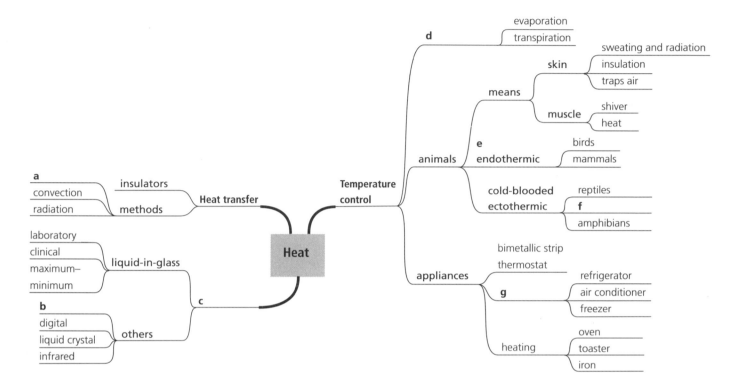

2   Temperature control in animals

Read the text and underline the correct word from the two choices given.

Some animals, such as birds and mammals, can keep a 1 (constant / changing) body temperature whatever the temperature of their surroundings. These animals are said to be endothermic or 2 (cold-blooded / warm-blooded). Other animals, such as reptiles, fish and amphibians, are ectothermic or 3 (cold-blooded / warm-blooded), because their body temperature is affected by the temperature of their surroundings.

4 (Ectothermic / Endothermic) animals that live in water are in an environment where temperature changes very little. Ectothermic animals that live on land have different ways to survive in the 5 (constant / changing) temperature of their environment. Those that live on the 6 (bottom / surface) of the land, such as lizards, may change their behaviour at different times of the day in order to keep their body 7 (temperature / heat) more constant. For example they bask in the sun on the top of an exposed rock during the morning to raise their body temperature above that of the air around them. However, as air temperature 8 (rises / lowers) and gets too hot, they move to shade where it is cooler. In this way they can keep body temperature more constant, which is better for all the 9 (biological / chemical) processes which are going on inside them.

Endothermic mammals can keep their 10 (internal / external) body temperature at around 37°C, and birds at around 40°C, without using the heat changes in the environment. They need to do this because many of the chemical changes that happen inside the body work best at these temperatures. The human body temperature cannot drop below 35°C, or get higher than 42°C, for very long without death following rapidly.

3   Temperature control in plants

Fill the gaps in the sentences using these words

> cooler   damage   evaporation   hot   hotter   photosynthesis   radiation
> stomata   temperature   transpiration   wilted   wilting

Plants need ways of controlling 1 _____ in order to survive. On very hot days if the plant becomes

too hot, this could 2 _____ the plant. Plants need water for 3 _____. This water is

taken in at the roots and passes up the plant to the leaves in a process called 4 _____. Some of the

water then evaporates through the stomata in the surface of the leaves. The 5 _____ of the water

provides a cooling effect for the plant. When the temperature is 6 _____, the rate of transpiration

is faster and more water evaporates through the 7 _____ so the plant is cooled more. If it gets

very 8 _____, the plant may close the stomata because too much water is being lost. Then the

plant looks 9 _____ and drooping. This also means that the leaves are no longer held out to catch

all the light (and so all the heat 10 _____) from the Sun, which also helps to keep the plant 11

_____. The plant will recover from 12 _____ as it gets cooler and enough water is

available for transpiration to start again.

B   Working with sentences

4   The advantages and disadvantages of using mercury and alcohol in thermometers

Read the characteristics of mercury and alcohol for use in thermometers and sort the information into the table.

> a   can be used to measure very high temperatures since mercury boils at 365°C.
> b   can be used to measure very low temperatures since alcohol freezes at -117°C.
> c   cannot be used to measure very high temperatures since alcohol boils at 78°C.
> d   cannot be used to measure very low temperatures since mercury freezes at -39°C.
> e   cheap.
> f   conducts heat much faster than alcohol.
> g   does not conduct heat as quickly as mercury.
> h   does not wet the sides of the tube, so none left on the side when the liquid contracts – more accurate readings are obtained.
> i   expensive.
> j   flammable.
> k   is opaque therefore can be seen easily in the thermometer.
> l   is transparent so must be dyed before being used in the thermometer.
> m   not flammable.
> n   not poisonous in small amounts.
> o   poisonous.
> p   wets the side of the tube, so some remains on the side of the tube as the rest contracts back into the bulb – gives less accurate readings.

	Mercury	Alcohol
Opacity (how opaque something is)	1	9
accuracy	2	10
conductivity	3	11
high temperature usage	4	12
low temperature usage	5	13
cost	6	14
toxicity	7	15
flammability	8	16

5 **Processes used by skin to regulate body temperature on hot days and cold days**

Read the text and label the diagram with the following information

> a lot of blood flow close to the skin   arterioles constrict   arterioles dilate   hair erector muscles contract
> hair erector muscles relax   heat can be easily lost from the skin   heat is carried away as sweat evaporates
> heat is lost from the blood   layer of warm air trapped which keeps body warm
> less blood flow close to the skin   on a cold day   on a hot day   sweat   sweat gland (x2)

The skin has a number of techniques for keeping the body cool or warm on hot and cold days. On a hot day the hair erector muscles relax and the hairs lie flat so heat can be easily lost from the skin. Additionally, the arterioles dilate and a lot of blood flows closer to the skin. Here, heat is lost from the blood. Sweat glands produce sweat and while this evaporates on the surface of the skin, heat is carried away from the skin. On cold days, the hair erector muscles contract and the hairs stand up which traps a layer of warm air which keeps the body warm. The arterioles constrict and less blood flows close to the skin and the sweat glands do not produce sweat to evaporate on the skin and keep it cool.

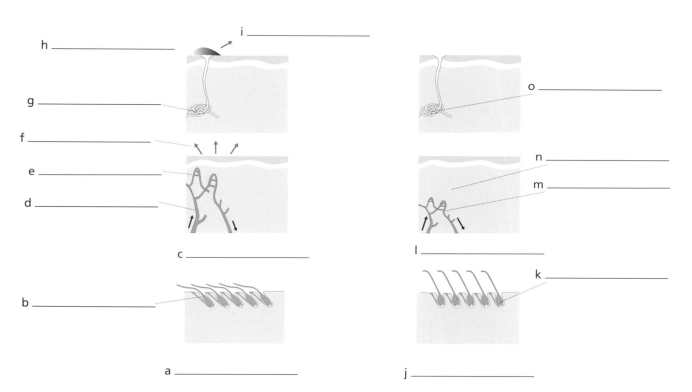

16 Coordination in humans

Translation

activate /ˈæktɪveɪt/	to make a machine or a piece of equipment start working or a process start happening. **verb [transitive]**	*The drug activates certain pathways in the brain.*
adrenaline /əˈdrenəlɪn/	a hormone that is produced in someone's body when they are frightened, excited, or angry. **noun [uncount]**	*The ride on the rollercoaster gave her an adrenaline surge.*
adrenal /əˈdriːn(ə)l/	one of two small glands above the kidneys that produce adrenaline. **noun [count]**	
axon /ˈæksɒn/	the long part of a neuron (=nerve cell) that carries the nerve impulses. **noun [count]**	
blood sugar /ˈblʌd ʃʊɡə/	sugars such as glucose that are present in healthy blood. **noun [uncount]**	*Insulin is important in regulating blood sugar.*
blow /bləʊ/	a hard hit from someone's hand or an object (also called: bump, injury). **noun [count]**	*The victim was killed by a blow to the head.*
broadening /ˈbrɔːd(ə)nɪŋ/	the process of becoming wider. **noun [uncount]**	*She noticed the broadening of his shoulders.*
central nervous system (CNS) /ˌsentrəl ˈnɜːvəs ˌsɪstəm/	the part of the nervous system that consists of the brain and the spinal cord. **noun [count]**	
cerebellum /ˌserəˈbeləm/	the back part of the brain that is responsible for balance and movement (plural: cerebella or cerebellums). **noun [count]**	*We use our cerebellum to help us ride a bicycle.*
cerebral haemorrhage /səˌriːbrəl ˈhemərɪdʒ/	an occasion when blood vessels in the brain rupture (=burst), so that blood leaks into the brain and causes damage = brain haemorrhage. **noun [count]**	
cerebrum /səˈriːbrəm/	the front part of the brain, where activities such as thinking, learning, and feeling take place. It is divided into two halves called cerebral hemispheres. **noun [count]**	
cluster /ˈklʌstə/	a small group of things that are very close to each other. **noun [count]**	*a cluster of nerve cells*
conscious /ˈkɒnʃəs/	done deliberately in a way that you can control and realize is happening. **adjective**	*A knee jerk in response to a stimulus is not a conscious movement.*
constant /ˈkɒnstənt/	continuing at the same rate, level, or amount over a particular period of time. **adjective**	*We maintain a constant temperature in the lab.*
coordinate /kəʊˈɔːdɪneɪt/	to control the movements of different parts of your body so that they work well together. **verb [transitive]**	*Children have to learn to coordinate eye and hand movements.*
coordination /kəʊˌɔːdɪˈneɪʃ(ə)n/	the ability to control the parts of your body so that they move well together. **noun [uncount]**	*Coordination is controlled by the nervous and endocrine systems.*
damage /ˈdæmɪdʒ/	physical harm. **noun [uncount]**	*a new drug to treat nerve damage*
deepening /ˈdiːp(ə)nɪŋ/	the process of becoming deeper or lower. **noun [uncount]**	*In boys, deepening of the voice occurs at puberty.*
dendrite /ˈdendraɪt/	a very short dendron. **noun [count]**	
dendron /ˈdendrɒn/	an extension of a neuron (=nerve cell) that links it to other neurons, or to a receptor (sense organ) or an effector (organ, muscle, or gland). **noun [count]**	
digestive juices /daɪˌdʒestɪv ˈdʒuːsɪz/	substances produced inside the body's digestive system that break down food. **noun [plural]**	
dorsal root /ˌdɔːsəl ˈruːt/	a structure in the spinal cord towards the back of the body (≠ ventral root). **noun [count]**	
ductless /ˈdʌktləs/	a ductless gland secretes directly into the blood, rather than into a duct (vessel). **adjective**	*Endocrine glands are ductless glands, while exocrine glands secrete into ducts such as lymph ducts.*
endocrine /ˈendəʊkraɪn/	the endocrine system is the system of glands that secrete hormones directly into the blood. **adjective**	*endocrine glands*

enlargement /ɪnˈlɑːdʒmənt/	the process of making something bigger or of growing bigger. noun [count/uncount]	*the abnormal enlargement of the lymph nodes*
excitement /ɪkˈsaɪtˌmənt/	the feeling of being excited. noun [uncount]	*The long wait only added to our excitement.*
exocrine gland /ˈeksəʊkraɪn ˌglænd/	a gland such as a sweat gland, salivary gland, or lymph gland that secretes chemicals into ducts (vessels) and not directly into the blood. noun [count]	
feedback mechanism /ˈfiːdbæk ˌmekənɪzm/	a mechanism for controlling reactions in the body where one action produces another action, which then inhibits the first action. noun [count]	
glucagon /ˈgluːkəgɒn/	a hormone produced by the pancreas which breaks down glycogen to glucose in the liver, regulating the amount of sugar in the blood. noun [uncount]	
glucose /ˈgluːkəʊz/	a simple sugar that is produced in plants through photosynthesis and in animals from the breaking down of carbohydrates in the body. It is important for providing energy to all cells. Chemical formula: $C_6H_{12}O_6$. noun [uncount]	
gonad /ˈgəʊnæd/	a sex organ in humans and other animals that makes cells that are used in producing babies or young. In men this sex organ is called a testicle, and in women it is called an ovary. noun [count]	*The gonads produce sex hormones.*
grey matter /ˈgreɪ ˌmætə/	the grey-brown tissue in the brain and spinal cord of vertebrate animals. It consists mainly of the bodies of neurons (=cells that carry messages to and from the brain). noun [uncount]	*The cerebrum contains a large amount of grey matter.*
homeostasis /ˌhəʊmiəʊˈsteɪsɪs/	the process by which a living organism or cell keeps its own state steady and continuous, despite changes in the environment around it. An example of homeostasis is the ability of warm-blooded animals such as humans to keep their body temperature at the correct level, despite the temperature changes around them. noun [uncount]	
hyperglycaemia /ˌhaɪpəglaɪˈsiːmiə/	a medical condition in which the level of sugar in someone's blood is too high. noun [uncount]	*The hypoglycaemia caused him to fall into a coma.*
hypoglycaemia /ˌhaɪpəʊglaɪˈsiːmiə/	a medical condition in which the level of sugar in someone's blood is too low. noun [uncount]	
hypothalamus /ˌhaɪpəʊˈθæləməs/	a small area on the lower part of the brain that controls the heartbeat and the temperature of the body. It also affects the pituitary gland. noun [singular]	*Special temperature sensors are found in the hypothalamus.*
impair /ˌɪmˈpeə/	to make something less good or effective by damaging it. verb [transitive]	*The disease impairs the body's ability to heal itself.*
impairment /ˌɪmˈpeəmənt/	the fact that a part of your body is unable to do something fully. noun [count/uncount]	*visual impairment*
impulse /ˈɪmpʌls/	an electrical signal that moves along a nerve fibre. noun [count]	
injection /ˌɪnˈdʒekʃ(ə)n/	a drug that is injected into the body, or the process of injecting it into the body. noun [count/uncount]	*Did the doctor give you a measles injection?*
injury /ˈɪndʒʊri/	physical harm. noun [count/uncount]	*an eye injury*
insulin /ˈɪnsjʊlɪn/	a hormone produced in the body that controls the level of sugar in the blood. People who have the disease diabetes do not produce enough insulin and have to inject artificially produced insulin. noun [uncount]	
intermediate neuron /ˌɪntəmiːdiət ˈnjʊərɒn/	a type of neuron that transmits nerve impulses between two other neurons, for example a sensory neuron and a motor neurone = relay neuron. noun [count]	
involuntary action /ɪnˈvɒləntəri ˌækʃ(ə)n/	an action that is not controlled consciously by the mind but automatically by the brain. noun [count]	*Blinking is an involuntary action.*
islet of Langerhans /ˌaɪlət əv ˈlæŋgəhænz/	one of the small clusters of endocrine cells that is found in the pancreas. noun [count]	
itch /ɪtʃ/	if your skin itches, it gives you a tickly feeling that makes you want to scratch it. verb [intransitive]	*This shirt makes my stomach itch.*
knee cap /ˈniː ˌkæp/	the bone at the front of the knee = patella. noun [count]	

long-term /ˈlɒŋtɜːm/	continuing to exist, be relevant, or have an effect for a long time in the future. **adjective**	*An infection can cause long-term damage to the nervous system.*
malfunctioning /mælˈfʌŋkʃənɪŋ/	the fact of no longer working in the right way. **noun [uncount]**	*The condition is caused by the malfunctioning of brain neurotransmitters.*
medulla oblongata /meˌdʌlə ˌɒblɒŋˈɡɑːtə/	the lowest part of the brain that is connected to the spinal cord. It controls the way the heart and lungs work. **noun [singular]**	
metabolic rate /ˌmetəbɒlɪk ˈreɪt/	the speed at which chemical processes occur in the body, especially the processes of breaking down food. **noun [singular]**	
motor neuron /ˈməʊtə ˌnjʊərɒn/	a type of neuron (nerve cell) that passes messages from the brain or spinal cord to a muscle or gland. **noun [count]**	
myelin sheath /ˌmaɪəlɪn ˈʃiːθ/	the protective layer around the axon (=long part) of a nerve cell. **noun [singular]**	
nervous system /ˈnɜːvəs ˌsɪstəm/	the system of nerves that control the body and the mind. **noun [singular]**	*The nervous system enables us to respond to our surroundings.*
neuron /ˈnjʊərɒn/	a cell that sends messages to the brain and receives messages from the brain. **noun [count]**	*Nerve cells are also called neurons.*
neurotransmitter /ˈnjʊərɒn/	a chemical substance that crosses the synapse (=space) between nerve cells, transmitting the nerve impulse from one neuron to another. **noun [count]**	
node of Ranvier /ˌnəʊd əv ˈrænvieɪ/	a gap in the myelin sheath of a nerve cell. **noun [count]**	
oestrogen /ˈiːstrədʒ(ə)n/	a hormone that makes women and other female mammals develop typical female sexual features. **noun [uncount]**	*The ovaries produce oestrogen.*
ovary /ˈəʊv(ə)ri/	one of the two organs in the body of a woman or other female animal that produce eggs and the sex hormones progesterone and oestrogen. In mammals, the eggs travel from the ovaries down the Fallopian tubes to the uterus. If the eggs are fertilized, an embryo will develop (plural: ovaries). **noun [count]**	
pancreas /ˈpæŋkriəs/	the small organ behind the stomach that produces insulin and enzymes to help with the process of digestion. **noun [count]**	
parathyroid /ˌpærəˈθaɪrɔɪd/	a gland next to the thyroid that produces a hormone that regulates calcium levels in the body. **noun [count]**	
pelvic girdle /ˌpelvɪk ˈɡɜːd(ə)l/	the bones that form the hips and pelvis. **noun [count]**	
peripheral nervous system (PNS) /pəˌrɪfərəl ˈnɜːvəs ˌsɪstəm/	the part of the nervous system that consists of the nerve fibres, as opposed to the brain and spinal cord. **noun [count]**	
pineal (gland) /ˈpɪniəl/	a pea-sized conical gland in the brain that secretes a hormone. **noun [count]**	
pituitary (gland) /pɪˈtjuːɪt(ə)ri/	the small gland at the base of the brain that produces the hormones that the body needs to control its growth and development. It is the main endocrine gland in the body, and controls many other endocrine glands. **noun [count]**	*The pituitary gland is sometimes called the master gland.*
polio /ˈpəʊliəʊ/	a serious infectious disease caused by a virus that can destroy muscles and affect the ability to control movement. It mainly affects children and young adults. Polio is short for poliomyelitis. **noun [uncount]**	
precise /prɪˈsaɪs/	exact and accurate. **adjective**	*The device gives a very precise measurement.*
rabies /ˈreɪbiːz/	a very serious viral disease that affects the central nervous system. It is passed on in the saliva of an infected animal, and so it can be caught by being bitten. **noun [uncount]**	*The dog had rabies and was foaming at the mouth.*
range /reɪndʒ/	all the numbers, ages, measurements etc that are included within particular limits, from the highest to the lowest possible. **noun [count]**	*Levels of calcium in the body have to be kept within a particular range.*
rapid /ˈræpɪd/	happening, moving, or acting quickly. **adjective**	*Rapid changes happen to the body at puberty.*
reflex action /ˌriːfleks ˈækʃ(ə)n/	a movement that one of your muscles makes without you thinking about it or being able to control it. **noun [count]**	
reflex arc /ˌriːfleks ˈɑːk/	the simple nerve pathway involved in a reflex action, involving an effector, a receptor, and the spinal cord. **noun [count]**	

regulate /ˈregjʊleɪt/	to control something so that it operates effectively or at the right level. verb [transitive]	Insulin regulates the level of sugar in the blood.
release /rɪˈliːs/	to let a substance or energy spread into the area or atmosphere around it, especially as part of a chemical reaction. verb [transitive]	Oxygen from the water is released into the atmosphere.
require /rɪˈkwaɪə/	to need someone or something. verb [transitive]	Breathing does not require conscious control.
respond /rɪˈspɒnd/	to react to something. verb [intransitive]	I called his name. but he didn't respond.
response /rɪˈspɒns/	the way that the body reacts to something, for example to bacteria. noun [count]	We're studying the body's immune response to the virus.
secrete /sɪˈkriːt/	to produce a liquid such as saliva. verb [transitive]	
scratch /skrætʃ/	to pull your nails along your skin, because you have an itch that makes you want to do this. verb [transitive/intransitive]	Will you scratch my back for me?
sensory impulse /ˌsensəri ˈɪmpʌls/	a nerve message that comes from a receptor (sense organ). noun [count]	
sensory neuron /ˌsensəri ˈnjʊərɒn/	a type of neuron (nerve cell) that passes messages from the sense organs to the brain or spinal cord. noun [count]	
stimulate /ˈstɪmjʊleɪt/	to make cells or a part of someone's body become more active. verb [transitive]	drugs to stimulate the production of hormones
stimulus /ˈstɪmjʊləs/	something that produces a reaction in a living thing (plural: stimuli /ˈstɪmjʊlaɪ/). noun [count/uncount]	The aroma of the food acted as a stimulus to his salivary glands, making his mouth water.
stretch /stretʃ/	if you stretch something, or if it stretches, it becomes longer or wider when you pull it. verb [transitive/intransitive]	
stroke /strəʊk/	illness caused by a blocked or broken blood vessel that can make someone suddenly unable to speak or move. noun [count]	Leni suffered a stroke last year, and is unable to walk.
sweat /swet/	liquid containing waste substances that forms on the skin when someone is hot. The evaporation of sweat helps to cool the body. noun [uncount]	She wiped the sweat off her forehead with a towel.
synapse /ˈsaɪnæps/	a space between nerve cells, across which nerve impulses travel using neurotransmitters. noun [count]	
target organ /ˈtɑːgɪt (ɔːgən/	an organ in the body on which a particular hormone acts. noun [count]	
testes /ˈtestiːz/	the male sex organs. noun [plural]	
testosterone /teˈstɒstərəʊn/	a sex hormone that causes men to develop the physical features that are typical of males, for example hair on the face and a deep voice. Testosterone belongs to the group of hormones called steroids. noun [uncount]	Testosterone is produced in the testes of males.
thymus /ˈθaɪməs/	an endocrine gland situated near the top of the spinal cord. noun [count]	
thyroid /ˈθaɪrɔɪd/	a gland in the neck that produces hormones that control the metabolism. noun [count]	She had an enlarged thyroid gland caused by a lack of iodine in her diet.
thyroxin /θaɪˈrɒksiːn/	the main hormone produced by the thyroid in humans and other vertebrates. It increases metabolic rate and controls growth and development. noun [uncount]	The low levels of thyroxin in her blood were making her lethargic.
transmission /trænzˈemɪʃ(ə)n/	the process of sending electronic signals such as radio or television signals, or a signal that is sent in this way. noun [count/uncount]	The transmission of nerve impulses is extremely fast.
transmit /trænzˈmɪt/	to send an electronic signal such as a radio or television signal. verb [transitive]	Nerve cells transmit nerve impulses from the brain and spinal cord to muscles and glands.
ventral root /ˌventrəl ˈruːt/	a structure in the spinal cord towards the front of the body (≠ dorsal root). noun [count]	
vertebra /ˈvɜːtəbrə/	one of the small bones that form a row down the centre of the back (plural: vertebrae /ˈvɜːtəbreɪ/). noun [count]	The spinal cord is protected by the vertebrae.
voluntary action /ˈvɒlənt(ə)ri ˌækʃ(ə)n/	an action that you choose to make and can control (≠ involuntary action). noun [count]	
white matter /ˈwaɪt ˌmætə/	the white tissue in the brain and spinal cord of vertebrate animals. It consists mainly of nerve fibres. noun [uncount]	

A   Working with words

1   Coordination word map

Fill in these words and phrases on the word map.

> brain   endocrine system   hormones   involuntary responses   peripheral nervous sytem (PNS)   thyroid

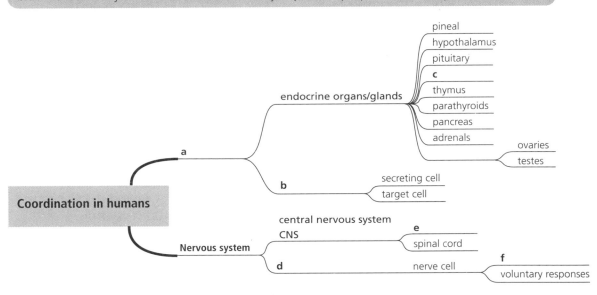

2   The adrenal gland

Read the text and complete with these words.

> adrenaline   danger   glucose   heart rate   kidney   respond   stimuli   stress

The adrenal glands are located on the top of each 1 _____. They release several hormones, one of which is 2 _____. This is designed for coping with 3 _____, excitement and 4 _____; and causes changes in the body such as increased 5 _____; increased blood supply to the brain and muscles; decreased blood supply to the skin and gut; increased 6 _____ levels in the blood. Adrenaline is often referred to, as the fight or flight hormone, since it brings about changes that causes the body to 7 _____ suddenly and quickly to certain 8 _____.

3   The pituitary gland

Read the text and complete with these words.

> endocrine glands   feedback mechanism   homeostasis   hypothalamus
> master gland   ovaries   pea-sized   target glands

The pituitary gland is a 1 _____ gland located at the base of the brain. It produces many hormones that control the functions of other 2 _____ and organs in the body, such as the 3 _____, testes and kidneys. This is why it is sometimes called the 4 _____. The levels of hormones secreted by the pituitary are partly controlled by the 5 _____, which monitors conditions in the body, and partly by the hormones that are made in the 6 _____ that the pituitary hormones stimulate. The hormones in the blood from the target glands inhibit the production of the hormone from the pituitary that stimulated them. This creates a balance in the body, called 7 _____, which keeps the internal environment of the body constant. This sort of interaction, where one action produces another action, which then inhibits the first action, is called a 8 _____. There are many examples of this in the endocrine system, such as the control of excretion of water by the kidney.

4 Neurone structures

Label the diagram with these words.

> axon (x2)   cell body (x2)   dendrite   dendron   intermediate or relay neurone
> motor neurone   myelin sheath   node of Ranvier   sensory neurone

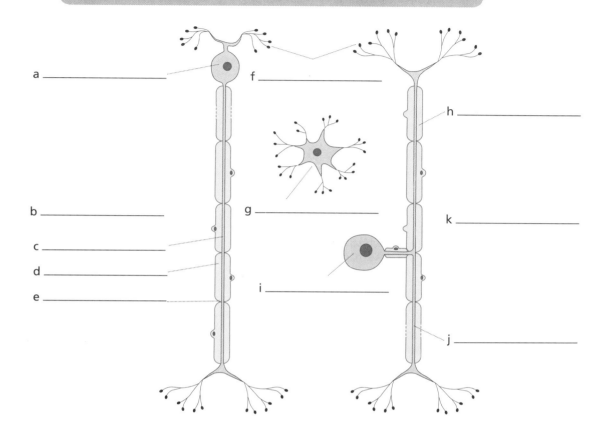

a _____

f _____

h _____

b _____

g _____

k _____

c _____

d _____

i _____

e _____

j _____

> **B   Working with sentences**

5 The endocrine system

The endocrine system is a collection of ductless glands. These glands secrete chemical messages or hormones into the bloodstream. Each hormone has a specific target organ. Here it reacts with receptor cells and stimulates the receptor organ to bring about changes. There are many endocrine glands in the human body. Have a look at the ones below and match these names with their descriptions.

> the adrenal gland   the gonads   the pancreas   the pituitary gland   the thyroid gland

1 _____ – this gland is a pea-sized gland located at the base of the brain. It produces many hormones that control the functions of other endocrine glands and organs in the body, such as the ovaries, testes and kidneys.

2 _____ – this gland is located on the top of each kidney. They release several hormones, one of which is adrenaline.

3 _____ – this gland is located in the neck and secretes the hormone thyroxin. Thyroxin increases the overall metabolic rate as well as regulates growth and development of the individual.

4 _____ – this is the name for the organs which produce male and female sex cells. The hormones that they release into the blood lead to the development of secondary characteristics at puberty.

5 _____ – this organ has exocrine cells as well as endocrine cells. The exocrine cells secrete digestive juices into a duct that leads into the small intestine. The endocrine cells are found in small clusters which are called the islets of Langerhans. These produce the hormones insulin and glucagon that are secreted into the bloodstream.

6 Coordination in humans

Match the beginnings and endings of the sentences.

Beginnings

1 The nervous system and the endocrine system control
2 The endocrine system consists of
3 Hormones are chemical messages that affect
4 Some human endocrine glands are:
5 The islets of Langerhans in the pancreas produce
6 The pituitary gland is often called the master gland because most of the hormones it produces control
7 The release of hormones by the pituitary is controlled partly by
8 The nervous system consists
9 The brain and spinal cord of the CNS and the nerves of the PNS are made up of
10 The brain is composed of three main parts:
11 The cerebrum controls
12 The medulla oblongata are responsible for
13 The tiny space between nerve cells is called
14 Messages travel through the neurones as
15 Messages pass across synapses

Endings

a a synapse.
b chemical neurotransmitters.
c coordination in humans.
d electrical impulses.
e endocrine organs (or glands) and hormones.
f involuntary movements.
g nerve cells.
h of the central nervous system (CNS) and the peripheral nervous system (PNS).
i pancreas, sex organs, adrenal glands, thyroid glands and pituitary gland.
j target organs.
k the cerebrum, cerebellum and the medulla oblongata.
l the function of the other endocrine glands.
m the hormone insulin, which regulates blood sugar levels.
n the level of the hormones that it stimulates to be released, in a feedback mechanism.
o voluntary movement.

1 ☐ 2 ☐ 3 ☐ 4 ☐ 5 ☐ 6 ☐ 7 ☐ 8 ☐ 9 ☐ 10 ☐ 11 ☐ 12 ☐ 13 ☐ 14 ☐ 15 ☐

C Working with texts

7 The structure and function of the nervous system

Read the text on the structure of the nervous system. Then place these words and phrases in the correct place in the diagram.

> brain   central nervous system (CNS)   nerve fibres   nervous system
> peripheral nervous system (PNS)   spinal cord

The nervous system responds quickly to changes (stimuli). It receives information from the environment, and passes it through the body to the point where the body can make sense of the information and respond to it. The nervous system has two main parts: the central nervous system (CNS) and the peripheral nervous system (PNS). The CNS is the main control centre in the human body and it consists of the brain and the spinal cord. The PNS is an extensive network of nerves extending from the CNS throughout the body.

The nervous system links receptors with effectors. Receptors, such as the sense organs, receive information from the environment. They respond to a change in the surrounding environment, which is called a stimulus, by sending a message through the peripheral nervous system to the central nervous system. In the CNS, a decision is made about how to respond and a message is sent through the peripheral nervous system to an effector, such as a muscle. The action that is made is called the response or action. For example, when you see a ball heading towards you, the eye is the receptor and sends a message from the eye to the brain. Then, the brain decides that the best way to respond is to kick the ball. Lastly, the brains sends messages to the leg and foot muscles to prepare to kick the ball.

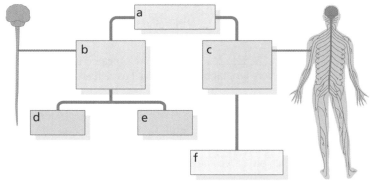

8 Voluntary actions

Read the text and label the diagram with these sentences.

A decision can be made here about whether or not to turn.
If the decision is to turn and look, a response is sent to motor neurones.
Motor neurones transmit response message to the neck muscles, known as the 'effectors'.
Neck muscles are activated causing the head to turn.
Receptors in the skin sense stimulus.
Sensory neurones transmit the stimulus message.
The message is interpreted in the brain.
The shoulder is tapped.

An example of a voluntary movement is where someone responds to a tap on the shoulder by turning their head in the direction where the touch was applied. When the shoulder is tapped, receptors in the skin respond to the touch stimulus by sending a message along a nerve to the spinal cord and brain. At this point a decision can be made about whether to turn and see what caused the stimulus or not to turn because there is something more important to look at. If the decision is to turn and look, an impulse is sent from the brain through a nerve to the muscles in the neck, which are the effectors. This makes the muscles move to turn the head in the direction of the tap.

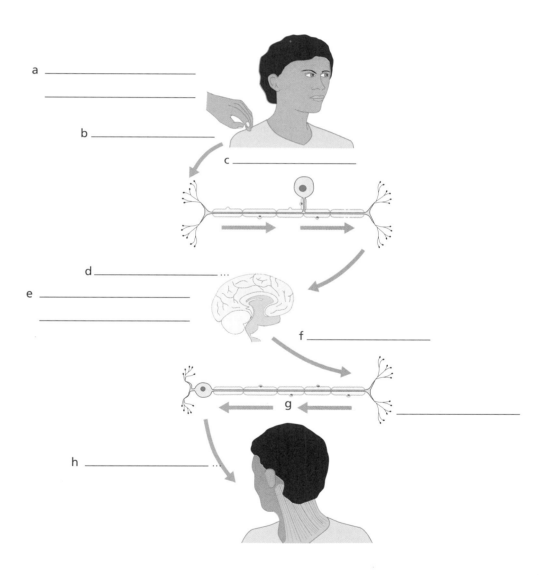

a _____

_____

b _____

c _____

d _____ ...

e _____

_____

f _____

g _____

_____

h _____ ...

17 Energy sources and pollution

Translation

absorb /əbˈzɔːb/	to take in a gas, liquid or other substance. **verb [transitive]**	*The timber expands as it absorbs moisture from the atmosphere.*
abundant supply /əˌbʌndənt səˈplaɪ/	large quantities of something, at least as much as is needed. **noun [count]**	*The area has an abundant supply of natural resources.*
acid rain /ˈæsɪd ˌreɪn/	rain that contains a high level of acid that can damage the environment. The acid forms when harmful gases from industry and vehicles mix with water in the atmosphere. **noun [uncount]**	*The trees had been killed by acid rain.*
acidification /æˌsɪdɪfɪˈkeɪʃ(ə)n/	the process of becoming an acid or starting to contain more acid. **noun [uncount]**	*the acidification of the soil*
aerosol /ˈeərəsɒl/	a container in which a liquid such as paint or perfume is kept under high pressure so that it can be sprayed. **noun [count]**	
air pollution /ˈeə pəˌluːʃ(ə)n/	pollution (damage caused by chemicals or other substances) that affects the air. **noun [uncount]**	*Motor traffic is a major cause of air pollution in cities.*
alternative energy /ɔːlˌtɜːnətɪv ˈenədʒi/	non-traditional sources of energy such as wind, wave and solar power. **noun [uncount]**	*Electricity companies were criticized for failing to look into alternative energy.*
animal excreta /ˌænɪməl ɪkˈskriːtə/	waste products excreted (removed from the body) by animals. **noun [uncount]**	
arsenic /ˈɑːs(ə)nɪk/	a poisonous grey solid element that is a metalloid. It is used to make alloys. Chemical symbol: As. **noun [uncount]**	*She was accused of murdering her husband by putting arsenic in his food.*
aviation fuel /eɪviˈeɪʃ(ə)n ˌfjuəl/	fuel used by aircraft. **noun [uncount]**	*There are concerns about pollution caused by aviation fuel.*
bioaccumulation /ˌbaɪəʊəˌkjuːmjʊˈleɪʃ(ə)n/	the process of chemicals or harmful substances becoming more concentrated in the bodies of living things. **noun [uncount]**	
biodegradable /ˌbaɪəʊdɪˈɡreɪdəb(ə)l/	decaying naturally in a way that is not harmful to the environment. **adjective**	*The food packaging was biodegradable.*
biomagnification /ˌbaɪəʊmæɡnɪfɪˈkeɪʃ(ə)n/	the process by which chemicals or harmful substances become more concentrated in the bodies of living things as they move up the food chain. **noun [uncount]**	
biomass /ˈbaɪəʊˌmæs/	**1** all the living things found in a particular area. **noun [uncount]** **2** plant and animal substances used for fuel. Biomass fuels produce less carbon dioxide than fossil fuels such as coal and oil. **noun [uncount]**	
biosphere /ˈbaɪəʊˌsfɪə/	the parts of the Earth's surface and atmosphere where living things can exist. **noun [singular]**	
bitumen /ˈbɪtʃʊmɪn/	a black sticky substance that is used for making the surfaces of roads, and for covering roofs (= tar). **noun [uncount]**	
blackening /ˈblækənɪŋ/	the process of becoming black, or making something black. **noun [uncount]**	*Soot causes blackening of surfaces.*
boiling point /ˈbɔɪlɪŋ ˌpɔɪnt/	the temperature at which a liquid boils. **noun [count/uncount]**	*The boiling point of water is 100°C.*
burning /ˈbɜːnɪŋ/	the process of using fuel to produce heat or energy. **noun [uncount]**	*Lead compounds are produced from the burning of gasoline containing lead.*
butane /ˈbjuːteɪn/	a type of gas in liquid form that is used as a fuel. **noun [uncount]**	
cadmium /ˈkædmiəm/	a blue-white chemical element that is a metal. It is used in electronics, in making batteries, in making fillings for teeth and for electroplating. Chemical symbol: Cd. **noun [uncount]**	
carbon dioxide /ˌkɑːbən daɪˈɒksaɪd/	the gas that is produced when humans and other animals breathe out and when fossil fuels are burned. It is used by plants in the process of photosynthesis. Carbon dioxide is a greenhouse gas. Chemical formula: CO_2. **noun [uncount]**	

carbon monoxide the poisonous gas that is produced by the engines of vehicles. /ˌkɑːbən mɒˈnɒksaɪd/ Chemical formula: CO. noun [uncount]

They were killed by carbon monoxide fumes from the faulty gas heater.

catalyst /ˈkætəˌlɪst/
a substance that causes a chemical reaction to happen more quickly but is not affected itself. An enzyme is a type of catalyst. noun [count]

CFC /ˌsiː ef ˈsiː/
chlorofluorocarbon: a gas used in refrigerators and in some aerosols. CFCs can damage the ozone layer of the Earth's atmosphere. noun [count]

chemical energy /ˌkemɪk(ə)l ˈenədʒi/
energy in the form in which it is stored in fuels, that can be released as other forms of energy (such as heat or light) when the fuel is burned. noun [uncount]

climate change /ˈklaɪmɪt ˌtʃeɪndʒ/
important and possibly harmful changes that some scientists believe are taking place in the world's weather because of increased pollution in the atmosphere. This pollution is thought to be the cause of the greenhouse effect, which is responsible for global warming and a rise in sea levels. noun [uncount]

combustion /kəmˈbʌstʃ(ə)n/
the chemical reaction in which oxygen combines with another substance, producing energy such as heat or light. noun [uncount]

The release of energy from food and coal are examples of combustion.

commercial use /kəˈmɜːʃ(ə)l ˌjuːs/
use in business. noun [uncount]

The new buildings are for commercial use.

complete combustion /kəmˌpliːt kəmˈbʌstʃ(ə)n/
burning that occurs when there is an abundant supply of oxygen, which does not give out much light and produces carbon dioxide but no carbon monoxide or soot. noun [uncount]

Complete combustion takes place in the burners of a gas stove.

compound /ˈkɒmpaʊnd/
a chemical substance that consists of two or more elements that together form a molecule. Each different compound has a fixed ratio of elements, for example the water compound (H_2O) always consists of two hydrogen atoms and one oxygen atom. noun [count]

condense /kənˈdens/
if gas or steam condenses, or if something or someone condenses it, it changes into a liquid, usually when it becomes cooler. verb [transitive/intransitive]

The steam condensed on the cold window, causing it to mist up.

convection current /kənˈvekʃ(ə)n ˌkʌrənt/
a constant movement of warm particles upwards and cooler particles downwards. noun [count]

The air in an oven circulates by convection currents.

convert into /kənˈvɜːt ˌɪntu/
to change something from one form to another. phrasal verb

Solar cells convert the Sun's energy into electricity.

coolant /ˈkuːlənt/
a liquid used for preventing machines from getting too hot. noun [count/uncount]

coral reef /ˌkɒrəl ˈriːf/
a hard natural structure under the sea that is formed from coral. Coral reefs are an important habitat for many types of fish and other forms of sea life. noun [count]

Water pollution in the sea is damaging the coral reefs.

crude oil /ˌkruːd ˈɔɪl/
oil in its natural state, before it has been refined for use. noun [uncount]

The tanker was carrying a shipment of crude oil.

cylinder /ˈsɪlɪndə/
a metal container for gas or liquid. noun [count]

a cylinder of natural gas

decay /dɪˈkeɪ/
to be gradually broken down by bacteria or fungi. verb [intransitive]

As dead plants decay, they release mineral salts into the soil.

deforestation /diːˌfɒrɪˈsteɪʃ(ə)n/
the process of cutting down and removing trees, especially from large areas of land. Deforestation is bad for the environment, as there are fewer trees to take in carbon dioxide and this can lead to an increase in global warming. It also involves the destruction of habitats and can cause soil erosion. noun [uncount]

The demand for more land for building has caused widespread deforestation.

deplete /dɪˈpliːt/
to reduce the amount of something or the number of things. verb [transitive]

We are depleting the world's natural resources.

destruction /dɪsˈtrʌkʃ(ə)n/
damage that is so severe that something cannot exist as it was before. noun [uncount]

the destruction of the rainforest

detergent /dɪˈtɜːdʒənt/
a liquid or powder that is used for washing clothes or dishes. noun [count/uncount]

diesel /ˈdiːz(ə)l/
heavy oil that is used as fuel instead of petrol in some engines. noun [uncount]

The truck runs on diesel.

digester /daɪˈdʒestə/
a tank in which organic matter is left to decay anaerobically (without oxygen) so that a gas is produced that can be used as fuel. noun [count]

Useful energy can be released from biomass in a digester.

dioxin /ˈdaɪˈɒksɪn/	a poisonous chemical produced during the process of making pesticides (chemicals for killing plants). **noun [count]**	
domestic use /dəˈmestɪk ˌjuːs/	use inside the home. **noun [uncount]**	*heating appliances for domestic use*
drilling /ˈdrɪlɪŋ/	the action of making a hole using a drill, in order to extract something such as oil or gas from under the Earth's surface. **noun [uncount]**	*The company is involved in drilling for petroleum.*
emission /ɪˈmɪʃ(ə)n/	a substance, especially a gas, that is released into the air. **noun [count]**	*a proposal to reduce carbon dioxide emissions*
energy /ˈenədʒi/	the ability to do work and to make things work. Electricity, heat and light are all forms of energy. Energy can change from one form to another, for example light can turn into heat. **noun [uncount]**	*Switching off lights is a good way to save energy.*
energy efficient /ˈenədʒi ɪˌfɪʃ(ə)nt/	using less energy to achieve the same result. **adjective**	*Energy-saving light bulbs are more energy efficient than standard ones.*
enhanced /ɪnˈhɑːnst/	made better or more powerful. **adjective**	*The image can be digitally enhanced to make it clearer.*
ethane /ˈiːθeɪn/	a gas that has no colour and no smell and burns very easily. It is obtained from petroleum and natural gas and is used as a fuel. **noun [uncount]**	
eutrophication /juːtrəʊfɪˈkeɪʃ(ə)n/	excess of nutrients in a lake or other area of water, usually caused by pollution from artificial fertilizers, leading to the dense growth of plants in the water. **noun [uncount]**	*In fresh water, phosphorus accelerates eutrophication.*
evaporate /ɪˈvæpəˌreɪt/	if a liquid evaporates, it slowly changes into a vapour at a temperature below its boiling point. **verb [intransitive]**	
exhaust fumes /ɪgˈzɔːst ˌfjuːmz/	waste gases released into the air from vehicle engines. **noun [plural]**	*Exhaust fumes can trigger asthma and other breathing difficulties.*
extraction /ɪkˈstrækʃ(ə)n/	the process of taking something from somewhere. **noun [count/uncount]**	*the extraction of crude oil from under the ground*
ferment /fəˈment/	if organic molecules ferment, or if they are fermented, microorganisms cause them to separate into simpler substances and to produce heat and gases when doing this. For example sugar is changed to alcohol by the action of yeast. **verb [transitive/intransitive]**	*Compost heaps get warm as the rotting matter in them ferments.*
fertile /ˈfɜːtaɪl/	**1** fertile land is able to produce good crops or plants. **adjective** **2** a fertile person, animal, or plant is able to produce babies, young animals, or new plants (≠ infertile). **adjective**	
fertilizer /ˈfɜːtəˌlaɪzə/	a substance that is added to soil in order to help plants to grow. **noun [count/uncount]**	*We do not use any artificial fertilizers.*
finite /ˈfaɪnaɪt/	existing only in limited numbers or amounts. **adjective**	*Fossil fuel resources are finite.*
fossil fuel /ˈfɒs(ə)l ˌfjʊəl/	a fuel such as coal, oil, or natural gas made from decayed material from organisms that lived many millions of years ago. **noun [count/uncount]**	
fractional distillation /ˌfrækʃ(ə)n(ə)l ˌdɪstɪˈleɪʃ(ə)n/	the process of using a volatile mixture to separate substances that have different boiling points, by first heating the mixture and then condensing and collecting the separated parts as they turn to liquids. **noun [uncount]**	*Crude oil is refined by fractional distillation.*
fumes /ˈfjuːmz/	waste gases released into the air, especially harmful ones. **noun [plural]**	*traffic fumes*
gasohol /ˈgæsəˌhɒl/	a fuel made from a mixture of ethanol (=alcohol) and petrol. **noun [uncount]**	
gasoline /ˈgæsəˌliːn/	petrol. **noun [count/uncount]**	
geothermal /ˌdʒiːəʊˈθɜːm(ə)l/	relating to the heat at the centre of the Earth. **adjective**	*geothermal energy*
geothermal energy /ˌdʒiːəʊˈθɜːm(ə)l ˈenədʒi/	energy in the form of heat obtained from hot moving groundwater. It is found in areas of volcanic activity such as New Zealand. **noun [uncount]**	*Geothermal energy can be obtained from deep underground.*
give off /ˌgɪv ˈɒf/	to produce something such as heat or a smell (= emit). **phrasal verb**	*When they die, plants give off gases.*
global warming /ˌgləʊb(ə)l ˈwɔːmɪŋ/	the increase in the temperature of the Earth that is believed to be caused by increasing amounts of carbon dioxide in the atmosphere. **noun [uncount]**	

grease
/'gri:s/
a thick substance similar to oil, used on machine parts for making them work smoothly. noun [uncount]

greenhouse effect
/'gri:nhaʊs ɪˌfekt/
the process by which the Earth's surface and lower atmosphere is getting warmer, which is believed to be the result of pollution by gases such as carbon dioxide. The heat from the sun cannot escape, leading to a general increase in the Earth's temperature called global warming. noun [singular]

gush
/gʌʃ/
if a liquid gushes, it flows quickly and in large quantities. verb [intransitive]

Oil gushed out of the well.

habitat
/'hæbɪˌtæt/
the type of place that a particular organism usually lives in, for example a desert, forest, or lake. noun [count]

The rainforest is the natural habitat for thousands of species.

halogen lamp
/'hælədʒən ˌlæmp/
a lamp that uses a bulb containing halogen gas. noun [count]

harness
/'hɑ:nɪs/
to get control of something in order to use it for a particular purpose. verb [transitive]

Humans first harnessed the power of electricity over 200 years ago.

heavy metals
/ˌhevi 'met(ə)lz/
a metal that has a high density. noun [uncount]

Heavy metals can cause pollution.

high tide
/ˌhaɪ 'taɪd/
the time when the sea reaches its highest level. noun [count/uncount]

hot spring
/ˌhɒt 'sprɪŋ/
a place where hot water comes up out of the ground and forms a pool. noun [count]

Thermal energy can be obtained from hot springs.

hunting
/'hʌntɪŋ/
the activity of catching and killing animals. noun [uncount]

hydrocarbon
/ˌhaɪdrəʊˈkɑːbən/
a chemical substance that contains only hydrogen and carbon, for example methane. Many fuels are hydrocarbons. noun [count]

hydropower
/ˌhaɪdrəʊˈpaʊə/
electricity produced from the energy in falling water (= hydroelectricity). noun [uncount]

incomplete combustion
/ˌɪnkəmpliːt kəmˈbʌstʃ(ə)n/
burning that occurs when there is a limited supply of oxygen, which produces soot, carbon monoxide and carbon dioxide, as well as heat and light. noun [uncount]

Incomplete combustion takes place when a candle burns.

industrial waste
/ɪnˌdʌstrɪəl 'weɪst/
waste products such as chemicals produced by industrial processes. noun [uncount]

the safe disposal of industrial waste

insulation
/ˌɪnsjʊˈleɪʃ(ə)n/
1 material that is used for preventing heat, cold, sound, or electricity from passing through something. noun [uncount]
2 protection from heat, cold, sound, or electricity. noun [uncount]

kerosene
/'kerəˌsiːn/
a clear oil with a strong smell that is obtained from petroleum and is used as fuel (also called: paraffin). noun [uncount]

The room was illuminated by a kerosene lamp.

landfill
/'læn(d)ˌfɪl/
a large hole in the ground where rubbish from people's homes or from industry is buried. noun [count]

lead
/led/
a soft heavy grey metal element whose compounds can be poisonous. It is used to make containers that protect against harmful radiation. It is also a bad conductor of electricity that does not corrode easily. Chemical symbol: Pb. noun [uncount]

Vehicle exhaust fumes contain harmful lead compounds.

lead-free
/ˌledˈfriː/
lead-free petrol and paints do not contain lead. adjective

liquefaction
/ˌlɪkwəˈfækʃ(ə)n/
the process of becoming a liquid or making something become a liquid. noun [uncount]

The natural gas is cooled until liquefaction takes place, then transported.

liquefied
/'lɪkwɪˌfaɪd/
changed into liquid form. adjective

liquefied petroleum gas

long lasting
/'lɒŋ ˌlɑːstɪŋ/
continuing for a long time. adjective

long-lasting damage

low-energy
/ˌɛləʊˈenədʒi/
using relatively little energy. adjective

a low-energy lightbulb

LPG
/ˌel piː 'dʒiː/
liquefied petroleum gas: a fuel that is a mixture of hydrocarbon gases in liquid form. noun [uncount]

LPG is much less polluting than petrol.

lubricate
/'lu:brɪˌkeɪt/
to put oil on the parts of a machine in order to make them move more smoothly. verb [transitive]

luminous flame
/ˌluːmɪnəs 'fleɪm/
a flame that occurs when there is a limited supply of oxygen, that gives out heat and light and produces soot. noun [count]

A luminous flame is bright yellow and unsteady.

melting ice-cap
/ˌmeltɪŋ 'aɪsˌkæp/
one of the large areas of ice that covers the land and sea around the North and South Poles, that are now melting. This is thought to be the result of global warming. noun [count]

17 ENERGY SOURCES & POLLUTION

mercury /ˈmɜːkjʊri/	a very heavy silver metal element that is liquid at room temperature. It is used in thermometers and for making pesticides. Chemical symbol: Hg. noun [uncount]	*She died from mercury poisoning caused by high levels of mercury in the fish she had eaten.*
methane /ˈmiːθeɪn/	a natural gas with no colour or smell that is used as a fuel. Chemical formula: CH_4. noun [uncount]	*Biogas contains methane.*
naphtha /ˈnæfθə/	one of the substances produced when crude oil is refined, that is used in making solvents and also in gasoline. noun [uncount]	
natural gas /ˌnætʃ(ə)rəl ˈgæs/	a gas consisting mainly of methane and other hydrocarbon gases that is found underground and is used for heating and cooking. noun [uncount]	
nitric acid /ˌnaɪtrɪk ˈæsɪd/	a very corrosive chemical that is used in industry, and for making bombs and in rocket fuels. noun [uncount]	
nitrogen dioxide /ˌnaɪtrədʒ(ə)n daɪˈɒksaɪd/	a very poisonous brown gas often present in smog and exhaust from vehicles. Chemical formula: NO_2. noun [uncount]	*Nitrogen dioxide is an example of an air pollutant.*
non-luminous flame /nɒnˌluːmɪnəs ˈfleɪm/	a flame that occurs when there is an abundant supply of oxygen, that gives out heat but not much light. noun [count]	*A non-luminous flame is blue and steady.*
non-renewable /ˌnɒnrɪˈnjuːəb(ə)l/	non-renewable energy, fuel, or other raw materials exist in limited amounts only and cannot be replaced once they have been used. Oil is an example of a non-renewable resource. adjective	
oil pollution /ˈɔɪl pəˌluːʃ(ə)n/	pollution (damage to the environment) caused by oil. noun [uncount]	*the problem of marine oil pollution*
oil rig /ˈɔɪlˌrɪg/	a large structure with equipment on it for getting oil out from underground or under the sea. noun [count]	*He used to work on an oil rig.*
oil slick /ˈɔɪl ˌslɪk/	a layer of oil on the surface of a large area of water, for example after a ship has sunk. noun [count]	*The oil slick spread out from the wreaked oil tanker.*
oil spill /ˈɔɪl ˌspɪl/	an occasion when oil is accidentally or deliberately released into the environment, for example from a tanker. noun [count]	*The oil spill has affected hundreds of miles of coastline.*
oil well /ˈɔɪl ˌwel/	a deep narrow hole that is dug in order to obtain oil. noun [count]	*There was a fire at the oil well.*
OTEC /ˌəʊ tiː iː ˈsiː/	Ocean Thermal Energy Conversion: a way of collecting and using solar energy absorbed by the sea. noun [uncount]	
outflow /ˈaʊtˌfləʊ/	a flow of water, gas, waste etc out of a pipe. noun [count]	*The beach had been contaminated by a sewage outflow.*
over-fishing /ˌəʊvəˈfɪʃɪŋ/	fishing that damages a river or an area of sea because too many fish are caught. noun [uncount]	
ozone depletion /ˈəʊzəʊn dɪˌpliːʃ(ə)n/	a reduction in the amount of ozone gas in the Earth's atmosphere. noun [uncount]	*This excessive radiation is thought to be the result of ozone depletion.*
ozone layer /ˈəʊzəʊn ˌleɪə/	a layer of ozone gas in the Earth's atmosphere that protects the Earth from some of the harmful effects of the Sun. noun [singular]	*Holes in the ozone layer allow harmful rays from the Sun to reach the Earth.*
pesticide /ˈpestɪˌsaɪd/	a chemical used for killing insects that damage crops. noun [count/uncount]	*Fruit must always be washed before eating it to remove any traces of pesticides.*
petroleum /pəˈtrəʊˌliəm/	a mixture of oils that is found under the ground or under the bottom of the sea. It is a mixture of hydrocarbons and is used for making petrol and other chemical products. noun [uncount]	
phenol /ˈfiːnɒl/	a chemical made from coal, used for killing bacteria. noun [count]	
pollutant /pəˈluːt(ə)nt/	a substance that is harmful to the environment, especially a chemical. Large amounts of noise, heat, etc can also be pollutants. noun [count]	
polystyrene /ˌpɒlɪˈstaɪriːn/	a very light artificial substance, used especially for making containers or as a protective material in packaging. noun [uncount]	
porous /ˈpɔːrəs/	with a lot of very small holes that air and water can pass through. adjective	*Water is found in the porous rock layer.*
power-station /ˈpaʊə ˌsteɪʃ(ə)n/	a large building that contains machines that produce power, especially electricity. noun [count]	
propane /ˈprəʊˌpeɪn/	a hydrocarbon gas obtained from natural gas or petroleum and used as a fuel for cooking and heating. noun [uncount]	*The gas cooker was attached to a cylinder of propane.*
refining /rɪˈfaɪnɪŋ/	the process of separating out unwanted substances from something such as oil or sugar in its crude form. noun [uncount]	

refuse /ˈrefjuːs/	things that you throw away (= waste). **noun [uncount]**	
renewable /rɪˈnjuːəbl/	renewable energy and natural materials replace themselves by natural processes, so that they are never completely used up. **adjective**	*Sunlight is a renewable resource.*
sea-going tanker /ˌsiːɡəʊɪŋ ˈtæŋkə/	a large ship that transports oil or petrol across the sea. **noun [count]**	
sewage /ˈsuːɪdʒ/	waste from people's bodies that is removed from houses and other buildings by a system of large underground pipes called sewers. **noun [uncount]**	*Raw sewage released into the sea can cause pollution.*
silicon /ˈsɪlɪkən/	a metalloid element that is found in sand, clay and other minerals. It is used especially for making computer chips. Chemical symbol: Si.	
sluice /sluːs/	a passage that water flows along, with a gate that can be closed to control the flow. **noun [count]**	
smog /smɒɡ/	polluted air that forms a cloud close to the ground. **noun [uncount]**	
soil erosion /ˈsɔɪl ɪˌrəʊʒ(ə)n/	the process by which soil is gradually removed by the rain, wind, or sea. It is sometimes made worse by farming practices such as cutting down trees, leaving the ground without any plant cover, or using heavy vehicles on slopes. **noun [uncount]**	
solar /ˈsəʊlə/	relating to the Sun, or coming from the Sun. **adjective**	*solar energy*
soot /sʊt/	a dirty black powder that is produced when you burn something such as coal. **noun [uncount]**	
sterile /ˈsteraɪl/	completely clean, with no bacteria. **adjective**	
sticky /ˈstɪki/	made of or covered with a substance that sticks to other things. **adjective**	*Bitumen is a sticky black substance used in road surfaces.*
sulphur dioxide /ˌsʌlfə daɪˈɒksaɪd/	a poisonous gas with a strong smell. It is used for preserving things. **noun [uncount]**	
sulphuric acid /sʌlˌfjʊərɪk ˈæsɪd/	a strong acid that has no colour and can harm flesh. It is used in batteries, fertilizers, and detergents, and in many other compounds. Chemical formula: H_2SO_4. **noun [uncount]**	
thermal pollution /ˌθɜːm(ə)l pəˈluːʃ(ə)n/	pollution (damage to the environment) caused by heat being released into streams, lakes, or other areas of water. **noun [uncount]**	
thermo-cracking /ˈθɜːməʊˌkrækɪŋ/	a process in which large hydrocarbon molecules are broken down into smaller, more useful ones by heating at a high temperature without air. **noun [uncount]**	
tidal system /ˈtaɪd(ə)l ˌsɪstəm/	the regular movement of the sea towards and away from the land. **noun [uncount]**	*The tidal system can be utilised to provide energy from moving water.*
toxic /ˈtɒkˌsɪk/	poisonous, and therefore harmful to humans and other animals, or to the environment. **adjective**	*He choked on the toxic gas fumes.*
ultraviolet radiation (UV) /ˌʌltrəˈvaɪələt reɪdiˈeɪʃ(ə)n/	a type of radiation coming mostly from the sun, that has waves with shorter wave-lengths than light that humans can see. **adjective**	*Over-exposure to ultraviolet radiation can cause sunburn and skin cancer.*
unburnt gas /ˌʌnbɜːnt (ɡæs/	gas that is not burning during a combustion process, for example the gas in the middle of a candle flame. **noun [uncount]**	
viscous /ˈvɪskəs/	viscous liquid is thick and sticky. **adjective**	
wave power /ˈweɪv ˌpaʊə/	power produced by the movement of waves in the ocean. **noun [uncount]**	
wax /wæks/	a soft, natural or artificial substance that becomes liquid when heated, used for making candles and models, for making wooden furniture shine, and for protecting objects from water. **noun [uncount]**	
wind /wɪnd/	a natural current of air that moves fast enough for you to feel it. **noun [count/uncount]**	*ways of harnessing the wind's energy*

A   Working with words

1   Energy sources and pollution word map

Write these words in the correct place on the word map.

> alternative energy sources   biomass   crude oil   flames   fossil fuels   hydropower

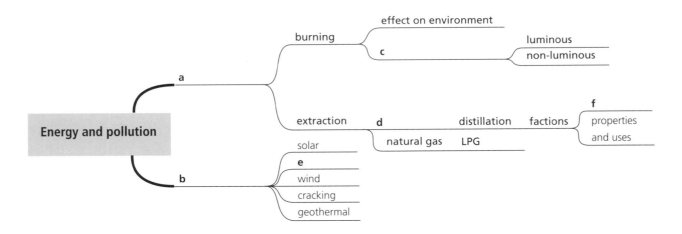

2   Energy from plants and animals

Fill in the gaps in the sentences with these words.

> biomass   cylinders   decay   digester   ethanol   ferment   fertilizer   methane   petrol   wood

1   _____ energy comes from plant material and animal excreta.

2   Plant material, such as _____, has been burnt for thousands of years to obtain heat directly.

3   However, we now also _____ plant material to obtain alcohol which can be used to power vehicles.

4   In most cases the _____ that is made is mixed with petrol to form a mixture called gasohol.

5   This is used as an alternative to _____.

6   Biogas is a gas produced from the anaerobic _____ of organic matter, vegetable refuse or animal excreta.

7   Biogas mainly contains the hydrocarbon gas _____ or natural gas.

8   Like natural gas, biogas can be used directly or stored in _____ for later use.

9   After the biogas is formed the remains are removed from the tank, called the _____.

10 This is used as a _____ because it is rich in nitrogen, phosphorus and potassium, which are essential for proper plant growth.

3 Energy from the ground

Underline the correct word in each sentence.

1 Heat (runs / swims / flows) outwards from the Earth's core.

2 It (makes / turns / forces) rock deep below the Earth's surface hot.

3 This heat energy is called geothermal energy and can be (collected / harnessed / burnt) and used directly.

4 In colder countries pipes are (hidden / used / buried) about 15 m underground, where the temperature is almost (constant / continuous / irregular).

5 Liquid circulating through the pipes becomes (colder / warmer / boiling).

6 It can be (made / used / stored) to heat the buildings above.

7 Below the surface of the Earth water can be (established / found / lost) at temperatures as high as 400°C.

8 This hot water is usually (flown / shipped / brought) to the surface as steam, which is used to power turbines in order to (deliver / generate / burn) electricity. Hot springs are a result of geothermal energy.

B Working with sentences

4 Refining crude oil

Put these sentences in the correct order. Use the diagram to help you.

a Gasoline changes next and is used in fuels for cars.
b Bitumen is heaviest in hydrocarbons and stays at the bottom.
c Fuel oils for ships and heating in factories change next, followed by lubricating oils for engines and machines.
d The larger, heavier ones such as greases and waxes change first.
e The lightest gases, such as butane and propane, come off at the top of the column.
f Kerosene fuel for aircraft and stoves changes next and then comes naphtha, used for making chemicals such as solvents.
g Diesel fuel for large vehicles and trains has a boiling point between 260–320°C.

1 ☐ 2 ☐ 3 ☐ 4 ☐ 5 ☐ 6 ☐ 7 ☐

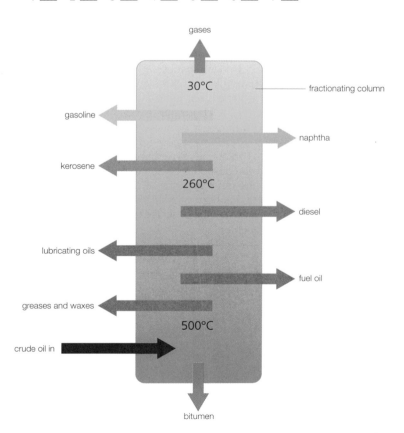

5   The extraction of crude oil and natural gas

Read the text and label the diagram.

Crude oil needs to be extracted from deep below the ground by drilling wells and using an oil rig to pump it to the surface. The oil is not located everywhere under the Earth's surface. Usually geologists find it by using explosives underground where they suspect that oil may be present. This illustration shows an oil rig at sea. Geologists use measurements of reflected sound waves from the explosions to help them discover whether oil is present or not. Then they do a test drill breaking through a cap of solid rock. The layer above the oil is a layer of soft rock (chalk or sandstone) and oil. The layer below is porous rock containing salt water. If oil is located, it is pumped to the surface. An oil storage buoy is placed above the location of the drill. If there is a lot of natural gas trapped in a pocket along with the crude oil, a 'gusher-type' well develops where the oil gushes to the surface requiring very little pumping. Natural gas is commonly used in houses all over the world. Oil tankers are used to transport the oil.

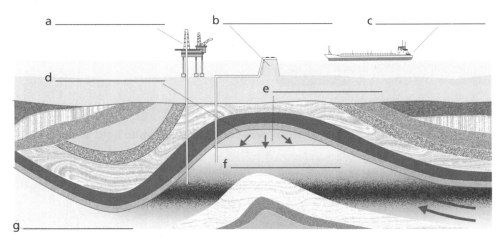

6   Luminous flames and non-luminous flames

Read the text and sort the different characteristics of luminous and non-luminous flames into the correct columns.

A luminous flame occurs when there is a limited supply of oxygen during burning. This results in incomplete combustion, which forms soot, carbon monoxide, as well as carbon dioxide that is the main gas formed. The soot is pure carbon, and causes the blackening of lampshades or the bottom of pans. Carbon monoxide is a toxic gas. It is dangerous because it bonds with haemoglobin in the blood, preventing it from transporting oxygen to the cells in the body. If carbon monoxide poisoning is not treated immediately, it will result in death. A luminous flame is a large, bright yellow flame, which generally burns unsteadily. Also, as the name suggests, the luminous flame gives out light. This is because the tiny particles of carbon soot glow when they get very hot. These flames are common in a burning candle, a gas lamp, or a Bunsen burner when the air hole is closed.

Non-luminous flames occur when there is an abundant supply of oxygen, which results in complete combustion. The main product of complete combustion is carbon dioxide. No carbon monoxide or soot is formed. The non-luminous flame does not give out much light since it contains no carbon which can get hot. These flames have a characteristic blue colour and burn steadily. They give out a roaring sound and so are also known as 'roaring' flames. Non-luminous flames can be observed when the burners of a gas stove are lit, or when the air hole of a lit Bunsen burner is open.

Luminous flame	Non-luminous (roaring) flame

18 Aquatic and terrestrial environments

absorb /əbˈzɔːb/	**1** to absorb liquid into a living cell through its cell membranes, for example by osmosis. verb [transitive] **2** to take in nutrients through the walls of the intestines into the blood. verb [transitive]	*Root hairs absorb water containing plant nutrients.* *Special lymph cells in the small intestine absorb fats.*
acidity /əˈsɪdəti/	the amount of acid in a substance, often measured in pH. noun [uncount]	*The acidity of the water in a lake can affect the organisms living in it.*
agricultural /ˌægrɪˈkʌltʃərəl/	relating to agriculture. adjective	*agricultural methods*
agriculture /ˈægrɪˌkʌltʃə/	the work, business, or study of farming. noun [uncount]	*She studied agriculture at college.*
algae /ˈældʒiː, ˈælgiː/	simple plants that have no roots, stems, or leaves and that usually grow in water. Most types of algae are small and green but some are large and brown, like some types of seaweed. Algae are an important part of food chains as many fish, insects, larvae etc feed on them. (singular alga /ˈælgə/). noun [plural]	
algal blooming /ˌælg(ə)l ˈbluːmɪŋ/	rapid growth of algae (simple plants that grow in water). noun [uncount]	
alkali /ˈælkəˌlaɪ/	a base that dissolves in water and has a pH of more than 7. Alkalis turn litmus paper blue. A common alkali used for cleaning is ammonium hydroxide. noun [count/uncount]	
ammonium salt /əˈməʊniəm ˌsɒlt/	a salt (chemical compound) formed by the reaction of ammonia with a base. noun [count]	
aquatic /əˈkwætɪk/	living in or near water. adjective	*Herons are aquatic birds.*
bare fallowing /ˈbeə ˌfæləʊɪŋ/	the practice of leaving land uncultivated (with nothing planted on it) for a time, allowing air to get into the soil and nutrients that have been used up by plant growth to be replenished. noun [uncount]	
bedrock /ˈbedˌrɒk/	the solid rock under the ground that supports the soil above it. noun [singular]	*The nature of a soil depends on the underlying bedrock.*
blowhole /ˈbləʊˌhəʊl/	a hole in the top of the head of a sea mammal such as a whale or dolphin, through which it breathes. noun [count]	
carbonate /ˈkɑːbəneɪt/	a salt (chemical compound) formed by the reaction of carbon with a base. noun [count]	
carbon cycle /ˈkɑːb(ə)n ˌsaɪk(ə)l/	movement of carbon between living organisms and their environment. Carbon dioxide is taken from the atmosphere and is used by plants. It then moves from plants eaten as food to animals, and is returned to the atmosphere by the respiration of plants and animals and by the burning of plant material. noun [uncount]	
carbonic acid /kɑːˌbɒnɪk ˈæsɪd/	a very weak acid formed when carbon dioxide dissolves in water. noun [uncount]	
carnivore /ˈkɑːnɪˌvɔː/	an animal that eats other animals. noun [count]	
cast /kɑːst/	to throw a fishing net into the water. verb [transitive]	*The fishermen cast their nets early in the morning.*
chalk /tʃɔːk/	a type of soft, white rock that consists of almost pure calcium carbonate. It is a type of sedimentary rock. noun [uncount]	*Chalk often contains fossils of sea creatures.*
chemical weathering /ˌkemɪk(ə)l (weðərɪŋ)/	the process by which rocks and minerals are broken into very small pieces by the action of chemicals, for example by oxidation reactions (with the oxygen in the air) or by being dissolved in water or carbonic acid. noun [uncount]	
clay /kleɪ/	a type of heavy wet soil that becomes hard when it is baked in a kiln (=oven), used for making cups, plates, and other objects. noun [uncount]	*Soil containing lots of clay easily becomes waterlogged.*

Term	Definition	Example
coastline /ˈkəʊstˌlaɪn/	the land along a coast, or the shape that it makes. noun [count]	*The coastline was very rocky.*
cone-shaped /ˈkəʊnˌʃeɪpt/	shaped like a cone, with a point at one end and a circular surface or space at the other. adjective	*He poured the liquid through a cone-shaped funnel.*
consumer /kənˈsjuːmə/	a living thing that feeds on other living things in the food chain. A living thing such as a plant that can make its own food is called a producer. noun [count]	*Rabbits are consumers.*
contour ploughing /ˌkɒntʊə ˈplaʊɪŋ/	a method of ploughing in which the land is ploughed along horizontal lines of the same height, for example on the side of a hill or mountain. This helps to prevent soil erosion, as it is less likely that the soil will get washed away when it rains. noun [uncount]	
coral /ˈkɒrəl/	**1** a hard substance that grows in the sea. It is made from the skeletons of corals. noun [uncount] **2** a small tropical sea animal that lives in large groups that look like plants. noun [count/uncount]	*She was wearing a coral necklace.* *Coral reefs contain millions of individual coral organisms.*
crop rotation /ˈkrɒp rəʊˌteɪʃ(ə)n/	the practice of regularly changing the type of crop that is grown on a particular area of land, in order to keep the soil healthy. noun [uncount]	
crop yield /ˈkrɒp ˌjiːld/	the amount of crop that is produced. noun [count]	*Fertilizers are used to improve crop yields.*
cycle /ˈsaɪk(ə)l/	to rotate; to move in a cycle through something. verb [intransitive]	*Elements such as oxygen cycle continuously between the living and non-living parts of the ecosystem.*
decay /dɪˈkeɪ/	to be gradually broken down by bacteria or fungi. verb [intransitive]	*Teeth may start to decay if they are not cleaned regularly.*
decomposer /ˌdiːkəmˈpəʊzə/	an organism, especially a bacterium or fungus, that causes organic matter to decay. noun [count]	*Decomposers help to recycle nutrients in nature.*
decomposition /ˌdiːkɒmpəˈzɪʃ(ə)n/	the process of decaying or decomposing (=breaking down through a slow natural process into basic elements). noun [uncount]	*The organic material in soil is formed through the decomposition of living things.*
denitrifying bacteria /dɪˌnaɪtrɪfaɪɪŋ bækˈtɪəriə/	bacteria in soil that break down nitrates in the soil and produce some of the nitrogen that exists in the air. They undo the useful work done by nitrifying bacteria. noun [plural]	
deplete /dɪˈpliːt/	to reduce the amount of something by using it, or to be reduced in this way. verb [transitive/intransitive]	*Cultivation depletes the nutrients in the soil.*
depletion /dɪˈpliːʃ(ə)n/	the process of becoming depleted, or of depleting something. noun [uncount]	*the depletion of the Earth's natural resources*
drainage /ˈdreɪnɪdʒ/	the process of taking water or waste liquid away from something such as land, or of allowing it to flow away. noun [uncount]	*Drainage is more difficult in heavy clay soil.*
dust storm /ˈdʌst ˌstɔːm/	a storm during which a strong wind blows a lot of dry soil around. noun [count]	
earthworm /ˈɜːθˌwɜːm/	a type of worm that lives in soil. noun [count]	*Earthworms have an important part to play in aerating the soil.*
echo sounder /ˈekəʊ ˌsaʊndə/	an instrument for measuring the depth of the seabed, or for detecting objects in water, by using sound echoes. noun [count]	
ecosystem /ˈiːkəʊˌsɪstəm/	all the plants, animals and other organisms in a particular area, considered in relation to the environment that they live in and the way they all depend on each other. noun [count]	*A desert is an example of an ecosystem.*
effluent /ˈefluənt/	liquid waste that a place such as a factory or farm allows to flow into a river or the sea. noun [count/uncount]	*The river was polluted by effluent from the nearby factory.*
eutrophication /juːˌtrəʊfɪˈkeɪʃ(ə)n/	excess of nutrients in a lake or other area of water, usually caused by pollution from artificial fertilizers, leading to the dense growth of plants in the water. noun [uncount]	*In fresh water, phosphorus accelerates eutrophication.*
fertility /fɜːˈtɪləti/	the ability of the soil to produce a lot of good crops or other plants. noun [uncount]	*Adding manure increases the fertility of the soil.*
food chain /ˈfuːd ˌtʃeɪn/	the natural process in which one organism is eaten by another, which is then eaten by another, etc. noun [count]	*Green plants are at the beginning of most food chains.*
fossilization /ˌfɒsɪlaɪˈzeɪʃ(ə)n/	the process by which things that were living become preserved in rock or in the form of rock. noun [uncount]	*Coal is formed by the fossilization of decayed plant matter.*
gully erosion /ˈgʌli ɪˌrəʊʒ(ə)n/	a type of erosion (wearing away of soil) in which flowing water cuts deep channels through the earth. noun [uncount]	
harvesting /ˈhɑːvəstɪŋ/	the process of collecting a crop from the fields. noun [uncount]	*Harvesting can be very labour-intensive.*

herbivore /ˈhɜːbɪˌvɔː/	an animal that eats only plants. noun [count]	*Rabbits and cows are herbivores.*
high tide /ˌhaɪ ˈtaɪd/	the time when the sea reaches the highest level (≠ low tide). noun [count/uncount]	*The beach is under water at high tide.*
hoeing /ˈhəʊɪŋ/	the action of working the soil with a hoe (tool with a blade at one end) in order to break up the surface of the soil or remove weeds. noun [uncount]	
horizon /həˈraɪz(ə)n/	a layer of soil or minerals in the ground that is different from the layer above or below it. noun [count]	*The soil was made up of several different horizons.*
humus /ˈhjuːməs/	plants and leaves that decay on the ground and improve the soil for the growth of other plants. noun [uncount]	*The soil was fertile and rich in humus.*
inorganic /ˌɪnɔːˈɡænɪk/	not consisting of or produced from a living organism (≠ organic). adjective	*Inorganic fertilizers can be added to soil as an alternative to organic manure.*
leaching /ˈliːtʃɪŋ/	the process in which a chemical or mineral is removed from something such as soil as a result of water passing through it. noun [uncount]	*During heavy rain, essential nutrients may be lost from the topsoil by leaching.*
limestone /ˈlaɪmˌstəʊn/	a type of white or grey stone that consists mainly of calcium carbonate and is formed from the skeletons and shells of sea animals. Limestone is a sedimentary rock. noun [uncount]	
loam /ləʊm/	a type of soil that is extremely good for plants to grow in. It is a mixture of sand, silt, clay, and humus. noun [uncount]	*The rich loam soil was very fertile.*
low tide /ˌləʊ ˈtaɪd/	the time when the sea is at its lowest level (≠ high tide). noun [count/uncount]	*The mud flats are exposed at low tide.*
mechanical weathering /məˌkænɪk(ə)l ˈweðərɪŋ/	the process by which rocks and minerals are broken into very small pieces by physical forces, for example by the action of water, ice, wind, and changes in temperature (also called: physical weathering). noun [uncount]	
mulch /mʌltʃ/	decaying leaves or other plant material used for protecting the roots of plants and improving the soil. noun [count/uncount]	*A thick layer of mulch was spread around the stems of the growing crop.*
nitrate /ˈnaɪˌtreɪt/	a salt formed from nitric acid that is used for improving the quality of soil. Nitrates are an important part of the nitrogen cycle. Chemical formula: NO_3. noun [count/uncount]	*Most inorganic fertilizers contain nitrates.*
nitrite /ˈnaɪˌtraɪt/	a salt formed from nitric acid that is part of the nitrogen cycle. Chemical formula: NO_2. noun [count/uncount]	
nitrogen cycle /ˈnaɪtrədʒ(ə)n ˌsaɪk(ə)l/	the series of processes by which nitrogen in the atmosphere is changed into nitrogen compounds in soil, is taken up by plants, then eaten and released in waste by animals and decaying organic matter. It is then changed back into nitrogen in the atmosphere. These processes include nitrogen fixation, nitrification, and denitrification. noun [singular]	
nitrogen-fixing bacteria /ˈnaɪtrədʒ(ə)n ˌfɪksɪŋ bækˈtɪəriə/	bacteria that change nitrogen from the atmosphere into compounds in the soil that plants and other organisms can use. noun [plural]	*Legumes have root nodules containing nitrogen-fixing bacteria.*
oil rig /ˈɔɪl ˌrɪɡ/	a large structure with equipment on it for getting oil out from underground. noun [count]	*He worked on an oil rig.*
oil spill /ˈɔɪl ˌspɪl/	an occasion when oil is accidentally or deliberately released into the environment, for example from a tanker. noun [count]	*The oil spill has affected hundreds of miles of coastline.*
oil tanker /ˈɔɪl ˌtæŋkə/	a large ship that carries oil. noun [count]	
omnivore /ˈɒmnɪˌvɔː/	an animal that eats both plants and other animals. An animal that eats only plants is called a herbivore and an animal that eats only other animals is called a carnivore. noun [count]	*Humans are omnivores.*
organic /ɔːˈɡænɪk/	consisting of or produced from a living organism (≠ inorganic). adjective	*Inorganic fertilizers can be added to soil as an alternative to organic manure.*
organic compound /ɔːˌɡænɪk ˈkɒmpaʊnd/	a compound that contains carbon. noun [count]	
oxidation /ˌɒksɪˈdeɪʃ(ə)n/	the process of a substance gaining oxygen or losing hydrogen. noun [uncount]	*Aquatic plants cause oxidation of the surrounding water.*
oxygen cycle /ˈɒksɪdʒən ˌsaɪk(ə)l/	the series of processes by which oxygen moves between plants and animals, being released into the air by photosynthesis from plants and used in respiration (breathing) and combustion (burning). noun [singular]	

phosphate /ˈfɒsˌfeɪt/	a chemical compound containing phosphorus that is used for making plants grow. **noun [count/uncount]**		*Many inorganic fertilizers contain phosphates.*
physical weathering /ˌfɪzɪk(ə)l ˈweðərɪŋ/	the process by which rocks and minerals are broken into very small pieces by physical forces, for example by the action of water, ice, wind, and changes in temperature (also called: mechanical weathering). **noun [uncount]**		
phytoplankton /ˈfaɪtəʊˌplæŋktən/	microscopic organisms that exist in large numbers in water and are eaten by fish. **noun [uncount]**		
porous /ˈpɔːrəs/	with a lot of very small holes that air and water can pass through. **adjective**		*Water drips down through the porous rock.*
primary consumer /ˈpraɪməri kənˌsjuːmə/	a living thing that feeds on plants at the bottom of the food chain, and is itself eaten by a secondary consumer (=first level consumer, herbivore). **noun [count]**		
producer /prəˈdjuːsə/	an organism such as a green plant that makes its own food from simple inorganic compounds and is itself used as food by other organisms. **noun [count]**		
quarternary consumer /ˈkɔːtən(ə)ri kənˌsjuːmə/	in a food chain, a carnivore (meat-eating animal) that feeds on another carnivore that itself feeds on another carnivore. Very few animals feed as quaternary consumers. **noun [count]**		
radar /ˈreɪdɑː/	a system that uses radio signals in order to find the position of something such as an aircraft or ship. **noun [count/uncount]**		
recreational /ˌrekriˈeɪʃ(ə)nəl/	done or used for enjoyment. **adjective**		*recreational sports*
reforestation /ˌriːfɒrɪˈsteɪʃ(ə)n/	the act of putting new trees into a place where the original trees have been cut down. **noun [uncount]**		
replenish /rɪˈplenɪʃ/	to bring something back to its previous level by replacing what has been used. **verb [transitive]**		*There are several ways to replenish nutrients in the soil.*
rod and line /ˌrɒd ənd ˈlaɪn/	a method of fishing using a long stick with a strong string attached to it. **noun [singular]**		
runoff /ˈrʌnɒf/	a flow of water or chemicals from one place to another, especially when this damages the environment. **noun [uncount]**		*Aquatic habitats can become polluted by runoff from farmland which contains fertilizers and pesticides.*
scoop net /ˈskuːp ˌnet/	a net used in fishing that catches fish close to the water surface. **noun [count]**		
sea grass /ˈsiː ˌɡrɑːs/	a type of plant with very long roots that live under the sea, usually in water that is not very deep. **noun [count/uncount]**		
seaweed /ˈsiːˌwiːd/	a simple green, red or brown plant that grows in the sea. **noun [uncount]**		
secondary consumer /ˈsekənd(ə)ri kənˌsjuːmə/	a living thing that feeds on primary consumers, which feed on plants at the bottom of the food chain (=second level consumer, carnivore). **noun [count]**		
sewage /ˈsuːɪdʒ/	waste from people's bodies that is removed from houses and other buildings by a system of large underground pipes called sewers. **noun [uncount]**		*Aquatic habitats are often polluted by sewage which has not been properly treated.*
sheet erosion /ˈʃiːt ɪˌrəʊʒ(ə)n/	a type of erosion (wearing away of soil) in which flowing water such as rain removes a thin layer of soil from the area over which it flows. **noun [uncount]**		
shoal /ʃəʊl/	a group of fish that swim together. **noun [count]**		*A shoal of silvery fish swam by.*
silt /sɪlt/	small particles of rock that are smaller than sand particles and bigger than clay. It is often found at the bottom of rivers, lakes etc, where it settles. **noun [uncount]**		*The river bed was covered with a layer of fine silt.*
soil profile /ˈsɔɪl ˌprəʊfaɪl/	a deep section of soil in which the different layers in the soil can be seen. **noun [count]**		*The soil profile showed a deep layer of topsoil.*
stagnant /ˈstæɡnənt/	stagnant water does not flow and often smells bad. **adjective**		*Mosquito larvae live in stagnant water.*
strip planting /ˈstrɪp ˌplɑːntɪŋ/	the way of reducing soil erosion by growing two or more different crops in alternate strips, which are harvested at different times to avoid leaving large areas of bare land. **noun [uncount]**		
submerged /səbˈmɜːdʒd/	completely under water. **adjective**		*This whole area is submerged at high tide.*
subsoil /ˈsʌbˌsɔɪl/	the layer of soil between the top layer and the rocks under it. **noun [uncount]**		*The topsoil had eroded, exposing the less fertile subsoil underneath.*

Term	Definition	Example
substrate /ˈsʌbˌstreɪt/	the material that a plant or an animal that does not move much feeds on or uses as support. noun [count]	*The plants were growing in a very rich substrate.*
surrounding net /səˈraʊndɪŋ ˈnet/	a net used in fishing that is laid out by a boat and catches large numbers of fish close to the water surface. noun [count]	
terracing /ˈterəsɪŋ/	land on the side of a hill that has been made into thin flat sections that look like steps so that it can be used for farming. noun [uncount]	*The terracing on the hillside could be clearly seen from a distance.*
terrestrial /təˈrestriəl/	living on land rather than in water. adjective	*Trees are terrestrial plants.*
tertiary consumer /ˈtɜːʃəri kənˌsjuːmə/	in a food chain, a carnivore (meat-eating animal) that feeds on another carnivore, for example a sea bird that eats a fish that itself eats smaller fish. noun [count]	
thermal pollution /ˌθɜːm(ə)l pəˈluːʃ(ə)n/	pollution (damage to the environment) caused by hot water being released into streams, lakes, or other areas of water. noun [uncount]	
topsoil /ˈtɒpˌsɔɪl/	the layer of soil that is near the surface of the ground, in which plants grow. Soil erosion can remove topsoil, making the land impossible to grow crops on. noun [uncount]	
toxic substance /ˌtɒksɪk ˈsʌbstəns/	a substance that is poisonous, and therefore harmful to humans and other animals, or to the environment. adjective	*Animals at the top of the food chain can build up large amounts of toxic substances in their bodies.*
trap /træp/	a piece of equipment that is used for catching animals. noun [count]	
trawling /ˈtrɔːlɪŋ/	a method of deep-sea fishing in which one or two boats tow a large net behind them. noun [uncount]	
treatment plant /ˈtriːtmənt ˌplɑːnt/	a place where something such as sewage (waste water and human waste products) is treated to make it safe. noun [count]	
uncultivated /ʌnˈkʌltɪˌveɪtɪd/	uncultivated land has not been used for growing crops. adjective	*The soil was uncultivated and covered with weeds.*
wetlands /ˈwetˌləndz/	low land that is often covered with water from the lake, river, or sea next to it. noun [plural]	*Wetlands form an important habitat for many aquatic organisms.*
zone /zəʊn/	a layer of soil or minerals in the ground (=horizon). noun [count]	
zooplankton /ˈzuːˌplæŋktən/	tiny animals that float in the surface water of the sea and feed on phytoplankton. noun [uncount]	

1 Terrestrial and aquatic environments word map

Write these words in the correct places on the word map.

clay eutrophication fertility omnivores primary producers radar terrestrial

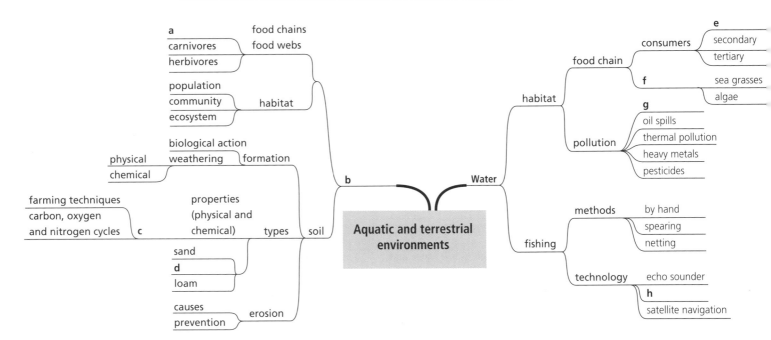

2 Oxygen cycle

Label the diagram with these phrases.

animals use oxygen for respiration
atmospheric oxygen
combustion uses oxygen
oxygen from plant photosynthesis

oxygen from soil organisms that photosynthesise
plants use oxygen for respiration
soil organisms use oxygen for respiration

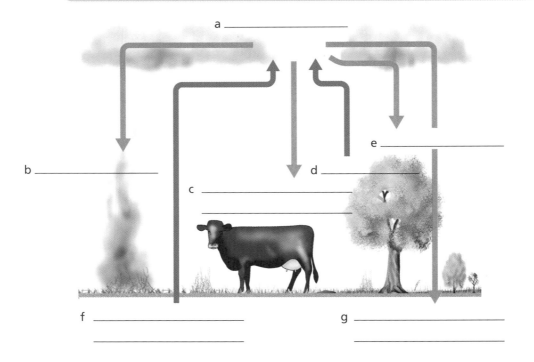

3 **Getting food in the aquatic environment**

Read the text and fill in the gaps with these words.

> carnivores consumers herbivores omnivores photosynthesise
> phytoplankton producers respiration seaweeds substrate

Aquatic organisms need to eat food to obtain energy during 1 _____, to move around, to repair cells and to carry out bodily functions. Aquatic plants, like terrestrial plants, 2 _____ and make their own food using energy from sunlight. Therefore they are called 3 _____.

Two main groups of aquatic plants are sea grasses and algae:

Sea grasses resemble land plants. However, they are rooted or anchored in the 4 _____ at the bottom of the water and are completely submerged in the water.

Algae are plants which do not have roots, leaves or stems, though they vary greatly in shape, structure and colour (red, green and brown). Some are microscopic and are called 5 _____. They float in the water, mostly near the surface. Some algae are very large and are called 6 _____.

Animals do not make their own food. Therefore they depend on plants for food, whether by directly eating the plant or by eating other organisms that feed on plants. Animals are therefore called 7 _____. Animals that eat only plants are called 8 _____. Animals that only feed on other animals are called 9 _____. Those that feed on both plants and animals and are called 10 _____.

B   Working with sentences

4   **Pollutants in the food chain**

Look at the diagram and label it with these sentences.

> 1   Pollutants are absorbed by the phytoplankton by diffusion and enter the food chain.
> 2   Primary consumers are eaten by secondary consumers who eat many of them and absorb a large concentration of pollutant.
> 3   Pollutants increase in each level of the food chain. This can be dangerous for the animals at the end of the food chain e.g. sea birds and humans, as they can build up toxic levels of pollutant which are damaging or even fatal.
> 4   Factories release harmful pollutants into aquatic environments.
> 5   Small crustaceans (primary consumers) eat microscopic plants and store pollutants in their bodies.

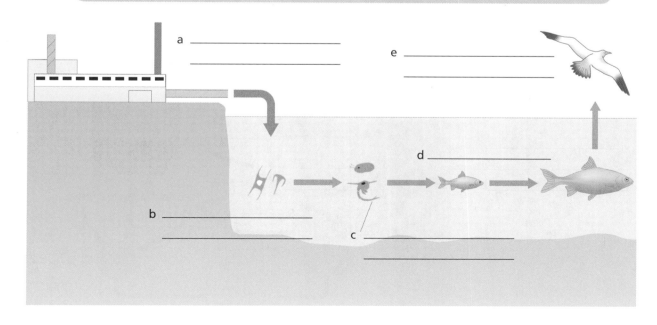

a _____

e _____

d _____

b _____

c _____

5 Terrestrial environment

Match the beginnings and endings of the sentences.

Beginnings

1 The main components of soil are
2 Soil formation results from
3 During a sedimentation test
4 Humus improves the crumb structure of
5 The three main types of soil are
6 Soil fertility depends on
7 Soil erosion is a process in which
8 Terracing, contour ploughing, reforestation, strip planting and use of organic fertilizers
9 Terrestrial food webs and food chains start with
10 Ecosystems contain
11 A community is
12 A population is
13 Oxygen, carbon and nitrogen

Endings

a all the animals and plants living in an ecosystem.
b all the members of a species in an ecosystem which are close enough to interbreed.
c chemical and physical weathering of rocks, along with biological action.
d cycle through the living and non-living parts of ecosystems.
e humus (from decaying plant and animal material) and fragments of rocks.
f many different habitats.
g particle size, mineral content, organic matter and soil pH.
h producers that are eaten by consumers.
i sand, clay and loam.
j soil, allowing for proper aeration and water retention without becoming waterlogged.
k the particles of soil settle out according to particle size, with the larger and heavier particles settling out first (to the bottom of the container).
l topsoil is removed either by wind or water.
m will assist in soil conservation.

1 ☐ 2 ☐ 3 ☐ 4 ☐ 5 ☐ 6 ☐ 7 ☐ 8 ☐ 9 ☐ 10 ☐ 11 ☐ 12 ☐ 13 ☐

C Working with texts

6 The nitrogen cycle

Read the text and label the diagram with these words or phrases.

> 1 absorbed   2 ammonium compounds in soil   3 death and decay   4 decay bacteria
> 5 denitrifying bacteria   6 eaten   7 nitrates in soil   8 nitrites in soil   9 nitrogen in the air
> 10 nitrogen-fixing bacteria   11 protein in animals   12 root nodule   13 urine and faeces
> 14 lightning   15 nitrogen fixation

The atmosphere contains about 79% nitrogen but very few organisms can use the gas because it is very unreactive. However plants need nitrogen in the form of nitrates for healthy growth. Some bacteria can convert atmospheric nitrogen directly into nitrites or nitrates by a process called nitrogen fixation. These are known as nitrogen-fixing bacteria. Some of these bacteria are found in the soil and others live in the roots of leguminous plants. Nitrates made by the bacteria can then be absorbed by the plants. Most of the nitrogen used by plants is in the form of nitrates that are released when dead plants and animals, and waste products such as urine and faeces, are decayed by decomposers. Nitrates can also be formed during thunderstorms where the lightning provides enough energy for oxygen and nitrogen in the air to combine and nitrogen fixation occurs. In water-logged soil, which doesn't contain enough oxygen, there are bacteria that change nitrates back to nitrogen. These bacteria are called denitrifying bacteria. So it is important to keep the soil well aerated where crops are growing, so that the nitrates are not lost.

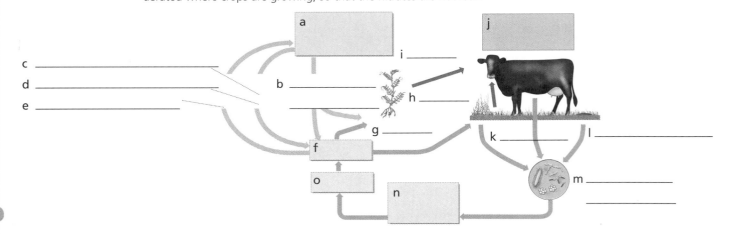

19 Atoms, elements and compounds

Translation

acid /'æsɪd/	a substance with a pH of less than 7. Acid turns damp litmus paper red. Some acids, for example citric acid in lemons, are weak and not harmful, while others, such as strong sulphuric acid, can seriously damage other substances. **noun [count/uncount]**	
alkali metal /'ælkəˌlaɪ ˌmet(ə)l/	a soft, white, metallic, very active element belonging to group 1 of the periodic table. For example, lithium, sodium, and potassium are alkali metals. **noun [count]**	
alkaline earth metal /ˌælkəˌlaɪn 'ɜːθ ˌmet(ə)l/	a silvery, soft low-density element that belongs to group 2 of the periodic table. For example, magnesium, calcium and radium are alkaline earth metals. **noun [count]**	
aluminium /ˌæləˈmɪniəm/	a light, silver-coloured metal element that does not corrode easily. Chemical symbol: Al. **noun [uncount]**	*She covered the meat with aluminium foil before roasting it.*
amphoteric /ˌæmfəʊˈterɪk/	an amphoteric substance that can act with both acids and alkalis. Many metals, for example zinc, lead and aluminium, are amphoteric. **adjective**	
argon /'ɑːɡɒn/	a gas that is an element that does not produce a chemical reaction with other substances. It is an inert gas that is used in electric lights, and also forms about 1% of air. Chemical symbol: Ar. **noun [uncount]**	
artificial /ˌɑːtɪˈfɪʃ(ə)l/	not natural, but made by people. **adjective**	*Most elements occur naturally but some such as plutonium are artificial.*
atom /'ætəm/	the smallest unit of all matter that has all the chemical properties of a particular element. An atom consists of a nucleus that is made of protons, which are positive, and neutrons, which are neutral. The nucleus has electrons, which are negative, travelling around it. The numbers of protons and electrons are equal so that atoms are neutral. **noun [count]**	
atomic mass unit /əˌtɒmɪk 'mæs ˌjuːnɪt/	a unit of mass that is used to express the masses of atoms and molecules. The abbreviations are u and Da. It is also called dalton. **noun [count]**	*One hydrogen atom has a mass of approximately 1 u.*
basic /'beɪsɪk/	forming the main or more important part or aspect of something. **adjective**	*Atoms are the basic building blocks of all matter.*
behave /bɪˈheɪv/	if a chemical substance, metal etc behaves in a particular way, it always reacts in that way because of its structure. **verb [intransitive]**	*All three compounds behave differently when heated.*
behaviour /bɪˈheɪvjə/	the way that a substance reacts in particular conditions. **noun [uncount]**	
beryllium /bəˈrɪliəm/	a light, hard, grey-white metal element that does not oxidize in air, used in alloys. Chemical symbol: Be. **noun [uncount]**	*Beryllium copper is a hard alloy of copper.*
bind /baɪnd/	if two substances bind, or if you bind two substances, they stick or mix together and become one substance. **verb [transitive/intransitive]**	*Atoms bind together to form molecules.*
boiling point /'bɔɪlɪŋ ˌpɔɪnt/	the temperature at which a liquid boils. **[count/uncount]**	*The boiling point of water is 100°C.*
boron /'bɔːrɒn/	a yellow-brown chemical element that is a metalloid. It is used in nuclear reactors and for making steel hard. It is also used for making glass and pottery. Chemical symbol: B. **noun [uncount]**	*Boron is a very poor conductor of electricity.*
calcium /'kælsiəm/	a silver-white chemical element that is very important for the normal growth and health of most living things, especially for bones and teeth. It is also used to make things such as plaster and cement. Chemical symbol: Ca. **noun [uncount]**	*Milk contains calcium.*

carbon
/ˈkɑːb(ə)n/
an important chemical element that exists in all living things. It is unusual because although it is not a metal, some forms of it can conduct electricity. Diamonds are a very pure form of carbon, and it is a major part of coal, petroleum, and natural gas. Chemical symbol: C. **noun [uncount]**

charge
/tʃɑːdʒ/
the amount or type of electrical force that something holds or carries. The protons in an atom have a positive charge, and the electrons have a negative charge. **noun [singular/uncount]**

chlorine
/ˈklɔːˌriːn/
a non-metal element that is a strong-smelling poisonous gas. It is a halogen, and very reactive. It is added to water as a disinfectant. Chemical symbol: Cl. **noun [uncount]**
Swimming pool water has chlorine added to it to kill germs.

compound
/ˈkɒmpaʊnd/
a chemical substance that consists of two or more elements that together form a molecule. Each different compound has a fixed ratio of elements, for example the water compound (H_2O) always consists of two hydrogen atoms and one oxygen atom. **noun [count]**

compress
/kəmˈpres/
to press something so that it fits into a smaller space. **verb [transitive]**

condense
/kənˈdens/
if gas or steam condenses, or if something or someone condenses it, it changes into a liquid, usually when it becomes cooler. **verb [intransitive/transitive]**
The steam from the kettle was condensing on the cold window.

copper
/ˈkɒpə/
a red-brown metal element that is a good conductor of electricity and heat. It is used to make electric wires, water and gas pipes and alloys. Chemical symbol: Cu. **noun [uncount]**
The saucepan had a copper bottom.

decrease
/diːˈkriːs/
1 to become less. **verb [transitive/intransitive]**
2 to reduce something. **verb [transitive/intransitive]**

electric charge
/ɪˌlektrɪk ˈtʃɑːdʒ/
a property of some sub-atomic particles such as protons and electrons. Electrons have a charge of –1 while protons have a charge of +1. **noun [count]**

electron
/ɪˈlekˌtrɒn/
the part of an atom that has a negative electrical charge. Electrons orbit the nucleus of atoms. Electrons moving through a conductor form an electric current. **noun [count]**
Hydrogen has one electron orbiting its nucleus.

element
/ˈelɪmənt/
a substance that consists of only one type of atom. **noun [count]**
Hydrogen and oxygen are two examples of elements.

evaporate
/ɪˈvæpəˌreɪt/
if a liquid evaporates, it slowly changes into a vapour at a temperature below its boiling point. **verb [intransitive]**
The water was slowly evaporating from the surface of the puddle.

fluorine
/ˈfluəˌriːn/
a poisonous yellow gas that is an element in the halogen group and is the most reactive element known. It is used in the treatment of water. Chemical symbol: F. **noun [uncount]**
Sodium fluoride, which is a compound of fluorine, is sometimes added to drinking water to help keep teeth healthy.

force of attraction
/ˌfɔːs əv əˈtrækʃ(ə)n/
a force that is attracted (=drawn) to another force, for example a negative to a positive charge. **noun [count]**
The forces of attraction that hold an individual molecule together are known as intramolecular attractions.

gas
/gæs/
one of the three main forms that matter takes, that is neither a solid nor a liquid. A gas has no fixed shape or volume and its molecules move to fill the space available. Molecules in a gas move faster than the molecules in liquids and solids. **noun [count/uncount]**

halogen
/ˈhælədʒen/
one of five non-metal elements of the periodic table that combine with metals to form salts. These include chlorine and iodine. **noun [count]**
The halogens all have seven electrons in their outer shell.

hardness
/ˈhɑːdnəs/
the quality of being hard, or the degree to which something is hard. **noun [uncount]**

helium
/ˈhiːliəm/
a gas that is lighter than air and is an element. It has the lowest boiling point of any substance. Chemical symbol: He. **noun [uncount]**
The helium-filled balloon floated upwards out of reach.

hydrogen
/ˈhaɪdrədʒən/
a chemical element that is a gas that has no colour or smell. It is the lightest element, and is the most common in the universe. Hydrogen combines with oxygen to make water, and is present in most organic compounds. In the sun and other stars, it is turned into helium by nuclear fusion which produces heat and light. Chemical symbol: H. **noun [uncount]**

identical
/aɪˈdentɪk(ə)l/
exactly the same. **adjective**
The atoms that make up each element are identical.

increase
/ɪnˈkriːs/
to become larger in number or amount, or to make something do this. **verb [transitive/intransitive]**

iron /ˈaɪən/	a chemical element that is a hard heavy metal used especially for making steel. Chemical symbol: Fe. noun [uncount]	*Iron was discovered thousands of years ago in the Iron Age.*
isotope /ˈaɪsəˌtəʊp/	one of the forms of a chemical element that have the same atomic number (=the same number of protons) but a different number of neutrons, and therefore have a different mass. noun [count]	*C-12 and C-14 are two isotopes of carbon.*
lead /led/	a soft, heavy, grey metal element whose compounds can be poisonous. It is used to make containers that protect against harmful radiation. It is also a bad conductor of electricity that does not corrode easily. Chemical symbol: Pb. noun [uncount]	*The heavy fishing weight was made of lead.*
liquid /ˈlɪkwɪd/	one of the three forms of matter that has a fixed volume but a changing shape. A liquid, for example water, can also flow. noun [count/uncount]	*It was a colourless liquid but he wasn't sure that it was water.*
lithium /ˈlɪθiəm/	a very soft, silver-white metal element that is lighter than all other metals. Chemical symbol: Li. noun [uncount]	*Lithium is always found bonded to other elements.*
magnesium /mægˈniːziəm/	a light grey metal element that burns very brightly. It is used in fireworks and in the flashes used for taking photographs. It is an important element in chlorophyll. Chemical symbol: Mg. noun [uncount]	*The burning magnesium gave off a dazzling light.*
mass /mæs/	the amount of matter that something contains. Mass is different from weight as the effects of gravity are not taken into account when it is measured. Symbol m. noun [uncount]	*The mass of an atom is made up of its protons and neutrons.*
mass number /ˌmæs ˈnʌmbə/	the number of protons and neutrons in an atomic nucleus (= nucleon number). noun [count]	
melting point /ˈmeltɪŋ ˌpɔɪnt/	the temperature at which a solid substance changes into a liquid. noun [count/uncount]	*The melting point of ice is 0°C.*
metalloid /ˈmetəlɔɪd/	a chemical element such as silicon that is not a metal but has some of the qualities that a metal has. noun [count]	*Silicon is called a metalloid because it is shiny and metallic-looking, but is not a metal.*
metal /ˈmetəl/	a hard, usually shiny element that is a good conductor of heat and electricity. Metals are used to make things such as tools, machines, pans, jewellery etc. Lead, iron, and gold are all types of metal. Mercury is the only metal that is liquid at room temperature. noun [count/uncount]	
neon /ˈniːɒn/	a colourless gas that is an element that turns orange when electricity is passed through it, used in lights and electric signs. Chemical symbol: Ne. noun [uncount]	*The nightclub entrance was lit up by many neon lights.*
neutron /ˈnjuːtrɒn/	a part of the nucleus of an atom that does not have an electrical charge. noun [count]	*Carbon has six neutrons in its nucleus.*
nickel /ˈnɪkəl/	a hard silver-white metal element, used in batteries and to make alloys. Chemical symbol: Ni. noun [uncount]	*Coins are often made from alloys of nickel.*
nitrogen /ˈnaɪtrədʒən/	an element that is a gas with no colour or smell. It makes up about 78% of the Earth's atmosphere. Chemical symbol: N. noun [uncount]	*Nitrogen is between carbon and oxygen in the periodic table.*
noble gas /ˈnəʊbəl ˌgæs/	a gas that does not react with other substances, from the group of gases that includes helium and neon. noun [count]	
non-metal /ˌnɒnˈmetəl/	a chemical element that is not a metal, for example carbon or oxygen. Non-metals are solids and gases and are not good conductors of heat and electricity. noun [count]	
nucleon number /ˌnjuːkliɒn ˈnʌmbə/	the number of protons and neutrons in an atomic nucleus (= mass number). noun [count]	
nucleus /ˈnjuːkliəs/	the central part of an atom, consisting of protons and neutrons, and containing most of its mass. (plural: nuclei /ˈnjuːkliaɪ/) noun [count]	*A carbon atom has six protons and six neutrons in its nucleus.*
outer shell /ˌaʊtə ˈʃel/	the outermost of the levels of an atom called energy levels, where electrons are found. noun [count]	
oxygen /ˈɒksɪdʒən/	an important element in the air that is a gas with no smell or taste. It makes aerobic respiration possible in organisms. It combines with most other elements. Chemical symbol: O. noun [uncount]	*Brain damage occurs when the supply of oxygen to the brain is interrupted. Blood absorbs oxygen from the air in the lungs.*
particle /ˈpaːtɪkəl/	1 an extremely small piece of matter, for example an atom or a molecule. noun [count] 2 a subatomic particle that is part of an atom, for example an electron, proton, or neutron. noun [count]	*Electrons are some of the smallest particles that exist.*
periodic table /ˌpɪəriɒdɪk ˈteɪbəl/	a list of chemical elements arranged according to the structure of their atoms. noun [singular]	*The periodic table divides the elements into groups and periods containing similar elements.*

period /ˈpɪəriəd/	a row of common elements in the periodic table. **noun [count]**	*All of the elements in a period have the same number of electron shells.*
phosphorous /ˈfɒsfərəs/	a chemical element, especially a form called white phosphorus that starts to burn by itself when air touches it. Chemical symbol: P. **noun [uncount]**	*Phosphorus is a very reactive element.*
potassium /pəˈtæsiəm/	a soft white metal element that is used for making soaps and fertilizers. Chemical symbol: K. **noun [uncount]**	*Most inorganic fertilizers contain potassium.*
precious metal /ˌpreʃəs (met(ə)l/	a valuable metal such as gold or silver. **noun [count]**	
property /ˈprɒpəti/	a quality or feature of something. **noun [count]**	*One of the properties of magnesium is that it is highly flammable.*
proton /ˈprəʊˌtɒn/	the part of the nucleus of an atom that has a positive electrical charge. In an atom, the number of protons equals the number of electrons and is the same as the atomic number of the element. **noun [count]**	
proton number /ˈprəʊtɒn ˌnʌmbə/	the number of protons in the nucleus of an atom (= atomic number). **noun [uncount]**	
reactive /riˈæktɪv/	a reactive substance combines easily with other substances. **adjective**	*Sodium and phosphorus are very reactive elements.*
reactivity /riˌækˈtɪvəti/	the degree to which a substance combines easily with other substances. **noun [uncount]**	
silicon /ˈsɪlɪkən/	a metalloid element that is found in sand, clay and other minerals. It is used especially for making computer chips. Chemical symbol: Si. **noun [uncount]**	*Rocks containing silicon are called silicates.*
sodium /ˈsəʊdiəm/	a very reactive chemical element that is a silver-white metal and is found in salt. Chemical symbol: Na. **noun [uncount]**	*Common table salt is a compound of sodium and chlorine.*
softness /ˈsɒftnəs/	the quality of being soft, or the degree to which something is soft. **noun [singular]**	
solid /ˈsɒlɪd/	a substance that does not change in shape or volume and is not a liquid or a gas. **noun [count]**	*Metals are usually solids at room temperature.*
solidify /səˈlɪdɪfaɪ/	to become solid, or to make something become solid. **verb [transitive/intransitive]**	*Water solidifies when it freezes.*
sulphur /ˈsʌlfə/	a yellow chemical element that burns with a strong smell. It is used to make sulphuric acid, matches, fungicides, and gunpowder. Chemical symbol: S. **noun [uncount]**	*Sulphur fumes were coming from the hot springs.*
symbol /ˈsɪmb(ə)l/	a mark, letter, or number that is used to represent something, for example in chemistry. **noun [count]**	*The symbol for calcium is Ca.*
tin /tɪn/	a chemical element that is a soft light silver metal. Chemical symbol: Sn. **noun [uncount]**	*There used to be tin mines all around this area.*
transition metal /trænˈzɪʃ(ə)n ˌmet(ə)l/	a metallic element such as copper or gold whose valency can vary. **noun [count]**	
unstable /ʌnˈsteɪb(ə)l/	**1** an unstable chemical element or compound reacts very easily with other substances. Some unstable substances, for example nitroglycerine, produce very violent reactions and are useful in making explosives. **adjective** **2** relating to a radioactive substance whose nucleus breaks down to release radioactivity. **adjective**	
vapour /ˈveɪpə/	the gas that is produced when a liquid evaporates below its boiling point. **noun [count/uncount]**	*The atmosphere contains water vapour.*

A Working with words

1 Atoms, elements and compounds word map

Write these words in the correct place on the word map.

elements matter mixtures molecules non-metal radium

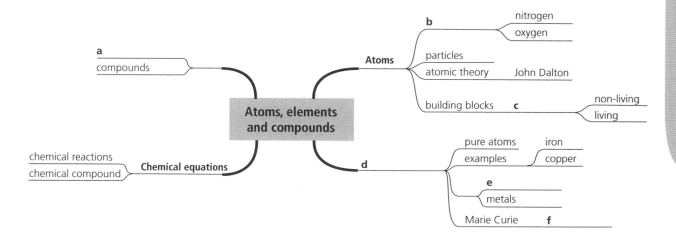

2 Atoms, elements and compounds

Match these words with the correct definition.

1	atom	a	A chemical substance that consists of two or more elements that together form a molecule.
2	particle		
3	compound	b	A substance that consists of only one type of atom.
4	element	c	The smallest unit of all matter that has all the chemical properties of a particular element.
5	gas	d	One of the three main forms that matter takes. It has no fixed shape or volume and its molecules move to fill the space available. Molecules move faster than the molecules in liquids and solids.
6	solid		
7	liquid		
8	helium	e	A gas that is lighter than air and is an element. It has the lowest boiling point of any substance. Chemical symbol: He.
9	metal		
10	nitrogen	f	One of the three forms of matter that has a fixed volume but a changing shape.
		g	Hard, usually shiny element that is a good conductor of heat and electricity.
		h	An element that is a gas with no colour or smell. It makes up about 78% of the Earth's atmosphere. Chemical symbol: N.
		i	An extremely small piece of matter, for example an atom or a molecule
		j	One of the three main forms of matter that does not change in shape or volume.

1 ☐ 2 ☐ 3 ☐ 4 ☐ 5 ☐ 6 ☐ 7 ☐ 8 ☐ 9 ☐ 10 ☐

3 Compounds

Read the text and fill in the gaps with these words.

> atoms   carbon monoxide   chemical formula   compounds   formula H_2O hydrogen and oxygen
> molecule   particles   sodium chloride   solid compound   symbol O   two oxygen atoms

Water molecules contain two different kinds of atoms: 1 _____. Molecules of the

poisonous gas 2 _____ contain one carbon atom combined with one oxygen atom. And molecules

of carbon dioxide, which plants use in photosynthesis, contain one carbon atom combined with

3 _____. Substances that are made of two or more different kinds of atoms are called

4 _____. A 5 _____ is a shorthand way of showing which elements are in a

compound. It also tells you how many atoms of each element are present in one 6 _____ of the

compound. For example, water has the 7 _____. This tells you that each molecule of water

contains two atoms of hydrogen (symbol H) and one atom of oxygen 8 (_____). In other words,

the hydrogen and oxygen are in the ratio 2:1. 9 _____ - common salt has the formula NaCl.

Sodium chloride is a 10 _____ with sodium and chloride 11 _____. There are

no separate molecules, but the formula tells you that there are equal numbers of sodium and chlorine

12 _____.

B   Working with sentences

4 Chemical equations

Match the beginnings and endings of the sentences.

1 When you mix iron and sulfur and heat the mixture
2 The iron and sulfur are the reactants
3 The iron sulfide is the product
4 The equation for the reaction is:
5 The product and reactant in a reaction can be solids,
6 Water molecules always contain two atoms
7 When water decomposes, two molecules of hydrogen are formed
8 When a compound is
9 The atoms in some molecules are more tightly
10 As a result, when molecules are rearranged during a chemical

a made, exact quantities of the different elements react.
b iron (Fe) + sulfur (S) → iron sulfide (FeS)
c reaction, energy may be needed or energy may be released.
d a chemical reaction occurs.
e liquids or gases.
f bonded together than in other molecules.
g – the substances you start with.
h of hydrogen bonded to every atom of oxygen.
i of the reaction.
j for every molecule of oxygen.

1 ☐   2 ☐   3 ☐   4 ☐   5 ☐   6 ☐   7 ☐   8 ☐   9 ☐   10 ☐

5 DNA

Put the words and phrases into the correct order to make sentences.

1 a compound called DNA, determines what you are like. is The basis of life which

_____

2 carbon, hydrogen, oxygen, nitrogen and phosphorus. contains It only the elements

_____

3 and can be combined DNA in millions of different ways. is very complex the various atoms

_____

4 are put together. from everybody else in the DNA in your body is the way in which makes you different the atoms What

_____

_____

5 and All matter are the building blocks can be divided into cells for living things. living and non-living things

_____

6 and all non-living things are made of are made of atoms and molecules. Cells elements and compounds, in turn which

_____

7 in your body is on the kitchen table. The salt the salt the same as

_____

8 and in an eggshell in limestone. in your bones is the same as The calcium carbonate the calcium carbonate

_____

9 and complex compounds. contain life is associated with Living things these very complex compounds

_____

10 and some day have been able to work out life itself. of living substances Scientists the structures they may be able to create

_____

_____

C   Working with texts

6 Common elements

Complete the text by choosing the correct word. There is one word too many.

aurum   capital   carbon   einsteinium   first   Greek   metals   non-metals   solids   symbol

Common elements can be classified into two main groups: 1_____ and non-metals. (The first

conduct electricity, and most 2 _____ do not.) The elements can also be classified according

to whether they are 3 _____, liquids or gases at room temperature (20°C). Each element

is represented by a 4 _____. This is a shorthand way of writing the name of the element.

Sometimes the symbol is the 5 _____ letter of the English name of the element: for example,

carbon, C. However, some elements have the same first letter: for example, 6 _____ and calcium.

In these cases a second letter is used: calcium, Ca. Note that the first letter is a 7 _____, but the

second letter is not. In some cases the symbol comes from a 8 _____ or Latin name. For example,

the symbol for gold is Au. This comes from the Latin word 9 _____, which means 'shining dawn'.

Some elements are named after famous people or places: for example, 10 _____ and francium.

Translation

alloy /ˈælɔɪ/	a metal made by combining two or more other metals. noun [count/uncount]	*Brass is an alloy of copper and tin.*
ammeter /ˈæmˌmiːtə/	a piece of equipment used for measuring the number of amps in an electric current. noun [count]	*The circuit contained a cell, and ammeter and a bulb.*
amp /æmp/	a unit for measuring the amount of flow of an electric current (also called: ampere /ˈæmpeə/). Symbol A. noun [count]	*The current in the circuit was 5 amps.*
analogue /ˈænəˌlɒg/	an analogue instrument has dials with numbers and hands (or pointers) that point to them. adjective	*Analogue meters are less easy to read than digital meters.*
attractive force /əˌtræktɪv ˈfɔːs/	the force by which one object attracts another. noun [count/uncount]	*Attractive force causes the north and south poles of magnets to move together.*
bar magnet /ˈbɑː ˌmægnɪt/	a magnet in the shape of a bar (=a long narrow rectangle). noun [count]	
battery /ˈbæt(ə)ri/	an object that fits into something such as a radio, clock, or car and supplies it with electricity. A battery consists of an electrical cell or a series of electrical cells (plural: batteries). noun [count]	*Several cells together are called a battery.*
blow (fuse) /bləʊ/	if something electrical blows, it stops working because a fault has caused an electrical circuit to break. verb [transitive/intransitive]	
bulb /bʌlb/	a glass object with a very thin wire called a filament inside, that produces light when it is connected to an electricity supply. noun [count]	
cell /sel/	a piece of equipment that uses chemicals, heat, or light to produce electricity. noun [count]	
charge /tʃɑːdʒ/	the amount or type of electrical force that something holds or carries. The protons in an atom have a positive charge, and the electrons have a negative charge. noun [singular/uncount]	
circuit /ˈsɜːkɪt/	the complete path that an electric current flows around. There are two main types of electrical circuit, a series circuit and a parallel circuit. noun [count]	
circuit breaker /ˈsɜːkɪt ˌbreɪkə/	a piece of equipment that is designed to stop an electric current automatically if it becomes dangerous. noun [count]	*The circuit breaker prevented him from getting an electric shock when he accidentally mowed over the lawnmower cable.*
coil /kɔɪl/	a long piece of wire that forms several circles, each on top of the other. noun [count]	*An electromagnet can be made from a coil of insulated wire wound around an iron rod.*
colour-coded /ˈkʌləkəʊdɪd/	marked with different colours to show the different features or uses. adjective	*Most electric flexes contain three colour-coded wires.*
compass /ˈkʌmpəs/	a piece of equipment used for finding your way, with a needle that always points to the north. noun [count]	*They knew how to use a compass so they didn't get lost.*
component /kəmˈpəʊnənt/	a part of a machine or piece of equipment. noun [count]	
conductor /kənˈdʌktə/	a substance that heat or electricity can pass through. noun [count]	*Metals are good conductors of electricity and heat.*
constantan /kənˈstæntən/	an alloy of copper and nickel. It is used to make resistors. noun [count]	
consumption /kənˈsʌmpʃ(ə)n/	the use of something such as energy or fuel, or the amount of something that people use or buy. noun [uncount]	*We've reduced our energy consumption by 10%.*
core /kɔː/	the iron rod in an electromagnet around which copper wire is wound. noun [count]	
current /ˈkʌrənt/	a flow of electricity. noun [count/uncount]	*Switching on the switch caused a current to flow through the circuit.*
decrease /diːˈkriːs/	1 to become less. verb [transitive/intransitive] 2 to reduce something. verb [transitive/intransitive]	

device /dɪˈvaɪs/	a machine or piece of equipment that does a particular job. noun [count]	*A resistor is a device that reduces the flow of current through a circuit.*
digital /ˈdɪdʒɪt(ə)l/	a digital instrument shows information as a row of numbers. adjective	*Digital meters are easy to read.*
earth /ɜːθ/	the wire in a piece of electrical equipment that makes it safe by connecting it to the ground. noun [singular]	*The earth wire in a plug connects the electrical device to Earth.*
earth leakage breaker /ˌɜːθ ˈliːkɪdʒ ˌbreɪkə/	a device that quickly cuts off the electric current to a piece of electrical equipment if a fault occurs in the circuit or if the person using the equipment receives an electric shock. noun [count]	
electrolyte /ɪˈlektrəˌlaɪt/	a liquid containing ions that electricity can pass through. noun [count]	*Water is an electrolyte.*
electromagnet /ɪˌlektrəʊˈmægnət/	a powerful magnet that uses an electric current passed in a wire around it to produce its magnetic force. It stops being a magnet when the supply of electricity is stopped. noun [count]	*Metal is moved around in a scrapyard by electromagnets.*
electromagnetism /ɪˌlektrəʊ ˈmægnəˌtɪz(ə)m/	magnetism that is produced by means of an electrical current. noun [uncount]	*A doorbell works by using electromagnetism.*
electromotive force /ɪˌlektrəʊˌməʊtɪv ˈfɔːs/	the force created by an electrical source which pushes the electrons around an electrical circuit. Voltage means the same. noun [uncount]	
electron /ɪˈlektrɒn/	the part of an atom that has a negative electrical charge. Electrons orbit the nucleus of atoms. Electrons moving through a conductor form an electric current. noun [count]	
energy conservation /ˈenədʒi ˌkɒnsəˌveɪʃ(ə)n/	the careful use of resources such as electricity so that the fuels that produce it are not wasted. noun [uncount]	*Everyone can play their part in energy conservation.*
energy-saving /ˈenədʒiˌseɪvɪŋ/	energy-saving equipment is designed so that it uses as little energy as possible. adjective	*Energy-saving light bulbs last much longer than normal light bulbs.*
fault /fɒlt/	a problem with a machine or piece of equipment that stops it from working correctly. noun [count]	
flex /fleks/	a plastic covered wire that is used for carrying electricity. noun [countable]	*Make sure that flexes are not frayed.*
flow /fləʊ/	the continuous movement of something. noun [count/uncount]	*The flow of electric current is controlled by a switch.*
fluorescent /flɔːˈres(ə)nt/	a fluorescent substance produces light when electricity passes through it. adjective	*The room was illuminated by fluorescent tubes.*
fuse /fjuːz/	an object in electrical equipment that contains a thin piece of wire that breaks and makes the equipment stop working when there is too much electricity flowing through it. noun [count]	*The hairdryer wouldn't work because the fuse in the plug had blown.*
fuse box /ˈfjuːz ˌbɒks/	a box containing the fuses for the electrical system in a building. noun [count]	
graphite /ˈgræfaɪt/	a soft black type of carbon that is used in pencils and for making electrodes. noun [uncount]	*The battery contained graphite electrodes.*
hammer /ˈhæmə/	a part that hits something in order to make a sound. An electric bell contains a hammer that hits a gong to make the bell ring. noun [count]	
in accordance with /ɪn əˈkɔːd(ə)ns ˌwɪð/	in a way that follows a rule, system, or someone's wishes. phrase	
incandescent /ˌɪnkænˈdes(ə)nt/	producing light as a result of being made very hot. adjective	*Incandescent bulbs are not very energy-efficient.*
increase /ɪnˈkriːs/	to become larger in number or amount, or to make something do this. verb [transitive/intransitive]	
in parallel /ˌɪn ˈpærəlel/	when components in an electrical circuit are connected in parallel, there is more than one route through which the current can travel. adverb	*Most electric wiring in the home is done in parallel.*
in series /ˌɪn ˈsɪəriːz/	when components in an electrical circuit are connected in series, the current can only travel through one route. adverb	*a string of lights connected in series*
insulate /ˈɪnsjʊˌleɪt/	to cover something in order to prevent heat, cold, sound, or electricity from passing through it. verb [transitive]	*Wires are insulated to prevent electric shocks.*

insulation /ˌɪnsjʊˈleɪʃ(ə)n/	**1** material that is used for preventing heat, cold, sound, or electricity from passing through something. **noun [uncount]** **2** protection from heat, cold, sound, or electricity. **noun [uncount]**	*The insulation around the cable had worn away, making it dangerous.*
insulator /ˈɪnsjʊˌleɪtə/	a substance that reduces the amount of heat, cold, sound, or electricity that can pass through something. **noun [count]**	*Electrical cables are covered with plastic, which is a good insulator.*
ion /ˈaɪən/	an atom or group of atoms that has become charged. A positive ion has an electrical charge caused by losing electrons, and a negative ion has an electrical charge caused by gaining them. **noun [count]**	
iron filings /ˌaɪən ˈfaɪlɪŋz/	very small pieces of iron. **noun [plural]**	
kilowatt-hour /ˌkɪləwɒt ˈaʊə/	a unit for measuring electrical energy, equal to the work done by one kilowatt in one hour. Symbol kWh. **noun [count]**	*According to the electricity bill, we had used over 150 kilowatt-hours of electricity.*
like poles /ˌlaɪk ˈpəʊlz/	when like poles (=both north or south) of two magnets face each other, they repel each other. **noun [plural]**	
live /laɪv/	a live wire or piece of equipment is connected to the electricity supply and has electricity going through it. **adjective**	*She didn't realise the wire was live and received an electric shock.*
magnetic field /mæɡˌnetɪk ˈfiːld/	the area that the force of a magnet affects. **noun [count]**	*The Earth has its own magnetic field.*
magnetism /ˈmæɡnəˌtɪz(ə)m/	the ability that a magnet has to attract iron or steel. **noun [uncount]**	*The magnetism of the iron rod was strong enough to attract several paper clips.*
manganin /ˈmæŋɡəˌnɪn/	an alloy of copper, manganese and nickel. It is used to make resistors. **noun [uncount]**	
molten /ˈməʊlt(ə)n/	molten rock, metal or glass has become liquid because it is very hot. **adjective**	
negatively charged /ˌneɡətɪvli ˈtʃɑːdʒd/	a negatively charged particle has the same electrical charge as an electron. **adjective**	*The flow of negatively charged electrons within a material is called an electric current.*
neutral /ˈnjuːtrəl/	a neutral wire is not live. It is the wire that is blue in a plug. **adjective**	
nichrome /ˈnaɪkrəʊm/	an alloy of nickel and chromium. It is used to make resistors. **noun [uncount]**	
nickel /ˈnɪk(ə)l/	a hard silver-white metal element, used in batteries and to make alloys. Chemical symbol: Ni. **noun [uncount]**	
non-conductor /ˌnɒnkənˈdʌktə/	a material that does not allow an electric current to pass through it. **noun [count]**	*Paper, plastic and rubber are non-conductors.*
ohm /əʊm/	a unit used for measuring resistance in an electrical circuit. Symbol: Ω. **noun [count]**	
Ohm's Law /ˌəʊmz ˈlɔː/	a law of physics discovered by the 19th century scientist Georg Ohm. It states that the current flowing through a resistor is directly proportional to the voltage across it. **noun [singular]**	
opposite poles /ˌɒpəzɪt ˈpəʊlz/	when opposite poles (=one north and one south) of two magnets face each other, they attract each other. **noun [plural]**	
orientation /ˌɔːriənˈteɪʃ(ə)n/	the position of an object, or the direction in which it is pointing. **noun [count]**	*The orientation of two magnets decides whether they will attract or repel each other.*
overload /ˌəʊvəˈləʊd/	to damage an electrical system or a piece of electrical equipment by putting too much electricity through it. **verb [transitive]**	*The computer crashed because the system was overloaded.*
parallel circuit /ˌpærəlel ˈsɜːkɪt/	an electric circuit in which all the parts are connected directly to the voltage supply, so that each receives a part of the current. **noun [count]**	*All lamps in a parallel circuit shine with equal brightness.*
particle /ˈpɑːtɪk(ə)l/	**1** an extremely small piece of matter, for example an atom or a molecule. **noun [count]** **2** a subatomic particle that is part of an atom, for example an electron, proton, or neutron. **noun [count]**	
path (circuit) /pɑːθ/	a route around which something can travel or flow. **noun [count]**	*The complete path around which an electric current flows is called an electric circuit.*
permanent magnet /ˌpɜːmənənt ˈmæɡnɪt/	a magnet that is a magnet all the time. It is made from iron, or from iron mixed with aluminium, nickel or cobalt. **noun [count]**	

pole /pəʊl/	one of the two ends of a magnet. noun [count]	*The north poles of two magnets will repel each other.*
potential difference /pəˌtenʃ(ə)l ˈdɪfrəns/	the work done in moving a unit of electrical charge between two points in an electrical circuit. noun [uncount]	*The potential difference in a circuit is measured in volts.*
power rating /ˈpaʊə ˌreɪtɪŋ/	the amount of electricity that an electrical appliance uses. noun [count]	*The power rating of a kettle is 1,5 kW.*
propeller /prəˈpelə/	a piece of equipment with blades that spin round. Propellers are used to move ships and aircraft. A turbine in a generator is like a large propeller. noun [count]	
reading (meter) /ˈriːdɪŋ/	a number or amount shown on a piece of measuring equipment. noun [count]	*Customers can do their own meter reading and inform the electric company.*
relay /ˈriːleɪ/	a type of electrical switch that opens and closes under the control of another electrical circuit. A relay allows a small electric current to be used to start a much larger electric current. Relays are used to control devices such as the starter motor on a car. noun [count]	
repel /rɪˈpel/	if one thing repels another, an electrical or magnetic force pushes them away from each other. verb [transitive]	*Two north or south poles repel each other.*
repulsive force /rɪˌpʌlsɪv ˈfɔːs/	a force such as electricity or magnetism that makes things move apart (≠ attraction). noun [count/uncount]	*The two north poles were pushed apart by a repulsive force.*
resistance /rɪˈzɪst(ə)ns/	the ability of a material or object to slow down an electric current. Good conductors, for example silver, have low resistance, and bad conductors, for example glass, have high resistance. noun [uncount]	
resistor /rɪˈzɪstə/	a piece of wire or other material that controls the level of current flowing in an electric circuit by providing resistance. noun [count]	
rheostat /ˈriːəˌstæt/	a resistor that allows the flow of electricity in an electrical circuit to be controlled without breaking the circuit. The volume control in a radio is a rheostat. noun [count]	
solar cell /ˈsəʊlə ˌsel/	a piece of equipment that uses the sun's energy to produce electricity. noun [count]	*Solar cells can produce electricity even in areas where there is not a lot of sunlight.*
spring /sprɪŋ/	a long thin piece of metal that is twisted into the shape of a coil that quickly returns to its original shape after you stop stretching it. An electric bell contains a spring which causes the hammer to hit the gong. noun [count]	
substation /ˈsʌbˌsteɪʃ(ə)n/	a place that electricity passes through on its way from where it is produced to where it is used. At the substation the voltage is reduced and the electricity is distributed to buildings. noun [count]	
surge /sɜːdʒ/	a sudden increase in electrical power that can damage equipment connected to it. noun [singular]	*a power surge*
swing (move) /swɪŋ/	to move backwards and forwards from a point, or to make something move in this way. verb [transitive/intransitive]	*When a magnet is suspended in the air it swings until its north pole points to the Earth's North Pole.*
switch /swɪtʃ/	something such as a button or key that turns an electric current on and off. When the switch is closed (on) the circuit is complete and the electric current flows; when it is open (off) the circuit is broken and electric current stops flowing. noun [count]	*a light switch*
thermostat /ˈθɜːməʊˌstæt/	a piece of equipment that controls the temperature in a building, machine, or engine. It consists of a switch containing metals that expand to a different degree when heated. The thermostat switches the heat off as the temperature rises, and switches it on as the temperature falls. noun [count]	*The oven had a faulty thermostat and kept overheating.*
three-pin plug /ˌθriːpɪn ˈplʌg/	an object to which the three insulated wires in a flex are connected. Each wire (earth, live and neutral) is connected to a particular metal pin and the three pins are inserted into a socket so that electrical current can flow to the appliance. noun [count]	
tidal energy /ˌtaɪd(ə)l ˈenədʒi/	energy produced by the movement of the tides of the sea, that can be used to produce electricity. noun [uncount]	
transformer /ˌtrænsˈfɔːmə/	a piece of electrical equipment that changes the voltage of a flow of electricity. A transformer can be used for connecting a piece of electrical equipment that uses one voltage to an electricity supply of a different voltage. noun [count]	*The electricity from the power station was converted to a high voltage in the transformer.*

20 ELECTRICITY & MAGNETISM

trip (circuit) /trɪp/	to make a switch turn off and stop the flow of an electrical current, especially to prevent wires from overheating or to prevent someone using electrical equipment from receiving an electric shock. **verb [transitive]**	*When a circuit breaker has been tripped, it has to be reset manually.*
turbine /ˈtɜːbaɪn/	a machine that produces power using the pressure of liquid or gas on a wheel. Turbines are used for generating electricity in power stations and for turning the propellers on ships. **noun [count]**	*Hydroelectric power stations use moving water to turn the turbines.*
U-shaped /ˈjuːʃeɪpt/	in the shape of the letter U. **adjective**	
volt /vəʊlt/	a unit for measuring the potential difference of an electric current. The unit of electric current is the amp, and the unit of electrical power is the watt. Symbol V. **noun [count]**	*Domestic electricity is normally supplied at 240 volts.*
voltage /ˈvəʊltɪdʒ/	the amount of potential difference in an electric current, measured in volts. **noun [count/uncount]**	
voltmeter /ˈvəʊltˌmiːtə/	a piece of equipment used for measuring voltage. **noun [count]**	*The circuit contained a voltmeter.*
watt /wɒt/	a unit for measuring electrical power, measured in joules per second. The unit of electric current is the amp and the unit of potential difference is the volt. Symbol W. **noun [count]**	*The kettle had a power rating of 3.5 kilowatts (or 3500 watts).*
wind power /ˈwɪnd ˌpaʊə/	electricity that is created using the power of wind. Large turbines are put in windy places and the energy is harnessed to generate electricity. **noun [uncount]**	

A   Working with words

1   Electricity and magnetism word map

Write these words in the correct place on the word map.

analogue   electricity   electric circuits   permanent   power   series

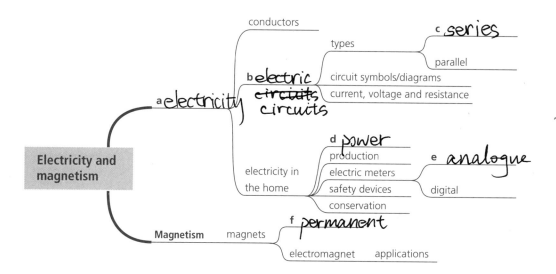

Electricity and magnetism

a *electricity*

b *electric circuits*   circuits
 conductors
 types
  c *series*
  parallel
 circuit symbols/diagrams
 current, voltage and resistance

electricity in the home
 d *power*
 production
 electric meters   e *analogue*
 safety devices   digital
 conservation

Magnetism   magnets
 f *permanent*
 electromagnet   applications

2   Voltage

Read the text and fill in the gaps in the sentences with these words.

circuit   electrons   force   negative   parallel   positive
potential   symbol   voltage (x2)   voltmeter   unit

Voltage is the 1 *force* that pushes electrons through the electrical circuit. The greater the force (voltage) the greater the number of 2 *electrons* that pass through the circuit in one second. That is, a larger 3 *voltm* will increase the flow of electrons (current) through the 4 *potential*. The change in voltage between any two points in a circuit is called the 5 *circuit* difference between those points. The voltage can be measured using a 6 *voltmeter*. The voltmeter must always be connected in 7 *parallel* to the appliance or component in the circuit across which it will measure the voltage. Also the 8 *negative* terminal of the voltmeter should connect to the wires coming from the negative terminal of the battery and the 9 *positive* terminal to the positive terminal of a battery. Voltage (potential difference) is given the 10 *symbol* V. The 11 *unit* of voltage is the volt which has the symbol V. Cells and batteries available on the market usually have a 12 *voltage* of between 1.5 and 12 volts (1.5–12 V).

3 Symbols

Look at the symbols and label them with the correct component. Then add the correct explanation of each component.

Component	Symbol	Explanation
a ammeter 5.k		j Gives out heat and light when current passes. The second symbol represents a bulb in a holder.
b bulb 2.j		
c cell (one) and battery (more than one cell) 1	1 _____ 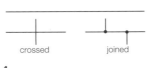	k Limits or controls the amount of current that passes through a circuit.
d connecting wires 4		l Measures the ability of the battery to push electrons through the circuit (voltage).
e fuse 8		
f resistor 7	2 _____	m Measures the rate of flow of electric current passing through a circuit or part of a circuit.
g switch 3		
h transformer 9		n The long line is the positive terminal and the short line is the negative terminal.
i voltmeter 6.l	3 _____ 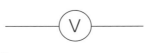	o Used to turn current on and off.
		p Usually made of copper which is a good conductor, and insulated with plastic. Wires that connect different parts of a circuit are often marked with a dot where they join, to distinguish them from wires that cross without joining.
	crossed joined	
	4 _____ 	q Consists of a thin metal wire that melts to break the circuit if too much electric current passes. Helps protect electrical appliances.
	5 _____ (A)	r Increases or decreases the voltage of electric current passing through a circuit.
	6 _____ (V)	
	fixed / variable	
	7 _____ 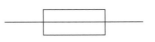	
	8 _____	
	9 _____ 	

1 . 2 . 3 . 4 . 5 . 6 . 7 . 8 . 9 .
c . b . g . d . a . i . f . e . h .
n . j . o . p . m . l . a . q . r

4 Circuits

Read the text and sort the sentences under the correct illustrations.

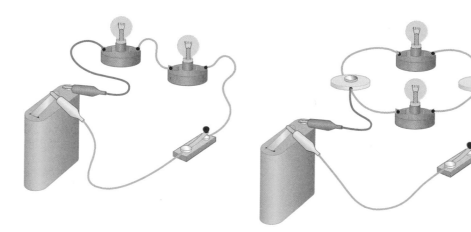

Series circuit

1 [a]   e. a. gc.
2 [c]
3 [e]
4 [g]

Parallel circuit

5 [b]   d. h. b f . i .
6 [d]
7 [f]
8 [h]
9 [i]

When there are several components in an electric circuit, they can be connected in series or in parallel.

a   all the components in the circuit are connected together in <u>one loop</u> and there is only one route through which the current can travel.

b   Also a defective or disconnected component in one part of a parallel circuit will not stop the flow of current to the remaining branches in the circuit.

c   If one of the components should become defective or disconnected, no electric current will flow through the circuit.

d   In a parallel circuit,

e   In a series circuit,

f   The current need not be the same in each of the branches.

g   The same current will flow through each part of the circuit.

h   there is more than one route through which current can travel around and back to the battery.

i   Therefore the current 'splits up' to supply each branch of the circuit with electric current.

5 Saving electricity

Match the beginnings and endings of the sentences.

Beginnings

1. Install ceiling and wall insulation and keep curtains closed during winter
2. Use awnings to shade windows
3. Turn off appliances, including lights,
4. Set the fans of air conditioners at high speed
5. Avoid opening the fridge door too much
6. Defrost the freezer before the ice builds up
7. Only use the dishwasher when there is a full load,
8. Use cooking pots and kettles with flat, wide bottoms
9. Keep lids on pans, pots and kettles while they are in use
10. Do not open the oven door regularly while in use
11. The oven and hot plates can be turned off before cooking is finished,
12. When boiling water,
13. Use fluorescent tubes and lights instead of incandescent light bulbs,

Endings

a. as cooler air will enter from outside.
b. as the ice prevents the efficient transfer of heat.
c. as the washer does not use less energy for smaller loads.
d. as these will use the heat most efficiently.
e. as this increases the amount of energy required to cool the inside.
f. because they use only one-quarter of the electricity and last up to four times longer.
g. do not boil more water than you need.
h. for greater efficiency.
i. so that heat does not escape into the air.
j. to make use of the residual heat.
k. to reduce heat gain in rooms that are being cooled.
l. to reduce heat loss.
m. when they are not in use.

1 [l] 2 [k] 3 [m] 4 [h] 5 [e] 6 [b] 7 [c] 8 [i] 9 [d] 10 [a] 11 [j] 12 [g] 13 [f]

C Working with texts

6 Electric current

Read the text and sort the different materials into the table.

All things on Earth are made up of tiny particles called atoms. There are many kinds of atoms, but they all consist of a dense central structure called the nucleus around which negatively charged particles called electrons orbit. The flow of these negatively charged electrons within a material is called an electric current. Not all materials conduct electricity. Substances such as metals and graphite, a form of carbon, have some electrons that can move freely between atoms. This means they can flow as an electric current through the materials. These substances are called electrical conductors. Metals such as copper and aluminium are excellent conductors of electricity and so are commonly used to make electrical wires. Some materials, such as paper, plastic, rubber and glass, do not allow an electric current to pass through them because their electrons are unable to move around freely. These materials are called insulators or non-conductors. Electrolytes are substances which contain charged particles called ions. When they are in solution or molten, they are free to move around and can carry an electric current. Sodium chloride (common salt) solution is an example of an electrolyte. Many of our body fluids are electrolytes, which is why the human body is a good conductor of electric current. We can get an electric shock if we touch an electric current so that it flows through our bodies.

Conductors 导体	Insulators 绝缘体	Electrolytes 电解质
human body copper aluminium	paper plastic rubber glass	sodium chloride body ~~fluid~~ fluids

21 Chemicals

acetic (ethanoic) acid /əˌsiːtɪk ˈæsɪd/	a type of acid that is the main part of vinegar. It is used in making drugs, plastics, fibres, and other products. noun [uncount]	*The acetic acid in vinegar gives it a sharp taste.*
acetone /ˈæsɪtəʊn/	a liquid that can be used to remove nail polish. It is also used in some types of paint and varnish to prevent them from becoming too thick. noun [uncount]	
acid /ˈæsɪd/	a substance with a pH of less than 7. Acid turns damp litmus paper red. Some acids, for example citric acid in lemons, are weak and not harmful, while others, such as strong sulphuric acid, can seriously damage other substances. noun [count/uncount]	*He had a nasty burn on his hand from the spilt acid.*
alkyl benzene /ˌælkɪl ˈbenziːn/	a chemical that is used to make soapless (or synthetic) detergents. noun [uncount]	
alum /ˈæləm/	aluminium potassium sulphate: a chemical substance used in dyes and for purifying water (=making dirty water safe to drink). noun [count]	
ammonium hydroxide /əˌməʊniəm haɪˈdrɒksaɪd/	a strong alkali that is a solution of ammonia in water. noun [uncount]	*Ammonium hydroxide is very corrosive.*
anhydrous sodium sulphate /ænˌhaɪdrəs ˌsəʊdiəm ˈsʌlfeɪt/	a chemical that is added to detergents in order to stop them absorbing moisture from the atmosphere. noun [uncount]	
antacid /æntˈæsɪd/	a medicine that reduces the amount of acid in the stomach. noun [count]	*She took an antacid to relieve her indigestion.*
antiseptic /ˌæntiˈseptɪk/	a substance that is used for cleaning injured skin and preventing infections. noun [count/uncount]	*The school nurse put some antiseptic on her grazed knee.*
approximate value /əˌprɒksɪmət ˈvæljuː/	approximate: not exact, but close to the exact amount or number. noun [count/uncount]	
aqueous /ˈeɪkwiəs/	containing water. adjective	
ascorbic acid /əˌskɔːbɪk ˈæsɪd/	vitamin C. noun [uncount]	*Citrus fruits contain ascorbic acid.*
baking powder /ˈbeɪkɪŋ ˌpaʊdə/	a white powder (sodium hydrogencarbonate) that is used in cooking for making cakes rise while they are baking, and in fire extinguishers. noun [uncount]	
baking soda /ˈbeɪkɪŋ ˌsəʊdə/	a white powder (sodium bicarbonate) that is used in cooking for making cakes rise while they are baking. It can also be used instead of toothpaste, and to relieve the pain of bee and wasp stings. noun [uncount]	
base /beɪs/	a chemical substance that turns red litmus paper blue. All alkalis are bases. noun [count]	*A base can be added to an acid to neutralize it.*
bleaching agent /ˈbliːtʃɪŋ ˌeɪdʒ(ə)nt/	a substance in a detergent that removes colour from fabric so that it becomes whiter and disinfects the fabric. noun [count]	
blotting paper /ˈblɒtɪŋ ˌpeɪpə/	special thick paper that you use for drying the ink when you have just finished writing with a fountain pen. noun [uncount]	
by-product /ˈbaɪ ˌprɒdʌkt/	an additional product that is made as a result of an industrial or chemical process. noun [count]	
calcium hydroxide /ˌkælsiəm haɪˈdrɒksaɪd/	a white alkaline chemical compound used in the treatment of acid soil and in making cement, plaster, and glass. noun [uncount]	*The acid soil was neutralized by adding lime (calcium hydroxide).*
carbonate /ˈkɑːbəneɪt/	a compound containing carbon and oxygen. noun [count]	*The common name for calcium carbonate is chalk.*
caustic soda /ˌkɔːstɪk ˈsəʊdə/	the chemical sodium hydroxide that is a strong alkali and is used for cleaning things that are very dirty. It is also used for making many other chemicals. It absorbs carbon dioxide gas. noun [uncount]	*She wore rubber gloves because the cleaning powder contained caustic soda.*

chloride /ˈklɔːraɪd/	a chemical that consists partly of chlorine, usually with one other element. noun [count/uncount]	Common table salt is sodium chloride.
citric acid /ˌsɪtrɪk ˈæsɪd/	an acid contained in the juice of fruits such as oranges and lemons. noun [uncount]	Lemons have a tangy taste because of the citric acid in them.
colloid /ˈkɒlɔɪd/	a substance that is between a solution and a suspension. Aerosols, foams and emulsions are all types of colloids. noun [count]	Acids are corrosive and can damage your skin.
corrosive /kəˈrəʊsɪv/	a corrosive substance contains chemicals that gradually cause damage. adjective	
crystalline /ˈkrɪstəˌlaɪn/	consisting of crystals, or looking like crystals. adjective	Sugar is a crystalline solid.
dab /dæb/	to touch a surface gently several times with something such as a cloth, for example in order to dry it. verb [transitive/intransitive]	You could try dabbing at the stain with dilute hydrogen peroxide.
deodorise /diˈəʊdəˌraɪz/	to make something smell better by removing odours. verb [transitive]	Bleaching agents are added to detergents because they deodorise fabrics.
detergent /dɪˈtɜːdʒənt/	a liquid or powder that is used for washing clothes or dishes. noun [count/uncount]	Detergents for use in the home can be soapy or soapless.
discolouration /dɪsˌkʌləˈreɪʃn/	the process of becoming discoloured (=losing colour). noun [uncount]	Bleach should be used with care as it can cause discolouration.
disinfectant /ˌdɪsɪnˈfekt(ə)nt/	a chemical substance that kills bacteria, viruses and fungi that may spread disease. noun [count/uncount]	Clean kitchen surfaces regularly with a disinfectant.
dissolve /dɪˈzɒlv/	if a solid substance dissolves in a liquid, or if someone dissolves it, it mixes into the liquid and becomes included in it. verb [transitive/intransitive]	Gases dissolve in the moist surface of the air sacs.
droplet /ˈdrɒpˌlɪt/	a very small drop of liquid. noun [count]	
Enos salts /ˈiːnəʊz ˌsɔːlts/	a medicine that reduces the amount of acid in your stomach. noun [plural]	
Epsom salts /ˈepsəm ˌsɔːlts/	a medicine that helps you to empty your bowels when you are constipated (=cannot go to the toilet). noun [plural]	
ethanoate /ˈeθənəʊeɪt/	a salt of acetic acid (=the acid contained in vinegar). noun [count]	
filter paper /ˈfɪltə ˌpeɪpə/	paper that is used in a filter and allows some substances to pass through it. noun [uncount]	She passed the dirty water through filter paper to clean it.
fluorescer /fləˈresə/	a substance that is added to detergent to make clothes look brighter or whiter after washing (= optical brightener). noun [count]	
formic acid /ˌfɔːmɪk ˈæsɪd/	an acid that irritates the skin. It is present in ant bites. noun [uncount]	
Glauber's salt /ˈglɔːbəz ˌsɔːlt/	a medicine that helps you to empty your bowels when you are constipated (=cannot go to the toilet). noun [uncount]	
heterogeneous mixture /ˌhetərəʊˈdʒiːnɪəs ˌmɪkstʃə/	a mixture in which each component retains its identity and can easily be distinguished. noun [count]	
homogeneous mixture /ˌhəʊməʊˈdʒiːnɪəs ˌmɪkstʃə/	a mixture in which the separate components cannot be identified and which looks the same throughout. noun [count]	
hydrochloric acid /ˌhaɪdrəˌklɒrɪk ˈæsɪd/	a strong liquid chemical that is used in industry and in laboratory work. Hydrochloric acid is present in the stomach in a weak form, and helps make conditions suitable for digestion. noun [uncount]	
hydrogen carbonate /ˌhaɪdrədʒən ˈkɑːbəneɪt/	a salt containing the negatively-charged ion HCO_3 (= bicarbonate). noun [count]	Water molecules split into positive hydrogen ions and negative hydroxide ions.
hydrogen ion /ˈhaɪdrədʒən ˌaɪən/	an ion of hydrogen that has a positive charge and is formed by removing an electron from a hydrogen atom. It is present in solutions of acids in water. The pH of a compound is a measure of the degree to which it produces hydrogen ions. noun [count]	
hydrophilic /ˌhaɪdrəˈfɪlɪk/	= water-loving. Detergent molecules have a hydrophobic and a hydrophilic end. The hydrophobic (=water-hating) ends surround the dirt particle, leaving the hydrophilic ends exposed. This makes it easier for the dirt to be washed away in water. adjective	

hydrophobic
/ˌhaɪdrəˈfəʊbɪk/
= water-hating. Detergent molecules have a hydrophobic and a hydrophilic end. The hydrophobic ends surround the dirt particle, leaving the hydrophilic (=water-loving) ends exposed. This makes it easier for the dirt to be washed away in water. adjective

hydroxide
/haɪˈdrɒkˌsaɪd/
a chemical compound that contains oxygen and hydrogen in the form OH. noun [count]

immiscible
/ɪˈmɪsɪb(ə)l/
immiscible liquids do not mix together to form a solution. adjective

Oil and water are immiscible.

indicator
/ˈɪndɪˌkeɪtə/
a chemical compound that changes colour in specific conditions. It can be used to test chemical substances, for example in order to discover how acid or alkaline something is. noun [count]

Adding universal indicator to something will tell you whether it is acidic or alkaline.

intermediate
/ˌɪntəˈmiːdiət/
in between two stages, places, levels, times etc. adjective

Colloids are intermediate between solutions and suspensions.

lactic acid
/ˌlæktɪk ˈæsɪd/
1 a substance that forms in muscles after physical exercise as a result of anaerobic respiration. It can cause cramp. noun [uncount]
2 an acid formed in sour milk. noun [uncount]

She suffered from cramp after the race because of the lactic acid in her muscles.

laxative
/ˈlæksətɪv/
a medicine that helps you to empty your bowels when you are constipated (=cannot go to the toilet). noun [count]

Rather than taking laxatives, try to eat more fibre.

litmus paper
/ˈlɪtməs ˌpeɪpə/
paper that contains litmus, used for testing whether something is an acid or an alkali. noun [uncount]

Acids turn blue litmus paper red.

methylated spirits
/ˌmeθəleɪtɪd ˈspɪrɪts/
a type of alcohol that is used as a fuel and is not suitable for drinking. noun [uncount]

Methylated spirits can be used to remove some stains.

micelle
/mɪˈsel/
a tiny droplet that consists of dirt and detergent molecules. noun [count]

Milk of magnesia
/ˌmɪlk əv mægˈniːziə/
a thick white liquid medicine that reduces the amount of acid in your stomach (Trademark).

miscible
/ˈmɪsɪb(ə)l/
miscible liquids mix together to form a solution. adjective

Syrup and water are miscible.

mist
/mɪst/
a mass of small drops of water in the air close to the ground. noun [count/uncount]

Mist is a colloid consisting of water and air.

mixture
/ˈmɪkstʃə/
a substance consisting of different substances that mix together without a chemical reaction taking place. The parts of a mixture can be physically separated. noun [count]

MSG
/ˌem es ˈdʒiː/
monosodium glutamate: a chemical added to food to improve its flavour. noun [uncount]

nail polish
/ˈneɪl ˌpɒlɪʃ/
a shiny coloured liquid that some women put on their nails. noun [uncount]

Acetone can be used to remove nail polish.

naked eye
/ˌneɪkɪd ˈaɪ/
if you can see something with the naked eye, you can see it without using an instrument such as a telescope or a microscope. phrase

The particles dissolved in a solution are too small to be seen with the naked eye.

neutralization reaction
/ˌnjuːtrəlaɪˈzeɪʃ(ə)n riˌækʃ(ə)n/
a reaction that takes place between an acid and a base/alkali. noun [count]

nitrate
/ˈnaɪtreɪt/
a salt formed from nitric acid that is used for improving the quality of soil. Nitrates are an important part of the nitrogen cycle. Chemical formula: NO_3. noun [count/uncount]

nitric acid
/ˌnaɪtrɪk ˈæsɪd/
a very corrosive chemical that is used in industry, and for making bombs and in rocket fuels. noun [uncount]

non-aqueous
/ˌnɒnˈeɪkwiəs/
not containing water. adjective

Petrol is a non-aqueous solution.

non-biodegradable
not able to decay naturally, and therefore harmful to the environment. adjective

The fields are sprayed with non-biodegradable insecticides.

oleum
/ˈɒliəm/
a form of sulphuric acid that is used to make soapless detergents. noun [uncount]

optical brightener
/ˌɒptɪk(ə)l ˈbraɪt(ə)nə/
a substance that is added to detergent to make clothes look brighter or whiter after washing (=fluorescer). noun [count]

oxalic acid
/ɒkˌsælɪk ˈæsɪd/
an acid that occurs naturally in plants such as rhubarb. noun [uncount]

oxide
/ˈɒksaɪd/
a chemical that consists of oxygen combined with another substance. noun [uncount]

Water is an oxide of hydrogen.

phenolphthalein /fiːˈnɒlfθæˌleɪn/	a chemical that is used in scientific experiments, for example as an indicator to show colour changes of solutions. noun [uncount]	
phosphate /ˈfɒsˌfeɪt/	a chemical compound containing phosphorus that is used for making plants grow. noun [count/uncount]	Many inorganic fertilizers contain phosphates.
pH scale /ˌpiː ˈeɪtʃ ˌskeɪl/	a number that describes how acid or alkaline a substance is. Pure water has a pH of 7, with a lower number showing a level of acidity and a higher number showing a level of alkalinity. noun [singular]	
pop /pɒp/	to make a sudden noise like a small explosion. The noise is also called a pop. verb [intransitive]	When hydrogen mixes with oxygen in the presence of a flame, it explodes, causing a popping sound.
potassium hydroxide /pəˌtæsiəm haɪˈdrɒksaɪd/	a white alkaline compound that is used for example in soap manufacture. noun [uncount]	
purification /ˌpjʊərɪfɪˈkeɪʃ(ə)n/	the process of making something clean by removing dirty or harmful substances from it. noun [uncount]	Alum is used in water purification.
purple cabbage /ˌpɜːpl ˈkæbɪdʒ/	a type of cabbage that has purple leaves. It can be used to make an indicator by being crushed with methanol or alcohol and added to filter or tissue paper. When the paper is dry it will have a particular colour which will change when an acid or alkali is added to it. noun [count/uncount]	
raising agent /ˈreɪzɪŋ ˌeɪdʒnt/	it is used in cooking for making cakes rise while they are baking. noun [count/uncount]	
reaction /riˈækʃ(ə)n/	a process in which a chemical change happens. noun [count]	Temperature can affect the rate of a chemical reaction.
reactivity /ˌriækˈtɪvəti/	the degree to which a substance reacts (=changes chemically) when put in contact with another substance. noun [uncount]	The reactivity of metals varies.
retain /rɪˈteɪn/	to keep something. verb [transitive]	
rhubarb /ˈruːbɑːb/	a plant with long red or pink stems that is cooked and eaten as a fruit. noun [uncount]	Rhubarb contains oxalic acid.
rust /rʌst/	the red-brown substance called iron oxide, that forms on the surface of iron or steel through a chemical reaction with water and air. noun [uncount]	The tools had been left out in the rain and had a layer of rust on them.
salt /sɔːlt/	a chemical compound formed from an acid. Solutions of salts can conduct electricity. noun [count]	When an acid is neutralized it forms a salt plus water.
saponification /səpɒnɪfɪˈkeɪʃ(ə)n/	the process of making soap, by heating fat or oil with an alkali such as sodium hydroxide. noun [uncount]	
scatter (light) /ˈskætə/	if a substance scatters light, it does not allow the light to pass through it completely. verb [transitive]	Suspensions appear cloudy because they scatter light.
scouring powder /ˈskaʊrɪŋ ˌpaʊdə/	a dry substance that is used for cleaning things. noun [count/uncount]	
slippery /ˈslɪpəri/	a slippery surface or object is difficult to hold because it is smooth and wet. adjective	Alkalis feel slippery because they react with fatty acids in the skin to form soap.
soapless /ˈsəʊpləs/	a soapless substance does not contain soap. adjective	soapless detergents
soapy /ˈsəʊpi/	covered in soap, or containing soap. adjective	
sodium hydroxide /ˌsəʊdiəm haɪˈdrɒksaɪd/	a chemical compound that is very alkaline and is used in making paper, soap, chemicals, and medicines (=caustic soda). noun [uncount]	Sodium hydroxide must be handled with care as it is very corrosive.
sodium stearate /ˌsəʊdiəm ˈstiːreɪt/	the chemical name for soap. noun [uncount]	
soiled /sɔɪld/	dirty. adjective	The trousers were soiled with mud.
solubility /ˌsɒljʊˈbɪləti/	1 the ability of a solute to dissolve in a solvent and become part of the new liquid solution. noun [uncount] 2 a measure of the ability of a solute to dissolve in a specific amount of a solvent at a specific temperature and pressure (plural: solubilities). noun [count]	The solubility of salt in water can be increased by warming the solution.
solute /ˈsɒljuːt/	a substance that has dissolved in a solvent and become part of the liquid so that they form a solution. noun [count/uncount]	In a sugar solution, sugar is the solute.

solution (true) /sə'luːʃ(ə)n/	a liquid mixture that is formed when a solute dissolves in a solvent and becomes part of the liquid. noun [count]	*Blue ink is a solution of blue pigments in water.*
solvent /'sɒlv(ə)nt/	the liquid part of a solution in which a solute dissolves. noun [count]	*In a sugar solution water is the solvent.*
sour /saʊə/	with a taste like that of a lemon. adjective	*Citric acid gives lemons their sour taste.*
sparingly soluble /ˌspeərɪŋli 'sɒljʊb(ə)l/	able to dissolve in a solution only to a small extent. adjective	*sparingly soluble salts*
stand (liquid) /stænd/	if a liquid stands, it is still and does not flow. verb [intransitive]	*If a suspension is left to stand, the solid particles settle at the bottom.*
stearic acid /ˌstɪərɪk 'æsɪd/	a solid fatty acid that is obtained from vegetable or animal fat. noun [count/uncount]	*Stearic acid is one of the ingredients of soap.*
sulphate /'sʌlfeɪt/	a chemical compound produced from sulphuric acid. Chemical formula: SO_4. noun [count/uncount]	*Some fertilizers contain ammonium sulphate.*
sulphuric acid /sʌlˌfjʊərɪk 'æsɪd/	a strong acid that has no colour and can harm flesh. It is used in batteries, fertilizers, detergents, and in many other compounds. Chemical formula: H_2SO_4. noun [uncount]	*Car batteries can be dangerous because they contain sulphuric acid.*
suspension /sə'spenʃ(ə)n/	a mixture that consists of a liquid containing very small pieces of solid material. noun [count]	*Some medicines such as cough mixtures are suspensions.*
table salt /'teɪbl ˌsɔːlt/	fine grains of salt that you can put on your food when you eat it. noun [uncount]	*The chemical name for table salt is sodium chloride.*
tartaric acid /ˌtɑːtərɪk 'æsɪd/	an acid that is used in baking powder and as a food additive. noun [uncount]	*Unripe grapes contain tartaric acid.*
turpentine /'tɜːpənˌtaɪn/	an oil with a strong smell that you use for removing paint from things. noun [uncount]	*He removed the paint from his hands with a rag soaked in turpentine.*
universal indicator /ˌjuːnɪ'vɜːs(ə)l 'ɪndɪˌkeɪtə/	a chemical solution that changes to different colours over a range of pH values and is used for finding out the degree to which a substance is an acid or an alkali. noun [count]	*The solution was green with universal indicator, which showed it to be neutral.*
varnish /'vɑːnɪʃ/	a clear sticky liquid that is put onto wood to protect it and make it shiny. noun [count/uncount]	*Varnish stains can be removed by rubbing with alcohol then washing in soap and water.*
vinegar /'vɪnɪgə/	a sour liquid that is used for preserving and adding flavour to food. noun [uncount]	*Vinegar contains acetic acid.*
washing soda /'wɒʃɪŋ ˌsəʊdə/	sodium carbonate: it is used to make soaps and as a water softener. noun [uncount]	
water softener /'wɔːtə ˌsɒf(ə)nə/	a substance that is used for removing unwanted minerals from water. noun [count]	*Sodium carbonate is used as a water softener.*

1 Chemicals word map

Write these words in the correct place on the word map.

colloids   detergents   indicators   mixtures   soapless   soapy

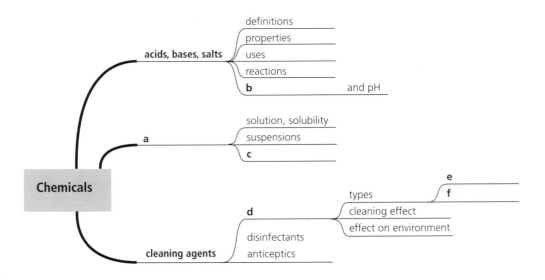

2 How do detergents clean?

Read the text and fill in the gaps with these words.

detergent   droplet   hydrogen   hydrophilic   hydrophobic   soapless   soluble

A detergent molecule, whether soapy or 1 _____, consists of two parts. There is a polar,

2 _____ (water-loving) end, which is soluble in water and is often called the 'head'. There is also a

non-polar, 3 _____ (water-hating) end, which is soluble in fats and oils and is called the 'tail'. The

tail is a long hydrocarbon chain, that is, a chain of carbon atoms with 4 _____ atoms attached to

them. Dirt clings to surfaces, skin or fabric, by an oil film that surrounds the dirt particle. The tail end of

5 _____ molecules will attach to the oil film around the dirt particle and completely surround it,

making a tiny 6 _____ or micelle. As all the tail ends are attached to the oil around the dirt particle,

only the hydrophilic end of the detergent molecules will be exposed to the surface. As these are

7 _____ in water, you can now wash away the dirt.

3 Common chemical substances and their uses in the home

Put the words and phrases in the correct places in the table. One item appears twice.

alum   antacid   citric acid   Glauber's salt   insect stings   laxative   monosodium glutamate   oven cleaner   raising agent   salt   sodium chloride   sodium hydrogencarbonate   sodium hydroxide   vinegar   washing soda

Common name	Chemical name (of active ingredient)	Type of chemical	Uses
caustic soda	1 _____	alkali	drain cleaner, 2 _____, grease remover
Milk of magnesia	magnesium hydroxide	alkali	3 _____
4 _____	acetic acid solution (ethanoic acid)	acid	cooking, pickling, cleaning and treating some 5 _____
baking soda	6 _____ _____	salt	raising agent in baking, an antacid, in dry powder fire extinguishers, treating insect bites, for cleaning
baking powder	sodium hydrogencarbonate	salt	7 _____ in baking
8 _____	sodium carbonate	salt	to make soaps and glass cleaners, also used as a water softener
Enos salts	sodium hydrogencarbonate and 9 _____	salt and acid	antacid
table (common) salt	10 _____	salt	cooking and preserving foods.
Epsom salts	magnesium sulphate	salt	11 _____
12 _____	sodium sulphate	salt	laxative
13 _____	sodium aluminium sulphate	salt	water purification, also baking powder
toothpaste	sodium monofluoroposphate	14 _____	prevents tooth decay
MSG	15 _____	salt	enhances flavour in food

4 Solutions

Underline the correct word in each sentence.

1   Solutions are (homogenous / heterogeneous) mixtures, which are formed when a solute completely dissolves in a solvent.
2   The (solute / solvent) is the substance that dissolves, while the (solute / solvent) is the substance that does the dissolving.
3   It is generally present in the (lesser / greater) quantity in the mixture.
4   When the solvent used to make the solution is water then the solution is said to be (aqueous / non-aqueous).
5   However when the solvent used is a liquid other than water, then the solution is said to be (aqueous / non-aqueous).
6   Liquid solutions are (translucent / transparent) but not necessarily colourless.
7   They allow (light / dark) to pass through without being scattered.
8   The dissolved particles are very small, from 0.1 nanometre to 1 nanometre therefore they cannot be seen with the (nude eye / naked eye) or even be removed by normal filter paper.
9   The dissolved (articles / particles) do not settle out if the solution is allowed to stand for some time.

5   Solvents in stain removal

Match these stains with the correct paragraph to show how the stain can be removed.

> blood   chocolate   coffee/tea   grease/oil   ink   nail polish   paint   varnish

1 _____ – Gloss is best removed whilst wet with turpentine or white spirit. Some water-based versions can be removed with hot water and detergent.

2 _____ – If the stain cannot be removed by warm water and soap, pour on boiling water, provided that this will not damage the fabric. Or use a biological washing powder. If this does not work, dab with dilute hydrogen peroxide.

3 _____ – If stains cannot be removed with soap and hot water, try a biological detergent which contains bleach.

4 _____ – Water-soluble versions of this substance can be removed by washing with soap and water. However, many stains made by this substance can be removed by soaking the stain in milk for 1 or 2 days, changing the milk as it becomes discoloured. Ethanedioic acid and methanol are non-aqueous solvents that can dissolve these stains.

5 _____ – Rub with alcohol. Then wash with warm water and soap.

6 _____ – Soak in cold water until stain turns lighter brown. Then wash in warm water and detergent.

7 _____ – Remove with acetone which is an organic solvent.

8 _____ – Wash in warm water and soap, or use clean white blotting paper, a piece on each side of the stain, and iron with a warm iron to remove as much of it as possible. Gasoline is a non-aqueous solvent that removes these stains.

6   Properties of acids and alkalis

Sort the characteristics of acids and alkalis in the correct columns. One of the characteristics applies to both.

Acids …	Alkalis …
1	7
2	8
3	9
4	10
5	11
6	12

a   … are corrosive.
b   … are slippery when touched, that is they feel soapy.
c   … are soluble in water.
d   … are the oxide or hydroxide of a metal.
e   … have a sour taste.
f   … react with acids to give a salt and water only.
g   … react with bases/alkalis to produce a salt and water only.
h   … react with fatty acids in the skin to form soap.
i   … react with many materials and some can damage human tissue.
j   … release hydrogen ions when dissolved in water.
k   … turn blue litmus paper red.

7   Types of solutions

Read the text and complete the table.

There are different types of solutions. We often think of solutions as being formed between a solid solute and a liquid solvent. However, gases and liquids can be solutes and solvents too.

There are solutions which are made up of a solid in a liquid where the solute is a solid and the solvent is a liquid. Examples of this are sugar in water, salt in water and iodine in ethanol.

Oxygen in water, carbon dioxide in water in fizzy drinks are examples of solutions where there is a gas in a liquid. This is where the solute is a gas and the solvent is a liquid.

It is also possible to have a solution which is a liquid in a liquid where both the solute and the solvent are liquids. Examples of this are alcohol in water and syrup in water.

Type of solution	Solute	Solvent	Examples
solid in liquid			
gas in liquid			
liquid in liquid			

22 Metals and plastics

Translation

adhesive /əˈdiːsɪv/	a substance that you use for making things stick together. noun [count/uncount]	
alloy /ˈælɔɪ/	a metal made by combining two or more other metals. noun [count/uncount]	
aluminium /ˌæləˈmɪniəm/	a light silver-coloured metal element that does not corrode easily. Chemical symbol: Al. noun [uncount]	*She covered the chicken with aluminium foil before roasting it in the oven*
amphoteric /æmˌfəʊˈterɪk/	able to act with both acids and alkalis. adjective	*Aluminium is amphoteric, which is unusual.*
anodising /ˈænəˌdaɪzɪŋ/	the process of coating a metal such as aluminium with an oxide layer, to prevent any more oxygen from getting into it. noun [uncount]	
Bakelite /ˈbeɪkəˌlaɪt/	a type of hard plastic that was used especially in the 1930s and 1940s for making things such as radios and telephones. It is not used much today (Trademark). noun [uncount]	*The house still had door handles made of bakelite.*
bend /bend/	to curve or fold something, or to be curved or folded. verb [transitive/intransitive]	*Some forms of plastic are easy to bend.*
brass /brɑːs/	a shiny yellow metal that is a mixture of copper and zinc. noun [uncount]	*Brass is harder than zinc.*
brittle /ˈbrɪt(ə)l/	hard and easily broken. adjective	*Cast iron is brittle.*
bronze /brɒnz/	a hard brown metal used for making statues and objects for decoration. It is made by mixing copper and tin. noun [uncount]	
buoyancy /ˈbɔɪənsi/	the quality of being able to float, or the ability of a liquid to make things float in it. noun [uncount]	*Being made of plastic gave the dingy buoyancy.*
cast iron /ˌkɑːst ˈaɪən/	very hard iron used for making objects such as cooking pans and fences. noun [uncount]	*Cast iron is used to make household utensils.*
conduct /kənˈdʌkt/	if something conducts heat or electricity, heat or electricity moves through it. verb [transitive]	
corrode /kəˈrəʊd/	if metal or another substance corrodes, or if something corrodes it, it is gradually destroyed by a chemical reaction. verb [transitive/intransitive]	*The metal had corroded and gone rusty.*
cupro-nickel /ˈkuprəʊˌnɪk(ə)l/	an alloy (=mixture) of copper and nickel that is hard and wears well. It is used to make coins. noun [uncount]	
dashboard /ˈdæʃbɔːd/	the part inside a car where the speedometer and other instruments are. noun [count]	
disposal /dɪsˈpəʊz(ə)l/	the process of getting rid of something. noun [uncount]	*Plastics can remain in the ground for many years after disposal.*
dry oxidation /ˌdraɪ ɒksɪˈdeɪʃ(ə)n/	the corrosion of metal in a water-free environment. noun [uncount]	*The oxidation of aluminium is an example of dry oxidation.*
ductile /ˈdʌktaɪl/	ductile metals are metals such as copper and aluminium that can be pulled into wires. adjective	*Copper is a ductile metal.*
durable /ˈdjʊərəb(ə)l/	able to stay in good condition for a long time, even after being used a lot. adjective	*Stainless steel is very durable.*
duralumin /djʊəˈræləmɪn/	an alloy (=mixture) of aluminium and copper. It is used to make kitchen utensils and frames for household appliances. noun [uncount]	
elastic /ɪˈlæstɪk/	able to stretch or bend and then return to the original shape. adjective	*Polyurethane is very elastic, which makes it suitable for making sportswear.*
forge /fɔːdʒ/	to heat metal until it is soft and then hit it with a hammer to form different shapes. verb [transitive]	*Iron can be forged.*
Formica /fɔːˈmaɪkə/	a hard plastic used for covering tables and working areas in kitchens (Trademark). noun [uncount]	*Formica is a thermosetting plastic.*
galvanize /ˈgælvənaɪz/	to cover iron or steel with zinc in order to prevent rusting. verb [transitive]	*The hut had a galvanized roof.*

gold /gəʊld/	a valuable yellow metal element that is used for making jewellery and in alloys. Chemical symbol: Au. noun [uncount]	*Her bracelet was made of solid gold.*
GRP /ˌdʒiː ɑː ˈpiː/	glass reinforced plastic: a material made of glass fibres and plastic. It is used for insulation and to make things such as boats and roofs. noun [uncount]	
inert /ɪenˈɪt/	an inert substance such as a gas does not produce a chemical reaction with other substances. adjective	*Platinum is a relatively inert metal.*
laminate /ˈlæmɪnət/	a substance that consists of several thin layers of wood, plastic, glass etc. noun [count]	*Melamine is used to make laminates.*
long-lasting /ˈlɒŋlɑːstɪŋ/	continuing for a long time. adjective	*Metals are long-lasting.*
lustrous /ˌlʌstrəs/	bright and shiny. adjective	*Metals are lustrous, which means they can be polished to look very shiny.*
Lycra /ˈlaɪkrə/	cloth made from polyurethane that is used for making sports clothes (Trademark). noun [uncount]	*Lycra running shorts*
malleable /ˈmæliəb(ə)l/	a malleable metal is easy to press into different shapes. adjective	*Aluminium is very malleable.*
man-made /ˈmænˌmeɪd/	something that is man-made has been made by people and does not exist naturally. adjective	*Rayon is a man-made fibre.*
melamine /ˈmeləˌmaɪn/	hard smooth plastic used for making the surfaces of things such as tables. noun [uncount]	*a melamine worktop*
melt /melt/	to change a solid substance into a liquid using heat, or to be changed from a solid substance into a liquid by the use of heat. verb [transitive/intransitive]	*Metals melt at very high temperatures.*
monomer /ˈmɒnəmə/	a simple molecule that can combine with other molecules to form a polymer. noun [count]	*Ethene is a monomer that links in a chain with other ethane molecules to form polythene.*
mylar /ˈmaɪlɑː/	a type of polyester that is used to make plastic films and sheets (Trademark). noun [uncount]	
non-metal /ˌnɒn ˈmet(ə)l/	a chemical element that is not a metal, for example carbon or oxygen. Non-metals are solids and gases and are not good conductors of heat and electricity. noun [count]	
organic /ɔːˈɡænɪk/	organic compounds contain carbon, and energy can be released from them. adjective	*Petrol and other fuels are organic compounds.*
overhead cable /ˌəʊvəhed ˈkeɪb(ə)l/	a thick wire that is used for carrying electricity high above the ground. noun [count]	*Aluminium is used to make overhead cables.*
Perspex /ˈpɜːspeks/	a strong transparent plastic that can be used in doors and windows instead of glass (Trademark). noun [uncount]	*Perspex softens when heated.*
platinum /ˈplætɪnəm/	a silver-grey metal element that is used in industry and for making expensive jewellery. Chemical symbol: Pt. noun [uncount]	*Her expensive wedding ring was made of platinum.*
plumbing /ˈplʌmɪŋ/	the system of pipes and equipment that are used for supplying and storing water in a building. noun [uncount]	*Copper and brass have many uses in plumbing.*
polyacrylamide /ˌpɒliəˈkrɪləmaɪd/	a type of plastic that absorbs water and then releases it on contact with salt. It is used in soil mixtures and in diapers. noun [uncount]	
polycyanoacrylate /ˌpɒlisaɪænəʊ ˈækrɪleɪt/	a type of plastic that sticks to almost anything and sets very quickly forming strong adhesive bonds. It is used in emergency surgery instead of stitches. noun [uncount]	
polymer /ˈpɒlɪmə/	a chemical compound consisting of large molecules made of groups of identical smaller ones called monomers joined together. Polymers can be natural or artificial. Starch, nylon, cellulose, and polythene are all polymers. noun [count]	*Polyethene is a polymer made from ethane monomers.*
polymerisation /ˌpɒlɪməraɪˈzeɪʃ(ə)n/	the process by which small molecules called monomers join together to form big ones called polymers. Polymerisation is used in making plastics. noun [uncount]	
polymethyl methacrylate /ˌpɒliˌmiːθaɪl meθəˈkraɪleɪt/	a type of plastic that is used to make Perspex. It softens when heated so it can be moulded. noun [uncount]	
polypropene /ˌpɒliˈprəʊpiːn/	a type of plastic that is used to make clothing, blankets and carpets. noun [uncount]	
polystyrene /ˌpɒliˈstaɪriːn/	a type of plastic that is used especially for making containers. Polystyrene foam is very light and is used as an insulator and in packaging. noun [uncount]	

polythene /ˈpɒlɪθiːn/	a strong light plastic made from ethene, used especially for making plastic bags and wrapping food in order to keep it fresh. **noun [uncount]**	*She put the bread in a polythene bag to stop it going stale.*
polyurethane /ˌpɒlɪˈjʊərəθeɪn/	a type of plastic that is used for making things such as paint and varnishes, and Lycra which is used to make sports clothing. **noun [uncount]**	
polyvinyl chloride /ˌpɒlivaɪn(ə)l ˈklɔːraɪd/	a type of plastic that is used for making clothes and cloth. **noun [uncount]**	
propathene /ˈprəʊpəθiːn/	the brand name for polypropene, a type of plastic that is used to make clothes, blankets and carpets. **noun [uncount]**	
property /ˈprɒpəti/	a quality or feature of something. **noun [count]**	
PTFE /ˌpiː tiː ef ˈiː/	a type of plastic that is stable at high temperatures and has a slippery surface. It is used as a coating for cookware and for some heavy duty clothing. **noun [uncount]**	
PVC /ˌpiː viː ˈsiː/	the brand name for polyvinal chloride, a type of plastic that is used for making clothes and cloth. **noun [uncount]**	*The raincoat was made from PVC.*
reactive /riˈæktɪv/	a reactive substance combines easily with other substances. **adjective**	*Sodium is a very reactive metal.*
reflect /rɪˈflekt/	1 if a surface reflects something, you can see the image of that thing on the surface. **verb [transitive]** 2 if something reflects light, heat etc, the light, heat etc comes back off it. **verb [transitive/intransitive]**	*Shiny metal surfaces reflect light like a mirror.*
reflective /rɪˈflektɪv/	a reflective surface shows the image of something. **adjective**	*Aluminium is highly reflective.*
resistant /rɪˈzɪstənt/	not harmed or affected by something. **adjective**	*Stainless steel is very resistant to rust.*
resonate /ˈrezəneɪt/	to produce or be filled with a deep clear sound that continues for a long time. **verb [intransitive]**	*The vibrations of the gong resonated through the temple.*
sacrificial protection /sækrɪˌfɪʃ(ə)l prəˈtekʃ(ə)n/	the use of a metal such as zinc to protect another metal such as iron from rust. The zinc rusts first, so that as long as there is some left, the iron will not rust. **noun [uncount]**	*Zinc is used on the iron hulls of ships for sacrificial protection.*
shiny /ˈʃaɪni/	something that is shiny has a bright surface that reflects light. **adjective**	*A shiny metal plate reflects the light of the headlamps forward.*
solder /ˈsəʊldə/	1 to join two metal surfaces together using solder. **verb [transitive]** 2 a soft metal that is a mixture of lead and tin. It becomes liquid when heated and is used for joining two other metal surfaces together. **noun [uncount]**	
sonorous /ˈsɒnərəs/	a sound that is sonorous is deep and strong in a pleasant way. **adjective**	*Metals are sonorous and so are used to make musical instruments.*
stainless steel /ˌsteɪnləs ˈstiːl/	steel that has been treated to stop rust forming on its surface. It is made from iron with small amounts of nickel and chromium and is used for making knives, tools, and cooking pans. **noun [uncount]**	
steel pan /ˌstiːl ˈpæn/	percussion instrument made out of an oil drum (also called: steel drum). **noun [count]**	
Styrofoam /ˈstaɪrəfəʊm/	a type of polystyrene that is very light and is used as an insulator and in packaging (Trademark).	
Superglue /ˈsuːpəˌgluː/	a type of very strong glue that sticks things together very quickly (Trademark). **noun [uncount]**	*Superglue is sometimes used instead of stitches in emergency surgery.*
surpass /səˈpɑːs/	to be better or bigger than something else. **verb [transitive]**	*Plastics can surpass natural materials, performing better than them in some circumstances.*
synthetic rubber /sɪnˌθetɪk ˈrʌbə/	rubber that is made from plastic rather than from a tropical plant. **noun [uncount]**	
tarnish /ˈtɑːnɪʃ/	if metal tarnishes, or if something tarnishes it, it loses its colour and becomes less shiny. **verb [transitive/intransitive]**	*Metal tarnishes as a result of the reaction between the metal and the gases in the air.*
Teflon /ˈteflɒn/	the trade name of a type of plastic called PTFE. Teflon is often put on pans to prevent food from sticking to them (Trademark). **noun [uncount]**	*Eventually the Teflon coating wears off and the pan has to be replaced.*
tensile strength /ˌhaɪ tensaɪl ˈstreŋθ/	the quality of being strong when stretched. Many metals have a high tensile strength. **noun [count]**	*Their high tensile strength means that metals are suitable for making fences, windows and doorframes.*

Terylene /ˈterɪˌliːn/	a type of polyester that is used to make clothes (Trademark). **noun [uncount]**	
thermoplastic /ˈθɜːməʊˌplæstɪk/	one of the two main types of plastic. Thermoplastics melt when heated and become hard when cooled. They can easily be remoulded. **noun [count/uncount]**	
thermosetting plastic /ˈθɜːməʊsetɪŋ ˌplæstɪk/	one of the two main types of plastic. Thermosetting plastics become permanently hard once they have been heated and moulded into form. **noun [count/uncount]**	
tin /tɪn/	a chemical element that is a soft light silver metal. Chemical symbol: Sn. **noun [uncount]**	*There used to be tin mines all around this area.*
waterproof /ˈwɔːtəˌpruːf/	waterproof clothes or materials do not let water pass through them. **adjective**	*Many types of plastic are waterproof.*
wear /weə/	if something wears well, it lasts for a long time. **verb [intransitive]**	*Plastic fibres are hard-wearing and stain-resistant.*
wet oxidation /ˌwet ɒksɪˈdeɪʃ(ə)n/	the corrosion of metal in an environment where water and air are both present. **noun [uncount]**	*The rusting of aluminium is an example of wet oxidation.*
white spirit /ˌwaɪt ˈspɪrɪt/	a liquid made from petrol, used for removing paint marks and making paint thinner. **noun [uncount]**	
wrought iron /ˌrɔːt (aɪən)/	iron that is used for making fences, gates etc especially for decoration. **noun [uncount]**	*Wrought iron can be made into many different shapes.*
zinc /zɪŋk/	a chemical element that is a blue-white metal. It is used to make alloys and as a surface layer to protect other metals, especially iron and steel. Chemical symbol: Zn. **noun [uncount]**	*The corrugated iron roof was coated with zinc to stop it going rusty.*

A Working with words

1 Metals and plastic word map

Write these words in the correct places on the word map.

chemical   corrosion   metals   pipes   sonorous   thermoplastics

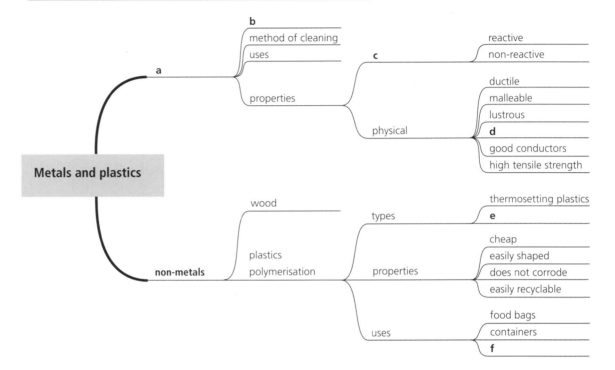

2 Plastics with special uses

Match these uses to the correct plastics.

a bouyancy tanks, sailboards, adhesives
b coatings for cookware, also some clothing for rough use, easy-gliding furniture
c in soil mixtures for houseplants; nappies
d sets very quickly forming strong adhesive bonds, used in emergency surgery to replace stitches
e windscreens, door panels, aircraft windows, optical fibres
f work surfaces, tableware, decorative laminates

Name of plastic	Example	Properties	Uses
PTFE	Teflon	stable up to 270–390°C, slippery surface	1
polyacrylamide		absorbs water, releases it on contact with salt	2
polyurethane		forms soft or rigid foams	3
polycyanoacrylate	Superglue	stable as monomer until moist, adheres to nearly anything	4
melamine resin	Melamine formica	resistant to heat and chemicals, hard, waterproof	5
polymethyl methacrylate	Perspex	glass-like, softens on heating so it can be moulded	6

3 Uses of metals related to their properties

First match these metals to their properties. Then put the missing uses in the correct places.

Metals
aluminium   copper   gold and platinum   iron   silver   tin   wrought iron   zinc

Uses
lining for steel cans in the food industry, especially for acid foods such as pineapple
ornaments, ornamental serving dishes and utensils
railings, horseshoes
used in cooking and for storing or packaging food – its highly reflective surface
prevents heat loss so it keeps foods warm for longer
used to make many common utensils

Metal	Properties	Uses
1	low density (light in weight); good conductor of heat and electricity	9
	malleable; high reflective surface	lightweight kitchen utensils, pans, cans and storage containers, industrial electrical wiring and overhead electrical cables
2	excellent conductor of heat and electricity; resistant to corrosion; soft, so easily bent and shaped; ductile, so easily stretched into wires; unreactive	electrical wires; pans, or the bottoms of pans made from another metal; pipes that carry gas and water since they can be bent easily and joined
3	does not corrode; lustrous	high quality jewellery and ornaments
	does not corrode; excellent electrical conductor	contacts in switches
4	strong (though cast iron is brittle); can be cast into moulds	10
	magnetic	used in magnets and electrical transformers to produce safer, low-voltage electrical supplies
	corrodes easily (rusts)	because iron rusts, it must be coated with other materials such as paint or zinc if it is to withstand the weather
5	soft; can be forged, hammered, welded	11
6	low melting point; does not corrode	12
7	low melting point; reactive	can coat iron / steel sheet to resist rusting since it corrodes before the iron; lining cans, coating roofing sheets, protecting automobile body panels
8	good conductor of heat; highly reflective does not corrode (but tarnishes slowly); not toxic	13

4 Metals and plastics

Match the beginnings and endings of the sentences.

Beginnings

1 Plastics are man-made products
2 Plastics are classified as
3 Plastics are hazardous to the environment because
4 Metals are useful
5 An alloy is a mixture of two or more metals that have been
6 Aluminium on exposure to air
7 Corrosion is the process
8 The type of corrosion, dry oxidation or wet oxidation,
9 Most metals
10 Corrosion on iron
11 Metals become tarnished

Endings

a because they are lustrous, strong, excellent conductors of heat and electricity, malleable, ductile and sonorous.
b by which metals react with substances in the environment to form the metal oxide and in some cases the sulphide or sulphate.
c corrode in moist air.
d depends on the environmental conditions.
e either thermoplastics or thermosetting plastics.
f is called rust.
g made by the process of polymerisation.
h many are non-biodegradable and burn to release toxic fumes.
i melted together and thoroughly mixed, e.g. brass is a mixture of copper and zinc.
j produces a protective oxide coat (aluminium oxide) over the metal.
k when a thin layer of metal oxide, sulphide or carbonate is formed on the surface when the metal reacts with gases in the air.

1 ☐ 2 ☐ 3 ☐ 4 ☐ 5 ☐ 6 ☐ 7 ☐ 8 ☐ 9 ☐ 10 ☐ 11 ☐

5 Plastics that form fibres

Read the text and fill in the missing information in the table.

Polypropene is a plastic which forms fibres; an example is propathene. It is a tough, waterproof plastic which is stain resistant and is used in clothing, blankets and carpets. Another plastic used in fibrous form is polyamide which gives us nylon. It is a strong, hard wearing and elastic material which is chemically resistant and self lubricating. It is used for the production of clothing, upholstery, in rope making, in gear wheels, fuel tanks, curtain rails and combs. Lycra is an example of polyurethane plastic which forms elastic fibres and is used in making stretch clothing, for example, ski suits. Polyester gives terylene mylar which has strong cotton-like waterproof fibres and is used in clothing manufacturing. Though it's not so good in hot climates, it can take permanent creases or pleats.

Name	Example	Properties	Uses
1	propathene	2	clothing, blankets, carpets
3	4	strong, hard wearing, elastic chemically resistant, self lubricating	clothing, upholstery, ropes, gear wheels, fuel tanks, curtain rails, combs
polyurethane	Lycra	5	6
polyester	7	strong waterproof cotton-like fibres	8

23 Forces and motion

acceleration
/ək,selə'reɪʃ(ə)n/
the rate at which a moving object increases its speed. **noun [singular]**
Acceleration continues for as long as the force continues to act upon the object.

action
/'ækʃ(ə)n/
something that happens that has an effect. **noun [count]**
Newton's third law states that for every action there is an equal and opposite reaction.

act on
/'ækt ,ɒn/
to start to have an effect. **verb [intransitive]**
It is possible for more than one force to act on an object at the same time.

aerodynamic
/,eərəʊdaɪ'næmɪk/
shaped in a way that makes it easier for something to move through the air smoothly and quickly. **adjective**
The car's streamlined, aerodynamic shape made it very attractive.

anticlockwise
/,ænti'klɒkwaɪz/
moving in a circle in the direction opposite to the direction of the hands of a clock. **adjective, adverb**

at rest
/,ət 'rest/
not moving. **phrase**
An object at rest will remain at rest unless acted on by an external force.

axle
/'æks(ə)l/
a metal bar that connects a pair of wheels on a car or other vehicle. **noun [count]**

ball bearing
/,bɔːl (beərɪŋ)/
one of several small metal balls that are used between moving parts of a machine to help the parts move smoothly. **noun [count]**
The bike gears contained several ball bearings.

bump
/bʌmp/
a raised part on a surface. **noun [count]**
a bump in the road

centre of gravity
/,sentə(r) əv 'grævɪti/
the point in an object around which its weight balances. **noun [count]**
All objects have a centre of gravity.

centrifugal force
/sen,trɪfjʊg(ə)l 'fɔːs/
a force that makes things move away from the centre of something when they are moving around that centre. It is the reaction force to the centripetal force. **noun [uncount]**

centripetal force
/sen,trɪpɪt(ə)l 'fɔːs/
a force that makes things move towards the centre of something when they are moving around that centre. Gravity is the centripetal force that keeps the planets orbiting around the sun. **noun [uncount]**

circular path
/,sɜːkjələ 'pɑːθ/
a direction in which something is moving that is in the shape of a circle. **noun [count]**
An object moving in a circular path experiences a centripetal pull.

clockwise
/'klɒk,waɪz/
moving in a circle in the same direction as the hands on a clock. **adjective, adverb**

counteract
/,kaʊntə'rækt/
to reduce the effect of something by doing something that has an opposite effect. **verb [transitive]**
Astronauts in space do special exercises to counteract the effects of weightlessness.

crest
/krest/
the top part of something, for example a wave or a hill. **noun [count]**

decelerate
/diː'seləreɪt/
to move more slowly. **verb [intransitive]**
A ball moving along a level surface will decelerate and then stop.

efficient
/ɪ'fɪʃ(ə)nt/
working well and producing good results. **adjective**
Ball bearings are very efficient in making the moving parts of machines work smoothly.

effort
/'efət/
the force used on a machine of any type in order to make it able to move an object. **noun [singular/uncount]**
He needed a great deal of effort to make the scissors cut the thick paper.

equilibrium
/,iːkwɪ'lɪbriəm/
a state in which an object is not moving in any way or is moving at the same rate all the time because there is a balance between any forces affecting it. An object that is not moving in any way is said to be at rest. **noun [count/uncount]**
The rocket drifted through space in a state of equilibrium.

exert
/ɪg'zɜːt/
to put force or physical pressure on something. **verb [transitive]**
When a force is exerted on an object, it brings about a change in the object.

external force
/ɪk,stɜːn(ə)l 'fɔːs/
a force that is outside an object and acts on it. **noun [count]**
When you push a shopping trolley, you are the external force that is acting on the trolley.

first law of motion /ˌfɜːst lɔː(r) əv ˈməʊʃ(ə)n/	one of the laws about movement that were first expressed by Isaac Newton. It states that an object at rest will remain at rest, and an object in motion will move in a straight line with constant speed, unless acted on by an external force. **noun [singular]**	
force /fɔːs/	a power that makes an object move or that changes the way it moves. **noun [count]**	*Gravity is the force that holds objects to the Earth's surface.*
freewheel /ˈfriːˌwiːl/	to ride on a bike without turning the pedals. **verb [intransitive]**	*He freewheeled down the hill.*
friction /ˈfrɪkʃ(ə)n/	the force that resists the movement of one object against another. Rough surfaces and objects create more friction than smooth ones. **noun [uncount]**	*Friction can be reduced by using oil.*
fulcrum /ˈfʊlkrəm/	the point on which a lever balances or turns. **noun [count]**	*The fulcrum of a wheelbarrow is the wheel.*
geostationary orbit /ˌdʒiːəʊsteɪʃ(ə)n(ə)ri ˈɔːbɪt/	an orbit of the Earth made by an artificial satellite that moves at the same rate as the Earth spins, with the result that it is always above the same point on the Earth's surface. **noun [count]**	*Satellites that transmit TV signals are usually in a geostationary orbit.*
GPS /ˌdʒiː piː ˈes/	global positioning satellite: a satellite (=an object that goes around the Earth high in the sky) that is used to provide a reference point for navigation aids (=devices that tell you where you are). **noun [count]**	
gravitational /ˌɡrævɪˈteɪʃ(ə)nəl/	relating to the force of gravity. **adjective**	*On the Moon the gravitational force is less than on the Earth.*
gravitational pull /ˌɡrævɪteɪʃ(ə)nəl ˈpʊl/	the force of gravity that one object with mass exerts on another. **noun [uncount]**	*The gravitational pull of the Earth stops us from floating off into space.*
gravity /ˈɡrævəti/	the force that makes any two objects that have mass move towards each other. The most common example of this is when an object falls to the ground. **noun [uncount]**	*The force of gravity keeps the Moon in orbit around the Earth.*
grip /ɡrɪp/	to hold a surface firmly without slipping. **verb [intransitive]**	
hinder /ˈhɪndə/	to stop something from making progress. **verb [transitive]**	*Friction hinders the motion of a moving object.*
hinge /hɪndʒ/	an object by which a door is attached to a wall, or a lid to a container, and which allows it to open and shut. **noun [count]**	*It is easier to close a door by pushing it from the side furthest away from the hinge.*
hollow /ˈhɒləʊ/	an area on a surface that is lower than the areas around it. **noun [count]**	
ignition /ɪɡˈnɪʃ(ə)n/	the process of making something start to burn. **noun [uncount]**	*The heat produced from friction is enough to cause ignition.*
interlock /ˌɪntəˈlɒk/	to join things together by means of parts that fit into other parts, or to be joined in this way. **verb [transitive/intransitive]**	*The two surfaces interlock, which hinders motion.*
law of moments /ˌlɔː(r) əv ˈməʊmənts/	a law of physics that states: when an object is in equilibrium (=balanced), the sum of the clockwise movements is equal to the sum of the anticlockwise movements about the same pivot (=point). **noun [singular]**	
law of motion /ˌlɔː(r) əv ˈməʊʃ(ə)n/	one of the laws about movement that were first expressed by Isaac Newton. **noun [count]**	
level /ˈlevəl/	at the same height. **adjective**	*A bike that is freewheeling along a level surface will come to a stop because of friction.*
load /ləʊd/	the amount of weight or pressure that something has to bear. **noun [count]**	*Placing a load on the top of a bus makes it unstable.*
lubricant /ˈluːbrɪkənt/	an oil that you use to lubricate a machine. **noun [count/uncount]**	*The engine had seized up due to a lack of lubricant.*
maintain /meɪnˈteɪn/	to make something stay the same. **verb [transitive]**	*A low centre of gravity is important to maintain the stability of moving objects.*
mass /mæs/	the amount of matter that something contains. Mass is different from weight as the effects of gravity are not taken into account when it is measured. Symbol: m. **noun [uncount]**	*Our mass is the same on the Moon as it is on Earth, even though our weight is different.*
moment /ˈməʊmənt/	the tendency of a force to produce movement of a load. It is measured by multiplying the force by the distance from the fulcrum. Symbol: Nm. **noun [singular/uncount]**	*A lever is balanced if the moments on either side of the fulcrum are equal.*

Term	Definition	Translation
neutral equilibrium /ˌnjuːtrəl iːkwɪˈlɪbriəm/	when the centre of gravity of an object is always at the same height, it is said to be in neutral equilibrium. noun [uncount]	
newton /ˈnjuːt(ə)n/	a unit for measuring force, equal to the force that causes a mass of one kilogram to accelerate at one metre a second every second. Symbol N. noun [count]	Weight is measured in newtons.
non-contact force /ˌnɒnˌkɒntækt ˈfɔːs/	a force that works without actually touching the object. Gravity is a non-contact force. noun [count]	
oil /ɔɪl/	to put oil on something. verb [transitive]	If you oil a machine, you will make it work more smoothly.
opposite /ˈɒpəzɪt/	completely different; the reverse. adjective	Action-reaction forces are equal in size and opposite in direction.
orbit /ˈɔːbɪt/	the path that is taken by an object such as a planet that is moving around a larger object in space. noun [count]	Space stations are designed to remain in orbit for years.
pivot /ˈpɪvət/	a fixed point or pin that something turns on or balances on (=fulcrum.) noun [count]	The pivot point of something is its central point.
plumbline /ˈplʌmˌlaɪn/	a piece of string with a metal object fixed to the bottom. It is used to check that things are straight, or to draw straight lines. noun [count]	You can use a plumbline to find the centre of gravity of an irregular shape.
press together /ˌpres təˈgeðə/	if two things press together, they push against each other. If you press two things together, you cause them to do this. verb [transitive/intransitive]	
prevent from /prɪˈvent ˌfrəm/	to stop something from happening. verb [transitive]	Friction prevents surfaces from sliding against each other.
pull /pʊl/	a strong physical force that causes things to move in a particular direction. noun [singular]	the pull of gravity
push /pʊʃ/	a movement in which you push someone or something. noun [count]	If you give an unstable object a push, it will probably fall over.
quantity /ˈkwɒntəti/	the amount of something. noun [uncount]	They check both the quantity and quality of materials used.
resistance /rɪˈzɪst(ə)ns/	a force that makes a moving object move more slowly. noun [uncount]	The wind resistance caused the runners to slow down.
resultant force /rɪˌzʌltənt ˈfɔːs/	the total force that is acting on an object. If the forces are acting in the same direction, you add them together; if they are acting in opposite directions, you subtract them. noun [count]	If the force from one direction is 10 N and the force from the other direction is also 10 N, the resultant force is zero.
result in /rɪˈzʌlt ˌɪn/	to cause or produce something. phrasal verb	Overheating can result in metal surfaces fusing together.
roll /rəʊl/	to move forwards while turning over and over, or to make something do this. verb [transitive/intransitive]	The pencil went rolling across the floor.
roller /ˈrəʊlə/	something shaped like a tube or a ball that is used to move an object over a surface. noun [count]	Ball bearings are the most common rollers used today.
rollerblade /ˈrəʊləˌbleɪd/	a type of boot with a single row of small wheels along the bottom, used for moving along quickly, especially for fun or as a sport (Trademark). noun [count]	
rotate /rəʊˈteɪt/	to move in a circle around a central point, or to move something in this way. verb [transitive/intransitive]	The Earth rotates 360 degrees every 24 hours.
roughness /ˈrʌfnəs/	the quality of being rough (= not smooth). noun [uncount]	You light a match by rubbing it against a rough surface on the box.
rub /rʌb/	to move your hands or an object firmly over a surface. verb [transitive/intransitive]	
satellite /ˈsætəˌlaɪt/	1 an object that is sent into space to travel round the Earth in order to receive and send information. noun [count] 2 a natural object such as a moon that moves around a planet. noun [count]	We have pictures of the disaster live via satellite (=by satellite).
second law of motion /ˌsekənd lɔː(r) əv ˈməʊʃ(ə)n/	one of the laws about movement that were first expressed by Isaac Newton. It states that a force accelerates the movement of an object. noun [singular]	
seize /siːz/	if the parts of an engine or machine seize, they stick together and the machine stops working. verb [intransitive]	
skid /skɪd/	to slide across the ground in an uncontrolled way. verb [intransitive]	The car skidded on the oily road.
slide /slaɪd/	to move smoothly and quickly across a surface, or to make something move in this way. verb [transitive/intransitive]	Friction prevents objects from sliding out of our hands.

slow down /ˌsləʊ ˈdaʊn/	if you slow something, or if it slows, you reduce the level or amount of it. **phrasal verb**	*Moving friction slows down moving objects.*
smooth /smuːð/	completely flat and even with no rough areas. **adjective**	*Even surfaces that look completely smooth are actually rough when viewed under a microscope.*
speed /spiːd/	how fast an object travels. **noun [uncount/count]**	*The car was travelling at high speed.*
spin /spɪn/	to turn round and round quickly, or to make someone or something do this. **verb [transitive/intransitive]**	*The Earth spins on its axis.*
spring balance /ˈsprɪŋ ˌbæləns/	a piece of equipment used for weighing things, consisting of a spring that is measured to see how much it stretches when something is hung from it. **noun [count]**	
stability /stəˈbɪləti/	the ability of an object to stay balanced so that it does not move. **noun [uncount]**	*The stability of an object can be increased by lowering its centre of gravity.*
stable /ˈsteɪb(ə)l/	able to stay balanced and not move. **adjective**	*Objects in a stable position have large bases on which they stand.*
static friction /ˌstætɪk ˈfrɪkʃ(ə)n/	the force that prevents stationary objects from moving. **noun [uncount]**	
streamlined /ˈstriːmˌlaɪnd/	a streamlined shape allows air or liquid to pass over it easily. **adjective**	*Fish have streamlined bodies to allow them to move easily through the water.*
support /səˈpɔːt/	to hold the weight of someone or something so that they do not move or fall. **verb [transitive]**	*The plants were supported with wire.*
surface /ˈsɜːfɪs/	the top layer or outside part of something. **noun [count]**	*a rough surface*
third law of motion /ˌθɜːd lɔː(r) əv ˈməʊʃ(ə)n/	one of the laws about movement that were first expressed by Isaac Newton. It states that every action has an equal and opposite reaction. **noun [singular]**	
turning effect /ˈtɜːnɪŋ ɪˌfekt/	when a force acts along a line which does not pass through the centre of gravity of an object, it produces a turning effect. The turning effect of a force is also called the moment of a force. **noun [count]**	
twist /twɪst/	an action of bending or turning something. **noun [count]**	*He gave the doorknob a twist.*
unstable /ʌnˈsteɪb(ə)l/	an unstable object is likely to move or change because of the forces affecting it. For example, a pencil lying on a desk is stable (=not likely to move or change), but a pencil standing on its end on a desk is unstable and will fall over. **adjective**	
upright /ˈʌpˌraɪt/	in or into a steady vertical position. **adjective, adverb**	*Carrying any load low down will help a motorbike stay upright.*
waste away /ˌweɪst əˈweɪ/	to gradually become thinner and weaker over a period of time. **phrasal verb [intransitive]**	*The muscles of astronauts in space waste away, as a result of weightlessness.*
wear and tear /ˌweə(r) ənd ˈteə/	the changes or damage that normally happen to something that has been used a lot. **phrase**	*Friction causes wear and tear to tyres and shoes.*
weight /weɪt/	a measurement of how heavy something is. For scientists, weight is a measure of the force that attracts an object towards the Earth, and the scientific unit of weight is the newton. A 100g mass is attracted to the Earth with a force of about 10 newtons (=10N). **noun [uncount]**	*It was about 12 pounds in weight.*
weightlessness /ˈweɪtləsnəs/	the state of having no weight, because of being outside the Earth's atmosphere. **noun [uncount]**	*Weightlessness causes many practical problems for astronauts.*

1 Forces and motion word map

Write these words in the correct places on the word map.

acceleration   centripetal force   equilibrium   fulcrum   moments   second law

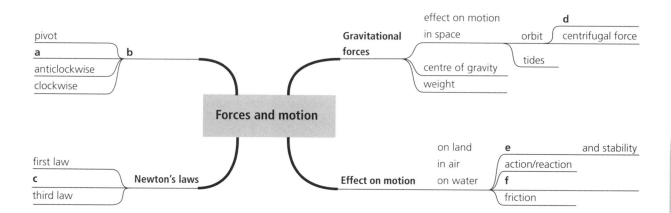

2 Overcoming friction

Read the text and fill in the gaps with these words.

effort   hinders   lubricant   oil   plastic   rolling   rotates   rub   slide   smoother

Try pushing a heavy book over the surface of your desk, then placing the same book on a few round pencils and pushing the book again. 1 _____ the book on the pencils will require least 2 _____ to move the book. On the desk, the tiny crests and hollows on the surface of the book interlock with those on the surface of the desk and this 3 _____ motion. But when the book is placed on the pencils, the surfaces no longer have to 4 _____ across each other. Making one or both of the surfaces 5 _____ will also reduce the friction force between them. For example, if heavy furniture has to be dragged across the floor, pads of the 6 _____ PTFE can be fixed to it. This is a very smooth solid and makes moving the furniture much easier. A 7 _____ is a slippery material which is not fixed to the moving object, but goes between it and the fixed surface. The lubricant forces the two surfaces apart so that they do not 8 _____ against one another. 9 _____ is a common lubricant. Most machinery uses a lubricant wherever two surfaces move over one another, such as where an axle 10 _____ inside a bearing or a valve slides up and down in a tube.

3 Law of moments

Underline the correct word in each sentence.

1 A ruler is balanced and the central point is the pivot point or (fulcrum / vacuum / pendulum / Velcro).
2 If a 25 g mass is placed on the right-hand side of the ruler, its weight, or (factor / fraction / force / faction), will cause the ruler to turn in a clockwise direction.
3 The moment of the force is the (present / product / addition / deduction) of the force and its distance from the pivot point.
4 This (anticlockwise / clockwise) moment can be counteracted by another force on the left-hand side of the pivot, to turn the ruler anticlockwise.
5 By shifting that (weight / load / mass / product) along the ruler it will reach a distance from the fulcrum where its turning force equals that of the first mass.
6 The ruler balances. The clockwise moment of the 25 g mass at a perpendicular distance of 16 cm from the (pivotal / hinge / pivot / pendulum) is exactly equalled by the anticlockwise moment of the 10 g mass at a distance of 40 cm from the pivot.
7 This is (added / calculated / totalled / summed) up in the law of moments. This law states that when an object is in equilibrium the sum of the clockwise moments is equal to the sum of the anticlockwise moments about the same pivot.

B Working with sentences

4 Examples of forces

Put the sentences in the correct order.

A Paddling a boat

a The answer is that the two forces act on different objects.
b The reaction to this acts on the man, who is attached to the boat, and pushes them in the opposite direction – forwards.
c First, a man paddling a boat applies a force to the water, trying to push it backwards with the paddle.
d This means that the paddle acts on the water and the water acts on the paddle.
e You may ask why, if the action and reaction are equal and opposite, the boat moves at all.

1 ☐ 2 ☐ 3 ☐ 4 ☐ 5 ☐

B Firing a rifle

a The rifle 'kicks' against the person holding it.
b These forces only act as long as the bullet is inside the rifle.
c They vanish when the bullet leaves the muzzle.
d This results in the reaction of a backward force exerted on the rifle.
e When a rifle is fired it exerts a forward force on the bullet (action).

1 ☐ 2 ☐ 3 ☐ 4 ☐ 5 ☐

C The jet engine

a Here it is expelled at high speed.
b So the plane moves forwards.
c The engine forces the gases backwards.
d The jet engine forces air from the front of the engine through to the back.
e The reaction to this is the forwards force exerted by the gas on the engine and hence, the plane.

1 ☐ 2 ☐ 3 ☐ 4 ☐ 5 ☐

5 Motion and the force of gravity

Put the phrases in the correct order to make sentences.

1 a ball, falls to the ground. like a coin, or a piece of paper, the object If you drop an object

_____

_____

2 because force gravity. is of of the This

_____

3 a force that works a non-contact force, Gravity is an example of that is,
the object. without actually touching

_____

_____

4 and then holds them causes down on the Earth's surface. Gravity objects
that have no support to fall,

_____

_____

5 any objects exists between Gravitational force the force. the greater the greater
the masses, which have mass;

_____

_____

C Working with texts

6 Centre of gravity and stability

Read the text. Then put the phrases under the appropriate diagrams.

> **a** centre of gravity closer to body   **b** centre of gravity further away from body
> **c** chair easier to lift   **d** chair harder to lift   **e** greater force exerted on muscles
> **f** greater risk of falling over   **g** greater turning effect   **h** less risk of falling over
> **i** smaller force exerted on muscles   **j** smaller turning effect

The centre of gravity is very important in relation to balance and stability. Which way do you think will be easier to lift the chair and why? It is much harder to lift an object when its centre of gravity is far away from your body. When the centre of gravity of the object is far away from your body it produces a greater turning effect. This means that, in order to lift the chair, your back muscles would need to exert a greater force to balance those turning forces. This could cause both you and the chair to topple to the floor.

1 ☐ 2 ☐ 3 ☐ 4 ☐ 5 ☐ 6 ☐ 7 ☐ 8 ☐ 9 ☐ 10 ☐

Translation

appear as /ə'pɪə(r) ˌəz/	to be or seem to have a particular form or nature. **verb [intransitive]**	*Kinetic energy also appears as heat energy.*
apply /ə'plaɪ/	to use physical force to make something happen or work. **verb [transitive]**	
balancing point /'bælənsɪŋ ˌpɔɪnt/	the fixed point on which a lever turns or pivots. **noun [count]**	
block-and-tackle pulley /ˌblɒk ənd ˌtæk(ə)l 'pʊli/	a piece of equipment that consists of fixed and moveable pulleys mounted in frames called blocks. **noun [count]**	
bottle opener /'bɒt(ə)l ˌəʊp(ə)nə/	a small tool used for removing the lid from a bottle. A bottle opener is a second class lever. **noun [count]**	
break down /ˌbreɪk 'daʊn/	if a substance breaks down or is broken down, it separates into the parts that it is made up of. **phrasal verb**	*When food is digested, it is broken down into smaller structures.*
cause /kɔːz/	to make something happen. **verb [transitive]**	*Heat energy causes objects to expand and liquids to evaporate.*
chemical energy /ˌkemɪk(ə)l 'enədʒi/	energy that is stored in the chemical structure of a substance, for example in the food that we eat. Chemical energy is a form of potential energy. **noun [uncount]**	*When food is digested, this releases the chemical energy that was stored in it.*
collision /kə'lɪʒ(ə)n/	what happens when two or more objects collide (=crash into each other). In an inelastic collision, the objects are deformed (=change shape) and the kinetic energy is converted into heat and sometimes light. In an elastic collision, all of the kinetic energy is transferred from one object to another and kinetic energy is not wasted in the form of heat or light. **noun [count/uncount]**	*When two pool balls collide, this is an elastic collision.*
conservation /ˌkɒnsə'veɪʃ(ə)n/	the maintenance of a quantity of something such as energy or mass at a constant amount. **noun [uncount]**	*The law of conservation of energy states that energy can neither be created nor destroyed.*
consist of /kən'sɪst ˌəv/	to be made of particular parts or things. **phrasal verb**	*A pulley is a simple machine that consists of a rope wrapped into the groove of a wheel.*
convert /kən'vɜːt/	to change from one thing to another or to make something do this. **verb [transitive/intransitive]**	*Energy is always converted from one form to another.*
deform /diː'fɔːm/	to change shape, or to make something change its shape. **verb [transitive/intransitive]**	*When two vehicles collide head on, they become deformed.*
distance /'dɪstəns/	the amount of space between two people or things. **noun [count/uncount]**	
distance multiplier /'dɪstəns ˌmʌltɪˌplaɪə/	a system that places the force that is needed to move an object close to a fulcrum, in order to increase the distance the object can be moved. **noun [count]**	
double /'dʌb(ə)l/	to become twice as big, twice as much, or twice as many or to make something do this. **verb [transitive/intransitive]**	*If you use two pulleys to lift something, the effort is halved but the distance moved by the effort is doubled.*
downward pull /ˌdaʊnwəd 'pʊl/	a pull in a downward (=towards the ground) direction. **noun [count]**	
drive in /ˌdraɪv 'ɪn/	to push one thing into another using force. **verb [transitive]**	*A sharp wedge is easier to drive into an object.*
efficiency /ɪ'fɪʃ(ə)nsi/	The efficiency of a machine is the ratio between the useful energy used to do work and the total energy put in. **noun [uncount]**	*The efficiency of a machine is usually expressed as a percentage.*
effort /'efət/	the force used on a machine of any type in order to make it able to move an object. **noun [singular/uncount]**	*An efficient machine is one that uses a small effort to lift a heavy load.*
elastic collision /ɪˌlæstɪk kə'lɪʒ(ə)n/	In an elastic collision, all of the kinetic energy is transferred from one object to another and kinetic energy is not wasted in the form of heat or light. **noun [count]**	
electrical energy /ɪˌlektrɪk(ə)l 'enədʒi/	a type of energy that is carried by very small moving particles called electrons (=electricity). **noun [uncount]**	

energy /ˈenədʒi/	the ability to do work and to make things work. Electricity, heat, and light are all forms of energy. Energy can change from one form to another, for example light can turn into heat. noun [uncount]	*Switching off lights is a good way to save energy.*
first class lever /ˌfɜːst klɑːs ˈliːvə/	a type of lever where the fulcrum is between the effort and the load. Hammers, scissors and see-saws are first class levers. noun [count]	
fishing rod /ˈfɪʃɪŋ ˌrɒd/	a long thin pole that is used for catching fish. A fishing rod is a third class lever. noun [count]	
fixed point /ˌfɪkst ˈpɔɪnt/	the point on which a lever turns or pivots. noun [count]	
fixed pulley /ˌfɪkst ˈpʊli/	a type of pulley where the pulley is attached to a fixed surface with a rope passing over it. Pulling on one end of the rope raises or lowers the load on the other. A flagpole is an example of a fixed pulley. noun [count]	
force multiplier /ˈfɔːs ˌmʌltɪplaɪə/	a system that reduces the force needed to move something, while increasing the distance over which the force acts. noun [count]	*A crowbar is an example of a force multiplier.*
free /friː/	not held, tied or fixed somewhere. adjective	*Hand me the free end of the rope.*
fulcrum /ˈfʊlkrəm/	the point on which a lever balances or turns. noun [count]	*The fulcrum of a wheelbarrow is the wheel.*
gain /ɡeɪn/	to get more of something, usually as a result of a gradual process. verb [transitive]	*The truck gained momentum as it rolled down the hill.*
gear /ˈɡɪə/	a device that consists of rotating wheels with evenly sized and spaced teeth around the edges. The teeth of one gear mesh (=connect) with the teeth of the other and make it move. noun [count/uncount]	
generate /ˈdʒenəˌreɪt/	to produce power or heat. verb [transitive]	*Seventy-five percent of the country's electricity is generated by nuclear reactors.*
give out /ˌɡɪv ˈaʊt/	to produce. phrasal verb	*The sun gives out energy in the form of heat and light.*
halve /hɑːv/	to reduce something to half its original size or amount, or to become half the original size or amount. verb [transitive/intransitive]	*When two pulleys are used, the effort required to lift the load is halved.*
head-on /ˌhed ˈɒn/	if two vehicles crash head-on, the front of one hits the front of the other. adjective/adverb	*a head-on crash between a car and a truck*
heat /hiːt/	the energy that is produced when the temperature of something changes. noun [uncount]	*These chemical processes generate a lot of heat.*
inelastic collision /ˌɪnəˌlæstɪk kəˈlɪʒ(ə)n/	in an inelastic collision, the objects are deformed (=change shape) and the kinetic energy is converted into heat and sometimes light. noun [count]	
inclined plane /ˌɪnklaɪnd ˈpleɪn/	a flat surface that forms a slope, making an angle of less than 90 degrees with a horizontal surface. It is considered to be a simple machine because it takes less force to roll or slide an object up the slope than to lift it straight upwards. noun [count]	
inefficiency /ˌɪnɪˈfɪʃənsi/	the inefficient way in which someone does something or something happens. noun [count/uncount]	*Lubrication reduces inefficiency by making it easier for surfaces to move over each other.*
interconversion /ˌɪntəkənˈvɜːʒ(ə)n/	the process by which two things can be converted (=changed) into each other. noun [uncount]	
interconvert /ˌɪntəkənˈvɜːt/	to cause two things to be converted (=changed) into each other. verb [transitive]	*Einstein's famous equation states that energy and mass can be interconverted.*
joule /dʒuːl/	a unit for measuring work or energy, equal to the work done when a force of one newton moves an object a distance of one metre. Symbol J. noun [count]	
kinetic energy /kaɪˌnetɪk ˈenədʒi/	the energy that an object has as a result of moving. This energy depends on the mass and velocity of the object. Symbol KE. noun [uncount]	*A bullet fired from a gun has a huge amount of kinetic energy.*
lever /ˈliːvə/	a solid bar, often made of metal, that you put under a heavy object to move it. A lever is a simple machine that turns on a fulcrum (=balance point) to apply the effort (=force) in order to move a load. noun [count]	*Scissors are an example of a lever.*
lift /lɪft/	the force that makes an aircraft leave the ground and stay in the air. noun [uncount]	*The shape of an aircraft's wings gives it lift.*

light energy /'laɪt ˌenədʒi/	energy in the form of light. It comes mainly from the Sun. **noun [uncount]**	*Without light energy, plants would not be able to make food.*
limit /'lɪmɪt/	**1** the greatest amount or level of something that is possible. **noun [count]** **2** to prevent something from increasing past a particular point. **verb [transitive]**	*There is a limit to the size of load a person can lift.* *Your strength limits the size of load you can lift.*
lower /'ləʊə/	**1** below another thing of the same kind. **adjective** **2** to move something down from a higher position. **verb [transitive]**	*You can use a pulley to raise or lower an object.*
mass energy /'mæs ˌenədʒi/	mass and energy regarded as interconvertible according to the laws of relativity. **noun [uncount]**	
mechanical advantage /mə'kænɪk(ə)l əd'vɑːntɪdʒ/	the mechanical advantage of a machine is the ratio of the load it moves to the effort that is needed to move the load. A machine that uses a small effort to move a heavy load will have a greater mechanical advantage. **noun [count/uncount]**	
mesh /meʃ/	if parts of an engine or other machine mesh, they connect tightly with each other and work together. **verb [intransitive]**	*The teeth of one gear wheel mesh with the teeth of the other.*
momentum /məʊ'mentəm/	the tendency of a moving object to keep moving unless another force stops it or slows it down. It is equal to the mass of the object multiplied by its velocity. Symbol: p. **noun [uncount]**	*The momentum of the ball increased as it rolled down the hill.*
moveable pulley /ˌmuːvəb(ə)l 'pʊli/	a pulley that is not attached to a fixed surface but is attached to the load and moves with it. **noun [count]**	
movement energy /'muːvmənt ˌenədʒi/	another name for kinetic energy. **noun [uncount]**	
narrow /'nærəʊ/	if something is narrow, there is only a short distance from one side of it to the other. **adjective**	*A needle is narrower than a pencil.*
nuclear energy /ˌnjuːkliə 'enədʒi/	**1** energy that is released during a nuclear reaction. **noun [uncount]** **2** electricity produced by a nuclear reactor. **noun [uncount]**	*Nuclear power stations harness nuclear energy to make electricity.*
nuclear fission /ˌnjuːkliə 'fɪʃ(ə)n/	the process of splitting the nucleus of an atom, for example the nucleus of a radioactive uranium atom, in order to release nuclear energy. **noun [uncount]**	
nuclear fusion /ˌnjuːkliə 'fjuːʒ(ə)n/	the process of combining the nuclei of particular atoms, for example hydrogen atoms, in order to release energy. This process takes place continuously in stars such as the sun. **noun [uncount]**	
pay back /ˌpeɪ 'bæk/	to give something in return for something else. **phrasal verb**	*If an inclined plane is used to lift a load, what is gained in smaller effort is paid back as a longer distance through which the effort is applied.*
pivot /'pɪvət/	a fixed point or pin that something turns on or balances on (=fulcrum). **noun [count]**	*The pivot point of something is its central point.*
plutonium /pluː'təʊniəm/	a radioactive element that is very toxic and is used in the production of nuclear power. Chemical symbol: Pu. **noun [uncount]**	*The nuclear bomb contained plutonium.*
possess /pə'zes/	to own or have something. **verb [transitive]**	*A stationary object possesses potential energy.*
potential energy /pə,tenʃ(ə)l 'enədʒi/	the energy that an object or system has stored because of its position or condition. For example, a raised weight has potential energy. Symbol: PE. **noun [uncount]**	*Water stored in reservoirs has considerable potential energy.*
pulley /'pʊli/	a simple machine used for lifting heavy things, consisting of a wheel with a rope around it. The rope is pulled in order to raise a load (plural: pulleys). **noun [count]**	*They lifted the heavy engine from the car using a pulley.*
raise /reɪz/	to lift something to a higher place or position. **verb [transitive]**	*They used pulleys to raise the boxes onto the truck.*
reduce /rɪ'djuːs/	to make something smaller or less in size, amount, importance, price etc. **verb [transitive]**	*Using a moveable pulley reduces the effort required to lift a load.*
release /rɪ'liːs/	to let a substance or energy spread into the area or atmosphere around it, especially as part of a chemical reaction. **verb [transitive]**	*Oxygen from the water is released into the atmosphere.*
require /rɪ'kwaɪə/	to need someone or something. **verb [transitive]**	*The more pulleys you have, the less effort is required to move a load.*
rotate	to move in a circle around a fixed point, or to move something in this way. **verb [transitive]**	*The Earth rotates 360 degrees every 24 hours.*
run /rʌn/	if a machine or engine is running, it is operating. **verb [intransitive]**	*Don't leave the car engine running.*

Term	Definition	Example
scissors /ˈsɪzəz/	a tool for cutting paper, with two blades that open and shut. noun [plural]	*A pair of scissors is an example of a first class lever.*
screw /skruː/	a thin pointed piece of metal that you push and turn with a screwdriver in order to fasten one thing to another. It has a raised line that curves around it called a thread. noun [count]	*A screw is a simple machine.*
second class lever /ˌsekənd klɑːs ˈliːvə/	a type of lever where the fulcrum is at one end and the effort at the other, with the load in between. Bottle openers and wheelbarrows are second class levers. noun [count]	
sharp /ʃɑːp/	a sharp object has an edge that can cut or an end that is pointed. adjective	*a sharp knife*
sloping surface /ˌsləʊpɪŋ ˈsɜːfɪs/	a surface that is neither horizontal nor vertical. noun [count]	*An inclined plane is a sloping surface.*
solar energy /ˌsəʊlə(r) ˈenədʒi/	the energy released by nuclear fusion reactions in stars such as the sun. noun [uncount]	*Solar energy comes mainly in the form of light and heat.*
sound energy /ˈsaʊnd ˌenədʒi/	energy in the form of sound waves. noun [uncount]	*Sound energy travels by vibrating particles so it cannot travel through a vacuum.*
spade /speɪd/	a tool used for digging that consists of a handle and a flat part that you push into the earth. noun [count]	*A spade is an example of a first class lever.*
spiral inclined plane /ˌspaɪrəl ɪnklaɪnd ˈpleɪn/	an inclined plane (=sloping surface) that has a spiral shape (=a line curving around a central line). noun [count]	*A screw is an example of a spiral inclined plane.*
split /splɪt/	to divide something into several parts, or to be divided into several parts. verb [transitive/intransitive]	*When the nucleus of an atom is split, a large amount of energy is released.*
steep slope /ˌstiːp ˈsləʊp/	a steep slope rises quickly and is difficult to climb. noun [count]	*The steeper the slope, the more effort is required to raise a load.*
store /stɔː/	to keep something in a particular place. verb [transitive]	*Energy is stored in the food we eat.*
strike /straɪk/	to hit against something. verb [transitive]	*When a moving ball strikes a stationary ball of the same mass head on, the stationary ball moves away.*
third class lever /ˌθɜːd klɑːs ˈliːvə/	a type of lever where the load is in the middle with the fulcrum and the effort at opposite ends. Tweezers and fishing rods are third class levers. noun [count]	
transfer /trænsˈfɜː/	to move something or someone from one place to another. verb [transitive]	*In an elastic collision, all the kinetic energy is transferred from one object to the next.*
tweezers /ˈtwiːzəz/	a tool that you use for picking up very small objects or for pulling out hairs. It consists of two narrow pieces of metal joined at one end. noun [plural]	*Tweezers are an example of a third class lever.*
uranium /jʊˈreɪniəm/	a silver-white, radioactive metal element. It is used in the production of nuclear energy. Chemical symbol: U. noun [uncount]	*Nuclear power stations use uranium as a source of nuclear energy.*
velocity /vəˈlɒsəti/	the speed at which something moves in one direction. It is measured by dividing the distance travelled in metres by the time taken in seconds. noun [uncount]	*The plummeting skydiver eventually reached a terminal velocity.*
waste /weɪst/	to use more of something than is necessary, or to use it in a way that does not produce the best results. verb [transitive]	*When energy is converted into a different form, some of it is wasted.*
wedge /wedʒ/	two inclined planes fastened back to back so that the sides of the two planes meet in a point. Axes, knives and chisels are wedges. The points of a nail, pin, needle and screw are also examples of wedges. noun [count]	*A wedge is a simple machine.*
wheel and axle /ˌwiːl ənd ˈæksl/	a wheel with a metal bar passing through the centre of it. noun [count]	*A wheel and axle is a kind of lever.*
wheelbarrow /ˈwiːlˌbærəʊ/	a large open container with a wheel at the front and handles at the back. You use it outside for moving things such as dirt, wood or supplies. noun [count]	*A wheelbarrow is an example of a second class lever.*
windlass /ˈwɪndləs/	a piece of equipment used for lifting heavy things. It uses a motor to wind a rope or chain around a large round cylinder. noun [count]	
work /wɜːk/	the process of changing energy from one form into another, usually in order to make something move or operate. Work is equal to the amount of force used on the object, measured in newtons, multiplied by the distance, measured in metres, over which it is used. Work is measured in units called joules. Symbol *W*. noun [uncount]	

1   Energy and machines word map

Write these words in the correct places on the word map.

efficiency   elastic collisions   kinetic energy   momentum   nuclear fission   pulleys

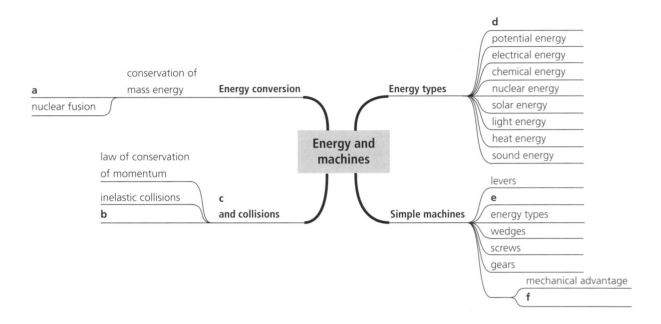

2   Forms of energy

Match the types of energy with the correct definition.

1 Kinetic energy (KE)
2 Potential energy (PE)
3 Electrical energy
4 Chemical energy
5 Nuclear energy
6 Solar energy
7 Light energy
8 Heat energy
9 Sound energy

a comes mainly from the Sun. However, we also get it from other luminous sources, such as an electric light bulb, fires and stars.

b is carried by moving electrons. Most appliances in the home use this energy to do work.

c is described as energy of motion and is commonly known as movement energy.

d is energy stored in the chemical structure of a substance. For example, this energy is stored in the food we eat.

e is energy stored in the nuclei of atoms.

f is energy that comes from the Sun. The Sun gives out energy, mainly in the form of heat and light.

g is the energy carried through a material through which vibrating molecules travel. Every day we use a lot of this energy.

h is the energy stored in an object because of its potential to change, such as position above ground or its shape.

i is the energy which is passed from a hot object to a cooler object. The molecules of objects that have been heated are moving at a faster rate than they did when cold.

1 ☐ 2 ☐ 3 ☐ 4 ☐ 5 ☐ 6 ☐ 7 ☐ 8 ☐ 9 ☐

3 Moveable pulley

Read the text and fill in the gaps with the correct word. Use the diagram to help you.

> attached   doubled   downward   effort   equally   half   halved   load   reduced

The moveable pulley, is not 1 _____ to a fixed surface, but is attached to the 2 _____ and moves with it. When you pull on the rope any extra in the length marked (a) has come from both (b) and (c), so the load only goes up by 3 _____ the distance moved by the effort. This results in less effort being required to move the load. In the system shown the effort is 4 _____ to half the load because the sections (b) and (c) of the rope each hold up the load 5 _____. Although the effort to lift the load has been 6 _____, the distance moved by the effort has been 7 _____. A combination pulley system, in which there is more than one pulley working together, saves a lot of 8 _____. The moveable pulley reduces the effort needed to lift the load, while the fixed pulley makes the work easier by allowing the 9 _____ pull.

b

c

a

moveable
pulley

fixed
pulley

effort

load

4   Energy and machines

Match the beginnings and endings of the sentences.

Beginnings

1 Energy is the ability
2 Kinetic energy and potential energy are the two basic forms
3 The principle of the conservation of energy states
4 Nuclear fission is the splitting
5 Nuclear fusion involves combining
6 Collisions may be either elastic
7 A machine is any device
8 Energy = distance moved
9 The efficiency of a machine is reduced
10 Mechanical advantage is the ratio

Endings

a of load to effort.
b by effort x effort.
c or inelastic.
d two or more small nuclei to produce energy.
e of energy.
f that increases the effect of a force.
g to do work.
h by friction between moving parts.
i of the nucleus of an atom and produces large amounts of energy.
j that energy can neither be created or destroyed but can be converted from one form to another.

1 ☐ 2 ☐ 3 ☐ 4 ☐ 5 ☐ 6 ☐ 7 ☐ 8 ☐ 9 ☐ 10 ☐

5   A series of energy conversions

Read the text and label the diagrams with these forms of energy. One form of energy needs to be used three times.

1 chemical energy   2 heat energy   3 kinetic energy (in the moving hammer)
4 potential energy (stored in the raised hammer)   5 sound energy (as hammer hits wall)

Can you deduce the series of energy changes that occur when a carpenter hammers a nail into a piece of wood? Here are some questions to help you analyse the energy changes that take place.

● What energy does the carpenter have in his or her body before beginning work?
  Chemical energy is stored in the carpenter's body, from the food eaten.
● What energy is present in the raised hammer?
  When the hammer is raised to any height above ground it has potential energy.
● As the carpenter moves the hammer down to the nail, what form of energy will the moving hammer have?
  As the hammer moves downward to the nail the potential energy is converted to kinetic energy (energy of motion). Chemical energy from the carpenter's muscles adds to this kinetic energy.
● What happens when the hammer hits the nail?
  When the hammer hits the nail the kinetic energy is converted to sound and heat energy.
  Therefore the series of energy conversions that take place when a hammer is used to hit a nail in a piece of wood is as follows:

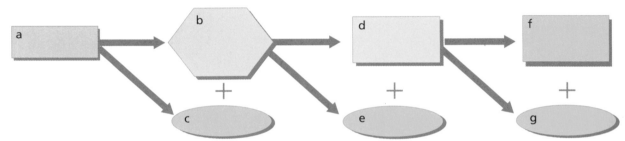

6   Other examples of levers

Read the text and label the diagrams with the correct words.

effort   first class   fulcrum   load   second class   third class

The fulcrum of the lever is not always between the effort and the load. There are three different arrangements of fulcrum, effort and load, which means there are three different classes of levers, which are used for different purposes.

● First class levers – the fulcrum is between the effort and the load. These are the more common types of levers, such as scissors, crowbar, hammer, spade and seesaw.

● Second class levers – the fulcrum is at one end and the effort at the other, with the load in the middle. Examples of second class levers are a bottle opener, nutcracker, spade and a wheelbarrow. Second class levers allow a large load to be lifted by a smaller effort.

● Third class levers – the effort is in the middle with the load and the fulcrum at opposite ends of the lever. For example: tweezers and fishing rod. A third class lever allows a small load to be lifted by a larger effort. However the load will move through a larger distance than the effort.

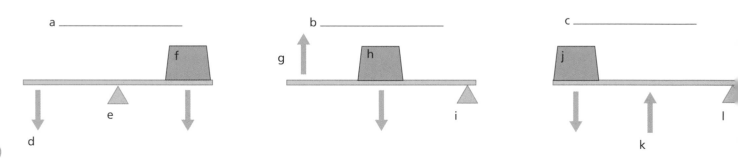

25 Light and sight

		Translation
accommodation /əˌkɒməˈdeɪʃ(ə)n/	the change in shape of the lens of the eye when it changes its focus to look at something nearer or further away. **noun [uncount]**	*the eye's accommodation to focus on a distant object*
additive theory of light /ˌædɪtɪv ˌθɪəri əv ˈlaɪt/	the theory that white light is a combination of red, green and blue, and that combining any two of these colours produces different colours. **noun [singular]**	
angle of incidence /ˌæŋɡ(ə)l əv ˈɪnsɪdəns/	the angle between a ray of light and a line that is perpendicular to a surface, at the point where the ray touches it. **noun [singular]**	*The angle of incidence was 30 degrees.*
angle of reflection /ˌæŋɡ(ə)l əv rɪˈflekʃ(ə)n/	the angle between a reflected ray of light and a line that is perpendicular to a surface, at the point where the ray is reflected. **noun [singular]**	*The angle of reflection was equal to the angle of incidence.*
apparent depth /əˌpærənt (depθ/	the distance that there appears to be between the surface of the water and an object that is beneath the surface. This distance is smaller than the real depth. **noun [uncount]**	
aqueous humour /ˌeɪkwiəs ˈhjuːmə/	the transparent liquid that fills the eye between the back of the cornea and the front of the iris and lens. **noun [uncount]**	
argon /ˈɑːɡɒn/	a gas that is an element that does not produce a chemical reaction with other substances. It is an inert gas that is used in electric lights, and also forms about 1% of air. Chemical symbol: Ar. **noun [uncount]**	*The light bulb was filled with argon.*
beam /biːm/	a line of light or other form of energy. **noun [count]**	*The torch shone a beam of light into the room.*
bend /bend/	to become curved or folded and not straight. **verb [intransitive]**	*Tools that will not bend or break under stress.*
blind spot /ˈblaɪnd ˌspɒt/	the part of the retina in the eye that is not sensitive to light. It is the place where the optic nerve leaves the eye. **noun [count]**	
blue printing /ˈbluː ˌprɪntɪŋ/	the process of making a copy of a drawing by shining light onto a drawing done on special paper. The copy is white on a blue background. **noun [uncount]**	
chromatography /ˌkrəʊməˈtɒɡrəfi/	a method of finding out which different gases or liquids are included in a mixture by passing it through or over substances that absorb the different parts at different rates. **noun [uncount]**	*The colours in inks can be separated by chromatography.*
ciliary muscle /ˈsɪliəri ˌmʌs(ə)l/	a muscle in the eye that controls the lens. **noun [count]**	*The ciliary muscle contracts to make the lens fatter so we can focus on a near object.*
complementary colour /kɒmplɪˌmentəri ˈkʌlə/	a colour that produces white light when it is mixed with a secondary colour. **noun [count]**	*Cyan's complementary colour is red.*
concave /ˈkɒnkeɪv/	curved inwards. **adjective**	*a concave lens*
condensing lens /kənˈdensɪŋ ˌlenz/	a lens which makes light rays move towards each other after they hit it. **noun [count]**	
cone /kəʊn/	a cell shaped like a cone in the retina of the eye. Cones make it possible for people and animals to see colours in bright light. **noun [count]**	
converging beam /kənˌvɜːdʒɪŋ ˈbiːm/	a beam of light in which the rays come together. **noun [count]**	
converging mirror /kənˌvɜːdʒɪŋ ˈmɪrə/	a mirror that makes light rays move towards each other after they hit it. **noun [count]**	
convex /ˈkɒnveks/	a convex surface curves outwards. **adjective**	*a convex lens*
cornea /ˈkɔːniə, kɔːˈniːə/	the transparent layer that covers the outside of the eye. **noun [count]**	*The cornea bends the light as it enters the eye.*

correction /kəˈrekʃ(ə)n/	the use of spectacles or contact lenses to make light focus on the retina of someone's eye, not in front of it or behind it, so they can see better. **noun [uncount]**	*the correction of short-sightedness*
cylindrical tube /sɪˌlɪndrɪk(ə)l ˈtjuːb/	a long thin round tube. **noun [count]**	*A fluorescent lamp is a cylindrical tube with electrodes at each end.*
demagnifier /diːˈmægnɪˌfaɪə/	something which makes an image appear smaller. **noun [count]**	*A concave lens is a demagnifier.*
developer /dɪˈveləpə/	a chemical substance that is used to develop photographs. **noun [uncount]**	*Developer reacts with the chemicals on the photographic paper, turning some areas black.*
diaphragm /ˈdaɪəfræm/	part of a camera which controls the amount of light allowed through the lens to the film. **noun [count]**	
dim /dɪm/	**1** if a light dims, or if someone dims it, it becomes less bright. **verb [transitive/intransitive]** **2** not bright or clear. **adjective**	*a dim light*
dispersion of light /dɪsˌpɜːʃ(ə)n əv ˈlaɪt/	the separation of a beam of light into several different colours. **noun [uncount]**	
diverging beam /daɪˌvɜːdʒɪŋ ˈbiːm/	a beam of light in which the rays spread out from a source. **noun [count]**	
diverging mirror /daɪˌvɜːdʒɪŋ ˈmɪrə/	a mirror that reflects rays of light outwards. **noun [count]**	
dye /daɪ/	**1** a substance used for changing the colour of something such as cloth or hair. **noun [count/uncount]** **2** to use dye to change the colour of something. **verb [transitive]**	*The molecules in the dye are attracted to the fibres in the fabric.* *The fibres are dyed and then made into fabric.*
eclipse /ɪˈklɪps/	a short period when all or part of the Sun or Moon becomes dark, because of the positions of the Sun, Moon, and Earth in relation to each other. A total eclipse is when the Sun or Moon is completely covered. An eclipse of the Sun is called a solar eclipse, and an eclipse of the Moon is called a lunar eclipse. **noun [count]**	
electromagnetic radiation /ˌelektrəʊmægˌnetɪk reɪdiˈeɪʃ(ə)n/	light, including light we can see and light we cannot see. **noun [uncount]**	*X-rays and ultraviolet rays are part of the spectrum of electromagnetic radiation.*
elongated /ˈiːlɒŋˌɡeɪtɪd/	longer and narrower than is usual. **adjective**	*The lens of your eye becomes elongated when you look at a distant object.*
eye lash /ˈaɪ ˌlæʃ/	the hairs along the edges of your eyelids. **noun [plural]**	
field of view /ˌfiːld əv ˈvjuː/	an area that a person or a piece of equipment can see at any one time. **noun [count]**	*the field of view of a camera*
filament /ˈfɪləmənt/	the thin wire inside a light bulb. **noun [count]**	*The filament glowed white-hot when the light was switched on.*
fluorescent lamp /flɔːˌres(ə)nt ˈlæmp/	an electric light that consists of a glass tube with a gas inside and two electrodes at each end. **noun [count]**	
fluorescent source /flɔːˌres(ə)nt ˈsɔːs/	something which produces fluorescent light. **noun [count]**	*a lighting fixture around a fluorescent source*
focal length /ˈfəʊk(ə)l ˌleŋθ/	the distance from the centre of a lens or mirror to its focal point. **noun [count]**	*The lens had a short focal length.*
focal point /ˈfəʊk(ə)l ˌpɔɪnt/	the point where light rays meet after being reflected by a mirror or passing through a lens, or the point from which they seem to start to spread. **noun [count]**	*The focal point of a convex mirror appears to be behind it.*
fovea /ˈfəʊvɪə/	a central part of the retina that contains a large number of cone cells, so that detailed images can be seen. **noun [count]**	
frosted glass /ˌfrɒstɪd ˈɡlɑːs/	glass that has a rough surface so that you cannot see clearly through it. **noun [uncount]**	*a frosted glass window*
glare /gleə/	a very bright light that reflects off a surface and makes things difficult to see. **noun [uncount]**	*Glare on glossy pages can make them difficult to read.*
glossy /ˈglɒsi/	shiny. **adjective**	*glossy pages*
goggles /ˈɡɒɡ(ə)lz/	special glasses that are worn to protect the eyes. **noun [plural]**	*You should always wear goggles when playing squash.*
grain /ɡreɪn/	a tiny piece of something. **noun [count]**	*grains of silver halide*

hypermetropia /ˌhaɪpəmeˈtrəʊpɪə/	the problem of not being able to see things clearly when they are near to you (=long-sightedness). noun [uncount]	
incandescent source /ɪnkænˌdes(ə)nt ˈsɔːs/	something that produces light as a result of being made very hot. noun [count]	*The filaments of light bulbs are incandescent sources.*
incident ray /ˈɪnsɪd(ə)nt ˌreɪ/	a ray of light that hits a surface. noun [count]	*The incident ray hit the mirror at a shallow angle.*
indigo /ˈɪndɪgəʊ/	between dark blue and purple in colour. adjective	
inert gas /ɪˌnɜːt ˈgæs/	a gas that does not produce a chemical reaction with other substances. noun [count]	*Light bulbs are filled with an inert gas.*
infrared /ˌɪnfrəˈred/	a type of light felt as heat that cannot be seen and has wavelengths that are longer than those of light that can be seen, but shorter than those of radio waves. noun [uncount]	*Infrared cameras produce thermal images of objects and organisms.*
iris /ˈaɪrɪs/	the coloured part of the eye in vertebrate animals. The iris controls the amount of light that reaches the retina by changing in size. noun [count]	
lateral inversion /ˌlætərəl ɪnˈvɜːʃ(ə)n/	the change that happens to an image in a flat mirror, when it appears the correct way up, but with the right side on the left and the left side on the right. noun [uncount]	
light-sensitive /ˈlaɪtˌsensətɪv/	affected by the presence of light. adjective	*light-sensitive photographic film*
long-sightedness /ˌlɒŋˈsaɪtɪdnəs/	the problem of not being able to see things clearly when they are near to you. noun [uncount]	*Long-sightedness is corrected by wearing spectacles with convex lenses.*
magnification /ˌmægnɪfɪˈkeɪʃ(ə)n/	the power of a piece of equipment to make something appear bigger than it really is. noun [uncount]	*the magnification of a telescope*
microwave /ˈmaɪkrəʊˌweɪv/	a type of electromagnetic wave used in radar, cooking and radio communication. noun [count]	*Mobile phone signals are transmitted by microwaves.*
myopia /maɪˈəʊpɪə/	the problem of not being able to see things clearly if they are far away from you. noun [uncount]	
negative /ˈnegətɪv/	an image on film in which dark things appear light, and light things appear dark. noun [count]	*The image on the negative is black.*
non-luminous /ˌnɒnˈluːmɪnəs/	not producing or reflecting light. adjective	*a non-luminous object*
normal (line) /ˈnɔːməl/	an imaginary line that is drawn at a 90° angle to a surface at a point where light hits the surface. noun [count]	*The light bends away from the normal.*
opaque /əʊˈpeɪk/	an opaque substance does not allow light to pass through it. adjective	
optic nerve /ˌɒptɪk ˈnɜːv/	the large nerve that sends signals relating to sight from the retina in the eye to the brain. noun [count]	*He was blind in one eye because the optic nerve had been damaged.*
optical effect /ˌɒptɪk(ə)l ɪˈfekt/	the special way that something looks because of the way light is reflected. noun [count]	*The optical effect of a pencil appearing to bend at the point it enters a glass of water.*
optical fibre /ˌɒptɪk(ə)l ˈfaɪbə/	a very long thin piece of transparent glass, used in telephone and computer systems for sending information in the form of light. noun [count/uncount]	*Telephone cables contain bundles of optical fibres.*
parallel beam /ˌpærəlel ˈbiːm/	a beam of light in which the rays are an equal distance from each other. noun [count]	
penumbra /ˌpenˈʌmbrə/	an area covered by the outer part of a shadow, so that it is not completely dark. noun [count]	
periscope /ˈperɪˌskəʊp/	a long tube with mirrors set at a 45° angle at each end, used for looking over the top of something, for example from a submarine. noun [count]	*He was able to see over the crowd using a periscope.*
perpendicular /ˌpɜːpənˈdɪkjʊlə/	forming a 90° angle with another surface or line. adjective	*The normal to a mirror is an imaginary line drawn perpendicular to the mirror's surface.*
phosphor powder /ˈfɒsfə ˌpaʊdə/	a substance that is used in fluorescent lamps to coat the inside surface of the cylindrical tube and produces a bluish light when hit by ultraviolet radiation. noun [uncount]	
photochemical reaction /ˌfəʊtəʊˌkemɪk(ə)l riˈækʃ(ə)n/	a change that produces a new substance, caused by light. noun [count]	*Photosynthesis and sun-tanning are photochemical reactions.*

photochromic lens /ˌfəʊtəʊˌkrəʊmɪk ˈlenz/ — a type of lens that becomes darker in sunlight. noun [count]
spectacles with photochromic lenses

photography /fəˈtɒɡrəfi/ — the skill, job, or process of taking photographs. noun [uncount]
the light-sensitive chemicals used in photography

photoluminescent material /ˌfəʊtəʊluːmɪˈnes(ə)nt məˈtɪəriəl/ — a material that produces light when a voltage is applied to it. noun [count]
photoluminescent materials used for the backlights of watches

primary colour /ˌpraɪməri ˈkʌlə/ — one of the colours red, blue, or yellow that are combined to make the other colours. They can also be combined to make white light. noun [count]

pupil /ˈpjuːp(ə)l/ — the black round part in the centre of the iris of the eye, where light enters. noun [count]
The bright light caused his pupils to constrict.

radio wave /ˈreɪdiəʊ ˌweɪv/ — an electromagnetic wave that radio signals can be sent on. noun [count]
Radio reception was poor in the valley because the surrounding hills obscured the radio waves.

rays /reɪz/ — a line of light, heat or energy. noun [count]
A collection of equally spaced rays of light is called a beam.

real depth /ˈriːl ˌdepθ/ — the actual distance from the surface of water to an object that is beneath the surface. noun [uncount]

reflected ray /rɪˌflektɪd ˈreɪ/ — a ray of light that is reflected from a surface. noun [count]

reflux /ˈriːflʌks/ — to heat a liquid in a container, whilst condensing the vapour released and returning it to the liquid, to make it more concentrated. verb [transitive]
The solvent is refluxed with the source of the pigment.

refraction /rɪˈfrækʃ(ə)n/ — **1** the way in which light bends when it passes from one substance to a different substance, for example from air to water. noun [uncount]
2 the ability of the eye, especially the lens, to bend light in order to focus it on the retina. noun [uncount]
The fish in the aquarium looked bigger than they actually were because of the refraction of light.

retina /ˈretɪnə/ — the part that covers the inside surface of the eye and sends signals to the brain along the optic nerve. The retina contains special cells called rods and cones that react to light of different strengths and colours. noun [count]

rod /rɒd/ — a cell shaped like a rod in the retina in the eye. Rods make it possible for people and animals to see when there is not much light. noun [count]

scattered /ˈskætəd/ — spread over a large area. adjective
the scattered light rays that are reflected from a rough surface

sclera /ˈsklɪərə/ — the outer layer of the eyeball that forms the white of the eye. noun [count]
The sclera of the eyeball is continuous with the transparent cornea at the front of the eyeball.

secondary colour /ˌsekənd(ə)ri ˈkʌlə/ — the secondary colours of light are yellow, magenta, and cyan. noun [count]

self-luminous /ˈselfˌluːmɪnəs/ — something that is self-luminous produces its own light. adjective
The sun is a self-luminous light source.

shade /ʃeɪd/ — an object used for covering a light to prevent direct light from damaging people's eyes. noun [count]
a light shade

short-sightedness /ʃɔːˈsaɪtɪdˌnəs/ — the problem of not being able to see things clearly if they are far away from you. noun [uncount]
Short-sightedness is corrected by wearing spectacles with concave lenses.

shutter /ˈʃʌtə/ — the part inside a camera that quickly opens and closes to let in light. noun [count]

silver halide /ˌsɪlvə ˈheɪlaɪd/ — a chemical which changes to give atoms of silver and bromine when it is exposed to sunlight. noun [uncount]

skin cancer /ˈskɪn ˌkænsə/ — cancer of the skin, often caused by ultraviolet light. noun [uncount]
Getting severe sunburn can increase your risk of skin cancer.

soft light /ˌsɒft ˈlaɪt/ — a light that is not very bright. noun [uncount]
Bulbs with frosted glass produce a softer light.

solvent extraction /ˈsɒlvənt ɪkˌstrækʃ(ə)n/ — the process of removing coloured pigments from their natural source, using a suitable solvent. noun [uncount]

speed of light /ˌspiːd əv ˈlaɪt/ — the speed of light in a vacuum which is equal to 3×10^8 metres per second. noun [uncount]
Nothing travels faster than the speed of light.

Term	Definition	Example
subtractive theory of light /səb,træktɪv 'θɪəri əv 'laɪt/	the theory that the colour we see from a coloured object depends on the colours of light that are reflected away from the object. noun [singular]	
sunburn /'sʌn,bɜːn/	sore skin that is caused by staying in the sun for too long. noun [uncount]	*Ultraviolet rays from the sun cause sunburn.*
sun-tanning /'sʌn,tænɪŋ/	a process of staying in the sun so that your skin becomes darker. noun [uncount]	
suspensory ligament /sə,spensəri 'lɪgəmənt/	a set of tissue fibres that supports an organ or another body part, especially the one that holds the lens of the eye in place. noun [count]	
tear gland /'tɪə ,glænd/	a gland in the eye where tears are produced. noun [count]	
telescope /'telɪ,skəʊp/	a piece of equipment shaped like a tube that makes distant objects look closer and larger. Telescopes contain a system of mirrors or lenses, or both. noun [count]	
total internal reflection /,təʊt(ə)l ɪn,tɜːn(ə)l rɪ'flekʃ(ə)n/	a situation that exists when light is refracted so much when it enters a dense medium that is sent backwards. noun [uncount]	
translucent /træns'luːs(ə)nt/	a translucent surface is clear enough for light to pass through it, but not completely clear. If you look through a translucent surface, you can see the general shape and colour of objects on the other side, but not the details. adjective	
transparent /træns'pærənt/	a transparent surface is clear enough to allow a lot of light to pass through it. If you look through a transparent surface, you can clearly see objects on the other side. adjective	
ultraviolet /,ʌltrə'vaɪələt/	ultraviolet light has waves with shorter wave-lengths than light that humans can see. Ultraviolet comes mostly from the Sun, and can cause skin cancer (= UV). adjective	*ultraviolet radiation*
umbra /'ʌmbrə/	a very dark shadow, sometimes inside an area of lighter shadow. noun [count]	
uniformly /'juːnɪ,fɔːmli/	in the same way. adverb	*All the light rays are reflected uniformly from a smooth surface.*
upside down /,ʌpsaɪd 'daʊn/	with the top part at the bottom or lower than the bottom part. adverb	*The image appears upside down.*
violet /'vaɪələt/	blue-purple in colour. adjective	
virtual /'vɜːtʃuəl/	something that seems to be something but in fact is not. adjective	*the virtual focal point*
virtual image /,vɜːtʃuəl 'ɪmɪdʒ/	an image formed by light rays from an object passing through a concave lens. noun [count]	*The virtual image formed is upright.*
visible /'vɪzɪb(ə)l/	able to be seen. adjective	*visible light*
visible spectrum /,vɪzɪb(ə)l 'spektrəm/	the seven colours that make up white light, that can be seen when white light passes through something such as water droplets or a diamond. noun [singular]	
X-ray /'eks ,reɪ/	**1** a type of dangerous radiation with a very short wavelength that is used for producing images of the inside of things, for example the inside of the human body. noun [count] **2** a picture of the inside of someone's body that is taken using X-rays. noun [count]	*The X-ray showed that he had broken his arm.*

A Working with words

1 Light and sound word map

Write these words in the correct places on the word map.

curved mirrors   fluorescent   incident ray   reflection   translucent   umbra

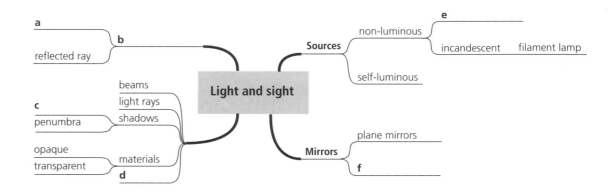

2 Refraction of light

Read the text and fill in the gaps with these words.

bend   incidence   light   normal   optical effect   refracted   refraction   transparent

When a pencil is half submerged in a beaker of water, the pencil should appear to bend at the point it enters the water. This 1 _____ is due to refraction. When light passes from one 2 _____ medium to another, such as from air to water, its speed changes. This change in speed causes the light to 3 _____. When light travels from a less dense medium, such as air, to a denser medium, such as glass or water, 4 _____ bends towards the normal but when it travels from a denser medium to a less dense medium it bends away from the 5 _____. The angle between the incident ray and the normal is called the angle of 6 _____, and the angle between the 7 _____ ray and the normal is called the angle of 8 _____.

3 Fluorescent lamps

Read the text and underline the correct words.

The fluorescent lamp is a sealed 1 (cylindrical / circular) glass tube that contains mercury at 2 (high / low) pressure and electrodes at either ends of the tube. Sometimes a small amount of inert gas, such as 3 (boron / argon), is placed in the tube. A phosphor powder coats the inside of the glass. When the lamp is turned on, the current flows through the electrical circuit to the electrodes, which shoot 4 (protons / electrons) into the mercury vapour causing it to emit a bluish light and 5 (extraviolet / ultraviolet) radiation. We are unable to see ultraviolet radiation but, when it hits the phosphor powder coating the glass tube, it causes the coating to emit 6 (visible / violent) light. These lamps do not produce much heat. Incandescent light bulbs glow because the 7 (filament / element) is heated to a very high temperature. So a lot of energy is wasted as heat. Therefore 8 (luminous / fluorescent) lamps are more economical than conventional 9 (candescent / incandescent) light bulbs, even though the initial installation cost of the fluorescent lamp is 10 (lower / higher).

B   Working with sentences

4   Real and apparent depth

Match the beginning and endings of the sentences.

Beginnings

1   When observing an object in water from
2   This optical effect
3   An observer sees the object when light rays leave the object and travel
4   However, as the light rays leave the water and enter the air, they are bent
5   This means that although the eye receives the light rays from the object, they appear
6   The angle of refraction is so large that all of the ray has been refracted
7   This is called

Endings

a   back into the denser medium as though it had been reflected.
b   is also due to refraction.
c   above it seems closer to the surface than it actually is.
d   to the surface of the water and enter the observer's eyes.
e   'total internal reflection'.
f   away from the normal.
g   to have come from a point above the location of the actual object.

1 ☐   2 ☐   3 ☐   4 ☐   5 ☐   6 ☐   7 ☐

C   Working with texts

5   How does light travel?

Read the text and the fill in the gaps on the diagram with these words.

cannot be seen   converging beams   diverging beams   parallel beam   visible

Light travels in a straight line, which is why we cannot see around corners. In diagrams light is generally represented as straight lines with arrowheads pointing in the direction in which the light travels. A single ray of light cannot be seen but when they come together they become visible. These lines are called rays and a collection of equally spaced rays is called a beam of light. There are different types of beams. Rays which do not meet are known as a parallel beam of light. Those rays which start from a source and spread out from this point are called a diverging beam and rays which come together to a point are known as a converging beam.

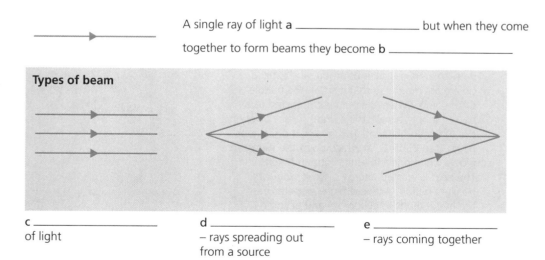

A single ray of light **a** _____ but when they come

together to form beams they become **b** _____

Types of beam

c _____
of light

d _____
– rays spreading out
from a source

e _____
– rays coming together

6 ## The effect of different types of material on light

Read the text and then fill in the gaps on the diagram with these words.

> any light   completely   difficult   do not   easy   impossible
> opaque   some light   translucent   transparent

Opaque materials and objects block the passage of light, that is, they do not allow any light to pass through them. So it is impossible to see through them to objects on the opposite side. However, not all materials are opaque. Transparent materials allow light to pass through completely. As a result it is easy to see things clearly on the other side of a transparent object. Clear glass and plastic wrap are examples of materials that are transparent. Translucent materials on the other hand only allow some light to pass through them, so it is difficult to see objects on the other side clearly. Examples of materials that are translucent are tracing paper, grease paper and frosted glass.

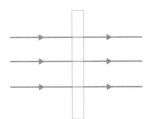 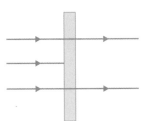 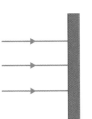

a _____ materials allow light to pass through b _____, making it c _____ to see through them.

d _____ objects only allow e _____ to pass through, making it f _____ to see through them clearly.

g _____ objects h _____, allow i _____ to pass through, making it j _____ to see through them.

7 ## The filament lamp

Read the text and label the diagram.

A filament lamp is an incandescent source of light, that is, it gives off light because it is very hot. The filament light bulb has a very thin tungsten filament coil, which is connected to electrical foot contacts via two stiff pieces of support wire. The support wires are enclosed in insulation at the base of the glass mount. The filament is enclosed in a glass case or bulb filled with an inert gas such as argon, and is fixed on a glass mount so that it sits in the middle of the bulb. When the bulb is connected to a power supply, an electric current passes through the tungsten filament. This makes the filament heat up to 2500°C, at which point the tungsten glows white hot and emits light and heat. The heat is wasted energy since it produces no illumination. At these high temperatures the metal tends to evaporate and become condensed on the sides of the bulb, gradually darkening it. The inert gas in the bulb slows down this process and prevents oxidation of the tungsten which would happen if air was used to fill the bulb. Some bulbs have a screw thread to allow them to be securely fixed into a lamp.

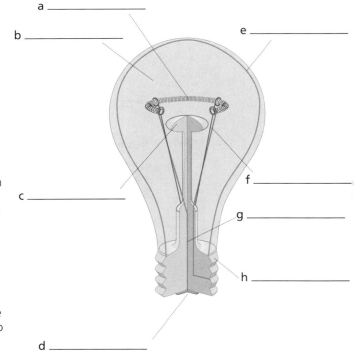

a _____
b _____
c _____
d _____
e _____
f _____
g _____
h _____

8 Slide projector and camera

Read the text and label the diagram with these words.

> concave mirror   condensing lenses   convex lens (x2)   diaphragm   film   image
> image inverted right way up   light source   object   shutters   slide inserted upside down

A slide projector uses an internal light source to illuminate a transparent slide. Light from the light source is collected by a large, double lens called the condensing lens, which then makes the light rays converge towards the slide. The slide is placed upside down in front of the light source and at a suitable distance behind the convex lens. The light passes through the transparency of the slide and then through the lens which refracts the light rays and converges them onto a screen, to give a large inverted image. However, the image will occur right side up if the slide (object) was placed in the projector upside down. A camera is basically a lightproof box, which contains a light-sensitive film behind a convex lens. When a photograph is taken, a shutter behind the diaphragm and lens opens and closes quickly. During the brief period that the shutter is open, light enters the camera from the object. The lens first converges the light rays causing them to cross and so produce a small inverted image on the light-sensitive film. The film is later developed into a permanent picture. The illustration shows how an image is formed on the film inside a camera.

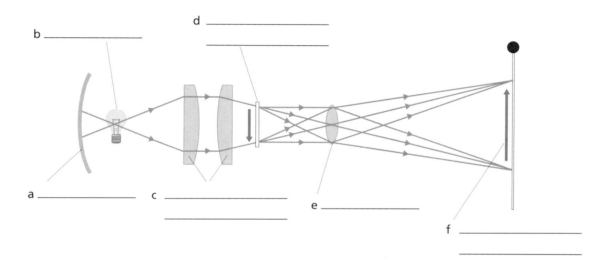

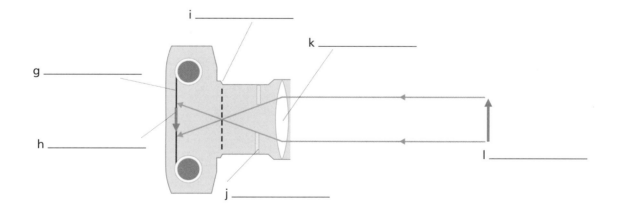

26 Sound and hearing

Translation

amplitude /ˈæmplɪˌtjuːd/	half of the total height of a wave, for example of sound or electricity, used as a measurement of how strong it is. The amplitude of a sea wave is its height above the level of water when the water is calm and still. **noun [uncount]**	
amplitude modulation, AM /ˈæmplɪˌtjuːd mɒdjʊˈleɪʃ(ə)n/	one of the two ways in which a radio wave is altered to carry the sound information from a radio transmitter to a receiver. The amplitude (=strength) of the wave is altered to show the sound information. AM has a long range and is simple to produce and receive, which is why it is used for short-wave broadcasting. However, it is subject to static and other electrical noise. **noun**	
anvil /ˈænvɪl/	a small bone in the middle ear between the hammer and the stirrup. **noun [count]**	*The hammer, anvil and stirrup amplify sounds and transmit them from the outer to the inner ear.*
auditory canal /ˌɔːdɪt(ə)ri kəˈnæl/	the passage that leads from the outer ear to the inner ear. **noun [count]**	
auditory nerve /ˌɔːdɪt(ə)ri ˈnɜːv/	a nerve in the ear that sends signals relating to hearing and balance from the inner ear to the brain. **noun [count]**	*His auditory nerves were damaged, causing deafness.*
carrier wave /ˈkærɪə ˌweɪv/	a high frequency radio wave that carries sound from a radio transmitter to a receiver. **noun [count]**	*The carrier wave is modulated in a transmitter.*
cochlea /ˈkɒkliə/	a part of the inner ear that has a spiral shape. It contains very small hairs that move when sound waves come into the ear. **noun [count]**	*The cochlea converts sound waves into electrical signals which are sent to the brain.*
compression /kəmˈpreʃ(ə)n/	the process of compressing (=pressing or squeezing) something. When sound travels through a material, the molecules in the material are alternately compressed (=pushed together) and rarefied (=pulled apart). **noun [uncount]**	*During compression the air pressure is a little above normal.*
cycle /ˈsaɪk(ə)l/	a series of events that happen again and again in the same order or at the same time. When a vibrator has completed one up and down or side to side movement, this is referred to as a cycle. **noun [count]**	*The complete cycle of a vibration can be represented as a double curve.*
decibel /ˈdesɪˌbel/	a unit for measuring how loud a sound is. The voices of most people measure between 45 and 60 decibels. Symbol dB. **noun [count]**	*Zero decibels is defined as the faintest sound that the human ear can detect.*
ear drum /ˈɪəˌdrʌm/	the membrane (=thin layer of tissue) inside the ear that vibrates when sound reaches it. (=tympanum). **noun [count]**	*Sound waves cause the eardrum to vibrate.*
flick /flɪk/	to make something move quickly and suddenly, usually with a quick movement of the hand. **verb [transitive]**	*He flicked a speck of dust off his sleeve.*
frequency /ˈfriːkwənsi/	**1** the rate at which a sound wave, light wave, or radio wave vibrates. **noun [count/uncount]** **2** the wavelength on which a radio programme is broadcast. **noun [count]**	*The higher the frequency of the sound, the higher the note or pitch.* *He found the radio station by tuning in to the correct frequency.*
frequency modulation, FM /ˈfriːkwənsi mɒdjʊˈleɪʃ(ə)n/	one of the two ways in which a radio wave is altered to carry the sound information from a radio transmitter to a receiver. The frequency of the wave is altered to show the sound information. FM is of high quality and not subject to interference, but FM signals can easily be blocked and sometimes good antenna are needed to receive them. **noun [uncount]**	
hammer /ˈhæmə/	one of the three small bones in the middle ear. Also called the malleus. **noun [count]**	*The hammer, anvil and stirrup amplify sounds and transmit them from the outer to the inner ear.*
hertz /hɜːts/	a unit for measuring the frequency of sound waves and radio waves. Symbol Hz (plural: hertz). **noun [count]**	
infrasound /ˈɪnfrəˌsaʊnd/	very low frequency sound waves that are below the normal range heard by humans. **noun [uncount]**	*Infrasound is used to move air around in cooling systems.*
inner ear /ˌɪnə ˈɪə/	the inside part of the ear that controls balance and the ability to hear. The inner ear includes the semicircular canals and the cochlea. **noun [singular]**	

long wave, LW /ˈlɒŋ ˌweɪv/	a radio wave of more than 1,000 metres, used for broadcasting. **noun [uncount]**	*The station is broadcast on long wave.*
loudness /ˈlaʊdnəs/	the quality of being loud or the degree to which something is loud. **noun [uncount]**	*The loudness of the music was such that they couldn't hear themselves speak.*
medium wave, MW /ˈmiːdiəm ˌweɪv/	a range of radio waves between 100 and 1,000 metres in length, used for broadcasting. **noun [uncount]**	*AM is susceptible to static and other forms of electrical noise.*
middle ear /ˌmɪdl ˈɪə/	the part of the ear that is between the inner ear and the eardrum. **noun [singular]**	*The middle ear contains the three small bones called hammer, anvil and stirrup.*
modulation /mɒdjʊˈleɪʃ(ə)n/	the process by which a high frequency radio wave (called the carrier wave) is altered to carry sound information. **noun [uncount]**	*There are two types of modulation, frequency modulation and amplitude modulation.*
noise /nɔɪz/	any sound that has no regular pattern or frequency. **noun [uncount]**	*The station is broadcast on medium wave.*
ossicle /ˈɒsɪk(ə)l/	a very small bone, especially in the inner ear. **noun [count]**	*The inner ear contains three ossicles.*
outer ear /ˌaʊtə(r) ˈɪə/	the part of the ear in humans and many other mammals that can be seen. It consists mainly of cartilage, and its job is to collect sound waves. **noun [count]**	*Some animals can move their outer ears to pick up sounds efficiently.*
oval window /ˌəʊv(ə)l ˈwɪndəʊ/	an opening covered by a membrane (=thin layer of tissue) between the middle ear and the inner ear that sound vibrations pass through. **noun [count]**	*The stirrup bone rests against the oval window and transmits sounds through it to the inner ear.*
overtone /ˈəʊvəˌtəʊn/	one of the frequencies that a musical instrument has in addition to the main frequencies. They give each instrument its particular sound quality. **noun [uncount]**	
pinna /ˈpɪnə/	the part of the ear which sticks out from the side of the head. **noun [count]**	
pitch /pɪtʃ/	the high or low quality of a sound that is controlled by the rate of the vibrations that produce it. **noun [uncount]**	*She uttered a high-pitched scream.*
pluck /plʌk/	to pull the strings of a musical instrument with your fingers in order to produce a sound. **verb [transitive/intransitive]**	*Her slender fingers plucked the strings of the harp.*
rarefaction /ˌreərəˈfækʃ(ə)n/	the process by which the molecules in a material are pulled apart as sound waves travel through them. **noun [uncount]**	*During rarefaction the air pressure is a little below normal.*
receiver /rɪˈsiːvə/	the part of a television or radio that receives electronic signals and changes them into pictures and sounds. **noun [count]**	*Radio waves are sent out by a transmitter and picked up by a receiver.*
round window /ˌraʊnd ˈwɪndəʊ/	an opening in the middle ear and inner ear that is covered by a membrane. **noun [count]**	
rupture /ˈrʌptʃə/	if something ruptures, or if you rupture it, it bursts or tears suddenly. **verb [transitive/intransitive]**	*A sudden burst of noise can rupture the eardrum.*
saccule /ˈsækjuːl/	a fluid-filled cavity in the inner ear that help us keep our balance. **noun [count]**	
semicircular canal /ˌsemiˌsɜːkjʊlə kəˈnæl/	one of the three tubes in the inner ear that is shaped like half of a circle and is important for balance. **noun [count]**	*The semicircular canals contain special nerve endings that detect movement and help with balance.*
short wave, SW /ˈʃɔːt ˌweɪv/	a type of radio wave that is used for broadcasting across large distances. **noun [count]**	*The ship's radio broadcast on a short wave (SW) frequency.*
side-to-side /ˌsaɪd tə ˈsaɪd/	moving from left to right, then from right to left, then back again. **adjective/adverb**	*A sound is produced when a vibrator moves up and down or side to side.*
skull /skʌl/	the bones of the head. **noun [count]**	*The middle and inner ear are protected by the bones of the skull.*
sound waves /ˈsaʊnd ˌweɪvz/	a type of wave movement that can be heard. It starts when something vibrates and causes further vibrations. Sound waves can travel through gases, liquids, and solids but not through empty space. **noun [count]**	*The hammer, anvil and stirrup amplify sounds and transmit them from the outer to the inner ear.*
static /ˈstætɪk/	the unpleasant noise that you hear on a radio, television, or telephone that is caused by electricity in the air. **noun [uncount]**	
stirrup /ˈstɪrəp/	one of the three small bones in the middle ear. Also called the stapes. **noun [count]**	
susceptibility /səˌseptəˈbɪlɪti/	the tendency to be easily affected or influenced by something. **noun [uncount]**	*One disadvantage of AM is its susceptibility to electrical noise.*
syringe /sɪˈrɪndʒ/	to spray warm water into the ear using a tube called a syringe, in order to remove wax that has built up in the auditory canal. **verb [transitive]**	*He needed his ears syringing because wax had built up in the ear canal, causing temporary deafness.*

taut /tɔːt/	stretched tight. **adjective**	*The pitch of a string can be raised by making the string more taut.*
tension /'tenʃ(ə)n/	the degree to which something such as a string is pulled tight. **noun [uncount]**	*The tension of a string is one of the factors that controls its pitch.*
transmitter /trænz'mɪtə/	a piece of electronic equipment that is used for sending radio, television, or telephone signals through the air. **noun [count]**	*The radio transmitter was positioned high up on top of a mast.*
tympanum /tɪm'pɑːnəm/	the membrane (=thin layer of tissue) inside the ear that vibrates when sound reaches it. Also called the ear drum. **noun [count]**	*The sound of the bomb blast perforated his ear drum, causing deafness.*
ultrasound /'ʌltrəˌsaʊnd/	sound that has a higher frequency than the range of sounds that humans can hear. **noun [uncount]**	*The ship's depth meter worked by bouncing ultrasound waves off the seabed.*
ultra high frequency, UHF /ʌltrə haɪ 'friːkwənsi/	a type of radio wave that is used for television broadcasting. **noun [uncount]**	
utricle /'juːtrɪk(ə)l/	a fluid-filled cavity in the inner ear that helps us keep our balance. **noun [count]**	
very high frequency, VHF /'veri haɪ 'friːkwənsi/	a range of radio waves that produces good sound quality. **noun [uncount]**	*Most radio programmes are transmitted on VHF.*
vestibular apparatus /vesˌtɪbjʊlə æpəˈreɪtəs/	the two fluid-filled cavities (called the saccule and the utricle) in the inner ear that help us keep our balance. **noun [singular]**	
vibrate /vaɪ'breɪt/	to shake very quickly with small movements; to make something do this. **verb [transitive/intransitive]**	*Sound waves travel through air and other media by vibrating the particles.*
vibration /vaɪ'breɪʃ(ə)n/	a small, fast, backward and forward movement such as that which sets up a sound wave. **noun [count/uncount]**	*A small amplitude in vibration causes a soft sound.*
wavelength /'weɪvˌleŋθ/	the distance between two waves of light or radio waves. **noun [count]**	*The longer the wavelength, the lower the sound.*
wax /wæks/	a dark yellow substance in the ears. **noun [uncount]**	*A build-up of wax can cause temporary deafness.*

26 SOUND & HEARING

A   Working with words

1   Sound and hearing word map

Write these words in the correct places on the word map.

amplitude   cochlea   ear   frequency   ultrasound   VHF (very high frequency)   waves

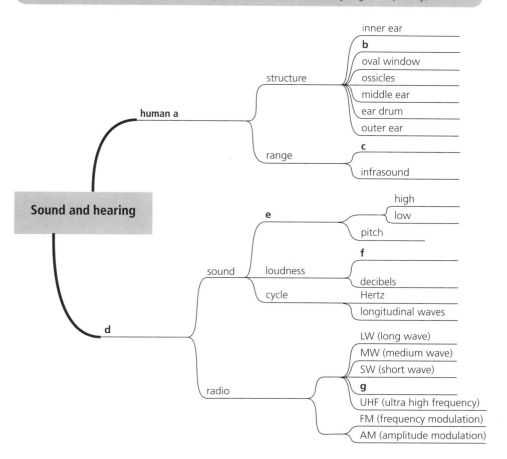

2   Sound waves

Read the text and fill in the gaps with the correct form of the word vibrate.

vibrate   vibrator(s)   vibrating   vibration(s)

Sounds are produced when things 1 _____. Try plucking a stretched rubber band or flicking a plastic ruler at the edge of a table to see this effect. The object that is 2 _____ is often called a 3 _____. A sound is produced when the 4 _____ is pushed aside, up or down and then released. In some 5 _____ you can actually see or feel the 6 _____ that give rise to the sounds. Musical instruments are 7 _____ that produce sounds through 8 _____: strings such as piano, guitar and violin; air in pipes such as the clarinet, saxophone and flute; part of the instrument itself, as in percussion instruments such as drums, cymbals, triangles and steel pans. When a 9 _____ has completed one up-and-down, or side-to-side movement, it is said to have completed one 10 _____ or one cycle.

3 The structure of the ear

Label the diagram with these words.

> anvil   auditory canal   auditory nerve   bones of skull   cochlea   hammer
> muscle attached to ossicle   ossicles   pinna   round window   saccule
> semicircular canals   stirrup   to throat   utricle   vestibular apparatus

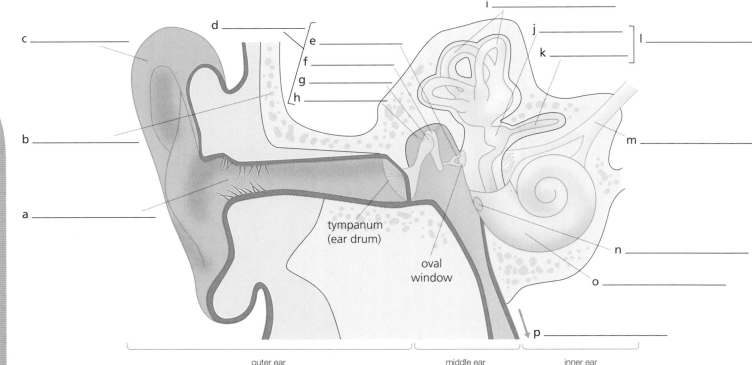

c _____   d _____
e _____
f _____
g _____
h _____

b _____

a _____

i _____

j _____
k _____
l _____

m _____

tympanum
(ear drum)

oval
window

n _____

o _____

p _____

outer ear   middle ear   inner ear

B   Working with sentences

4 Structure and function of the ear

Put these sentences in the correct order.

We are able to hear sounds because they stimulate the auditory cells of the ear.

a   As the oval window picks up the vibrations, it transfers them to the cochlea in the inner ear.
b   As the vibrations pass between the ossicles they are amplified.
c   At the end of this passage is the eardrum or tympanic membrane. As the sound waves hit the eardrum, they cause it to vibrate.
d   Hearing begins with the outer ear, when the pinna or earflap collects sound waves and directs them down the external auditory passage (ear canal).
e   The base of the stirrup vibrates against the oval window, which is a membrane that separates the middle ear from the inner ear.
f   The cochlea contains the sensory cells that produce impulses in the auditory nerve.
g   The vibrations from the eardrum are received by the hammer, which passes them to the anvil and then to the stirrup.
h   These impulses are transmitted to the brain where they are interpreted. At the end of the cochlea is the round window which functions as a pressure 'safety valve' releasing the pressure in the cochlea caused from the vibrations of the oval window.
i   These are called the hammer, anvil and stirrup.
j   The vibrations of the eardrum are picked up by three small bones in the middle ear called the ossicles.

1 ☐   2 ☐   3 ☐   4 ☐   5 ☐   6 ☐   7 ☐   8 ☐   9 ☐   10 ☐

5 Loudness of sound

Put the phrases in the correct order to make sentences.

1 A ruler that   and produces sound.   at the edge of a table   is flicked   vibrates

_____

2 by the ruler   the distance   moved up and down   of the vibration.   the amplitude   We call

_____

3 loud   of a sound wave   or soft.   The amplitude   the sound is   whether   will determine

_____

4 a small amount of energy   If   is flicked only a little,   is supplied   the ruler   then   to the ruler.

_____

5 a small amplitude   a soft sound   and   causes   in vibration   is heard.   This

_____

6 and   and a large energy   However,   if the ruler   is larger   is flicked more strongly,   is supplied,   louder.   the amplitude   the sound will be

_____

7 on the ruler,   that occurs.   The harder   the louder   the sound   you pluck

_____

8 a guitar.   applies   of   on the strings   The same   to plucking

_____

9 can be   cycle   graphically.   of   represented   The complete   the vibrations

_____

10 A   a   amplitude.   greater   has   louder   sound

_____

6 Frequency or pitch of sounds

Match the beginnings and endings of sentences.

Beginnings

1 Pitch is a musical term which is similar
2 The frequency of a sound represents the number
3 However the sensations of these frequencies are
4 Objects that vibrate more rapidly, that is have
   more vibrations per second,
5 So, on a guitar, the strings that produce notes
   with a higher pitch
6 The unit for frequency is

Endings

a commonly referred to as the pitch of a sound.
b cycles per second or hertz (Hz).
c in meaning to the scientific term frequency.
d of vibrations that occur in one second.
e vibrate faster than those with a lower pitch.
f will have a higher pitch than objects that vibrate
   more slowly.

1 ☐   2 ☐   3 ☐   4 ☐   5 ☐   6 ☐

7 AM and FM radio

Read the text and make notes on the advantages and disadvantages of AM and FM radios.

There are two ways of modifying the carrier wave. Amplitude modulation (AM): here the strength (amplitude) of the carrier wave is altered to show the sound information. Three separate frequencies are transmitted, the carrier frequency which is constant, a lower sideband (LSB) below the carrier frequency, and an upper sideband (USB) above the carrier frequency. These sidebands are 'mirror images' of each other and contain the same sound information. Frequency modulation (FM) is the method where it is the frequency of the carrier, not its amplitude, which is altered. Amplitude modulation and frequency modulation each have their own advantages and disadvantages. AM signals have a long range and provide good coverage of the area outside the transmitter. AM has the advantage of being easy to produce in a transmitter and AM receivers are simple in design. Disadvantages of AM include its susceptibility to static and other forms of electrical noise. Despite this, AM is simple to tune on ordinary receivers, which is why it is used for almost all short-wave broadcasting. The big advantage of FM is its audio quality and immunity to noise. Most forms of static and electrical noise (for example, lightning) is naturally AM, and a FM receiver will not respond to AM signals. But FM signals are readily obstructed and in some areas good antennae may be needed to receive signals at all.

	Advantages	Disadvantages
AM		
FM		

Translation

active /ˈæktɪv/	an active volcano is likely to erupt (=explode) at any time. **adjective**	*the alternating rise and fall in sea level*
alternating /ˈɔːltəˌneɪtɪŋ/	changing from one thing to another. **adjective**	
asphalt /ˈæsfəlt/	a black sticky substance that is used for making the surface of a road. **noun [uncount]**	
avalanche /ˈævəˌlɑːntʃ/	a large amount of snow that suddenly falls down a mountain. **noun [count]**	*The skier was buried by the avalanche.*
basalt /ˈbæsɔːlt/	a dark-green or black rock formed when hot liquid rock from a volcano becomes solid. It is a type of igneous rock. **noun [uncount]**	
bend /bend/	to curve or to make something curve. **verb [transitive/intransitive]**	*A build-up of pressure causes the rocks to bend and buckle.*
boundary /ˈbaʊndəri/	the edge of an area of land, or a line that marks the edge. **noun [count]**	*95% of earthquake energy is released at plate boundaries.*
bowl-like /ˈbəʊlˌlaɪk/	shaped like a bowl. **adjective**	*the bowl-like crater at the top of a volcano*
bowl-shaped /ˈbəʊlʃeɪpt/	shaped like a bowl. **adjective**	*a bowl-shaped depression in the land*
buckle /ˈbʌk(ə)l/	to bend, or to make something bend under pressure. **verb [transitive/intransitive]**	*The rocks began to bend and buckle.*
catastrophic /ˌkætəˈstrɒfɪk/	causing a lot of damage or suffering. **adjective**	*catastrophic floods*
cinder /ˈsɪndə/	a small piece of something that has been burnt almost completely. **noun [count]**	*Cinders fall around the vent of the volcano.*
cinder cone /ˈsɪndə ˌkəʊn/	used for describing a type of volcano with a hill around the vent that explodes violently when it erupts. **adjective**	
cold front /ˈkəʊld ˌfrʌnt/	the place where a moving mass of cold air meets a mass of warm air. Cold fronts usually cause heavy rain and they sometimes cause thunder. **noun [count]**	
combustible /kəmˈbʌstɪb(ə)l/	able to burn easily. **adjective**	*an underground store of combustible material*
composite /ˈkɒmpəzɪt/	used for describing a type of volcano that is tall and made of layers of ash, cinder and hardened lava. **adjective**	
consistency /kənˈsɪstənsi/	the degree to which a substance is thick, smooth or firm. **noun [uncount]**	*The Earth's mantle flows with the consistency of asphalt.*
continental polar /ˌkɒntɪˌnent(ə)l ˈpəʊlə/	an air mass that forms over high cold land and is therefore usually cold and dry. **noun [count]**	
continental tropical /ˌkɒntɪˌnent(ə)l ˈtrɒpɪk(ə)l/	an air mass that forms over tropical land and is therefore usually hot and dry. **noun [count]**	
converging /kənˈvɜːdʒɪŋ/	coming to the same place from different places or directions. **adjective**	*two converging air masses*
coral reef /ˌkɒrəl ˈriːf/	a hard natural structure under the sea that is formed from coral. Coral reefs are an important habitat for many types of fish and other forms of sea life. **noun [count]**	
crater /ˈkreɪtə/	the round hole at the top of a volcano. **noun [count]**	*They climbed up the volcano and stood on the rim of the crater.*
crumple /ˈkrʌmp(ə)l/	to crush something so that it forms untidy folds. **verb [transitive]**	*The waves pile on top of the waves in front of them, like crumpling a rug against a wall.*
crust /krʌst/	the outer layer of rock on the Earth. **noun [count/uncount]**	*The Earth's crust is a comparatively thin layer.*

cumulonimbus cloud /ˌkjuːmjʊləʊˈnɪmbəs ˌklaʊd/	a large thick cloud. It usually brings heavy rain and sometimes brings thunder. **noun [count/uncount]**	
cyclone /ˈsaɪˌkləʊn/	a severe storm in which the wind spins in a circle. Hurricanes and tornadoes are types of cyclone. **noun [count]**	
cyclonic storm /saɪˌklɒnɪk ˈstɔːm/	a cyclone. **noun [count]**	
dense /dens/	a dense substance is very heavy in relation to its size. **adjective**	*a dense mixture of volcanic gases, rock fragments, pumice and hot ash*
devastating /ˈdevəsˌteɪtɪŋ/	causing a lot of harm or damage. **adjective**	*a devastating earthquake*
disastrous /dɪˈzɑːsˌtrəs/	very bad or harmful. **adjective**	*disastrous floods*
dormant /ˈdɔːmənt/	not active or developing now, but possibly becoming active in the future. **adjective**	*a dormant volcano*
earthquake /ˈɜːθkweɪk/	a sudden movement of the ground, often causing a lot of damage to buildings etc. Earthquakes usually take place along geological faults or in volcanic areas. The strength of earthquakes is measured on the Richter scale.	
eject /ɪˈdʒekt/	to make something leave a place, especially with a lot of force. **verb [transitive]**	*Gases and ash are ejected from the top of the volcano.*
epicentre /ˈepɪˌsentə/	the area of land directly over the centre of an earthquake. **noun [count]**	*The epicentre of the earthquake was in the middle of the Pacific Ocean.*
erupt /ɪˈrʌpt/	if a volcano erupts, it explodes inside and flames, rocks, and lava come out of the top. **verb [intransitive]**	
extinct /ɪkˈstɪŋkt/	an extinct volcano is no longer active and no longer erupts. **adjective**	
eye /aɪ/	the calm area at the centre of a storm. **noun [count]**	*the eye of the hurricane*
fault /fɔːlt/	a crack on or below the Earth's surface. **noun [count]**	*The San Andreas Fault has been the site of many earthquakes in the past.*
flooding /ˈflʌdɪŋ/	a situation in which water from a river or from heavy rain covers large areas of land. **noun [uncount]**	*Heavy rain resulted in severe flooding.*
focus /ˈfəʊkəs/	the place under the ground where an earthquake starts. **noun [count]**	
front /frʌnt/	a line where a large area of cold air meets a large area of warm air. **noun [count]**	*The weather map showed a cold front approaching from the west.*
frontal system /ˈfrʌnt(ə)l ˌsɪstəm/	a system of air masses with particular characteristics. **noun [count]**	
granite /ˈɡrænɪt/	a type of very hard stone, used especially for building, that is grey, black, or pink in colour. It is a type of igneous rock. **noun [uncount]**	*The tall cliffs were made of granite.*
hemisphere /ˈhemɪˌsfɪə/	one half of the Earth. The northern hemisphere is the part of the world north of the equator, and the southern hemisphere is the part south of it.	
high tide /ˌhaɪ ˈtaɪd/	the time when the sea reaches the highest level. **noun [count/uncount]**	
hurricane /ˈhʌrɪkən, ˈhʌrɪkeɪn/	a violent storm with extremely strong winds and heavy rain. **noun [count]**	*The hurricane caused extensive structural damage.*
inner core /ˌɪnə ˈkɔː/	the central solid part of the Earth that contains nickel and iron. **noun [singular]**	
intensify /ɪnˈtensɪˌfaɪ/	if something intensifies, or if you intensify it, it becomes greater, stronger, or more extreme. **verb [transitive/intransitive]**	*The graph shows how the vibrations intensify and then ease off during an earthquake.*
intersect /ˌɪntəˈsekt/	if lines or the edges of something intersect, they cross each other, or they join. **verb [intransitive]**	*places where the Earth's tectonic plates intersect*
lava /ˈlɑːvə/	**1** rock in the form of extremely hot liquid that flows from a volcano. **noun [uncount]** **2** the solid rock that forms when liquid lava becomes cold. **noun [uncount]**	*Molten lava spewed out of the erupting volcano.*
low tide /ˌləʊ ˈtaɪd/	the time when the sea is at its lowest level. **noun [count/uncount]**	

magma /ˈmægmə/	hot liquid rock inside the Earth. When magma becomes cool it forms igneous rock. **noun [uncount]**	
magnitude /ˈmægnɪˌtjuːd/	the size of something. **noun [count]**	*The magnitude of the earthquake was 7.4 on the Richter scale.*
mantle /ˈmænt(ə)l/	the part of the Earth that is deep below the surface and surrounds the core. **noun [singular]**	*The Earth's mantle is mostly composed of solid rock.*
maritime polar /ˌmærɪtaɪm ˈpəʊlə/	an air mass that forms over cold ocean water and is therefore cold and humid. **noun [count]**	
maritime tropical /ˌmærɪtaɪm ˈtrɒpɪk(ə)l/	an air mass that forms over tropical seas and is therefore usually warm and humid. **noun [count]**	
micro-earthquake /ˌmaɪkrəʊ ˈɜːθkweɪk/	a small earthquake measuring between 0 and 2 on the Richter scale. **noun [count]**	
molten /ˈməʊltən/	molten rock, metal or glass has become liquid because it is very hot. **adjective**	
neap tide /ˈniːp ˌtaɪd/	a tide that has the least amount of change between the highest and lowest levels of the sea. **noun [count]**	
nimbostratus /ˌnɪmbəʊˈstreɪtəs/	thick low cloud that carries rain and covers all of the sky. **noun [uncount]**	
occluded front /əˌkluːdɪd ˈfrʌnt/	a weather front that forms when a fast-moving cold front catches up with and overtakes a slower moving warm front, pushing the warm air between them upwards so that cloud forms. **noun [count]**	
ocean floor /ˌəʊʃ(ə)n ˈflɔː/	the land at the bottom of the ocean. **noun [singular]**	*The ocean floor is home to many animals and plants.*
outer core /ˌaʊtə ˈkɔː/	the central part of the Earth that consists of molten rocks, iron and nickel and surrounds the inner core. **noun [singular]**	
plate /pleɪt/	one of the layers of rock that form the surface of the Earth. **noun [count]**	*A fault is a deep crack between two of the Earth's plates.*
plume of ash /ˌpluːm əv ˈæʃ/	a long narrow cloud of dust, smoke etc that moves upwards. **noun [count]**	*The volcano released a plume of ash.*
precipitation /prɪˌsɪpɪˈteɪʃ(ə)n/	water that falls to the ground in the form of rain, snow, hail etc. These are all formed by the condensation of water vapour in the atmosphere. **noun [uncount]**	
pressure wave /ˈpreʃə ˌweɪv/	a type of seismic wave that pushes particles of ground together and then apart as it moves through the Earth. Also called P wave. **noun [count]**	
pumice /ˈpʌmɪs/	a very light grey stone from a volcano. **noun [uncount]**	
pyroclastic flow /ˌpaɪrəʊˌklæstɪk ˈfləʊ/	the large amount of hot ash, pumice, pieces of rock and gas that flows very quickly down the side of a volcano when it erupts. **noun [count/uncount]**	
recover /rɪˈkʌvə/	to return to a previous healthy state. **verb [intransitive]**	*After a volcano erupts, it can take many years for the area to recover.*
Richter scale /ˈrɪktə ˌskeɪl/	a scale from 1 to 10 which is used for measuring the strength of earthquakes according to how much energy is released. A higher number represents a stronger force. **noun [singular]**	*The earthquake measured 5.5 on the Richter scale.*
rip off /ˌrɪp ˈɒf/	to remove something in a very violent way. **phrasal verb [transitive]**	*Powerful winds ripped off roofs and destroyed buildings.*
rush down /ˌrʌʃ ˈdaʊn/	to move very quickly down something. **phrasal verb [transitive]**	*the hot material that rushes down the side of a volcano when it erupts*
seismic waves /ˌsaɪzmɪk ˈweɪvz/	shock waves that are produced when a build-up of pressure causes rocks beneath the surface of the Earth to snap and move past each other. **noun [plural]**	*Two types of seismic wave are produced by earthquakes.*
seismogram /ˈsaɪzməʊˌgræm/	a written record of an earthquake, produced by an instrument called a seismograph. **noun [count]**	
seismograph /ˈsaɪzməˌgrɑːf/	an instrument used for measuring and recording the strength of earthquakes. Also called seismometer. **noun [count]**	
shear /ʃɪə/	a type of seismic wave that moves sideways as it passes through the Earth. Also called S wave. **noun [count]**	
shield /ʃiːld/	used for describing a type of volcano with a gentle slope caused by the lava that flows out of it spreading for miles before it goes hard. **adjective**	
shock waves /ˈʃɒk ˌweɪvz/	seismic waves. **noun [plural]**	*The shock waves of the earthquake were felt miles away.*

silicon /ˈsɪlɪkən/	a metalloid element that is found in sand, clay and other minerals. Chemical symbol: Si. **noun [uncount]**	
slip /slɪp/	if something slips, it slides out of the position it should be in. **verb [intransitive]**	*The rocks slip past each other, causing the ground to shake.*
snap /snæp/	to suddenly break with a short loud noise. **verb [intransitive]**	*A build-up of pressure makes the rocks snap.*
spring tide /ˌsprɪŋ ˈtaɪd/	a time when there is a big difference between the highest and lowest levels of the sea. **noun [count]**	
steep-sided /ˈstiːpˌsaɪdɪd/	having steep sides. **adjective**	*a steep-sided volcano*
stratiform clouds /ˌstrætɪfɔːm ˈklaʊdz/	clouds in layers that spread out over a large area. **noun [plural]**	
submarine earthquake /ˌsʌbməˌriːn ˈɜːθkweɪk/	an earthquake under the sea. **noun [count]**	
surface /ˈsɜːfɪs/	a type of seismic wave that travels along the surface of the ground. Also called longitudinal or L wave. **noun [count]**	
tectonic plate /tekˌtɒnɪk ˈpleɪt/	one of the pieces into which the Earth's crust is divided. **noun [count]**	
throw up /ˌθrəʊ ˈʌp/	to force something upwards, especially violently. **phrasal verb**	*The water is thrown up into great waves.*
thunderstorm /ˈθʌndəˌstɔːm/	a storm with thunder and lightning. **noun [count]**	
tidal bulge /ˌtaɪd(ə)l ˈbʌldʒ/	the effect of the gravitational pull of the moon and sun on the ocean, which causes changes in sea level. **noun [count]**	
tidal wave /ˈtaɪd(ə)l ˌweɪv/	**1** a large wave or mass of water in the sea that is sometimes produced at high tide. **noun [count]** **2** a tsunami. **noun [count]**	*The tidal wave wrecked several boats in the harbour.*
tides /taɪdz/	the regular movement of the sea towards and away from the land. **noun [count]**	*The tides are influenced by the phases of the moon.*
trailing wave /ˌtreɪlɪŋ ˈweɪv/	a wave behind another wave. **noun [count]**	*In a tsunami, the trailing waves pile on top of the waves in front of them.*
trembling /ˈtremblɪŋ/	a shaking movement. **noun [uncount]**	*Earthquakes are felt as a trembling in the ground.*
tremor /ˈtremə/	a small earthquake. **noun [count]**	
tsunami /tsuːˈnɑːmi/	a very large wave in the sea that is caused by an earthquake under the sea or by the eruption of a volcano. Tsunamis usually cause severe damage on land. **noun [count]**	
unstable /ʌnˈsteɪb(ə)l/	likely to change at any time, especially to something extreme or bad. **adjective**	*unstable weather*
uproot /ʌpˈruːt/	to pull a whole tree or plant from the ground. **verb [transitive]**	*The hurricane uprooted trees and overturned vehicles.*
vent /vent/	a hole in the Earth's surface through which lava or gas comes out. **noun [count]**	*A sudden vertical shifting of the sea floor causes a tsunami.*
vibration /vaɪˈbreɪʃ(ə)n/	a small, fast, backward and forward movement. **noun [count/uncount]**	*Seismic waves are vibrations which pass through the Earth's crust, causing earthquakes.*
violent /ˈvaɪələnt/	a violent wind, storm, or explosion happens with a lot of force and causes serious damage. **adjective**	
volcano /vɒlˈkeɪnəʊ/	an opening in the surface of the Earth through which hot gas, rocks, ash, and lava are pushed. Some volcanos are in the form of mountains, and some are under the sea. Some are not dangerous at the present time because they are not active and have become dormant. Others will never be dangerous again because they are completely extinct (plural: volcanos or volcanoes). **noun [count]**	
warm front /ˌwɔːm ˈfrʌnt/	the front edge of a mass of warm air that brings warm weather when it moves into an area. The front edge of a mass of cold air is called a cold front. **noun [count]**	
zonation /zəʊˈneɪʃ(ə)n/	the arrangement of different plants and animals at different points along the shore that depends on how long they are under the sea as the sea level rises and falls. **noun [uncount]**	

1   Forces and motion word map

Write these words in the correct places on the word map.

crust   earthquakes   fronts   hurricanes   magma   maritime tropical   neap   tsunamis

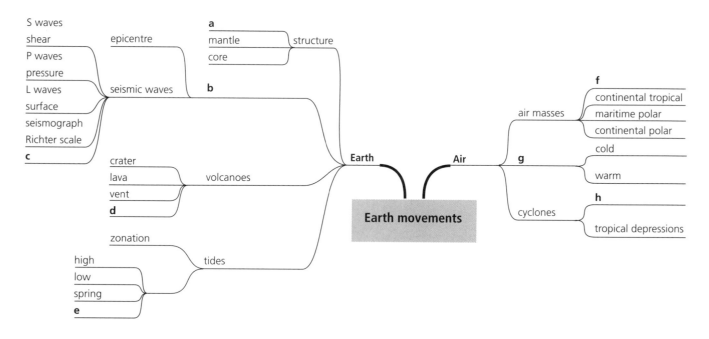

2   Earth movements

Fill in the gaps with these words.

crust   dormant   epicentre   lava   longitudinal   Richter   seismograph   slip   tsunamis   volcanoes

1   The Earth consists of three main layers: the core, mantle and _____.

2   Faults are cracks along which rocks _____.

3   The vibrations of an earthquake are greatest at the _____.

4   There are three types of seismic waves: pressure waves, shear waves and _____ waves.

5   A _____ measures the intensity of the vibrations of an earthquake.

6   The magnitude of an earthquake can be measured on the _____ scale.

7   Submarine earthquakes may result in_____.

8   _____ result when there is a build-up of heat and pressure beneath the Earth's surface.

9   Molten magma is called _____ when it reaches the Earth's surface.

10   Volcanoes are classified as active, _____ or extinct depending on their eruption history.

3 Types of seismic waves

Read the text and fill in the gaps with these words.

> earthquake   epicentre   longitudinal   P   seismic   shear   surface   tremors   wave

There are three types of 1 _____ wave. Pressure waves are also called 2 _____ waves.

When P waves slip through the Earth they push the particles of the ground together and then apart, similar

to what happens in a sound 3 _____. 4 _____ waves are also known as S waves.

These waves move sideways or in a transverse direction. They also twist, shake and distort solid substances as

they pass through them. Both S and P waves result from the movement of rocks. 5 _____ waves

are also known as longitudinal waves or L waves. When S and P reach the Earth's surface waves they become

6 _____ waves. These waves cause the most damage because they travel along the surface of the

ground. However, the intensity and damage caused by these waves reduces as they get further away from the

7 _____. Since there are three types of seismic waves it means that three kinds of

8 _____ are felt during an 9 _____.

4 Earth movements

Match the beginnings and endings of the sentences.

Beginnings

1   The Earth's crust is divided
2   The sudden trembling or movement of
    the Earth indicates
3   The three basic types
4   When the Moon, Earth and Sun are in
5   Neap tides are formed when the Moon
    and Sun are at right angles to one

Endings

a   line spring tides are formed.
b   that an earthquake is occurring.
c   into large plates.
d   another in relation to the Earth.
e   of volcano are cinder cone, shield and
    composite.

1 ☐   2 ☐   3 ☐   4 ☐   5 ☐

5 Fronts

Read the sentences and sort them into the correct columns.

a   As the front moves, the clouds get thicker and nimbostratus clouds develop which results in heavy rain or snow ahead of the front.
b   As the warm air rises, water vapour in it condenses into cumulonimbus clouds that stretch about 120 km before and behind the front.
c   Before the cold front passes, the temperature of the surroundings will be warm. However, as it passes, the temperature will fall (often by about 5°C) and the wind direction will change.
d   However, as the warm front line passes over, the precipitation decreases and the temperature increases (it gets warmer).
e   On a weather map, a warm front is drawn as a solid red line with semicircles. The bulging sides of the semicircles point in the direction in which the frontal system is moving.
f   On a weather map, the cold front is drawn as a solid blue line with triangles where the triangles point in the direction of the frontal movement.
g   The clouds burst into heavy rains, which end quickly. Sometimes thunderstorms may occur.
h   The warm front is generally accompanied by stratiform clouds, which extend up to 1600 km ahead of the warm front on the ground.
i   These are formed when an advancing cold, dry air mass pushes a warm, moist air mass ahead of it.
j   These occur when an advancing warm, moist air mass pushes a cold, dry polar air mass ahead of it.

Cold fronts	Warm fronts
1	6
2	7
3	8
4	9
5	10

6   Tides

Read the text and label the diagrams.

> 1 first quarter   2 full moon   3 highest tides   4 lowest tides
> 5 neap tides   6 new moon   7 spring tides   8 third quarter

Tides are the alternating rise and fall in sea level. This is produced by the gravitational attraction of the Moon and to a lesser extent the Sun on the large bodies of water on the Earth. The Moon has a stronger effect on the tides since it is four hundred times closer to the Earth than the Sun. The oceans stay on the Earth's surface due to the Earth's gravitational pull. However, the gravitational pull of the Moon and Sun on the surface of the waters will cause them to bulge. The Moon is constantly orbiting and changing its position relative to the Earth, so the tides are constantly changing. Since the Earth–Moon system rotates once in every 24 hours, there will be two high tides each day, one when a spot on Earth is nearest to the Moon and one when it is furthest away. Between the high tides there will be low tides, as water flows away following the Moon's pull. When the Moon, the Earth, and the Sun are in line, the gravitational pull of the Sun and Moon will be in the same direction on the ocean. This will create the highest high tide and the lowest low tide during the month, which is known as the spring tide. This happens twice every month, at full moon and new moon. When the Moon, the Earth, and Sun are at right angles to each other, at the first and third quarters, the gravitational pulls of the Moon and Sun act against each other. So we have the highest low tides and the lowest high tides. These are known as neap tides.

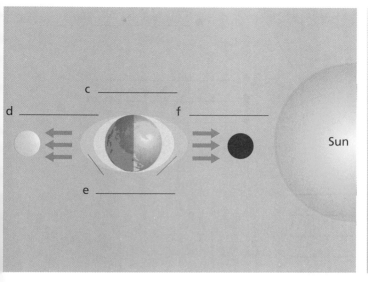

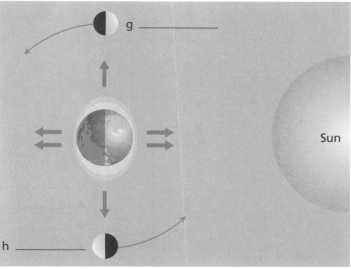

The layers of the Earth

Read the text and label the diagram with the correct information.

The Earth is the fifth largest planet in our solar system and the third planet from the Sun. The Earth is made up of three main layers. There is the crust which is the outer layer and is very thin, between 5 and 67 km thick. The crust consists of the land and sea. The land is mainly made up of two types of rocks: granite and basalt. Then there is the mantle. This is a thick layer which is about 3000 km thick that lies directly below the crust. It consists of hot dense rocks and compounds of magnesium, iron and silicon. The rocks of the mantle are much heavier than those in the crust. Lastly, there is the core. This is the centre of the Earth which consists of heavy metals. It has an inner and an outer layer. The outer core consists of molten rocks, iron and nickel and it is about 2000 km thick. The inner core is about 1500 km thick and is a solid structure containing nickel and iron. The temperature and pressure of the inner core of the Earth is so great that the metals are squeezed together making it difficult for them to move about like a liquid, instead they are forced to vibrate in one place like a solid.

1   1500 km thick
2   2000 km thick
3   3000 km thick
4   directly below the crust
5   granite and basalt
6   hot dense rock, compounds of magnesium, iron and silicon
7   inner core
8   land and sea
9   liquid, molten rocks, iron, nickel
10   metals vibrate in one place, like solid
11   outer core
12   outer layer, very thin, between 5 and 67 km think
13   solid structure, nickel and iron
14   the crust
15   the mantle

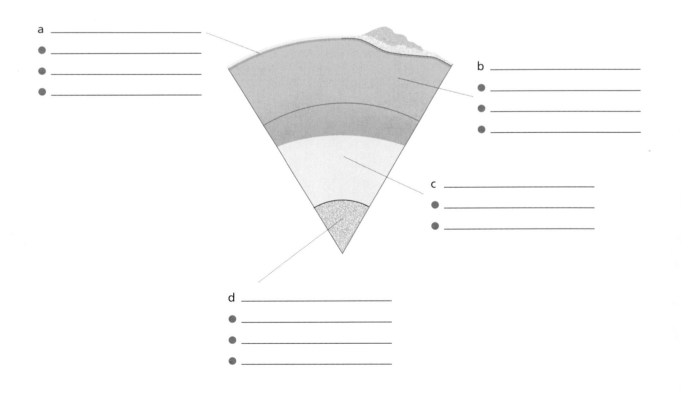

a _____

● _____

● _____

● _____

b _____

● _____

● _____

● _____

c _____

● _____

● _____

d _____

● _____

● _____

● _____

Translation

ammonia /əˈməʊniə/	a poisonous gas, with a strong unpleasant smell, or the gas dissolved in water. noun [uncount]	
Andromeda Galaxy /ænˈdrɒmɪdə ˌgæləksi/	a spiral galaxy (= group of stars and planets) about two million light years away and about twice as large as our galaxy. noun [singular]	
asteroid /ˈæstəˌrɔɪd/	a mass of rock that moves around in space. Most asteroids are found in the region of space between the planets Jupiter and Mars, a region known as the asteroid belt. noun [count]	
atmosphere /ˈætməsˌfɪə/	the air around the Earth or around another planet. It consists of three main layers, the lowest being the troposphere, the middle one the stratosphere, and the highest the ionosphere. noun [singular]	*The Earth's atmosphere is getting warmer.*
axis /ˈækˌsɪs/	an imaginary line through the middle of an object such as a planet, around which it seems to spin (plural: axes /ˈæksiːz/). noun [count]	*The Earth spins once on its axis every 24 hours.*
Big Bang /ˌbɪg ˈbæŋ/	the explosion of a very large mass of matter that is believed to have caused the Universe to begin to exist. The Big Bang is believed to have happened about 15 billion years ago, and this theory explains why the Universe is still increasing in size. noun [singular]	
black hole /ˌblæk ˈhəʊl/	an object in outer space that has such strong gravity that nothing near it can escape from it, not even light. Black holes are thought to be formed when a very large star stops existing. noun [count]	
blob /blɒb/	something that seems to have no definite shape. noun [count]	*She stuck the paper down with a blob of glue.*
bright /braɪt/	producing a lot of light. adjective	*Sirius is the brightest star in the night sky.*
Cassiopeia /ˌkæsɪəʊˈpeɪə/	a constellation (= group of stars) in the northern sky shaped like the letter W. noun [singular]	
Ceres /ˈseres/	the first asteroid to be discovered, which is also the largest. noun [singular]	
circular orbit /ˌsɜːkjʊlə ˈɔːbɪt/	a path in the shape of a circle that is taken by an object such as a planet moving around a larger object in space. noun [count]	*The space station has an almost circular orbit.*
comet /ˈkɒmɪt/	an object in space that leaves a bright stream of gas and dust behind it as it moves around the Sun. noun [count]	*The bright tail of the comet could be seen with the naked eye.*
compress /kəmˈpres/	to press or squeeze something so that it fits into a smaller space. verb [transitive]	
constellation /ˌkɒnstəˈleɪʃ(ə)n/	a group of stars that form a particular pattern in the sky. Most of the constellations we recognize have been given names, for example Orion the Hunter and the Great Bear. noun [count]	
crescent /ˈkrez(ə)nt/	a curved shape that is wide in the middle and pointed at the ends. noun [count]	*The moon first appears as a crescent.*
debris /ˈdebriː/	the broken pieces that are left when something large has been destroyed, especially by an explosion, fire or accident. noun [uncount]	
disturbance /dɪsˈtɜːbəns/	an occasion when something is prevented from operating in its usual way. noun [count/uncount]	*Events such as fires and strong winds can cause disturbance in forest ecosystems.*
Doppler effect /ˈdɒplə(r) ɪˌfekt/	the change that you notice in a sound, light etc as you get closer to it or further from it. noun [singular]	
eclipse /ɪˈklɪps/	a short period when all or part of the Sun or Moon becomes dark, because of the positions of the Sun, Moon, and Earth in relation to each other. A total eclipse is when the Sun or Moon is completely covered. An eclipse of the Sun is called a solar eclipse, and an eclipse of the Moon is called a lunar eclipse. noun [count]	

Word	Definition	Translation
elliptical /ɪˈlɪptɪk(ə)l/	in the shape of a circle that is longer than it is wide. **adjective**	*The Earth travels around the Sun in an elliptical orbit.*
enormous /ɪˈnɔːməs/	very large in size or quantity. **adjective**	*The impact created enormous amounts of dust.*
equator /ɪˈkweɪtə/	an imaginary line that goes around the centre of the Earth and divides it into northern and southern parts. **noun [singular]**	*In countries that are near the equator it is always hot.*
equinox /ˈiːkwɪˌnɒks/	one of the two days in the year when the day and night are the same length. The vernal equinox is on 20 or 21 March and the autumnal equinox is on 22 or 23 September. **noun [count]**	
fade /feɪd/	to gradually become less bright or strong. **verb [intransitive]**	*The supernovae increase to maximum brightness and then fade away.*
first quarter /ˈfɜːst ˌkɔːtə/	the phase (= shape) of the Moon when it appears as half a moon about a week after the new Moon. **noun [singular]**	
galaxy /ˈɡæləksi/	an extremely large group of stars and planets. **noun [count]**	*The Earth is part of a galaxy called the Milky Way.*
gibbous /ˈɡɪbəs/	a gibbous Moon is one that appears a few days before and after the full Moon, when it is less than full but more than half visible. **adjective**	
gravitational pull /ˌɡrævɪˈteɪʃ(ə)nəl ˈpʊl/	the force exerted by gravity, in which things are pulled towards a physical object such as the Earth. **noun [uncount]**	*The gravitational pull of the Earth keeps the Moon in orbit around it.*
greenhouse effect /ˈɡriːnhaʊs ɪˌfekt/	the process by which the Earth's surface and lower atmosphere is getting warmer as a result of pollution by gases such as carbon dioxide. The heat from the Sun cannot escape, leading to a general increase in the Earth's temperature called global warming. **noun [singular]**	
hazy /ˈheɪzi/	not clear because there is smoke, dust or water in the air. **adjective**	*Saturn's moon Titan has a hazy atmosphere.*
helium /ˈhiːliəm/	a gas that is lighter than air and is an element. It has the lowest boiling point of any substance. Chemical symbol: He. **noun [uncount]**	*The atmosphere contains very small amounts of helium gas.*
Hubble constant /ˌhʌb(ə)l ˈkɒnstənt/	the ratio of the speed at which a galaxy (=group of stars and planets) is moving away because the universe is expanding to its distance from the person looking at it. **noun [singular]**	
Hubble telescope /ˌhʌb(ə)l ˈtelɪskəʊp/	a very powerful telescope attached to a satellite that is orbiting the Earth. It is used to look at and photograph parts of the universe that are very far away. **noun [singular]**	*The Hubble telescope enables us to observe distant galaxies.*
hydrogen /ˈhaɪdrədʒən/	a chemical element that is a gas that has no colour or smell. It is the lightest element, and is the most common in the Universe. Hydrogen combines with oxygen to make water, and is present in most organic compounds. In the Sun and other stars, it is turned into helium by nuclear fusion which produces heat and light. Chemical symbol: H. **noun [uncount]**	
impact crater /ˈɪmpækt ˌkreɪtə/	a large round hollow area in a surface caused by something hitting the surface. **noun [count]**	
Jupiter /ˈdʒuːpɪtə/	the fifth planet from the Sun and the largest in the solar system. **noun [singular]**	*The orbit of Jupiter is in between those of Mars and Saturn.*
light year /ˈlaɪt jɪə/	the distance that light travels in a year, used as a unit for measuring distances in space. A light year is almost 9,500,000,000,000 kilometres. **noun [count]**	*The nearest star to us is several thousand light years away.*
liquid nitrogen /ˌlɪkwɪd ˈnaɪtrədʒən/	the element nitrogen (chemical symbol: N) in liquid form. **noun [uncount]**	
lump /lʌmp/	a solid piece of something that does not have a regular shape. **noun [count]**	*a lump of rock*
lunar eclipse /ˌluːnə(r) ɪˈklɪps/	a short period when the Moon becomes dark, because the Earth moves between the Sun and the Moon so that its shadow covers the Moon. **noun [count]**	*We all went outside to watch the total lunar eclipse.*
Mariner Valley /ˌmærɪnə ˈvæli/	a large area of deep valleys on the planet Mars. **noun [singular]**	
Mars /mɑːz/	the red planet that is fourth furthest from the Sun, between Venus and Earth. **noun [singular]**	*The planet Mars is named after the Greek god of war.*
Martian /ˈmɑːʃ(ə)n/	relating to the planet Mars. **adjective**	*an analysis of Martian rock samples*
Mercury /ˈmɜːkjʊri/	the planet that is smallest and nearest to the Sun. **noun [singular]**	*The temperature on Mercury ranges from −170°C at night to 350°C during the day.*

meteorite
/'miːtiəˌraɪt/
a piece of rock that has fallen from space and landed on the Earth. noun [count]
The meteorite fell onto the roof and cracked some tiles.

methane
/'miːθeɪn/
a natural gas with no colour or smell that is used as a fuel. Chemical formula: CH_4. noun [uncount]
Jupiter, Saturn, Uranus and Neptune are made of several gases, including methane.

Milky Way
/ˌmɪlki 'weɪ/
the galaxy (=group of planets and stars) that the Earth belongs to and that you can see at night as a band of pale light across the sky. noun [singular]

moonlet
/'muːnˌlət/
a small moon or an artificial satellite. noun [count]

nebula
/'nebjʊlə/
a very large cloud of dust and gas that exists in outer space (plural: nebulae /'nebjʊliː/). noun [count]
The Bug Nebula is about 4000 light years from Earth.

Neptune
/'neptjuːn/
the planet that is eighth furthest from the Sun, between Uranus and Pluto. It has a very stormy atmosphere and is the second coldest planet in the solar system. noun [singular]
Neptune is made up almost entirely of gas.

neutron star
/'njuːtrɒn ˌstaː/
a very small, very dense object in space that is mostly made of neutrons (=particles with no electrical charge) packed closely together. noun [count]

nitrogen
/'naɪtrədʒ(ə)n/
an element that is a gas with no colour or smell. It makes up about 78% of the Earth's atmosphere. Chemical symbol: N. noun [uncount]
We cannot make use of nitrogen so we breathe out the same amount as we breathe in.

North Pole
/ˌnɔːθ 'pəʊl/
the North Pole: the northern end of the Earth's axis. noun [singular]
Many explorers have reached the North Pole.

nuclear fusion
/ˌnjuːkliə 'fjuːʒ(ə)n/
the process of combining the nuclei of particular atoms, for example hydrogen atoms, in order to release energy. This process takes place continuously in stars such as the Sun. noun [uncount]

Olympus Mons
/əˌlɪmpəs 'mɒnz/
a volcano on Mars which is the largest volcano in the solar system. noun [singular]

optical illusion
/ˌɒptɪk(ə)l ɪ'luːʒ(ə)n/
something that appears to be very different from what it really is, for example because of the way it is lit. noun [count]
The canals on Mars turned out to be optical illusions, and were really just dry channels.

outer planet
/ˌaʊtə 'plænɪt/
one of the planets in the solar system that is furthest away from the Sun. noun [count]
The space probe was on a mission to the outer planets: Jupiter, Saturn, Uranus and Neptune.

parallax
/'pærəlæks/
the change in the position of an object that seems to take place when the person looking at the object changes their position. noun [count/uncount]

photochemical smog
/ˌfəʊtəʊˌkemɪk(ə)l 'smɒg/
smog (=polluted air forming a cloud close to the ground) caused by the chemical action of light. noun [uncount]
Photochemical smog can cause eye, nose and throat irritations.

Plough
/plaʊ/
the Plough: a group of seven bright stars that you can only see in the northern part of the world. The American name is the Big Dipper. noun [singular]

Pluto
/'pluːtəʊ/
the ninth and furthest planet from the Sun. noun [singular]
Pluto rotates in the opposite direction to all the other planets.

Polaris
/pəʊ'laːrɪs/
= the Pole Star. noun [singular]

Pole Star
/'pəʊl ˌstaː/
the Pole Star: a bright star that appears in the sky very near the North Pole. noun [singular]
The Pole Star is also called Polaris and is used in navigation.

Proxima Centauri
/ˌprɒksɪmə sen'tɔːri/
a faint red dwarf star that is the closest known star to the solar system. noun [singular]

radio telescope
/ˌreɪdəʊ 'telɪˌskəʊp/
a very large piece of equipment that receives and records the radio waves that come from stars and other objects in space. noun [count]
Many images of stars and nebulae have been taken by the Hubble telescope – a well-known radio telescope.

red giant
/ˌred 'dʒaɪənt/
a very big red star. noun [count]

revolution
/ˌrevə'luːʃn/
the movement of something in a circle around something else, either once or continuously. noun [uncount]
The revolution of the Earth around the Sun.

rotate
/rəʊ'teɪt/
to move in a circle around an axis. verb [intransitive]
Venus takes 243 Earth days to rotate once around its axis.

Saturn
/'sætɜːn, 'sæt(ə)n/
the planet that is sixth furthest from the Sun, between Jupiter and Uranus. Saturn is surrounded by large rings. noun [singular]

solar eclipse /ˌsəʊlə(r) ɪˈklɪps/	an eclipse in which the Moon passes between the Sun and the Earth, preventing all or part of the Sun's light from reaching the Earth's surface. noun [count]	*We are only able to see a total solar eclipse about once every 80 years.*
South Pole /ˌsəʊθ ˈpəʊl/	the southern end of the Earth's axis. noun [uncount]	
space probe /ˈspeɪs ˌprəʊb/	a vehicle containing cameras and other equipment that is sent into space to collect information and send it back to Earth. noun [count]	*The space probe was launched and began its journey to Mars.*
summer solstice /ˌsʌmə ˈsɒlstɪs/	the day of the year when the Sun is above the horizon for the longest amount of time, around 21st June in the northern half of the Earth and 21st December in the southern half. noun [count/uncount]	
sunrise /ˈsʌnˌraɪz/	the time in the early morning when the sun first appears in the sky. noun [count/uncount]	
sunset /ˈsʌnˌset/	the time in the evening when the sun goes down below the horizon and night begins. noun [count/uncount]	
supernova /ˌsuːpəˈnəʊvə/	an exploding star that produces an extremely bright light. noun [count]	
swell /swel/	the movement of the waves in the sea. noun [singular]	
tide /taɪd/	one of the regular movements of the sea towards or away from the land. noun [count]	*The tides are influenced by the phases of the Moon.*
tilted /ˈtɪltɪd/	not straight, but at a slight angle so that one side is lower than the other. adjective	*The Earth is tilted on its axis.*
Titan /ˈtaɪtən/	the largest of the moons of the planet Saturn. noun [singular]	
Triton /ˈtraɪtən/	the largest of the moons of the planet Neptune. noun [singular]	
universe /ˈjuːnɪˌvɜːs/	the universe: space and everything that exists in it, including the Earth, solar systems, and galaxies. noun [singular]	*The origins of the universe are still a mystery.*
Uranus /ˈjʊərənəs/	the planet that is seventh furthest away from the Sun, between Saturn and Neptune. It is made up mainly of the gases hydrogen and helium. noun [singular]	*Uranus is four times bigger than Earth and has 27 moons.*
Venus /ˈviːnəs/	the planet that is second furthest from the Sun, between Mercury and Earth. It is the hottest planet in the solar system, and, from Earth, it looks like a very bright star. noun [singular]	*The atmosphere of Venus is full of sulphuric acid.*
waning Moon /ˌweɪnɪŋ ˈmuːn/	the Moon when it is between a full Moon and a new moon, and less of it appears each night. noun [singular]	
waxing Moon /ˌwæksɪŋ ˈmuːn/	the Moon when it is between a new Moon and a full Moon, and more of it appears each night. noun [singular]	
white dwarf /ˌwaɪt ˈdwɔːf/	a star that does not shine very brightly and is at the end of its life. noun [count]	
winter solstice /ˌwɪntə ˈsɒlstɪs/	the day of the year when the Sun is above the horizon for the shortest amount of time, around 21st December in the northern half of the Earth and 21st June in the southern half. noun [count/uncount]	

A   Working with words

1   Solar system word map

Fill in these words and phrases on the word map.

~~gibbous moon~~   hemisphere   ~~planets~~   rotation   ~~Uranus~~   ~~Venus~~   ~~white dwarf~~

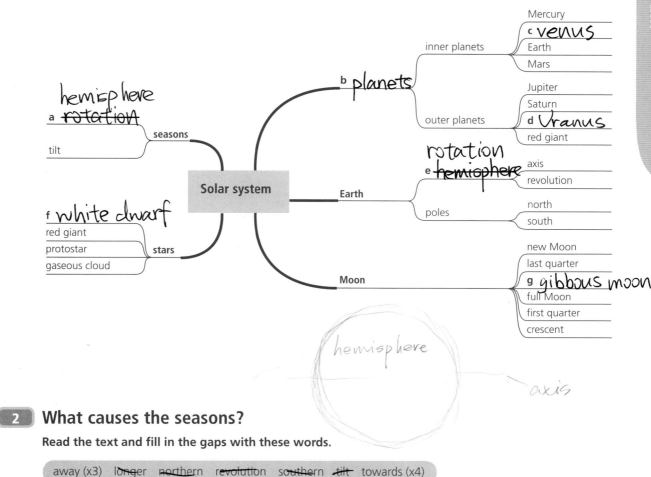

hemisphere
a **rotation**

tilt — seasons

Solar system

Earth

f **white dwarf**
red giant
protostar — stars
gaseous cloud

Moon

inner planets
- Mercury
- c **Venus**
- Earth
- Mars

outer planets
- Jupiter
- Saturn
- d **Uranus**
- red giant

rotation
e ~~hemisphere~~
- axis
- revolution

poles
- north
- south

- new Moon
- last quarter
- g **gibbous moon**
- full Moon
- first quarter
- crescent

hemisphere

axis

2   What causes the seasons?

Read the text and fill in the gaps with these words.

away (x3)   longer   ~~northern~~   revolution   southern   ~~tilt~~   towards (x4)

We divide the year into four seasons: spring, summer, autumn and winter. Summer is much warmer than winter, and the days are 1 __longer__. Seasons are caused by a combination of the 2 __tilt__ of the Earth's axis and the Earth's 3 __revolution__ around the Sun. The particular season depends on whether the Earth's axis is tilted 4 __towards__ the Sun or away from it. When the 5 __southern__ hemisphere is tilted towards the Sun, this means the northern hemisphere is tilted away from the Sun. Sunlight hits the southern hemisphere square-on, and shines over a smaller area. At the same time, sunlight hits the 6 __northern__ hemisphere at an angle and is spread out over a larger area of the Earth. The first sunlight warms the Earth more than the second does. So, where the sunlight hits the hemisphere tilted 7 __towards__ the Sun it would be summer, and where sunlight hits the hemisphere tilted 8 __away__ from it would be winter. Summer in Australia is when the southern hemisphere is tilted 9 __towards__ the Sun. In this position there is more of the southern hemisphere than the northern hemisphere in sunlight. Six months later we are on the other side of the Sun. The southern hemisphere is now tilted 10 __away__ from the Sun, and it is winter. The seasons in the southern hemisphere are the opposite of those in the northern hemisphere. If the southern hemisphere is tilted 11 __towards__ the Sun (summer), then the northern hemisphere is tilted 12 __away__ from the Sun (winter).

3 The planets

Read the text and fill in the gaps with these words.

asteroids   atmosphere   ~~belt~~   ~~compressed~~   ~~gas~~   ~~groups~~   hydrogen   ~~Mercury~~   ~~nitrogen~~   ~~rocky~~   ~~small~~

The planets are usually divided into two 1 _groups_ : the inner planets and the outer planets.
Inner planets are sometimes called the 2 _rocky_ planets and include Mercury, Venus, Earth and Mars.
They are the ones closest to the Sun, they have rocky surfaces and are all relatively 3 _small_ .
The outer planets, Jupiter, Saturn, Uranus and Neptune, are giant planets and are often called the 4
~~asteroids~~ gas planets. They consist mainly of the gases hydrogen, helium and methane. However, these
planets are so cold that the gases are 5 _compressed_ to a liquid or solid state. The two groups of planets
are separated by hundreds of thousands of tiny chunks of metallic rock called 6 _~~rocky~~ asteroids_. They
orbit the Sun between Mars and Jupiter in what is called the asteroid 7 _belt_ . There are so many
asteroids here that there is always a danger of collision for passing spacecraft. Most planets have a layer of gas,
called an 8 _~~asteri~~ atmosphere_ covering them. The inner planets have a relatively thin atmosphere, while the gas
planets have a much thicker atmosphere. Earth's atmosphere is a mixture of 9 _~~gas~~ nitrogen_ and oxygen
and smaller amounts of carbon dioxide and water vapour. Jupiter's thick atmosphere, on the other hand, consists
mainly of 10 _hydrogen_ and helium. The gases in the atmosphere are held close to a planet by its gravity.
On a large planet like Jupiter, where the gravity is 2.6 times greater than on Earth, the lightest gases are held in
the atmosphere. On Earth, however, these gases escape into space. 11 _Mercury_ is so small and hot
that it has no atmosphere at all.

B   Working with sentences

4 Phases of the Moon

Starting with the new Moon put these names and descriptions of the different stages of the moon in the correct order.

Names
the crescent Moon   the first quarter   the full Moon   the gibbous Moon   the last quarter   the new Moon

Descriptions
We see this Moon when it is one-quarter through its revolution around the Earth.
We see this Moon between the quarter and full Moon phases.
We see this Moon when it is three-quarters through its revolution around the Earth.
Between the quarter and new Moon phases we see this Moon.
When the Moon and the Sun are on opposite sides of the Earth, the entire side of
the Moon facing the Earth is lit up by the Sun and we see this Moon.
When the Moon and the Sun are on the same side of the Earth, the dark
side of the Moon faces the Earth and we don't see it at all.

	Names	Descriptions
1	The new Moon	When the moon and the sun are on the same side of the Earth. the dark side of the moon ··· see it at all.
2	The crescent moon	Between the quarter and the new moon phases we see this moon.
3	The first quarter	We see this moon when it is one-quarter through it's revolution around the Earth.
4	The gibbous moon	We see this moon between the quarter and full moon phases.
5	The full moon	When the moon and the sun are on opposite sides of the Earth. the entire side of the moon ··· see this moon
6	The last quarter	We see this moon when it is three quarters through it's revolution around the earth.

C Working with texts

5 Earth's revolution

Read the sentences. They are jumbled up. Put them in the correct order to make a text.

As well as revolving on its axis, the Earth travels through space around the Sun.

During this time the Earth rotates 365¼ times, which means there are 365¼ days in a year and this is very difficult to divide into equal parts for our days and weeks.

So we consider each year as having just 365 days and every fourth year, or leap year, we have 366 days.

The Earth rotates on its axis and revolves around the Sun, both in an anticlockwise direction viewed from space above the North Pole.

The Earth stays in its orbit because of the gravitational force of attraction between it and the Sun.

The time taken for one complete revolution of the Sun is one year.

This is almost circular, but slightly oval.

We say the Earth revolves around the Sun and the path it follows is called its orbit.

As well as revolving on its axis, the earth travels through the space the sun. We say the Earth revolves around the Sun and the path it follows is called it's orbit. This is almost circular. but slightly oval. The earth stays in its orbit because of the gravitational force of attraction between it and the sun. The time taken for one complete revolution of the Sun is one year. During this time the Earth rotates 365 1/6 times, which means there are 365 1/6 days in a year and this is very difficult to devide into equal parts for our days and weeks. So we consider each year as having just 365 days and every fourth year, or leap year, we have 366 days.

1: The Earth rotates on it's axis and revolves around the Sun, both in an anticlockwise direction viewed from space above the north pole

Index

H

N

O

INDEX

X

Y

Z

Answer key

Topic 1

1   a muscle   b mitochondrion   c vacuole   d epithelial   e larynx
f mouth   g muscles   h circulatory   i trachea

2   a cell membrane b nucleus c small vacuole d mitochondrion e glycogen granule f cytoplasm

3   1   muscle cells: cause the body to move by contracting;
2   white blood cells: kills bacteria and viruses;
3   red blood cells: transport oxygen around the body and help remove waste such as carbon dioxide;
4   epithelial cells: have the role of protecting the cells beneath them;
5   nerve cells: have the job of carrying messages around the body

4   1 breaks down   2 pumps   3 remove   4 produce   5 protects   6 produces   7 removes

5   1 oesophagus; large intestine   2 blood vessels   3 trachea; bronchi   4 penis; sperm duct
5 muscles   6 ovaries; Fallopian tubes   7 ureter urethra

6   1b   2j   3f   4h   5a   6c   7e   8g   9l   10d   11k   12i

7   1   Cells are the building blocks of all living organisms.
2   Unicellular organisms only consist of one cell, while multicellular organisms are made up of many cells.
3   The cytoplasm is the jelly-like material inside the cell in which the organelles are embedded.
4   The nucleus of a cell controls all the functions of a cell.
5   Mitochondria are the site of respiration where energy is released from food.
6   Plant cells differ from animal cells in that most have a large central vacuole, a cell wall and chloroplasts.

8   Plant cells and animal cells contain: nucleus; cytoplasm; mitochondria.
Plant cells contain: cell wall; chloroplasts; large central vacuole; possibly some small vacuoles; starch stores.
Animal cells contain: no cell wall; no chloroplasts; small vacuoles or none at all; glycogen stores.

Topic 2

1   a spores   b bulb   c cuttings   d stamen   e flower   f petals   g style   h pollination

2   a12   b8   c11   d4   e2   f5   g3   h6   i8   j2   k11   l1   m9   n7   o10

3   1 anther   2 stigma   3 style   4 pollen grain   5 ovary   6 ovule (containing egg)   7 pollen sacs

4   1 types   2 plants   3 cuttings   4 technique   5 soil   6 roots   7 hormones   8 potato

5   1 dispersal   2 drop   3 conditions   4 methods   5 external

6

Characteristics	Insect-pollinated flowers ...	Wind-pollinated flowers ...
Petals	... have large, brightly coloured petals.	... are usually small with small petals that are not very conspicuous.
Nectar production	... have sweet scented flowers which usually produce nectar.	... are odourless and produce no nectar.
Direction of flowers	... are generally directed upwards.	... hang down.
Location of stigmas	... have stigmas and anthers which are usually inside or partly enclosed in the flower.	... have stigmas and anthers which hang outside the flower for easy shaking in the wind.
Stigmas	... have rigid and smooth stigmas, which are sticky at the tip.	... have feathery stigmas to catch air-borne pollen grains.
Amount of pollen	... produce a relatively small amount of pollen.	... produce a large amount of pollen.
Pollen grains	... have relatively large pollen grains with rough or sticky surface.	... have small, light and smooth pollen grains.

7 1 corm   2 bulb   3 rhizome   4 stem tuber   5 root tuber   6 tap roots   7 runners

8 1 Coconuts are the best known seeds that are dispersed by water.
 2 They have a buoyant husk which is the mesocarp of the fruit.
 3 This enables them to float for long distances by sea before they are washed up onto shore.
 4 Their waterproof epicarp, the skin of the fruit, prevents them from becoming waterlogged during their journey.
 5 Some plants, such as the legumes, have a built-in mechanism that allows seeds to be scattered when the fruit suddenly bursts open when dry.
 6 As the fruit dries, tension builds up in parts of the seed coat until it splits along lines.
 7 The sudden 'explosion' scatters the seed quite widely.

Topic 3

1 a embryo   b ejaculation   c sexual organs   d sperm   e testis   f oviduct   g puberty

2 a oviduct   b ovary   c cervix   d uterus   e vagina

3 a oxygen   b placenta   c capillaries   d uterus   e deoxygenated   f waste   g umbilical cord
 h amnion   i embryo   j umbilical cord   k eye   l food   m oxygen

4 1 reproduction   2 penis   3 semen   4 gamete   5 gamete   6 ejaculation   7 cervix   8 semen
 9 uterus   10 Fallopian tubes   11 fertilize   12 penetrate   13 ovum   14 nucleus   15 fertilization

5 a8   b4   c5   d1   e2   f7   g3   h9   i6

6 1e   2d   3i   4c   5g   6h   7a   8f   9b   10j

7 1d   2g   3b   4c   5h   6k   7f   8l   9e   10a   11m   12i   13j

8 Females: Puberty starts between 8 and 16 years; marked increase in growth at start of puberty; breasts enlarge and develop; hair grows in armpits and genital region; hips get wider and fat deposits under skin increase here, giving a characteristic, curvier female shape; whitish, odourless vaginal secretions prior to the beginning of menstrual cycle; menstrual cycle begins when ovaries start to release mature ova (ripe eggs); perspiration (sweating) begins and body odours are more noticeable; acne may also result.

Males: Puberty starts between 10 and 17 years; rapid increase in height and weight; shoulders widen and voice deepens as voice box (Adam's apple) enlarges; hair grows on face, armpit, genitals and sometimes chest; muscles get bigger and penis and testicles enlarge; erections may be more frequent, especially when emotionally or sexually aroused, and may be accompanied by emissions of semen from penis (if this happens during sleep it is called nocturnal emissions or 'wet dreams'); testes are now able to produce sperm; perspiration (sweating) begins and body odours are more noticeable; endocrine (hormone) and sebaceous (oil secreting) glands increase their activity. Acne may also result.

Topic 4

1 a homozygous   b recessive   c cystic fibrosis   d parent   e division   f meiosis   g body cell

2 1 genetic disease   2 heterozygous   3 faulty   4 suffer from   5 blood tests   6 gene   7 amniotic fluid   8 foetus

3 a   This body cell has 4 chromosomes – humans have 46.
   b   Before cell division starts, the chromosomes duplicate so each has two strands.
   c   The chromosomes line up along the middle of the cell.
   d   The strands of the chromosomes are pulled apart – one copy of each chromosome goes to each side of the cell.
   e   The cell divides in two, each new cell has a full copy of the original chromosomes.
   f   Two pairs of similar chromosomes (total 4).
   g   Pairs of chromosomes line up across centre of cell. Each chromosome duplicates to make two strands.
   h   Cell divides in two – each new cell has two chromosomes.
   i   Cell division occurs again – each chromosome strand is separated.
   j   Each cell has copies of one chromosome from each original pair – half the chromosome number of the parent cell.
   k   Stages in mitosis.
   l   Stages in meiosis.

4 1d   2a   3g   4b   5f   6c   7e

5 1   Reproductive cells, like the sperm and ovum in humans, are formed not by mitosis but by a kind of cell division called meiosis.
   2   In this kind of cell division the parent cell divides to form four new daughter cells.
   3   Each of these cells has half the number of chromosomes that was present in the parent cell.
   4   In humans there are 46 chromosomes in the parent cell, so the gametes will have 23 chromosomes each.
   5   It is random which one of each chromosome pair becomes part of the new cell, so the gametes which are formed contain different chromosomes from each other.
   6   During fertilization, the nucleus of the sperm cell fuses with the nucleus of the ovum, so a new offspring will end up with the full number of 46 chromosomes like the parents.

6

Characteristics	Asexual reproduction	Sexual reproduction
name	mitosis	meiosis
production of new cells	produces new cells that are exact copies of the original parent cell	does not produce new cells that are exact copies of the original parent cell only half the number of chromosomes of the original cell exchange of genetic information between chromosomes
offspring	offspring all the same	every offspring is different and unique
chances of survival	in good conditions more offspring will be well adapted and will survive	variation means chance that some will survive in adverse conditions
mating	no mate needed	mate needed

Topic 5

1 a roots   b dissolved minerals   c leaves   d cells   e carbon dioxide   f cellulose

2 a petiole   b margin   c apex   d midrib   e lamina   f veins

3 a sun   b light energy   c carbon dioxide taken from the air   d chlorophyll
e oxygen given out   f glucose made in the leaves is taken to all parts of the plant
g water and minerals are taken from the soil by the plant's roots

4 1 Water and minerals are absorbed from the soil through the roots.
   2 The glucose that is made during photosynthesis is transported to other parts of the plant.
   3 Here it is used in respiration to provide energy for cell reactions.
   4 It also makes new materials such as complex sugars like sucrose.
   5 Cellulose is used to form cell walls.
   6 Proteins and fats are made from the glucose using minerals absorbed from the soil with water.
   7 Glucose is also converted to starch, which is stored in various parts of the plant such as stems, roots and seeds
      for use at another time.

5

Type of food	Test	Results
Reducing sugars (e.g. glucose)	Add one dropper full of Benedict's solution to a small sample of the food containing the reducing sugar.	A brick-red precipitate indicates the presence of a reducing sugar.
Non-reducing sugar (e.g. sucrose)	Add a few drops of dilute hydrochloric acid and warm gently. Neutralize the solution by gradually adding sodium carbonate until fizzing stops. Test with Benedict's solution.	The acid breaks the non-reducing sugar up into reducing sugars which produce a brick-red precipitate with Benedict's solution.
Starch	Add a few drops of iodine solution.	A blue-black colour indicates the presence of starch.
Proteins	Add 1 cm³ of 0.1 M sodium hydroxide followed by 2 drops of a 1% copper sulphate solution. This is called the Biuret test.	A purple colour indicates the presence of protein.
Fats	Rub the sample in paper and warm the area over a light bulb. Or add 2 cm³ ethanol to the food sample and shake vigorously.	If a translucent spot (grease spot) develops then the sample contains fat. A cloudy mixture indicates the presence of fat.

Topic 6

1 a balanced diet   b disorder   c malnutrition   d essential nutrients   e minerals   f food colouring

2 1 plant cell walls   2 carbohydrates   3 sugars   4 starch   5 provisions   6 peas   7 significant   8 energy
9 more quickly   10 deficiency

3 1b   2h   3a   4i   5c   6g   7d   8f   9e

4 1 Nutrition is the study of how the body uses the nutrients from the food we eat to provide energy needed for growth, repair and reproduction.
2 We get these nutrients from carbohydrates, proteins, fat, vitamins, and minerals.
3 The foods we eat and drink every day make up our diet.
4 To stay healthy, we need to eat a good balance of the different kinds of nutrients.

5 1T   2F   3T   4T   5F   6F   7T

6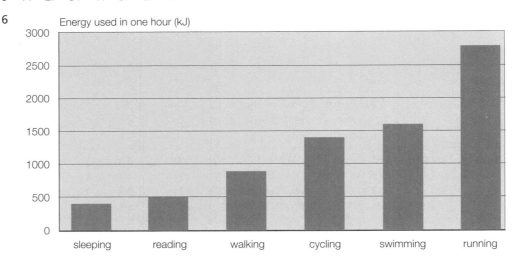

7

Mineral	Sources in food	How it is used in the body	Result of deficiency
calcium	cheese and milk green vegetables, dried peas and beans	formation and hardening of bone and teeth; also promotes healthy functioning of nerves and normal clotting of blood	rickets in children and osteomalacia in adults; brittle bones (increases risk of fracture)
sodium	table salt and sodium chloride in foods	contraction of muscles and transmission of nerve impulses	painful muscle cramps and poor transmission of nerve impulses
iron	dark green leafy vegetables and pumpkin; liver, kidney, fish, red meat	haemoglobin	can lead to anaemia (weakness and tiredness)
magnesium	green leafy vegetables, nuts, dried peas and beans	effective nerve and muscle functioning; energy production	tiredness and weakness

Topic 7

1 a fire extinguisher   b Accidents   c protective wear   d radioactive   e permission   f oxide of nitrogen

2 a corrosive   b explosive   c highly flammable   d harmful or irritant   e oxidising   f radioactive   g toxic

3 1 Precautions   2 fuel   3 fire   4 foam   5 Carbon monoxide   6 Air pollutants   7 hazard   8 injuries

4 a9   b7   c6   d4   e8   f2   g5   h1

5 a3   b7   c6   d9   e2   f1   g10   h4   i8   j12   k5   l11

6 A and B: 1d   2e   3i   4c   5h   6a   7g   8f   9b

Topic 8

1 a parasites   b pinworms   c house flies   d mosquitoes   e immunity against disease   f AIDS

2 1 infection   2 vaccinations   3 chickenpox   4 microorganism   5 lymphocytes   6 immunity   7 antibodies   8 vaccine

3 1 transmitted   2 Virus   3 immune   4 infected   5 transfusions   6 antibodies   7 opportunistic   8 Deficiency
   9 condom   10 prevent

4 rot   bacteria   decay   cycle   organisms   plants   unpleasant   ill

5 1f   2c   3i   4g   5a   6l   7j   8b   9k   10m   11d   12h   13e.

6 Cause: bacterium *Leptospira*; Ways of infection: Through urine/faeces of infected rats, mice and fleas. Other infected
   animals can also spread disease.
   Symptoms: high fever, severe headache, chills, muscle aches, vomiting, jaundice, red eyes, abdominal pain, diarrhoea
   and rash.
   Consequences: no treatment > kidney damage, meningitis, liver failure, respiratory distress, possibly death;
   Treatment: with antibiotics early in the course of the disease; Prevention: avoid contact with water that could be
   contaminated; wear protective clothing or footwear; get rid off rubbish around or in the house which may attract
   rodents.

7

technique used	name of method(s)	how	type of foods
temperature	heating / refrigeration	heat source / fridge, freezer	–
extraction of moisture	drying / salting / adding sugar	– / salt / sugar	fruits, vegetables, some kinds of meats and fish / meats and fish / fruit
use of acid	pickling	usually vinegar	–

Topic 9

1 a artery   b blood vessels   c left side   d right atrium   e pumps blood to lungs   f plasma   g platelets

2 1 pumping   2 cardiac   3 septum   4 upper   5 lower   6 valves   7 vena cava   8 pulmonary   9 atria   10 aorta

3 a deoxygenated blood from the head   b head, neck and arms   c oxygenated blood to the head
   d from head   e deoxygenated blood to the lungs   f lungs   g oxygenated blood to the head and body
   h to heart   i from body   j deoxygenated blood from body   k oxygenated blood to the body   l capillaries in the body

4 a Right Side   b Left Side   c aorta   d right pulmonary artery   e left pulmonary artery   f vena cava from the head
   g left pulmonary vein   h left atrium   i semilunar valves   j bicuspid valve   k right atrium   l tendon
   m tricuspid valve   n vena cava from the lower part of the body   o left ventricle   p septum   q right ventricle

5 a fibrous layer   b muscle and elastic layer   c small lumen   d endothelium – one cell thick   e fibrous layer
   f endothelium   g large lumen   h thin muscle and elastic layer
   i wall composed of a single layer of cells   j lumen – red blood cells pass in single file   k artery   l vein   m capillary

6 1 phagocytes   2 toxins   3 clotting   4 fibrin   5 forms   6 scab   7 foreign material

7 1 heart attack   2 angina   3 hypertension   4 arteriosclerosis   5 atherosclerosis   6 thrombosis

8 1 blood vessels   2 around the body   3 and capillary   4 away from the heart   5 them bursting   6 from the heart
   7 heart beats   8 the capillaries   9 one cell thick   10 easily damaged   11 cells of the body   12 cell in your body
   13 become veins   14 elastic fibres   15 when you walk   16 along the veins   17 walls of the veins
   18 blood in the veins

9 1 The pumping action of your heart is due to the regular and repetitive contractions and relaxations of the cardiac muscle.
2 This keeps the blood flowing constantly around your body.
3 When the heart muscles relax, blood enters the atria on both sides.
4 The valves open, allowing the heart to be filled with blood.
5 The heart muscles then contract immediately.
6 The contractions begin at the top of the atria and squeeze downwards.
7 This forces the blood into the ventricles through the valves.
8 The muscle of the ventricle walls then contracts, but this starts from the bottom and squeezes upwards.
9 The valves between the atria and ventricles are forced shut and the blood is pushed into the arteries.
10 The wall of the left ventricle is more muscular than the right ventricle.
11 Blood from the left side of the heart needs to be pushed all around the body.
12 This cycle of contraction and relaxation is called a heartbeat and it occurs about 70 times per minute while resting.

10 1 ✓ 2 ✗ 3 ✗ 4 ✓ 5 ✗ 6 ✓ 7 ✗ 8 ✓ 9 ✓ 10 ✓ 11 ✓ 12 ✓ 13 ✗ 14 ✗ 15 ✗ 16 ✓

Topic 10

1 a gastric juices b teeth c premolar d enzymes e inhibitors f digested food g anus

2 a teeth cut and grind food b tongue mixes food with saliva
c epiglottis closes entrance to trachea when food is being swallowed d salivary glands produce saliva
e trachea (breathing tube into lungs) f oesophagus g diaphragm h stomach mixes food with gastric juice
i liver produces bile j gall bladder stores bile k pancreas l duodenum m ileum
n small intestine digests and absorbs food o large intestine removes water from undigested food p caecum
q rectum r appendix s anus

3 1 human 2 digestion 3 incisors 4 canine 5 premolars 6 crush 7 grind 8 molars 9 jaw 10 wisdom

4 a incisors b canine c premolars d molars e enamel f dentine g pulp cavity h jaw bone

5 1 mouth 2 anus 3 gut 4 enzymes 5 small intestine 6 Physical digestion 7 Chemical digestion

6 1k 2e 3d 4i 5b 6j 7c 8g 9h 10a 11f

7 1 The process of absorption begins in the ileum.
2 The villi increase the surface area for absorption.
3 Inside the villus is a network of many blood vessels.
4 Anything in the ileum that is water-soluble, such as water-soluble vitamins, minerals, water, glucose, fructose and amino acids, is absorbed into the blood capillaries.

8 1b 2e 3h 4a 5c 6d 7f 8g

9

Parts of small intestine	duodenum	ileum
Receives juices from	pancreas and liver	–
Type of juice (name)	pancreatic juice and bile	–
Juice consists of …	pancreatic juice: trypsin, amylase, lipase	enzymes
Digestion of … by …	protein by trypsin / starch by amylase / fats and oils by lipase	sugars / polypeptides / fats and oils
Digested into …	polypeptides + amino acids / maltose + glucose / fatty acids + glycerol	fructose + glucose / polypeptides + amino acids / fatty acids + glycerol

Topic 11

1 a Animals   b humans   c bronchi   d gills   e pneumonia   f aerobic   g stomata

2 a nose   b mouth   c movement of air   d trachea opens to mouth and nose   e larynx (voice box)   f ring of cartilage
g trachea   h left bronchus   i left lung   j heart   k rib   l internal intercostals muscle   m external intercostal muscle
n bronchiole   o air sacs/alveoli   p pleural membrane   q pleural fluid   r diaphragm

3 1 food   2 aerobic and anaerobic   3 presence   4 occurs   5 Carbon dioxide   6 lactic acid   7 energy
8 noble   9 mechanical   10 trachea   11 sacs   12 gills   13 photosynthesize

4 1 human   2 ✓   3 carbonated   4 exercise   5 ✓   6 nuclear   7 ✓   8 are   9 ✓   10 leg   11 ✓   12 alternative

5 1 pneumonia   2 asthma   3 lung cancer   4 pollutants and respiratory problems   5 emphysema   6 bronchitis

6 1k   2a   3b   4e   5f   6c   7d   8j   9h   10m   11l   12g   13i

7 a   capillary transporting blood to the alveoli, has little oxygen, deoxygenated blood, high in carbon dioxide
  b   bronchiole
  c   capillary transporting blood from the lungs, has lots of oxygen, oxygenated blood, low concentration
      of carbon dioxide
  d   air sac or alveolus
  e   network of capillaries surrounding alveoli, gases are exchanged here
  f   air
  g   carbon dioxide
  h   oxygen
  i   deoxygenated blood
  j   oxygenated blood
  k   carbon dioxide
  l   capillary (wall is one cell thick)
  m   oxygen
  n   alveolus (wall is one cell thick)
  o   flow of blood in capillary

Topic 12

1 a vascular bundle   b phloem vessels   c transpiration   d root pressure   e roots   f cohesion

2 a a number of xylem vessels lie close together   b a number of phloem tubes lie close together
c cortex   d epidermis   e xylem   f vascular bundle   g phloem   h pith
i a transverse section through the stem of a dicotyledonous plant   j epidermis
k made up of a number of xylem vessels   l stele   m xylem   n phloem   o made up of a number of phloem vessels
p cortex   q the transverse section of a root of a dicotyledonous plant

3 1b   2a   3f   4g   5c   6d   7e

4 Root pressure: 1g   Capillarity: 3a, 4h, 5d   Transpiration: 6c, 7e, 8b, 9f

Topic 13

1 a digested food   b egestion   c part not required   d excreted via lung   e sweat pore   f urethra

2 a Bowman's capsule   b proximal convoluted tubule   c distal convoluted tubule   d cortex
e blood coming to kidney   f glomerulus (knot of capillaries)   g medulla   h capillaries   i blood leaving kidney
j collecting duct   k loop of Henlé   l urine

3 1 digested   2 small intestine   3 amino acids   4 excess   5 deamination   6 urea   7 carbohydrates   8 respiration
9 kidneys

4 a pain receptor   b sweat pore   c temperature receptor   d epidermis   e hair erector muscle   f dermis
g sebaceous gland   h capillary network   i hair follicle   j nerve fibre   k fatty layer below skin
l pressure receptor   m sweat gland epidermis

5 a The soluble substances, urea and salts, remain on the surface of the skin.
   b The water evaporates from the skin's surface.
   c The skin contains many sweat glands which are tubular structures that extend into the skin's surface.
   d The sweat is transported to the surface of the skin via the sweat duct.
   e The base of the glands are near blood capillaries which allows easy diffusion of waste products from the blood into the gland. The mixture of water, urea and salt, which is excreted from the sweat glands, forms a solution called sweat.
   f Blood carrying a lot of water flows along the capillaries and the waste diffuses from the blood into the sweat gland.
   g The blood continues along the capillary but contains less water.

6 1 Plants also form waste products.
   2 Plants do not require a complex excretory system like humans because most of their products can be re-used in other processes.
   3 Oxygen can be considered a waste product of photosynthesis, while carbon dioxide is a waste product of respiration.
   4 Both gases, oxygen and carbon dioxide, will diffuse out of the leaves via the stomata on the underside of the leaves.
   5 During daylight much of the carbon dioxide made in respiration may be used in photosynthesis, and at night oxygen that was made during photosynthesis may be used in respiration.
   6 Water made during respiration that is not needed by the plant will be lost through transpiration through the stomata.
   7 The leaves are the main excretory organs in plants.
   8 Waste products from other chemical reactions in the plant may be stored in different parts, like the leaves and seeds, which are destined to drop off the plant after some time.
   9 Some plants may store a large amount of waste in the vacuoles of their leaves.
   10 The accumulated waste eventually crystallises, and is lost when the leaf dies and drops off.

7 1e   2d   3a   4c   5b

8 A and B:

The lung as an excretory organ	The kidney as an excretory organ
7 The lungs excrete the gaseous waste product of respiration, carbon dioxide.	6 The kidneys are the main excretory organs in the human body.
5 This carbon dioxide which is formed in the cells during respiration diffuses into the bloodstream, which transports it to the lungs.	10 We have two of them, which are located to the back of the body just above the waist on either side of the spine.
3 On reaching the lungs the blood flows through a network of capillaries over the alveoli, which is the point of gaseous exchange in the lung.	2 Each kidney is about 12.5 cm long and 7.5 cm wide.
4 The carbon dioxide diffuses into the lung along with some water from the cells of the alveoli.	8 The main function of the kidneys is to remove excess water and nitrogenous waste from the blood.
1 Both the carbon dioxide and water vapour are excreted from the lungs into the atmosphere when you exhale.	9 This waste is urea, which was formed from the breakdown of amino acids in the liver.

Topic 14

1   a skeleton   b vertebral column   c lumbar   d joints   e ball-and-socket   f biceps   g extensor muscle

2   a spongy bone   b articular cartilage – functions as shock absorber   c compact bone   d synovial membrane
    e synovial fluid – lubricates joint reducing friction during movement   f ligament   g muscle at rest   h ligament
    i bone   j contracted muscle   k relaxed muscle   l bone moved to the left   m relaxed muscle   n contracted muscle
    o bone moved to the right

3   a cranium   b face   c clavicle   d scapula   e sternum   f ribs   g vertebral column   h pelvis   i humerus
    j ulna   k radius   l carpals   m metacarpals   n phalanges   o femur   p patella   q tibia   r fibula   s tarsals
    t metatarsals   u phalanges.

4   1d   2j   3f   4b   5h   6e   7i   8c   9g   10a

5   cervical vertebrae: They have a large neural canal since they are closest to the brain; Vertebrarterial canals are present;
    They have a short neural spine; They have short transverse processes.

    thoracic vertebrae: The neural canal is smaller than in the cervical vertebrae as these are further from the brain;
    They have a very long neural spine for attachment of back muscles;
    They have short transverse processes to accommodate rib bones on either side.

    lumbar vertebrae: The centrum is big and well developed to support the weight of body; The neural canal is small;
    They have a heavy, wide neural spine; They have long transverse processes for muscle attachment.

6   a flexing the arm   b tendons, attach muscle to bone   c triceps muscle (relaxes)
    d biceps muscle (contracts) (flexor muscle)   e radius (pulled)   f ulna   g arm bends or flexes   h extending the arm
    i biceps muscle (relaxes)   j radius   k triceps muscle (contracts) (extensor muscle)   l ulna (pulled)   m arm extends

Topic 15

1   a conduction   b bimetallic   c thermometers   d plants   e warm blooded   f fish   g cooling

2   1 constant   2 warm-blooded   3 cold-blooded   4 Ectothermic   5 changing   6 surface   7 temperature
    8 rises   9 chemical   10 internal

3   1 temperature   2 damage   3 photosynthesis   4 transpiration   5 evaporation   6 hotter
    7 stomata   8 hot   9 wilted   10 radiation   11 cooler   12 wilting

4   1k   2h   3f   4a   5d   6i   7o   8m   9l   10p   11g   12c   13b   14e   15n   16j

5   a on a hot day   b hair erector muscles relax   c heat can easily be lost from the skin   d arterioles dilate
    e a lot of blood flow close to the skin   f heat is lost from the blood   g sweat gland   h sweat
    i heat is carried away as heat evaporates   j on a cold day   k hair erector muscles contract
    l layer of warm air is trapped which keeps body warm   m arterioles constrict
    n less blood flow close to the skin   o sweat gland

Topic 16

1 a endocrine system   b hormones   c thyroid   d peripheral nervous system (PNS)   e brain   f involuntary responses

2 1 kidney   2 adrenaline   3 danger   4 stress   5 heart rate   6 glucose   7 respond   8 stimuli

3 1 pea-sized   2 endocrine glands   3 ovaries   4 master gland   5 hypothalamus   6 target glands   7 homeostasis
   8 feedback mechanism

4 a cell body   b motor neurone   c axon   d myelin sheath   e node of Ranvier   f dendrite
   g intermediate or relay neurone   h dendron   i cell body   j axon   k sensory neurone

5 1 the pituitary gland   2 the adrenal gland   3 the thyroid gland   4 the gonads   5 the pancreas

6 1c   2e   3j   4i   5m   6l   7n   8h   9g   10k   11o   12f   13a   14d   15b

7 a nervous system   b central nervous system (CNS)   c peripheral nervous system (PNS)
   d brain   e spinal cord   f nerve fibres

8 a   The shoulder is tapped.
   b   Receptors in the skin sense stimulus.
   c   Sensory neurons transmit the stimulus message.
   d   The message is interpreted in the brain.
   e   A decision can be made here about whether or not to turn.
   f   If the decision is to turn and look, a response is sent to motor neurons.
   g   Motor neurons transmit response message to the neck muscles, known as the 'effectors'.
   h   Neck muscles are activated causing the head to turn.

Topic 17

1 a fossil fuels   b alternative energy sources   c flames   d crude oil   e hydropower   f biomass

2 1 Biomass   2 wood   3 ferment   4 ethanol   5 petrol   6 decay   7 methane   8 cylinders   9 digester   10 fertilizer

3 1 flows   2 makes   3 harnessed   4 buried; constant   5 warmer   6 used   7 found   8 brought; generate

4 1b   2d   3c   4g   5f   6a   7e

5 a oil rig   b oil storage buoy   c oil tanker   d cap of solid rock   e natural gas trapped in a pocket
   f soft rock (chalk or sandstone) and oil   g porous rock containing salt water

7

Luminous flame	Non-luminous (roaring) flame
1 bright yellow	8 blue flame
2 unsteady	9 steady
3 lower temperature than a roaring flame	10 hotter than a luminous flame, highest temperature is at the tip of the inner cone
4 gives off soot (carbon)	11 no soot
5 gives off carbon monoxide	12 no carbon monoxide
6 occurs in a limited supply of air (oxygen) – incomplete combustion	13 occurs in an abundant supply of oxygen – complete combustion
7 quiet flame	14 noisy flame

Topic 18

1 a omnivores   b terrestrial   c fertility   d clay   e primary   f producers   g eutrophication   h radar

2 a atmospheric oxygen   b combustion uses oxygen   c animals use oxygen for respiration
   d oxygen from plant photosynthesis   e plants use oxygen for respiration
   f oxygen from soil organisms that photosynthesise   g soil organisms use oxygen for respiration

3 1 respiration   2 photosynthesise   3 producers   4 substrate   5 phytoplankton
   6 seaweeds   7 consumers   8 herbivores   9 carnivores   10 omnivores

4 a4   b1   c5   d2   e3

5 1e   2c   3k   4j   5i   6g   7l   8m   9h   10f   11a   12b   13d

6 a9   b10   c14   d15   e5   f7   g1   h12   i6   j11   k3   l13   m4   n2   o7

Topic 19

1 a mixtures   b molecules   c matter   d elements   e non-metals   f radium

2 1c   2i   3a   4b   5d   6j   7f   8e   9g   10h

3 1 hydrogen and oxygen   2 carbon monoxide   3 two oxygen atoms   4 compounds   5 chemical formula
   6 molecule   7 formula H_2O 8 symbol O   9 Sodium chloride   10 solid compound   11 particles   12 atoms

4 1d   2g   3i   4b   5e   6h   7j   8a   9f   10c

5 1 The basis of life is a compound called DNA, which determines what you are like.
   2 It contains only the elements carbon, hydrogen, oxygen, nitrogen and phosphorus.
   3 DNA is very complex and the various atoms can be combined in millions of different ways.
   4 What makes you different from everybody else is the way in which the atoms in the DNA in your body are
      put together.
   5 All matter can be divided into living and non-living things and cells are the building blocks for living things.
   6 Cells and all non-living things are made of elements and compounds, which in turn are made of atoms
      and molecules.
   7 The salt in your body is the same as the salt on the kitchen table. Alternative: The salt on the kitchen table is
      the same as the salt in your body.
   8 The calcium carbonate in an eggshell and in your bones is the same as the calcium carbonate in limestone.
      Alternative: The calcium carbonate in your bones is the same as the calcium carbonate in an eggshell and
      in limestone.
   9 Living things contain very complex compounds and life is associated with these complex compounds.
   10 Scientists have been able to work out the structures of living substances and some day they may be able to
      create life itself.

6 1 metals   2 non-metals   3 solids   4 symbol   5 first   6 carbon   7 capital   8 Greek   9 aurum   10 einsteinium

Topic 20

1 a electricity   b electric circuits   c series   d power   e analogue   f permanent

2 1 force   2 electrons   3 voltage   4 circuit   5 potential   6 voltmeter   7 parallel
   8 negative   9 positive   10 symbol   11 unit   12 voltage

3 1 c/n   2 b/j   3 g/o   4 d/p   5 a/m   6 i/l   7 f/k   8 e/q   9 h/r

4 1e   2a   3g   4c   5d   6h   7i   8f   9b

5 1l   2k   3m   4h   5e   6b   7c   8d   9i   10a   11j   12g   13f

6 Conductors: metals (copper, aluminium), graphite (form of carbon)
   Insulators: paper, plastic, rubber, glass
   Electrolytes: sodium chloride (salt), body fluids

Topic 21

1 a mixtures   b indicators   c colloids   d detergents   e soapy   f soapless

2 1 soapless   2 hydrophilic   3 hydrophobic   4 hydrogen   5 detergent   6 droplet   7 soluble

3 1 sodium hydroxide   2 oven cleaner   3 antacid   4 vinegar   5 insect stings   6 sodium hydrogencarbonate
   7 raising agent   8 washing soda   9 citric acid   10 sodium chloride   11 laxative   12 Glauber's salt
   13 alum   14 salt   15 monosodium glutamate

4 1 homogenous   2 solute / solvent   3 greater   4 aqueous   5 non-aqueous   6 transparent
   7 light   8 naked eye   9 particles

5 1 paint   2 coffee / tea   3 chocolate   4 ink   5 varnish   6 blood   7 nail polish   8 grease/oil

6 1a   2c   3e   4g   5j   6k   7b   8c   9d   10f   11h   12i

7 solid in liquid: solute = solid; solvent = liquid; examples: sugar in water, salt in water, iodine in ethanol.
   gas in liquid: solute = gas; solvent = liquid; examples: O2 in water, CO2 in water, (fizzy drinks).
   liquid in liquid: solute = liquid; solvent = liquid; examples: alcohol in water, syrup in water.

Topic 22

1 a metals   b corrosion   c chemical   d sonorous   e thermoplastics   f pipes

2 1b   2c   3a   4d   5f   6e

3 1 aluminium   2 copper   3 gold and platinum   4 iron   5 wrought iron   6 tin   7 zinc   8 silver
   9 used in cooking and for storing or packaging food – its highly reflective surface prevents heat loss so keeping foods
   warm for longer   10 used to make many common utensils   11 railings, horseshoes
   12 lining for steel cans in the food industry, especially for acid foods such as pineapple
   13 ornaments, ornamental serving dishes and utensils

4 1g   2e   3h   4a   5i   6j   7b   8d   9c   10f   11k

5 1 polypropene   2 tough, waterproof, stain resistant   3 polyamide   4 nylon
   5 forms elastic fibres   6 stretch clothing, e.g. ski suits   7 terylene mylar
   8 clothing (though not so good in hot climates) can take permanent creases or pleats

Topic 23

1 a fulcrum   b moments   c second law   d centripetal force   e equilibrium   f acceleration

2 1 Rolling   2 effort   3 hinders   4 slide   5 smoother   6 plastic   7 lubricant   8 rub   9 Oil   10 rotates

3 1 fulcrum   2 force   3 product   4 clockwise   5 mass   6 pivot   7 summed

4 A 1c   2b   3e   4a   5d
   B 1e   2d   3a   4b   5c
   C 1d   2a   3c   4e   5b

5 1 If you drop an object like a coin, a ball, or a piece of paper, the object falls to the ground.
   2 This is because of the force of gravity.
   3 Gravity is an example of a non-contact force, that is, a force that works without actually touching the object.
   4 Gravity causes objects that have no support to fall, and then holds them down on the Earth's surface.
   5 Gravitational force exists between any objects which have mass; the greater the masses, the greater the force.

6 Left diagram: 1a   2j   3i   4c   5h
   Right diagram: 6b   7d   8e   9f   10g

Topic 24

1 a nuclear fission b elastic collisions c momentum d kinetic energy e pulleys f efficiency

2 1c 2h 3b 4d 5e 6f 7a 8i 9g

3 1 attached 2 load 3 half 4 reduced 5 equally 6 halved 7 doubled 8 effort 9 downward

4 1g 2e 3j 4i 5d 6c 7f 8b 9h 10a

5 a1 b4 c2 d3 e2 f5 g2

6 a first class b second class c third class d effort e fulcrum f load g effort h load i fulcrum j load
k effort l fulcrum

Topic 25

1 a incident ray b reflection c umbra d translucent e fluorescent f curved mirrors

2 1 optical effect 2 transparent 3 bend 4 light 5 normal 6 incidence 7 refracted 8 refraction

3 1 cylindrical 2 low 3 argon 4 electrons 5 ultraviolet 6 visible 7 filament 8 fluorescent 9 incandescent 10 higher

4 1c 2b 3d 4f 5g 6a 7e

5 a ray of light b visible c parallel d diverging beams e converging beams

6 a transparent b completely c easy d translucent e some light f difficult g opaque h do not i any light j impossible

7 a tungsten filament b inert gas c glass mount d electrical foot contact e bulb f support wires g insulation
h screw thread contact

8 a concave mirror b light source c condensing lenses d slide inserted upside down e convex lens
f image inverted right way up g film h image i shutters j diaphragm k convex lens l object

Topic 26

1 a ear b cochlea c ultrasound d waves e frequency f amplitude g VHF (very high frequency)

2 1 vibrate 2 vibrating 3 vibrator 4 vibrator 5 vibrators 6 vibrations 7 vibrators 8 vibrating 9 vibrator 10 vibration

3 a auditory canal b bones of skull c pinna d ossicles e stirrup f anvil g hammer
h muscle attached to ossicle i semicircular canals j utricle k saccule l vestibular apparatus
m auditory nerve n round window o cochlea p to throat

4 1d 2c 3j 4i 5g 6b 7e 8a 9f 10h

5 1 A ruler that is flicked at the edge of a table vibrates and produces sound.
2 We call the distance moved up and down by the ruler the amplitude of the vibration.
3 The amplitude of a sound wave will determine whether the sound is loud or soft.
4 If the ruler is flicked only a little, then a small amount of energy is supplied to the ruler.
5 This causes a small amplitude in vibration and a soft sound is heard.
6 However, if the ruler is flicked more strongly, and a large energy is supplied, the amplitude is larger and the
sound will be louder.
7 The harder you pluck on the ruler, the louder the sound that occurs.
8 The same applies to plucking on the strings of a guitar.
9 The complete cycle of the vibrations can be represented graphically.
10 A louder sound has a greater amplitude.

6 1c 2d 3a 4f 5e 6b

7 Advantages AM: long range, good coverage, easy to produce in a transmitter, receivers are simple in design,
simple to tune on ordinary receivers;
Disadvantages AM: susceptible to static and other forms of electrical noise
Advantages FM: good audio quality and immunity to noise;
Disadvantages FM: readily obstructed and good antennae needed.

Topic 27

1   a crust   b earthquakes   c tsunamis   d magma   e neap   f maritime tropical   g fronts   h hurricanes

2   1 crust   2 slip   3 epicentre   4 longitudinal   5 seismograph   6 Richter   7 tsunamis   8 Volcanoes
     9 lava   10 dormant

3   1 seismic   2 P   3 wave   4 Shear   5 Surface   6 longitudinal   7 epicentre   8 tremors   9 earthquake

4   1c   2b   3e   4a   5d

5   A   1i   2b   3a   4c   5f
     B   6j   7h   8g   9d   1e

6   a7   b5   c4   d2   e3   f6   g1   h8

7   a   14, 12, 8, 5
     b   15, 3, 4, 6
     c   11, 9, 2
     d   7, 1, 13, 10

Topic 28

1   a hemisphere   b planets   c Venus   d Uranus   e rotation   f white dwarf   g gibbous Moon

2   1 longer   2 tilt   3 revolution   4 towards   5 southern   6 northern   7 towards
     8 away   9 towards   10 away   11 towards   12 away

3   1 groups   2 rocky   3 small   4 gas   5 compressed   6 asteroids   7 belt   8 atmosphere   9 nitrogen
     10 hydrogen   11 Mercury

5   1   the new Moon: When the Moon and the Sun are on the same side of the Earth, the dark side of the Moon faces the Earth and we don't see it at all.
     2   the crescent Moon: Between the quarter and new Moon phases we see this Moon.
     3   the first quarter: We see this Moon when it is one-quarter through its revolution around the Earth.
     4   the gibbous Moon: We see this Moon between the quarter and full Moon phases.
     5   the full Moon: When the Moon and the Sun are on opposite sides of the Earth, the entire side of the Moon facing the Earth is lit up by the Sun and we see this Moon.
     6   the last quarter: We see this Moon when it is three quarters through its revolution around the Earth.

6   As well as revolving on its axis, the Earth travels through space around the Sun. We say the Earth revolves around the Sun and the path it follows is called its orbit. This is almost circular, but slightly oval. The time taken for one complete revolution of the Sun is one year. During this time the Earth rotates 365¼ times which means there are 365¼ days in a year and this is very difficult to divide into equal parts for our days and weeks. So we consider each year as having just 365 days and every fourth year, or leap year, we have 366 days. The Earth stays in its orbit because of the gravitational force of attraction between it and the Sun. The Earth rotates on its axis and revolves around the Sun, both in an anti-clockwise direction viewed from space above the North Pole.

Macmillan Education
Between Towns Road, Oxford OX4 3PP
A division of Macmillan Publishers Limited
Companies and representatives throughout the world

ISBN: 978 0230 53502 2
ISBN: 978 0230 53505 3 (with CD Rom)
ISBN: 978 0230 53503 9 (with key)
ISBN: 978 0230 53506 0 (with key & CD Rom)

Text © Macmillan Publishers Limited 2008
Design and Illustration © Macmillan Publishers Limited 2008

First published 2008

Designed by Giles Davies Design Ltd
Illustrated by Raymond Turvey (Turvey Books Ltd) and Oxford Designers and Illustrators
Cover design by Giles Davies Design Ltd
Cover photos by Photodisc and Superstock
CD-ROM interface design and programming by e-s-p.

Author's Acknowledgements
The authors and publishers are grateful for permission to reprint the following copyright
material:

Definitions taken from the *Macmillan English Dictionary* second edition published 2007 ©
A&C Black Publishers Ltd 2007, also *Macmillan School Dictionary* first published 2004 ©
Bloomsbury Publishing plc 2004. Extracts from *CXC Biology* by Linda Atwaroo-Ali copyright
© Linda Atwaroo-Ali 2003, Series Editor Dr Mike Taylor. Extracts from *CXC Intregrated*
Science by Tania Chung-Harris copyright © Tania Chung-Harris 2005, Series Editor Dr Mike
Taylor. Extracts from pages 158 & 160 from *Science World 7*, 3rd edition by Peter Stannard
and Ken Williamson copyright © Peter Stannard and Ken Williamson 2006, first published
1995, 2000 and 2006. Reproduced by kind permission of Macmillan Education Australia.
Animations from *Science World* CD-Rom levels 7-10 3rd edition. Created by Chris Dent.
Copyright © Macmillan Education Australia 2006, first published 2006. Reproduced by kind
permission of Macmillan Education Australia. Extracts from pages 143, 150, 151, 155, 163,
164, 166, 171, 173 & 178 from *Science World 8*, 3rd edition by Peter Stannard and Ken
Williamson Copyright © Peter Stannard and Ken Williamson 2006, first published 1995,
2000 & 2006. Reproduced by permission of Macmillan Education Australia.

These materials may contain links for third party websites. We have no control over, and
are not responsible for, the contents of such third party websites. Please use care when
accessing them.

Printed and bound in Thailand by MPAL

2012 2011 2010 2009 2008
10 9 8 7 6 5 4 3 2 1